Social Capital in Developing Democracies

Drawing on extensive fieldwork in Nicaragua and Argentina, as well as public opinion and elite data, Leslie E. Anderson's *Social Capital in Developing Democracies* explores the contribution of social capital to the process of democratization and the limits of that contribution. Anderson finds that in Nicaragua strong, positive, bridging social capital has enhanced democratization, while in Argentina the legacy of Peronism has created bonding and non-democratic social capital that undermines the development of democracy. Faced with the reality of an antidemocratic form of social capital, Anderson suggests that Argentine democracy is developing on the basis of an alternative resource – institutional capital. Anderson concludes that social capital can and does enhance democracy under historical conditions that have created horizontal ties among citizens, but that social capital can also undermine democratization where historical conditions have created vertical ties with leaders and suspicion or noncooperation among citizens.

Leslie E. Anderson is a University of Florida Research Foundation Professor of Political Science at the University of Florida. She is a scholar of democracy, popular politics and protest, and democratic development. Professor Anderson is also the author of *The Political Ecology of the Modern Peasant: Calculation and Community* and *Learning Democracy: Citizen Engagement and Electoral Choice in Nicaragua, 1990–2001* (with Lawrence C. Dodd), in addition to multiple journal articles.

Social Capital in Developing Democracies

Nicaragua and Argentina Compared

LESLIE E. ANDERSON

CAMBRIDGE UNIVERSITY PRESS
Cambridge, New York, Melbourne, Madrid, Cape Town, Singapore,
São Paulo, Delhi, Dubai, Tokyo

Cambridge University Press
32 Avenue of the Americas, New York, NY 10013-2473, USA

www.cambridge.org
Information on this title: www.cambridge.org/9780521140843

© Leslie E. Anderson 2010

This publication is in copyright. Subject to statutory exception
and to the provisions of relevant collective licensing agreements,
no reproduction of any part may take place without the written
permission of Cambridge University Press.

First published 2010

Printed in the United States of America

A catalog record for this publication is available from the British Library.

Library of Congress Cataloging in Publication data
Anderson, Leslie (Leslie E.)
  Social capital in developing democracies : Nicaragua and Argentina
compared / Leslie E. Anderson.
    p. cm.
  ISBN 978-0-521-19274-3 (hardback) – ISBN 978-0-521-14084-3 (pbk.)
  1. Social capital (Sociology) – Argentina – History – 20th century. 2. Social
capital (Sociology) – Nicaragua – History – 20th century. 3. Argentina – Politics and
government – 20th century. 4. Nicaragua – Politics and government – 20th century.
5. Democracy – Argentina – History – 20th century. 6. Democracy – Nicaragua –
History – 20th century. I. Title.
  HM708.A52 2010
  302.0982–dc22   2009048077

ISBN 978-0-521-19274-3 Hardback
ISBN 978-0-521-14084-3 Paperback

Cambridge University Press has no responsibility for the persistence or
accuracy of URLs for external or third-party Internet Web sites referred to in
this publication and does not guarantee that any content on such Web sites is,
or will remain, accurate or appropriate.

For Elizabeth P. Anderson
BA Sarah Lawrence College, 1945
PhD in Biochemistry
Stanford University, 1951

All the people like us are We, and everyone else is They.
                                                    Rudyard Kipling

Contents

Preface	*page* ix
1 An Introduction	1
PART I CREATING SOCIAL CAPITAL	
People I Have Known: The Human Face of Popular Politics	27
2 Creating "We": Sandinismo and Bridging Social Capital	31
3 Creating "Us" and "Them": Peronism and Bonding Social Capital	68
PART II AN EMPIRICAL EXAMINATION OF THE ARGUMENT	
4 A Tale of Two Neighborhoods: Social Capital in Nicaragua and Argentina	115
5 Democracy and Its Competitors: Political Values in Nicaragua and Argentina	138
6 Participation, Democratic Institutions, and Procedures	172
PART III MAKING DEMOCRACY WORK WITHOUT SOCIAL CAPITAL: INSTITUTIONAL CAPITAL	
7 If You Build It They Will Come: Institutional Capital in Democratic Development	201
8 Conclusion	238
Appendix	273
Works Cited	277
Index	297

Preface

When I was a doctoral student at the University of Michigan I rode a Yamaha 150 motorcycle around Central America so that I could more easily reach the rural poor, my subject of study. I continued to ride that motorcycle long after I finished my dissertation because it was the best and cheapest way to get around in Nicaragua. But it was a rough-and-tumble way to do research, and I got into trouble plenty of times. I got stuck in the mud. I had flash floods reach up over the handlebars. I ran out of gas. I knocked the chain off the gear wheel. Whenever I got into trouble, the Nicaraguans helped me out, rescued me, found me a pint of gas somewhere, leveraged the bike out of two feet of oozing mud, fixed the bike, replaced and oiled the chain, kept it running.

The Nicaraguan people were poor, always and everywhere, but their generosity toward me and toward each other never ceased to amaze me. Those who had nothing always seemed to have something to give. Although the Nicaraguans were certainly not saints, they had a stoic kindness, a willingness to pitch in, reach out, buckle down, work together. That willingness was so evident everywhere in the country, in rural and urban areas, and so constant over time that in the first ten years of my research on Latin America, I came to take it for granted, to consider it Latin American.

Then I went to Argentina. I began researching Argentina in the early 1990s, not too long after the nation had returned to democracy after nearly seven years of brutal dictatorship. But cruelty was still evident to a foreign visitor. In 1992, on a street in downtown Buenos Aires, I saw a bus stop at a curb to pick up an elderly, crippled woman. She moved slowly and painfully to the open door as the driver waited for her to climb in. But just as she reached the stairs onto the bus, the bus suddenly crept forward a foot or two. She nearly fell but recovered her balance. Then she slowly moved forward the additional two feet and tried, once again, to climb onto the bus. But once again the bus rolled forward another couple of feet. This time I knew it was no accident. The bus driver was doing this deliberately. I watched aghast at the cruelty I was witnessing. No one in the street did or said anything. It appeared that no one but I had even noticed. Suddenly a wave of anger rushed over me, and I started toward the bus and the woman. In fluent Nicaraguan Spanish, that bus driver was about to get a piece of my mind. But at that moment, suddenly the driver pulled away entirely and drove off. The woman stared at the bus as it went away. I stood in the street stunned, shocked by what I had seen.

By the time I was researching Argentina in the late 1990s, nearly ten years later, I no longer saw events like the bus incident, and sometimes I witnessed acts of real kindness among citizens on the street. Every time I came to Argentina, people seemed kinder, more trusting; neighbors more willing to open their doors, talk on the streets, help each other out. But there was always an edge of caution and distrust in Argentina that was simply not there in Nicaragua. Why? Why would Argentines, who had so much and who, relatively speaking, were so wealthy, be so cautious, ungenerous, and guarded toward each other while Nicaraguans, who are clearly so very poor, were so often generous, trusting, and kind? And while Argentines appeared to grow more trusting over time, there was always a marked difference between the two societies. This book tries to uncover why.

The research for this book combined extensive fieldwork with public opinion and elite surveys in both Nicaragua and Argentina.[1] Between 1984 and 2009 I visited Nicaragua 16 times. My work in the 1980s addressed citizen involvement in the Sandinista revolution both before and after its 1979 triumph. I researched rural and urban revolutionary participation in 1984 and continued that work during a six-month visit in 1985. I returned for visits of two or three months in 1986, 1987, and 1990. During the 1990s I returned every twelve to eighteen months, and I observed national elections in 1990, 1996, 2001, and 2006, as well as the municipal elections of 2000, 2004, and 2008. I conducted interviews of citizens and political leaders in Nicaragua. Interviewees included citizen activists, former and current legislators, political leaders, party organizers, union activists, opposition activists, editors of the major newspapers, and presidential and vice-presidential candidates. During the 1996 and 2001 elections, I conducted nationwide public opinion surveys funded by the National Science Foundation and the Manning Dauer Research Fund at the University of Florida. These surveys asked questions about associational memberships, social activities, political participation, support for democratic institutions and processes, and democratic values, as well as about the elections themselves. In 2002 I conducted a survey about associational membership and political activism in a Sandinista neighborhood in Managua. Finally, between 2001 and 2003 I surveyed 53 members of the 92-member single-chamber legislature.

I visited Argentina nine times between 1992 and 2009. I began by focusing on social and human rights movements and developing democratic institutions. I spent six weeks in 1992 researching the role of social movements in Argentina's return to democracy. I returned as a Fulbright Scholar for four months in 1993 to continue research on popular movements and citizen

---

[1] These surveys are described in the Appendix.

Preface

initiative. I observed the national and midterm elections in 1995, 1997, and 2000. Funded by a Howard Foundation Fellowship from Brown University, I returned for five months in 1997 and 1998 to study the relationship among citizens, the legislature, and the president. I returned again in 1999, 2000, 2002, and 2005 for brief visits. In 2008 I received a second Fulbright Fellowship to continue my research on Argentina. I spent a full semester in Buenos Aires at that time, during which period I also taught a class of doctoral students at the University of Buenos Aires. I offered them a course on social capital in Argentina and elsewhere. I am appreciative of those students for their insights on my research in this book.

These visits allowed me to conduct in-depth interviews in Argentina with citizen leaders, social-movement activists, members and leaders of human rights organizations, political party activists and leaders, current and former legislators from both the Senate and the House of Deputies, political advisors, government ministers from the Alfonsín and Menem administrations, and former President Alfonsín. In 1997 and 2000 I conducted public opinion surveys funded by the Institutions Program, Department of Political Science, University of Florida and by a Humanities Award, also at the University of Florida. These surveys addressed associational memberships, social activities, political participation, support for democratic institutions and processes, and democratic values, as well as electoral opinion. In 2002 I conducted a survey about associational membership and political activism in a Peronist neighborhood in Buenos Aires. In 2002 and 2003 I surveyed 83 members of the national Congress.

A number of individuals expressed great faith in this project at different points in its development. One of the earliest true believers was my father, Thornton Hogan Anderson, who became excited about my theory even before this book became a manuscript. He was often on the phone, calling me in Argentina, asking what I had learned in my field research that week. I am sorry that he is not around to see the completed book now. I also thank Aimee and Bill Hagerty for the support they showed during my sabbatical year of 2003–4. I am greatly appreciative of my Kentucky cousins, who have kept careful track of the development of this project and supported it throughout its history: Mildred and Jack Woodruff, Elizabeth and Bernie Conrad, and Steve Woodruff. Although I have never lived there, my cousins have certainly given me a sense of my old Kentucky home. Other strong supporters include Nancy Bermeo, Robert Dahl, Daniel Levine, Guillermo O'Donnell, Robert Putnam, and Theda Skocpol. Powerful intellectual mentors, they inspired me to do my best, lest I disappoint them. I thank them for their interest and support.

At the University of Florida I have received support from multiple sources. I am indebted to H. Russell Bernard for helping me to discover the scholarship of social capital beyond political science. In the Department of Political Science, I have received strong encouragement from Richard Conley, Margaret Conway, Aida Hozic, Renee Johnson, Margaret Kohn, and Richard Scher. I am deeply grateful for their interest and enthusiasm. I have benefited from particular insights about the various issues of this book from several of my colleagues. On the desirability of participatory democracy, I have learned a lot from Dan O'Neill. On corruption, the perception of the common good, and differing visions of community, I have learned much from Beth Rosenson. And on the commonalities between German and Argentine culture, I have gained important help from Conor O'Dwyer. Won-ho Park helped with some aspects of the statistical analysis. Scholars who read an earlier version of this book and offered helpful comments include Elizabeth Anderson, Nancy Barber, H. Russell Bernard, Laurent Berthet, Margaret Conway, J. Samuel Fitch, Yael Harari, Goran Hyden, Daniel Levine, Cynthia McClintock, Dan O'Neill, Anne Pitcher, Beth Rosenson, and Katrina Schwartz. In the final stages of the revision process for this manuscript, the Latin American Collection at the Smathers Library of the University of Florida purchased the recent Latinobarometro data for inclusion in this book. I am grateful to Richard Phillips and Paul Losch for entertaining my purchase request in the midst of the economic crisis, and to John Ingraham, Associate Dean of Libraries, for authorizing the purchase of the Latinobarometro data for the University of Florida scholarly community. The graphics for this book were paid for by funds from my University of Florida Research Foundation Professorship. I would like to thank Carmen Diana Deere, Director of the Center for Latin American Studies, for nominating me to compete for the professorship. I also thank Associate Deans Allan Burns and Lou Gillette for encouraging me to compete for the professorship.

In Argentina and from Argentines, I have also received support that deserves particular recognition. To be Argentine today and still be able to acknowledge the true character of Peronism, including the knowledge that Argentina produced such a movement in the first place, is to display a level of personal courage and intellectual honesty that is difficult and rare. Individuals who have supported this work and displayed that level of courage include Aníbal Corrado, Carlos Escudé, Andrés Fontana, Ana Maria Mustapic, Enrique Peruzzotti, and Guillermina Seri, as well as Guillermo O'Donnell, mentioned above. Andrés, Ana Maria, Enrique, and Guillermo deserve a second mention for having waded their way through an early draft of this manuscript. Aníbal read a later version in its entirety and gave extensive detailed comments. Thanks to all of them. The book is better for their input. Nicaraguans who have supported this project include Ricardo Chavarría, Milagros and Gabriela Chavarría, Sergio Santamaría, and Marvin Ortega. The pollsters I have worked with have been invaluable: Maria Braun of MoriArgentina and Gerardo Androgué of KNACK, both in Argentina; Sergio Santamaria of CINASE in Nicaragua; and Gustavo Mendez of DOXA in Venezuela, who conducted the earlier polls in Nicaragua.

I would like to thank Charles Chamberlin and Erin Johnson of Erin Johnson Designs for meticulous work on the graphics for this book. At Cambridge University Press I received excellent input from two anonymous reviewers.

I also thank Eric Crahan, of Cambridge University Press, for believing in this book from early on and seeing it through to publication.

I thank Lyle and Teresa Sherfey, Tinker Harris, Helen Gould, and Randy and Cheryl Winter for keeping me riding and keeping me sane. I thank my husband, Lawrence C. Dodd, who has supported me and this project through it all. I will never know why I got to be so lucky as to have found him. Finally, this book is dedicated to my mother "who raised a banner and pointed the way." It is dedicated to her because, after all, we still need each other and because, although she finds it hard to believe given her fundamental faith in humanity, we still have a very long way to go.

Boulder County, Colorado
July 19, 2009

1

An Introduction

> There is no faith in America, between either men or nations. Treaties are papers; constitutions books; elections combat; liberty, anarchy, and life, a torment.
>
> *Simon Bolivar, Mirada Sobre America española*[1]

> ...conflicts are more threatening among people who distrust one another. Public contestation requires a good deal of trust in one's opponents. They may be opponents but they are not implacable enemies.
>
> Robert Dahl, *Polyarchy*[2]

Our mutual faith in each other is one fundamental essence of democracy. We must have faith that if we lose (an election, an argument) to "the other," we and our interests will nonetheless live to see another day, to make another argument, to discuss another issue, to contest another election.[3] We will not be destroyed forever by our loss today. Some scholars have called this faith in the system and argued that participants must believe that the system will protect them, within reasonable limits, even if they are the (temporary) losers. Moreover, that same system will provide them a level playing field so that, come the next contest, they will have every advantage and at least a reasonable likelihood of winning the next round. But the system, of course, consists of both the citizen members within it and the institutional framework around it. We must trust each other, or trust our institutions, or both before we can trust the system. The ability to trust one another, cooperate, and work together is a valuable asset in the development, consolidation, and continuation of democracy. Particularly when a democracy is new, but also as it consolidates, citizens need resources that they can use to confront authoritarian power and resolve differences among themselves peacefully. Citizens' mutual faith in each other is a resource to combat authoritarianism and resolve disagreements. It is a basis of democracy.

---

[1] Quito, (1929). Cited in Rippy (1963, p. 22).
[2] Taken from Dahl (1971, p. 152).
[3] Linz and Stepan (1978; 1996).

ECONOMIC AFFLUENCE OR SOCIAL CAPITAL?

The suggestion that citizens' faith in each other is a basis of democracy is an argument in favor of social capital that deemphasizes the importance of affluence to the health of democracy. Barrington Moore, for example, argued that a larger economic pie would allow more individuals to access resources, resources that citizens could then translate into political power.[4] Similarly, Seymour Martin Lipset suggested that the broad distribution of resources would facilitate democratization, while Tatu Vanhannen explored the link between affluence, intellectual and economic resources, and democracy.[5] However, Lawrence Dodd and I have demonstrated that national and individual poverty have not prevented democratization in Nicaragua, although that study does not explicitly address the creation of social capital.[6] The forward movement of democracy in many poor nations calls the argument about affluence into question.

One way to reconcile the steadfast development of democracy in low-income nations with arguments about affluence is to focus upon equality of resources rather than upon the sheer level of resources themselves. Resources per se may or may not be positively related to democratization, but the *relatively equal distribution* of the resources that do exist does, in fact, enhance democracy. The notion that resources are distributed relatively equally, regardless of the absolute amount of economic resources, levels the playing field among citizens in much the same way that Moore's larger economic pie did in more affluent societies. Focusing on equality also allows a connection between the resources argument and the social capital argument, since original arguments about citizen cooperation and associational life underscored the extent to which equality among citizens enhanced cooperation. Tocqueville, for example, in work that originally influenced social capital theory, stressed equality among American citizens along with his focus upon associational life as an explanation for democratic development.[7]

In contrast to affluence theories, arguments that democratization depends on social capital do not privilege national or personal affluence, although they do have an original basis in economics. Modern social science recognizes mutual faith and cooperation as assets and defines them as capital – social capital. But capital was originally economic. The notion of capital originates with Marx's description of economic relations in human society.[8] For Marx,

---

[4] Moore (1966); Andrew Janos (1992) has made a similar argument with respect to the current process of democratization in Russia.
[5] Vanhannen (1992; 1997).
[6] Anderson and Dodd (2005).
[7] Recent theory on equality and social capital criticizes Putnam's work for its lack of attention to Tocqueville's argument about equality. McLean et al. (2002).
[8] I am indebted to the criticisms of H. Russell Bernard for the discussion in this section. He forced me to look at the ways that disciplines other than political science have considered the concept of social capital.

capital was purely economic. It constituted the surplus created by the laboring classes but retained and controlled by capitalist industrial owners. This definition of capital saw it as a resource essential for building society but simultaneously connected it with exploitation. Capital created by workers was inappropriately expropriated by capitalists, and directed in ways that served them, but not the workers to whom it belonged. Marx's definition of capital constrained it further by defining it as a group phenomenon, something that resulted from the group efforts of many but belonged to no single individual in particular. An implied individual disempowerment inadvertently emerges from Marx's definition of capital, since it is not something created by one person nor can it necessarily be used by any single individual other than the uniquely-positioned capitalist. So while Marx abhorred the exploitation and disempowerment of the individual, his own theory did not see that same individual as capable of using or controlling the capital he or she created.

Later considerations of capital freed it from Marx's restriction of considering it purely economic and primarily a group phenomenon. Scholars began considering human capital something that belonged to one individual and comprised the assets that person brought to the world: education, skills, talents, intelligence, but also acquired or inherited goods. Once individualized in this manner, human capital became something that people could increase of their own volition and use according to their own decisions, thus empowering the individual. The notion of human capital also extended the definition beyond economics, although individual economic resources, particularly when used to increase individual capacities, remained a part of the definition.[9]

From the definition of human capital – which included all resources, some at least partially under individual control – the notion of social capital developed, although in a much more restricted fashion than political science uses it today. A large community of sociologists began studying social capital, defined as resources that individuals could gain through work with others, namely involvements beyond the individual self, as exemplified in the work of Nan Lin.[10] Specifically, we are talking about social networks and the resources that networks brought to the individual: personal connections, enhanced knowledge and wherewithal, and inside information. This understanding of social capital still included economic goods but was not confined to them. It also kept the individual central and personally able to access, control, and increase social capital resources. Sociologists acknowledged that individuals with more human capital (more money, a better job) would be better able to access social capital. Thus, while all people had some access to human capital to create social capital, some had more human capital and thus more social capital. The notion of inequality returned to the study of capital, although not the notion of exploitation. In addition, sociologists saw social

---

[9] Fernandez and Castilla (2001).
[10] Lin, et al. (2001).

capital as something that individuals could use to their own advantage, and so individualism predominated in their view of this resource.

This understanding of social capital allows sociologists to treat it as something quite specific, tangible, and measurable. If social capital consists of specific, tangible resources, sociologists ought to be able to identify it precisely and measure it quantitatively.[11] This expectation has sent sociology students of social capital off in pursuit of measures of social capital, both how much of it individuals possess (e.g., how many connections they have with what kinds of people) and how much it has enhanced their position (e.g., better jobs, more job offers, higher salaries).[12]

The working definition that political science today uses for social capital comes from this work in sociology and then moves beyond it. Robert Putnam suggests that social capital includes the increased resources that individuals gain from personal connections – the value of the rolodex. He acknowledges that such connections bring better capacities, access, and outcomes to the individual who holds such connections. But social capital, according to Putnam, is much more than just the additional resources one gains through connections. Social capital also includes the connections themselves, which are of inherent and intrinsic value both to the individuals and to society at large.

The difference between Putnam's and Lin's understanding of social capital can be captured in a simple example. Suppose X has a delivery to make but has no vehicle. Through her social connections (and access to social capital) she knows Y. Y, perchance, owns a bicycle – a specific, tangible resource that X lacks. X asks Y if she can borrow the bicycle; Y says "yes" and X makes her delivery that way. For Lin, social capital is the bicycle, a tangible, measurable resource that accrues directly to X as a result of her network connections to Y. For Putnam social capital is the relationship itself between X and Y. The bicycle is only a part of it. Putnam's understanding of social capital defines it as something much less tangible, less measurable, and something that accrues to society as a whole as well as to both X and Y as individuals.

Beyond this, political scientists studying social capital argue that the relationship itself and the myriad of relationships like it have a political effect. Here they move the definition of social capital beyond sociology entirely. Putnam suggests that the relationship between X and Y has a positive, enhancing effect on society at large and on the polity. Through such relationships, individuals learn to like, trust, and respect each other. They learn to work together. Eventually this mutuality translates into the basic faith in each other that is necessary for a society to resolve differences peacefully, make compromises and agreements, and ultimately to function in a democratic fashion. In this sense, many relationships between many Xs and Ys, particularly those enhanced and structured through organizations and associations, create the foundation of a democratic society.

---

[11] La Duke Lake and Huckfeldt (1998); Dietlind (1998); Smith (1999).
[12] Green and Brock (1998).

In political science today, social capital is individual, but not only individual. The strength of social capital lies primarily in the group, namely, in group cooperation. Social capital is thus social, with broad social advantages. Those social advantages have an important political effect.[13] In addition, the political science notion of social capital makes it far more intangible than sociology has understood it to be, and therefore harder to measure. This is not to say that social capital as understood in political science is immeasurable. But measuring something that is both intangible and of social and political value will be more difficult than measuring the much more individual, tangible, and restricted definition of social capital that many sociologists use.

In this movement beyond the sociological understanding of social capital, and toward viewing it as having a broad, amorphous political effect, political scientists have moved backward as well as forward. One hundred and fifty years ago, Alexis de Tocqueville, also a student of politics, fielded the notion that a democratic society was more likely to develop where human relationships and interactions were strong and positive. He wrote, "Feelings and opinions are recruited, the heart is enlarged, and the human mind is developed, only by the reciprocal influence of men upon each other. ... these influences...must be...created, and this can only be accomplished by associations."[14] "Thus," wrote Tocqueville, "the most democratic country on the face of the earth is that in which men have...carried to the highest perfection the art of pursuing in common the object of their common desires, and have applied this new science to the greatest number of purposes."[15] Thus, action within social associations was a key to why democracy was working in America.[16]

Tocqueville's argument is even more important for the study at hand and, in general, for the study of developing democracies than it is for the large body of political science literature that examines the state of democratic health in established democracies today. This is true for two reasons. First, Tocqueville looked at democracy at a much earlier stage in the development process when he considered the role of associations in American democracy in the mid-nineteenth century. Skocpol also studies associations and social capital in America during this period.[17] This perspective is closer to the subject of this book, since I examine the role of associations in the early stages of democratic consolidation and the relationship between social capital and democracy in its early years. But second, Tocqueville actually emphasized the role of *political* associations specifically in contributing to democracy.[18] In this way, my own

---

[13] For critiques of the prevailing political science perspective on social capital see Hero (2003) and Kohn (1999).
[14] Tocqueville (1956, p. 200).
[15] Tocqueville (1956, p. 199).
[16] Tocqueville (1956, esp. Chap. 29).
[17] Skocpol (1999; 2003).
[18] Hulliung (2002, p. 184). Hulliung is correct to point out that Tocqueville stressed political associations and that he saw them as *preceeding*, not following, general associations in the process of democratic development. But Tocqueville's argument itself is sometimes confusing

work is also closer to his than to more recent studies of social capital since the findings of this study will underscore the direct importance of political association for the early development of democratic politics. Tocqueville's stress on political associations is often missed in contemporary renditions of his argument about associations and democracy.[19]

Inherent in these arguments about social capital is the notion that capital – human, social, or otherwise – is something that is built slowly over time, with small incremental inputs, not unlike equity in a house or a retirement account. Also inherent in these arguments is the idea of a gradual, forward movement as a result of building on something that has happened in the past. X can use Y's bicycle now because she built a positive relationship with Y in the past. Tocqueville suggests that democracy moves forward better now because members of society joined and worked within associations previously.[20] Within this connection between past actions and positive results now or in the future is the notion of *learning*. Persons X and Y have learned to work together with positive results. Americans are more able to engage in a democratic polity because they learned to interact through their associations. Current theorists of social capital also embrace the notion of learning, although they do not say so explicitly in their arguments. Italians or Americans, the two groups Putnam studies, who have learned to interact with each other in the past are more constructive at making democracy work today. But those who have not learned such interactive lessons are unable or less able to contribute to making democracy work. This book also relies on the role of learning from the past as a key component in understanding how social capital can develop and what kind of social capital develops. That reliance forces us to incorporate history into our understanding of the development of social capital.

CREATING SOCIAL CAPITAL

If many political scientists agree that social capital has a political effect and is a basis for democracy, they are less certain of how societies develop or retain

---

since there are other places in his writing where he does specifically stress the importance of all kinds of civic associations in making democracy work in America. See Tocqueville (1956, esp. chap. 29).

[19] A decade before the more recent focus on social capital and during the 1980s, Benjamin Barber also noticed that citizens' confidence in national government was in decline while citizen involvement in local level politics was still high. He suggested that after a decade in which national government was characterized by "greed, narcissism and hostility to big government," citizens had turned instead to local and community affairs (1984, p. xi).

[20] Tocqueville's argument and other, more recent views of social capital all assume a stable society where members live in one place for long periods of time. Such assumptions do not apply in migrant societies where most members come and go, staying in one place for only a few years. Yet the evidence is that even in migrant societies, individuals are capable of creating supportive associational relationships, even if only on a small scale. These can be seen as a kind of mobile social capital. While her work is not about social capital and she does not

social capital. Putnam, following Tocqueville, argues for the centrality of citizen organization. The breeding ground of social capital lies in organizations that citizens join for enjoyment, relaxation, and social interaction.[21] These are often casual groups and may be devoted to a variety of activities that matter little for their direct contribution to democracy. It is the fact and habit of interaction, cooperation, and mutual support within these activities and organizations that cause citizens to develop capacities to interact in a democratic fashion – in other words, to develop social capital. Joining is itself the social good and the democratic contributor.

In his examination of social capital, especially in Italy, Putnam further argues that these organizations and the development of social capital trace far back into national history, requiring generations, even centuries to develop. Social capital is thus a slowly evolved good that societies can only expect to enjoy if they have had generations of associational experience. Where societies have a long history of mutual association, democracy will work better. Skocpol picks up on this historical perspective, as well, by examining voluntary associations in the United States in the nineteenth century.[22] There is, then, a strong precedent in the study of social capital for considering a nation's history, and particularly the history of that nation's popular organizations and associations. If democracy is governance by the voice of the people, then the history of the popular political experience, particularly the pre-democratic history of the people, ought to be of relevance as democracy takes shape.

The argument that social capital develops slowly contrasts with an earlier position that social interaction and democratic engagement may be attained in a much faster and more effective manner via social revolution.[23] According to this earlier argument, revolution breaks the ice of political tyranny, mobilizes and empowers the population rapidly, and forces the popular agenda onto the political stage in a manner that forever changes the nature of political relationships and power.[24] Although revolutions in the real world have not necessarily bred democracy, those outcomes are more due to leadership that later corrupted the revolutionary ideals than to the nature of citizen

---

consider the concept of mobile social capital, Lara Putnam (2002) describes mobile associational relationships developed by migrants in Caribbean Costa Rica.

[21] Crawford and Levitt (1999).

[22] Skocpol (2003).

[23] On the relationship between revolution and democracy in the United States, see G. Wood (1969; 1974). See also Elkins and McKitrick (1993). With respect to the relationship between revolution and democracy in France, Moore argues that the French Revolution marked a critical step toward democratic development in that country, first and foremost, by sweeping aside the ancienne regime and its upper classes who were so hostile to democracy (1966, p. 108). Also see Woloch (1994, pp. 91–92) and Hunt (1984). Even today, electoral studies in France emphasize ideology, related to social class, and deep social cleavages, as a result of the impact on democracy that has come from the French Revolution. The study of social cleavage, of course, is also of European origin (Lipset and Rokkan, 1967; Rokkan, 1970).

[24] For a consideration of changes in popular political culture after the Cuban revolution see Fagen (1969).

associations themselves. These, of course, did cooperate to end tyranny and create a visionary society, even if that vision was later lost by leaders who gained power without accountability. The argument in favor of a relationship between revolution and democracy remains because the revolutionary movement ended a tyrannical regime. And it differs from a social capital argument first in allowing for *rapid* advancement of the foundations for democracy and second in acknowledging that *disruptive* citizen organization, despite and indeed because of its dissenting characteristics, can help democracy develop.

THE NATURE OF SOCIAL ORGANIZATION

If we embrace the argument that citizen organization enhances democracy slowly, or we accept the earlier suggestion that revolutionary action builds democratic capacity rapidly by destroying tyranny and empowering citizens, either way we have assumed a positive kind of citizen organization that contributes constructively to democratic political development. Either position suggests that citizen organization has a long-term effect that is positive in its relation to human freedom. The outcome of such involvement is a better society, not a worse one.[25] Association, organization, joining, belonging, all of these activities lead individuals to think better and more positively toward others and to interact with more mutuality and respect. Whether they get there slowly through generations of associational activity or rapidly through revolution, the point at which they arrive has an enhancing effect on democracy. Such associational ties create a "we" that can work together to make society – and democracy – function.

Putnam has called these associational ties "bridging social capital." Bridging social capital teaches individuals and groups to overcome and even value difference and forces those individuals and groups to find a common ground on which to interact, build a relationship, and work toward a mutual future. Another genre of literature has called them "cross-cutting ties," which bind individuals to each other across natural lines of division, such as race, ethnicity, class, or religion. Ties that cut across such natural divisions reduce conflict in society. Reduced conflict enhances the possibilities of compromise and non-violent conflict resolution.[26]

---

[25] Even in studies of social capital that confine themselves to Latin America, here again the presumption is that social capital is a positive good that enhances democracy. This book challenges that assumption. See, for example, Klesner (2007).

[26] See Anderson (2002). Also Ross (1985; 1986; 1993). Cross-cutting ties theory has been used and explored by many authors. For an early description of it, contrasting it with other theories of conflict see Levine and Campbell (1972) who contrast cross-cutting ties methods of describing social divisions with "pyramidal segmentation," arrangements where social members are segmented into separate divisions in hierarchical order. These authors note that pyramidal segmentation is related to higher levels of conflict than are cross-cutting ties (see esp. chap. 4). See also Pruitt and Rubin (1986, p. 68). Similarly, Dahl argues that cross-cutting social contacts and checks are essential in making democracy possible (1956; 1971). For a study confirming the above theories see Harris (1972). In Harris' study, divisions in an Irish

But some scholars of social capital have questioned whether social organizations and associations are always positive.[27] Some scholars suggest that popular organizations do not always enhance respect, cooperation, mutuality, and social cooperation and do not always contribute to democracy.[28] Organizations differ: some enhance mutual respect, cooperation, or egalitarian interaction, while others do not.[29] Some encourage members to empower themselves, work together, reach outward, and create mutuality, cooperation, and respect. Others encourage associational members to view each other positively while viewing non-members negatively, with suspicion, caution, hostility, distrust. Some organizations bind members to each other in large part by defining them as special, different, and better than others, but not necessarily by encouraging them to work together. Some associations create "associational glue" by erecting barriers between members and non-members, insiders and outsiders, "us" and "them."

Putnam's work acknowledges the existence of "bonding social capital" within organizations that bind members to each other but do not enhance mutuality and social respect across society, and recognizes that this bonding social capital does not have a positive relationship with democracy. This aspect of his argument, however, is less developed.[30] The notion of bonding social capital remains largely unexplored and its relationship to democracy poorly understood. If bridging social capital fosters democracy, what does bonding social capital do to and for democracy? Studies of social capital in political science have left this issue largely unexplored and these questions mostly unanswered. Yet if we are to understand fully the relationship between social capital and democracy, we must comprehend the effect of bonding social capital on making democracy work.

The broader social context is also relevant here because organizations do not develop in a vacuum. Rather, they emerge in a social context with its own traditions, and they reflect the values of their social surroundings. Some societies have cultures conducive to relatively egalitarian ties and interactions. There, associations that develop are more likely to build horizontal ties among members and to encourage mutual respect among equals. But other societies have strong traditions of hierarchy, vertical ties, and deference by those at the bottom toward those at the top. Strong hierarchical or clientelist social traditions that encourage vertical ties make it particularly difficult to develop bridging social capital. Most observers agree that the social context in the United States encouraged horizontal cooperation. But in Italy, Putnam found that horizontal cooperation was more common in the north, while hierarchy

---

community paralleled each other rather than cutting across each other with the result that conflict was more extensive than it otherwise would have been.

[27] Fiorina (1999).
[28] Berman (1997).
[29] Wood (2002).
[30] Putnam (2000, chap. 22).

and vertical ties were more prevalent in southern Italy. Scholars studying civil society in Spain have also argued that hierarchy characterized social relations there, particularly before the return to democracy in 1975. A hierarchical civil society encouraged hierarchical forms of social control in Spain, including the Catholic Church and the fascist state, and the development of democracy had to overcome such hierarchical traditions.[31] Social context affects the nature of the organizations that are created in a particular society.

If organizations create at least two different kinds of ties within themselves – horizontal and vertical – the nature of those ties is determined in part by the style of leadership. In organizations where members consider each other peers and partners, horizontal ties are created, enhanced, and encouraged. Members look sideways toward each other, build and retain an awareness of each other, and consider each other resources. They are "tuned in" to each other. They learn ways of working together as equals. The horizontal ties among them become part of the strength and resources of the organization itself. Members learn that together they can do things that they would be unable to do alone. Horizontal ties empower associational members and encourage citizen initiatives. They build citizen faith in each other.

Vertical ties, on the other hand, emphasize the bond between each individual associational member and the leader. Organizations that encourage vertical ties stress the separate value of a direct connection between each individual and the leader. Individuals who cultivate a strong vertical tie to the leader can create great benefits for themselves. Organizations that promote vertical ties encourage members to look upward toward a leader rather than sideways towards each other. Members are to be loyal followers, and such loyalty may result in greater benefits from organizational membership. But vertical ties do not promote mutual cooperation among peers or faith in each other. In fact, members may not be tuned in to their peers at all because vertical orientation yields greater benefits than horizontal orientation. Vertical organizations may even discourage horizontal ties among members. Vertical ties can promote dependency, passivity, and an incapacity to work together.[32] Citizens tied vertically to a leader above them typically have less capacity for citizen initiative, and such an organization may lack the resources to accomplish tasks that individuals are unable to complete alone. Organizational members bound by vertical ties may even be less able to accomplish group tasks than they would be if they were not associational members because of induced passivity and dependency.

These differences in organizational style create two dimensions along which organizations may relate to democracy: internal relationships inside the organization and outward perspectives toward non-members. Organizations may produce horizontal ties of mutuality and empowerment along with positive or tolerant attitudes toward those outside the organization. Or they may

---

[31] Pérez-Díaz (1993).
[32] Madsen and Snow (1991).

produce vertical ties of dependency and passivity that induce powerlessness while fostering suspicion, caution, separateness, and even hostility toward nonmembers. The nature of relationships within an organization (both relationships among equals and ties to leaders) and the view members take of nonmembers are as much a part of the social learning experience as is the speed with which such associational experience evolves. The nature of internal ties and the character of external views determine the kind of social capital created.

CAUSALITY AND INGREDIENTS

The tendency to assume that associations are more likely to make a positive contribution toward democracy derives from studying societies that are already fully democratic and tracing causality backward. Scholars have looked at the democratic outcome and asked why. Their answer has been associations, regardless of whether those associations are pro-status quo or disruptive. But that is an answer made inevitable by a lack of observation during the process of democratic construction. Just as one cannot guess all the ingredients that have gone into making a cake after the cake is finished, so one cannot fully know all of the ingredients that have gone into making a democracy work.

The best way to know what is in a cake is to be present while it is being made. Similarly, studies of the relationships among associational membership, the social capital it creates, and the relative success or quality of democracy can be improved by a perspective that looks at causality in a forward direction. We can begin by studying citizen associations themselves and following their development forward through time. We can consider the history of those associations, the social context, the nature of internal ties, and the character of external views that they encourage among associational members. We can find citizen associations that fostered horizontal internal ties and positive outward views, and contrast them with associations that encouraged vertical internal ties and suspicious outward views. We can study the relationship between those two types of associations and the development of democracy. We can also ask what, apart from associations, is helping a new democracy develop. Such forward-looking examination of democratization, along with an analysis of the relationship between associations and democratic development, will help determine whether and when citizen associations contribute to democracy.

A TALE OF TWO DEMOCRACIES

If, in fact, associational life sometimes contributes to positive mutual relations and respect, but may also produce internal dependency and external suspicion, a relevant question is how and why societies create one type of social organization or the other. Under what historical, contextual, and ideological circumstances does each type of social organization develop? How does each type of social organization contribute to the development of democracy?

TABLE 1.1. *Standard Economic Indicators: Nicaragua and Argentina*

	GNP 2006	Per Capita Income 2005	Literacy	Infant Mortality 2007
Nicaragua	$17.33 billion	$910	67.5% (2003)	27.14/1000 births
Argentina	$608.8 billion	$4470*	97.2% (2001)	14.29/1000 births

Note: * per capital income in Argentina was $8909 in 1999 before the national recession
Sources: www.finfacts.ie/biz10/globalworldincomepercapita.htm; www.indexmundi.com; CIA World Fact Book, January, 2007.

This book explores these questions by examining the relationship between different types of social organizations and democratic development. We have chosen two modern societies with histories of extensive mass organization both of which are currently attempting to democratize. Unique among late twentieth-century Latin American nations, Nicaragua and Argentina each experienced a mass organizational phenomenon in which most low-income citizens joined or supported a single political organization. These were the Sandinista revolution in Nicaragua and Peronism in Argentina. Each of these two mass movements organized huge proportions of the population and fundamentally altered political loyalties among citizens. Each retains extensive popular loyalty in their respective countries today, despite long periods out of power. And yet each used a very different kind of social organization and left a very different legacy within civil society from which to develop democracy. This book studies the relationship between Sandinista or Peronist social organization and democratic development in Nicaragua and Argentina today.

The choice of Nicaragua and Argentina sets aside standard explanations about democratic development that emphasize economic resources, affluence, or industry. Standard economic indicators invariably advantage Argentina, as shown in Table 1.1.

As this book will show, despite these economic indicators, Argentina's democracy is not developing more smoothly or faster than Nicaragua's. In fact, democratization in Nicaragua is moving forward despite the poverty that these indicators reveal. This book focuses on social capital, its creation, and its limits in both nations, and redirects our attention away from economic development and toward citizen cooperation. If arguments about social capital are universally true, then they should travel easily irrespective of national affluence. Social capital theory does not claim to apply only to wealthy nations. Instead, social capital theory presents itself in a universalistic fashion. Accordingly, the relationship between social capital and democracy should be evident regardless of national context, both in a poor agrarian society and in a wealthy, industrial society. If social capital is a foundational asset for democracy, then its relationship to democracy should not be contingent upon national affluence but should be evident anywhere. This is the value of good theory.[33] In fact, the best test of social capital theory is to apply it in comparing two different nations where economic indicators would lead us to expect that the wealthier nation would have the democratic advantage.

Experiments are more difficult in social science than they are in the natural sciences, particularly experiments than engage entire nations. Yet if there was ever an opportunity to construct an experiment using contrasting types of mass movements, Nicaragua and Argentina are perfect examples to produce, combined, that experiment. Nicaragua is building its democracy based on an egalitarian revolutionary movement that depended upon and fostered horizontal ties of mutual cooperation among citizens. Argentina is building its democracy based on hierarchical authoritarian populism that depended on vertical ties from the grassroots to a single charismatic leader, and that fostered distrust and mutual suspicion toward those outside Peronism and even among those within it. The contrasting values these movements created in their loyalists underscore the need for political science to study different kinds of social capital in relationship to democratic development. A brief overview of the Nicaraguan and Argentine democracies illustrates the extent to which the standard focus on level of national development cannot explain differences in democratic development. We need to incorporate an understanding of social capital to begin to explain the differences in democratic development in these two cases.

We begin with Argentina because standard explanations about democratic development that privilege levels of economic development would give the advantage to Argentina. From the outside, Argentina should seem an obvious case for successful democratization. Relatively affluent, the most cosmopolitan and European of all Latin American nations, Argentina should move readily and swiftly toward democracy. Highly industrialized, potentially self-sufficient in industry and agriculture, and a producer of multiple commodities for the global market, Argentina has many of the economic advantages normally associated with democracy. Home to an educated, literate middle class, historically the base of organized, unionized labor, Argentina should be enjoying a civilized, educated, politicized, cosmopolitan population who can readily embrace democratic institutions and process. And yet Argentina's democracy seems always on the verge of, already deeply mired in, or just emerging from crisis. Since its return to a regular electoral calendar in December of 1983, it has suffered hyperinflation, several attempted coupes, an economic collapse, the resignation of several presidents, rampant corruption, the decline of its legal system and a lack of two-party contestation for office. Even now, as it appears to be enjoying competent governance, the presidency is still haunted by lack of effective party competition and suspicions of strong-man rule disguised as nepotism. An apparent *caudillista* control in presidential power is being greeted as positive. No one even seems to be troubled by the fact that the

---

[33] For a similar choice of very different cases to test the power of an argument in contrasting settings see E. Wood (2000).

presidency, which was continually staying within the same party, is now staying within the same family. Why? Why would a nation with so many apparent democratic advantages have so much trouble developing democracy?

The answers to Argentina's troubles do not lie in current events, or in the choice of a president, or in the failure of economic policy, or in investigations of the electoral capacity of political parties. These are immediate manifestations of more fundamental problems. Many observers have noticed that Argentines lack a basic ability to cooperate with each other and that deficiency has been evident over many decades as well as in contemporary problems. But the reasons behind that inability are historical and lie in the nature of Argentine society. By looking into historical context we can understand why Argentina's democracy appears to be so often troubled, and by understanding that we can find pathways out of that trouble. Whatever temporary measures Argentina takes to address its current problems, over the long term its democracy must address the fundamental issues of trust and cooperation if it is to survive.

In Nicaragua, by contrast, democracy seems to be developing against remarkable odds and multiple disadvantages.[34] Nicaragua is a tiny, poverty-stricken, agricultural nation whose entire economy depends on a few agricultural export crops. It has almost no industry and relies on foreign imports for much of the basis of its economy. Its people are poor, traditionally undereducated, and many have historically been illiterate. It has suffered intensive foreign imperialism for much of its history. It has all the disadvantages and few of the advantages that tend to auger well for democracy.

And yet, Nicaragua has moved slowly but steadily toward democracy ever since it began a regular electoral calendar in November, 1984.[35] Since then, each of its three major parties, the Liberals, the Conservatives, and the Sandinistas, have won and then lost national elections, and have left office on schedule. There has been no hyperinflation and no attempted coupes. Although there is poverty, there has been no major national crisis and no threat to default on international loans. No president has resigned. Its most corrupt president, Arnoldo Alemán (1996–2001), was tried and punished through the legal system – an effort led by the next president, Enrique Bolaños, who had been Alemán's own Vice President and a member of the same Liberal Constitutionalist Party.[36] Nicaraguans have engaged in thoughtful, reflective discussions in recent elections, in a manner similar to that of citizens in established democracies and one that has advanced democratic development in Nicaragua. This has occurred despite circumstances that theorists find antithetical to democratization.[37] In the most recent national election, the leftist Sandinistas won office legitimately and were allowed to take office peacefully. The new president, Daniel Ortega, who appears to be bent on personalistic

---

[34] Anderson and Dodd (2002; 2004; 2005).
[35] Anderson and Dodd (2002; 2009).
[36] Anderson (2006).
[37] Anderson and Dodd (2002; 2004; 2005; 2007).

Introduction

control, is being accused of *caudillista* politics and meets resistance at every turn. He faces firm opposition from the legislature, other members of the left, and from within his own party.[38] Nicaraguans are responding negatively to the attempted *caudillista* control, recognizing it as wrong and trying to stop its development.[39] While Nicaragua is not without its problems, it does not seem to have the repeated dramatic crises that plague Argentina. Personalized politics is greeted as a problem rather than a solution. Why? Why would a nation with apparently so few democratic advantages be developing its democracy in such a steady fashion?

As in the case of Argentina, current events and contemporary issues are not enough to explain Nicaragua's democratization. Current events reflect social relations underlying Nicaragua's progress. The outcome of one election, the role of domestic actors, domestic responses to international influences at a given moment in time, and strong electoral parties that win office and alternate in power are all manifestations of a deeper pattern of human relations that has facilitated Nicaragua's democracy in a remarkable way. As with Argentina, the answer to Nicaragua's democratization lies in historical context. Despite multiple disadvantages, Nicaragua has habits of social behavior that facilitate democratic development. Its citizens have a capacity for cooperation – a capacity that has been mildly present for generations but was dramatically encouraged by social revolution. Today it is causing democratization. The popular histories examined here have formed popular culture within each nation and it is that popular culture which determines social capital and its role in democracy.[40]

This tale of two democracies has also been told before, and the paths Nicaragua and Argentina travel have been taken before by older democracies that today are considered established democratic nations. Upon reaching the end of this book, the reader will understand how the stories of Nicaragua and Argentina also pertain to those of the developing democracies of France and

---

[38] Anderson and Dodd (2009).
[39] On legislative resistance to Ortega's caudillista maneuvers see *El Nuevo Diario*, December 1, 2, 3, 2007, p. 1. Leading the legislative resistance to Ortega's efforts to ignore constitutional law is Wilfredo Navarro, head of the legislative bloc for the Liberal Constitutional Party (PLC). For leftist resistance to Ortega's efforts to control power extra constitutionally see *El Nuevo Diario*, December 16, 2007, p. 1. Leading leftist resistance to Ortega's efforts to subvert aspects of constitutional rule is Edmundo Jarquin, 2006 presidential candidate for the center leftist party, Sandinista Renovating Movement. On this issue Jarquin raised questions about Ortega's mental fitness for office. On the 2006 election see Anderson and Dodd (2007).
[40] Jeffrey W. Rubin (2004) likewise seeks to understand the relationship between social movements and the cultural politics behind those movements. Like his, my approach requires contextual understanding of the different historical paths by which these movements have developed. Likewise, Nancy Bermeo (2003) uses historical and contextual analysis to inform her understanding of popular support for democracy across Europe and Latin America. Her analysis reveals findings that have gone unnoticed by scholars less steeped in historical analysis.

the United States, of Germany and Italy. For the struggles being played out in these two Latin American nations have also been played out before in other developing democracies in the early nineteenth century. This book places the cases studied here in the broader comparative context of history, and compares them to the development or failure of democracy elsewhere.

In Nicaragua we are looking at a nation with a revolutionary history. Chapter 2 will illustrate how that history has folded itself into every aspect of contemporary politics. In particular, it has affected how citizens relate to each other and how they view their leaders. It has also produced a particular brand of politics, strong with respect to mobilizational capacity and weak with respect to institutions. Those strengths and weaknesses shape Nicaraguan democratization today. But the story of the relationship between revolution and democracy does not belong to Nicaragua alone. In France and in the United States, many scholars have found the connection that popular cooperation and revolution have with democratic development. That story of revolution and democracy emphasizes the presence of horizontal ties of cooperation and mutuality, the strong development of associations and popular participation, and the importance of citizen participation.

Crucial to the relationship between revolution and democracy in Nicaragua is the role of alternation in power. Unlike the revolutions of Cuba, Russia, and China, Nicaragua's revolution benefited from the liberating aspects of popular revolution and then removed the revolutionary leaders from power before they could become totalitarians. Alternation in power allowed popular participation to flourish rather than crushing it at its height. Nicaragua's story reminds us that revolution was originally supposed to be a liberating movement against authoritarianism. By taking the liberating aspects and curtailing the totalitarian aspects of revolution, Nicaragua has put us back in touch with the democratizing potential of revolution.

In Argentina, by contrast, we are looking at a nation with a deep authoritarian culture and a history of repression toward the popular sectors that were never broken by revolution. Chapter 3 will show how that culture produced a popular social movement that only intensified the previous cultural tendencies toward vertical ties, clientelistic control, personalized, charismatic strong-man politics, and a lack of citizen cooperation or initiative. Argentina's political history, far more than Nicaragua's, is shared by many other Latin American nations. Clientelism and deep authoritarian patterns of leadership also characterize Brazil, Peru, and Mexico, to name but a few. A tendency to embrace personalized politics also characterizes the Dominican Republic and, until recently, even Venezuela. But Argentina's authoritarian political culture is not confined to Latin America. Chapter 3 will show that Argentina also shares the characteristics of authoritarian personalism and democratic breakdown with the European nations of Germany, Italy, and Spain.

This overview indicates that Argentina does not have the advantage in democratization that we would expect it to have given its status as a relatively wealthy industrialized nation. Nicaragua, on the other hand, looks more successful in its democratic development than we would expect it to be given its status as a poor agrarian nation. The argument of this book is that part of the answer to this contrast lies in social capital theory, and specifically in the kind of social capital these nations developed with the mass movements of the Sandinista revolution and Peronism. Differences in social capital, rather than differences in industrial or economic development, explain democratic development in these two cases.

But even there we do not have the full answers. Even by understanding social capital in these two nations, we fall short of a full explanation for democratic development in each context. Even if we allow that social capital is strong in agrarian Nicaragua because of the type of association Sandinismo created, and that social capital is weak in industrialized Argentina because of the type of social capital Peronism instilled, we still face the fact that modern Argentina is democratizing. In a determined fashion and in the face of extreme military brutality, Argentine democracy is lurching forward. Even if Argentine democratization is not as smooth and untroubled as we would expect it to be judging from the nation's level of industrial development, nevertheless, Argentina is making forward progress in the construction of a recognizable democracy.

This can only be possible upon the basis of some democratic foundation other than social capital. We find that, despite the popular culture of suspicion and distrust, despite clientelism and authoritarianism, or possibly precisely because of them, Argentina has attended to the development of its institutions – far more than Nicaragua. Indeed, it has given more attention to the establishment of democratic institutions than it has to the establishment of democracy itself. Argentina's story will focus our attention on the power of institutions and the capacity of institutions to create and protect democratic space, provide a bulwark against authoritarianism, and gradually grow into the role of democratic governance. Argentina's path to democracy is weak with respect to popular participation but strong with respect to institutional development. It is an alternative path to democracy that has received less attention.

By placing this tale of two democracies within the larger tale of democracy in Europe and Latin America, we will find the universal lessons about how the patterns of human relations and civil society influence the polity. By learning what those patterns are in Nicaragua and Argentina, we will be able to identify them elsewhere and to understand beforehand where and why democracy will develop with reasonable steadiness and where and why its development will be troubled. By having that knowledge, we can then inject human agency into the course of democracy, as, in fact, both the Nicaraguans and the Argentines have already done. Whether human agency comes in the form of mobilized, cooperative popular participation, or whether it comes by the deliberate careful construction of the institutions of state, either way human agency produces for itself a resource that can be used against authoritarianism.

It provides a space for dialogue and contestation with protection from authoritarian power. Either way, it provides a key to democratization.

I argued at the outset of this chapter that citizen cooperation and social capital represent resources that citizens can draw upon to develop democracy. They can use the resource of mutual faith and cooperative capacity – social capital – to combat authoritarianism, restrain power, and work together to resolve disagreements peacefully. The Argentine story tells us that societies may also have an alternative resource other than social capital – some other foundation that a nation can use to combat authoritarianism, restrain power, and resolve differences.

DEMOCRATIZATION WITHOUT SOCIAL CAPITAL

If nations need resources upon which to develop democracy, strong institutional development offers another resource. I call this "institutional capital," the slow gradual creation of strong resilient institutions that can combat authoritarianism, curtail power and provide space to resolve differences peacefully.[41] An alternative resource for democratic problem-solving lies in a nation's institutions – institutional capital. Quite apart from the history of social movements, revolution, and popular values, nations develop an institutional history. Within that unfolding history, nations may or may not begin to develop their institutions of state in a formal, procedural manner that creates a broad frame for the rule of law. Some nations move toward institutional construction early in their histories while others pay less attention to institutional development. By using the Argentine case and focusing on the institutions of state, particularly the legislature, this book will show that a long history of institutional development can create institutional capital, even where democracy has repeatedly broken down. Once established, institutions develop a life of their own and gradually become a place where differences can be worked out peaceably.[42]

---

[41] I define institutions as organizations or associations. I am particularly interested in the formal institutions of state, since these are directly involved in the development of democracy. The definition I use for "institutions" is more restrictive than the definition often associated with the "new institutionalism," wherein institutions are often defined as "sets of rules." On the other hand, I define institutions more broadly than rational choice approaches wherein "institutions" are seen as sets of rules *within* organizations. For excellent examples of the definition of institutions as sets of rules, see Bunce (1999) or Thelen (2004). For an important example of the approach that defines institutions as sets of rules within organizations, see Shepsle (1986, esp. p. 52). I am particularly indebted to conversations with Goran Hyden and Lawrence Dodd, who helped me clarify my own use of the term "institutions" and place it in comparative context.

[42] An important study of the role of institutions in causing political change is Valerie Bunce's work on the demise of socialism. While my work is a study of institutions as they differ in their ability to construct democracy in Latin America, Bunce's work is a study of how the nature of institutions can explain variation in the ways that socialism collapsed in Eastern Europe (1999).

Huntington tells us that personalities are dangerous.[43] At a minimum, sometimes some personalities can become dangerous. When dangerous personalities are also leaders, including even leaders of social movements, then nations must turn to institutions in order to find a way to restrain those leaders and protect society. This book argues that institutional capital and a long history of gradual institutional development can provide an alternative resource for democratization when social capital is in short supply. The Argentine case allows us to explore that argument and to see how Argentine democracy has been able to develop based on the strength of its institutions. The story holds relevance, and also holds out hope, for many other nations where clientelism, patronage, and vertical ties inhibit democratic development.

Chapter 7 explores where and how Argentina has certain democratic advantages over Nicaragua. Nicaragua's founders never defined a set of democratic institutions as carefully and thoroughly as the writers of Argentina's constitution did. Although Nicaragua developed parties, the formal institutions of state remained weak and poorly articulated until very recently. As a result, institutions are weaker in Nicaragua than they are in Argentina.

The discovery that Argentina is strong with respect to institutions but weak on social capital, while Nicaragua offers the opposite scenario, leads to the question of the relationship between social capital and institutions. Can a nation like Argentina that has relatively strong institutions use them to create social capital? Can strength in institutions be used to shore up weak social capital? Alternatively, can the strong foundation in social capital that Nicaragua enjoys be used to develop stronger institutions? What precisely is the relationship between social capital and institutions?

We will revisit this question throughout the book and summarize what we know at the end. But the question requires further investigation into the democratic consolidation process underway in each of these nations. Time and further progress toward consolidation in these two cases will help answer that question. For scholars of democracy, the great advantage of studying developing rather than established democracies is the opportunity it affords for us to understand how democracy actually unfolds, what different kinds of problems nations encounter along different paths, and how new democracies may use different responses to resolve similar problems.

THE DEBATE IN OTHER LANGUAGES

I have chosen to frame the issues of this book in the language of social capital and institutional development, what I call institutional capital. Social capital

---

[43] In modern political science, Huntington's advocacy of institutions is widely recognized. In point of fact, however, Huntington followed the earlier position of Edmund Burke, whose defense of institutions emerged in his criticism of the French Revolution. "We are afraid to put men to live and trade each on his own private stock of reason; because we suspect that the stock in each man is small, and that the individuals would do better to avail themselves of the general bank and capital of nations and of ages." (1790). See also Burke (1782, pp. 7, 94),

theory and its extension to institutional development is a robust and versatile way of exploring the complex issues of this book. In the puzzle of how democracy evolves, we gain the greatest mileage with this language. But other scholars at other times have used other terms to consider many of these same issues. Linz and Stepan used the terms "state centered" and "society centered" democratization, and the issues of this book can also be considered usefully from that vantage point (1978). Nicaragua is emerging in a more society-centered style of democratization, while Argentina is using a more state-centered path toward democracy. Each has advantages and limitations. Similarly, the issues raised by the Nicaraguan and Argentine cases reveal contrasts between mobilizational versus institutional democratic development: Nicaragua's style of democratization is more reliant on a powerful national capacity for popular mobilization, while Argentina's democratization is more dependent on institutional capacity. Nicaragua's democratization emphasizes participatory democracy, while Argentina's relies on representational democracy. Again, each has advantages and disadvantages, and we will return to these contrasts at the end of the book.

This book also asks "What difference does a revolution make for democracy today?" If mass participation in politics had already occurred before democracy arrived, that participation would impart popular values and experiences that would affect political trust and cooperation today. The question speaks to the contrast of tumultuous, participatory, and revolutionary participation versus a formal, hierarchical, and representative version of participation within democratization.

The book asks as well, "What difference do institutions make for democracy today?" When a nation's founders carefully laid down a framework for democratic institutional function, but that framework was subsequently ignored or used in only a minimal way, the mere existence of democratic institutions nonetheless represents a potential resource for democratic development. Once society begins to cast around for assets to use for democratization, that institutional framework can be turned to constructive purpose.

None of these languages, however, allows us to consider a society's investment in itself as fully as does the language of social capital. Using and expanding that language allows us to consider which form of capital a society has poured its positive, creative energies into, and therefore where it has the greatest pool of resources upon which to draw in the face of the challenges of democratization. We embark upon the study of these two contrasting cases using the language of social capital theory, and expanding it to include political and institutional capital as well. In the process, we learn how societies can make use of whatever liberating resources they have developed in the past for the task of developing a more humane society. Creating a better society

quoted in Herzog (1998, p. 15). Herzog suggests that Burke's preference for institutions (and his hope that they will not be overthrown in England as they were in France) lies in the fact that he sees individuals as less wise than institutions.

Introduction

is a tall order, indeed, and its cause is best served by flexible societies whose citizens and leaders are willing to use any assets they have at hand to move forward with the task.

THE CONTRAST IN OTHER PLACES

The issues raised in this book go far beyond the cases of Nicaragua and Argentina. In Latin America, Europe and other places around the world today, democracy is developing in many different contexts. Some of those contexts have benefited from an explosive liberating experience in the form of a revolution. Where revolution did not deteriorate into its own antithesis, it greatly enhanced democracy. The cases of the French and American revolutions first taught us about the positive relationship between revolution and democracy. The Nicaraguan case reminds us that the relationship is still there today and revolution can still enhance democracy.

But far more countries in Latin America and elsewhere are developing their democracies without the benefit of such an explosive, unpredictable, and dangerous event as a revolution. In many cases, democracy is attempting to emerge in contexts of strong authoritarian traditions, extensive clientelist practices, and vertical ties of patronage control. The Argentine case is one of them. In such contexts, hierarchical control, clientelism and vertical patronage networks greatly undermine citizen cooperation and the mutual faith necessary to establish democratic social capital. The Argentine case shows where societies like these might turn to find resources upon which to build democracy.

AN OVERVIEW OF THE BOOK

This book begins with social capital theory but moves beyond it in multiple ways. First, the book challenges the argument that social capital develops slowly over many generations. The Nicaraguan case forces us to look at the possibility of the rapid development of social capital in a poor agrarian context. Viewing revolution as a source of democratizing social capital in Nicaragua allows us to consider the possibility of the rapid development of social capital. Nicaragua's revolution emerged in the late 1960s and took power in 1979. Any social capital to which it contributed has formed within one or at most two generations. Nicaragua's rapid formation of social capital helps us expand the argument to new democracies. To allow for rapid associational experience and learning is to make the social capital argument pertinent to all democracies developing today, expanding the relevance of the original argument. It illustrates that nations and citizens can produce circumstances that enhance the development of social capital, and with it democratization, more rapidly than we originally thought.

Second, this book moves beyond current studies of social capital by scrutinizing the relationship between social capital and politics. The cases of Sandinismo and Peronism make us examine the powerful role of political associations beyond that of social associations or activities. Instead of assuming that social capital directly facilitates democracy and that all associations enhance democratic political participation, we consider both social organizations and political organizations in relation to political participation. That consideration reveals a second step in the causal movement from social interaction to democratic politics. That second step consists of a series of specifically *political* actions and attitudes, something that I call "political capital." Thus the argument developed here and the empirical basis upon which it rests scrutinize indicators of social capital *in relation to* political actions and attitudes that come from associational interactions among citizens. The analysis shows that democratic political capital comes from certain types of associations (and therefore from one type of social capital) but not from other kinds of associations. Social capital always has political ramifications but these may or may not be democratic.

This discovery takes us to a third way that the book moves beyond contemporary studies of social capital. Since the empirical findings uncover a type of citizen association or social capital that has anti-democratic implications, we must consider democratization in contexts of anti-democratic social capital. Peronism makes us consider the different and potentially anti-democratic results of some kinds of political organizations and the values they impart. Such contexts underscore the limits of social capital in facilitating democracy and demonstrate that some kinds of citizen associations actually undermine the development of trust, cooperation, and initiative. Associations that insist upon vertical loyalty to a leader will discourage citizen initiative, encourage dependency upon leadership, and produce individualist rather than cooperative efforts. The combination of low citizen initiative, dependency, and lack of cooperation will allow openings for clientelism and patronage. For those at the bottom, these become substitutes for cooperation to get their needs met, which has very negative implications for democratic development. For those at the top, clientelism and patronage become more convenient and less visible forms of control that can substitute outright repression. It is important, therefore, to understand the nature of the values citizens absorb when they join organizations, particularly political organizations, and when they participate through these organizations in mass politics. Mass politics can be revolutionary and empowering, but European history reminds us that mass politics also produced fascism. The Argentine story will make us remember that alternative side of associational interaction and mass mobilization.

The data for this study consist in comparative historical analysis, public opinion surveys, and mail surveys of elite opinion. The details of the data bases are presented in the Appendix. Part I (Chapters 2 and 3) presents the historical perspective and the argument drawn from it. Chapter 2 considers the history of Sandinismo and the type of social capital it created. Chapter 3 examines Peronism and the social capital it created. These chapters scrutinize each movement in historical and social context, and in contrast with other similar movements elsewhere in history. They examine the position of these two mass movements on the left–right spectrum and the implications of that position for democratic development today. They scrutinize the ideas behind each movement and the extent to which these contributed to feelings of social and political trust among associational members or, alternatively, the extent to which the mass associational experience rested upon ideas of superiority, rejection of "others," and exclusion. Chapters 2 and 3 also consider the political legacy of a movement that emphasized informal, tumultuous politics of the streets (Sandinismo), versus the legacy left by another movement that encouraged formal, hierarchical politics that inadvertently worked within preexisting institutions and accidentally reinforced institutionalization (Peronism).

Part II considers empirical evidence on social capital in Nicaragua and Argentina. The empirical analysis examines the argument made in Part I. The data analyzed come from several public opinion data sets collected in each country. These scrutinize social and political trust as indicators of the nature of social capital in each nation. With respect to social trust, the analysis uses many of the same empirical indicators that Robert Putnam has used to study social trust in the United States. The data on political trust move beyond the question of social trust to examine attitudes toward the institutions and processes of democracy. Chapter 4 considers the legacy of social capital that Sandinismo and Peronism have each left behind. Chapters 5 and 6 consider the more explicitly political results of that legacy of social capital. Chapter 5 considers political values across these two societies – between Sandinistas and non-Sandinistas in Nicaragua, and between Peronists and non-Peronists in Argentina. Chapter 6 considers political participation and political attitudes toward democratic institutions and procedures, and makes the same set of contrasts. The empirical evidence of Part II offers substantial support for the argument of Part I.

Part III addresses Argentine democratization in the absence of positive social capital. The chapter provides an historical and empirical examination of institutional development in each case. It scrutinizes the formal institutions of state in each nation, particularly the national legislature. Since the legislature is the most important institutional locus of popular opinion and national democratic debate, it seems appropriate to make it a central part of the study of democratic institutions. Chapter 7 considers the history of legislative development in Nicaragua and Argentina, and the relationship between the mass movements in each nation and the legislature. Chapter 7 asks how the legacies of Sandinismo and Peronism affected and continue to shape the contours of the national legislature, as well as the balance of national powers between the president and the legislature. The chapter is thus a consideration of the institutional legacy of the mass movements. It shows how institutions, particularly the legislature, can represent an alternative foundation for democracy in the absence of positive social capital. Chapter 7 also presents empirical evidence of legislative development in the two nations, data that support the importance of institutional capital.

The Conclusion considers the state of social capital and democratization in Nicaragua and Argentina. It steps back from these specific nations to ask what the implications of these findings are for democratic development and for the study of democratization and democratic consolidation. The popular experience is important in any understanding of democratic development because it determines the nature of civil society. The study of the social capital within any given nation must be a part of the study of democratization. Putnam is correct that social capital, of the positive kind, can help make democracy work. Yet a populist mass movement in and of itself does not necessarily enhance democratic development, and joining an association, any association, just for the sake of joining, does not automatically enhance democracy. Some mass movements help create social capital while others foster social isolation. The study of Peronism, as well as the realization that Peronism is not unique, illustrates, too, that mass organization and association can also have a non-democratic character to them. Accordingly, attention to the nature of the mass movement, the values it instills, the social organization it fosters, and the nature of social capital it produces is in order. These conclusions cause us to reconsider the kind of capital that derives from popular association. They expand our understanding of social capital, adding a perspective derived from a non-democratic society and its authoritarian history.

In the end, of course, a strong, healthy democratic nation needs both mechanisms for participatory democracy as well as channels for formal political involvement. Democracy needs an involved, attentive, and mobilized population prepared to take the initiative in favor of democratic movement forward, and also willing to take a stand to protect democracy from leaders or influences that threaten it. But a new democracy also needs institutions and a willingness to use them. These can substitute for a lack of participatory democracy or for a lack of democratically oriented participation. Democracy needs vibrant, independent democratic institutions that contribute to strengthening, deepening, and protecting the rule of law. Institutionalized and mobilized politics are *each* essential to democracy. That a new democracy would develop one without the other leaves it with significant weaknesses and vulnerabilities, as well as with work still to do in consolidating democracy. The book concludes with the question of how a nation that has one of them can develop the other.

PART I

CREATING SOCIAL CAPITAL

People I Have Known: The Human Face of Popular Politics

Ricardo became a Sandinista. Born in 1944 to a family of modest income in Managua, Nicaragua, Ricardo found himself drawn to religion when he was still a teenager. He began studying in the Catholic high school and decided to become a priest. He worked under the tutelage of then-Bishop Miguel Obando y Bravo. When he was old enough to join the university, Ricardo traveled to Europe, supported by the church, to complete his studies there. He attended a European seminary and met many Catholics from Spain, Belgium, and elsewhere. When he graduated and was ordained a priest, Ricardo returned to Managua to work among the poor. That's where he was on December 23, 1972, when, in the early morning hours, Managua was hit by the most severe earthquake of its history. With extraordinary good luck, Ricardo woke up and rushed out of his room and out into the courtyard of his residence, only to see the walls around him rock and begin to fall. "I saw a woman crushed by a wall," he told me. "After it fell, all you could see were her legs. It was terrible to see the damage and to see the people suffer. I walked among the ruins, and the people cried for help. All the poor people suffered so much. I always remember that." For the next several weeks, Ricardo joined with other clergy and international aid workers to try to rescue the victims of the earthquake and to bring them food, clothing, and emotional support as they mourned the loss of loved ones and anguished over the loss of their homes.

Ricardo's life plan, in his thirties, had been to remain a priest and to work with the poor for the rest of his days. He was well-suited to the task. He was a generous, patient man of few words, with a ready smile and a constant willingness to help others, particularly the poor who were most in need. But Ricardo fell in love. A lovely, kind Nicaraguan beauty, his new girlfriend posed for Ricardo one of the most stark choices of his young life: to marry or to remain in service to the church. Ricardo left the priesthood to marry the love of his life. But he retained his commitment to a life of service, his concern for the poor, and his willingness to work, together with others, to build a better world. These were values he now shared with his new wife.

Always interested in books and the world of the intellect, Ricardo left Nicaragua to pursue a Masters degree and then a doctorate at universities in the United States. For this reason, he was not in Nicaragua during the final years of the Nicaraguan Revolution and the Sandinista triumph over Somoza in July, 1979. But Ricardo watched such events closely from abroad and when the revolution triumphed, he returned to Nicaragua to join the new government. Ricardo had completed his Masters degree and except for the dissertation he had finished his doctoral research as well. But after joining the Sandinista cause, he never had a chance to return to the dissertation, and it remained incomplete. I asked him if he would ever finish the dissertation. "No," he said, "I don't need it for what I do."

Ricardo's life was full, exciting, fascinating, inspiring, and energizing. He became a civil servant, working within several ministries of the new Sandinista government. This position allowed him to return to the goals of service that had drawn him into the priesthood, but now he could serve from a position within a state that was itself dedicated to serving the poor. Ricardo played an extraordinary role in his new job. Drawing on his previous contacts within the church, his knowledge of the academic and professional world, and his friendly, nonjudgmental personality, Ricardo remained friends with everyone and enemies with none. He and his work exemplified a perpetual effort to build alliances, retain friendships, find common ground for cooperation even with those opposed to the government he loved, supported, and believed in so deeply. Ricardo kept many and even most doors open for himself and for his work because he chose to see the good in others and to work with the good part of others, even if he disagreed with them on most specifics.

When the Sandinistas were voted out of power in the election of 1990, Ricardo left the Chamorro government that cut back services to the poor. Seeking still to serve the poor, Ricardo now began work with a nongovernmental organization (NGO) that was devoted to many kinds of development work throughout Nicaragua. Ricardo worked for the NGO for the rest of his life until his death in 2000. He worked on many different projects but found himself most drawn to development work in the Atlantic Region of Nicaragua, the nation's poorest and most backward area.

I saw Ricardo many times throughout the 1990s. It was a tense time in Nicaragua as the Sandinistas struggled to retain influence on Nicaraguan politics from a position of opposition. Meanwhile, the political right sought to marginalize the Sandinistas as much as possible. Neither side was completely successful, but Ricardo appeared to move between individuals on both sides of the political divide. He always retained an ability to see the other person's perspective and to recognize the other person's contributions. The last time I saw Ricardo, he had come to say good bye. We hoped to see each other again at my next visit. He was rushing off for several days of development work in the Atlantic region. I was flying out of Managua to return to the United States. The last thing he said to me was, "That's a good book you're writing. Just keep writing. Whatever you do, just keep writing."

I was shocked and saddened to learn that Ricardo died in an airplane accident several months after I last saw him. He was returning from his development projects in the Atlantic region in a small commercial plane. The plane encountered a severe rainstorm and turbulence while flying over the high mountains in eastern Nicaragua. The pilot lost visibility, and the radar apparatus that should have guided the plane had been illegally removed before takeoff. I never saw Ricardo again. At his funeral his co-workers called him "the priest without a frock."

Lucinda became a Peronist. I first met her at an afternoon tea party in Buenos Aires. She appeared a fine lady, dressed in elegant clothing, a charming smile on her face, her voice deepened by years of smoking. But Lucy had not always been wealthy. She was born to a working class family in Buenos Aires in 1939. Her father and older brothers were factory workers who became caught up in the Peronist movement of the time. Lucy grew up in a household where the name "Perón" was part of nearly every conversation. His picture hung on the walls in the living room and kitchen. When Perón spoke, all the family members gathered around the radio to listen. As a very young girl, Lucy remembered being taken to the Plaza de Mayo outside the Presidential Palace to hear Perón speak. "There were so many people," she told me, "thousands and thousands of us, all calling Perón's name and waving our arms and calling to him. When he spoke it became so quiet you could hear your own heart. And it was so beautiful. He spoke and spoke. His voice resonated across the crowds. And he said such beautiful things, and we listened and learned and loved. We loved him so much."

Lucy was still a girl when Perón was ousted from power in 1955. But his name and the service he had done for the workers remained a part of the household dialogue for the rest of her girlhood. Her father and older brothers were firm union loyalists. They talked about the union a lot, but she could not understand much of what they said. They seemed to hate everyone not in the union. They blamed "them" for Perón's exile and talked a lot about how Perón could be brought back to Argentina. But they never seemed to have, or know, a plan of action, and Perón never returned.

When Lucy was 19, her father was killed in an industrial accident. Her girlhood home suffered a decline in its fortunes, but her brothers supported the family, including herself, her mother, and her little sister. Lucy was attending a local high school, but she says it was not a good school and there was lot of politics in the classroom. Sometimes the teacher did not show up, and the books were old and torn. When Lucy graduated, there was no question of her pursuing university studies. There was no money for such luxury, and Lucy went to work in a sewing factory. She remembers Argentine politics as being "angry all the time" during the 1950s and 1960s. "Everyone was always angry at everyone else," she recalls.

When Lucy was 22, she met and married her husband, Paulo. He had attended a Peronist high school and was deeply committed to the workers' movement and to Perón's return. Through the use of union funds, Lucy's husband was able to attend university for two years. He studied economics but dropped out when the funding ran short. He returned to work for the union, managing its financial affairs. Paulo divided his time between union meetings, bookkeeping, and factory work. Their household was again filled with talk about Perón and about his possible return.

The year 1970 was a turning point in Lucy's life. The union movement became more and more agitated over the return of Perón to Argentina. When Perón finally returned in 1973, it was a day of great rejoicing. "Now we'll show them," Paulo said, "all those who have kept us down. Now it is our turn again." Because of his loyalty and his training in economics, Paulo was invited to work for the Ministry of Economics under the new Peronist administration. He remained in that position throughout most of the three brief years of Peronism's return. During those years, Lucy's economic fortunes improved dramatically. Now there was money in the household. She began to dress well, buy make-up, and wear jewelry. "Those were good years," she remarks. "We finally began to have a little something."

But the good fortune did not last. In 1974 Perón died, and after that, the administration gradually collapsed under chaos. Paulo stayed with the ministry but then suddenly resigned one day. Lucy never understood why Paulo resigned, and his work appeared a mystery to her for several months after that. But then the military took over the government, and Paulo was not particularly upset. Once again he was hired by the economic ministry, "something to do with his relations with the labor unions."

I met Lucy in 1993. By that time, Argentina had been a new democracy for nearly 10 years, and many celebrated the newfound political freedom. But Lucy did not celebrate the democracy, and she became crafty and evasive when I tried to learn the specifics of hers and Paulo's relationship with the last Peronist administration and with the military government. "But you know," she told me, "the best government was the military. I mean, at least we have Menem, and he is one of us. But he does not make things as good as they used to be. And all this about human rights, it is all lies. No one disappeared. Don't believe everything they tell you," she warned me.

I met Lucy on a number of occasions at social events in Buenos Aires. I learned her life history gradually over those casual encounters. She fascinated me. I wondered how she thought and why she believed as she did. But she was never fully forthcoming with me. She would smile and change the subject, take my arm and rush me across the room to meet someone new or to refill my wine glass. When we talked, her face was always guarded and veiled. When she smiled, only her mouth smiled. Her eyes remained hard behind her elegant glasses. I learned not to trust Lucy. She clearly did not trust me. But then, I was not certain whom she really did trust, if anyone. Trust was not part of her world. Glitz and glitter, fine clothes and convenient contacts, getting by and managing with whoever was in power: These were her goals and they characterized Paulo's career, even when it was not clear to her precisely what he did in the government.

2

Creating "We"

Sandinismo and Bridging Social Capital

> And what the hell do I care if the banks reduce their interest rates by one and one half points?
>
> *Eduardo Mazo, Autorizado a Vivir*

> Look at this cross!... I am not a communist, as Somoza calls all who fight against his government. I am a Catholic and a Sandinista.
>
> *Nicaraguan revolutionary from the barricades of Estelí, 1978*[1]

> We did not invent the fundamental elements of our liberation ourselves. The vanguard gathered these ideas from Sandino... We found political, military, ideological, and moral elements in our people, in our own history.
>
> *Humberto Ortega Saavedra*[2]

Sandinismo was fundamentally a movement of the poorest of the poor, many of whom did not even have jobs, much less labor unions. It was born out of landlessness, exploitative agro-export capitalism, and urban squalor.[3] Although most Sandinistas were the lowest-income members of one of the poorest Latin American nations, Sandinismo was also a movement that joined together likeminded opponents of dictatorship who themselves came from many different walks of life. It was a movement deeply grounded in and aware of mainstream currents of political thinking and economic interdependence worldwide. Its leaders and thinkers exhibited profound awareness of the causes and consequences of wealth and poverty, even as many of its followers knew they were excluded from wealth and participation in the global economy.

Although Nicaragua is a poor nation lacking extensive natural resources, a vast market, or a strong economy, it benefits from its geographical location near the United States and at the heart of Latin America. Managua, the nation's capital, is only a few hours flight from Miami, roughly the same

---

[1] As reported by Jose Fajardo in *El Tiempo*, Bogota, Colombia, October 9, 1978 and quoted in Lernoux (1982, p. 102).
[2] La revolución a traves de nuestra direccion nacional, p. 9.
[3] Enriquez (1991, chap. 2); Téfel (1976).

31

distance from Mexico City, and even closer to Havana and the northern capitals of South America. While proximity to the United States has also brought heavy-handed meddling and efforts at political control of domestic affairs, Nicaragua's location has favored the dissemination of ideas from the United States and Europe, Mexico, Cuba, and Venezuela. This was true long before the Sandinista revolution, and would remain true throughout its formative years and its struggle for power.

By the time of the Sandinista revolution, this location mattered even more. The ease of communication and travel in the late twentieth century were considerable. While electronic communication had not yet arrived, air travel and telephone calls were easy, not to mention wire communication and fax machines. The nation's proximity to modern currents of communication and ideas helps explain the ideological configuration Sandinismo assumed: the origin of its ideas about resistance, nationalism, and revolutionary leftism; and the style of leadership and struggle that it used to seek power.

This chapter scrutinizes the citizens' experience within Sandinismo. Key elements in the creation of bridging social capital in Nicaragua were (1) the interchangeability of leadership, (2) the centralization of ideas rather than personality that underlay the cooperation of multiple leaders, (3) the fostering of grassroots initiatives, and (4) the creation of cross-class ties. Each of these four factors interacted with the others so that fostering one also enhanced the others, and they grew in tandem, intertwined. These four key elements originated with the beginning of Sandinista resistance to the dictatorship, continued and strengthened with the insurrectionary years, and formed the foundations of political society during the eleven years of the Sandinista regime. They also spawned social trust among revolutionaries and across Nicaraguan society as a result of the revolutionary movement.

THE INTERCHANGEABILITY OF LEADERSHIP

Although newscasts since 2006 have focused our attention on Daniel Ortega, we should not be deceived by such coverage into thinking that he represents the only current of opinion within Sandinismo.[4] Far from it. From its earliest inception as a tiny guerrilla movement, to and throughout its first eleven years in power, Sandinismo was led by many different leaders.[5] This interchangeability of leadership was made possible, in part, because the movement framed its struggle within the larger global effort against international imperialism and for self-determination and social justice within small nations. That struggle

---

[4] Anderson and Dodd (2009).
[5] Even today, the modern, electoral Sandinista party boasts a wide array of good leaders. Careful study of the party will find them located in the national legislature, in the mayoral and vice-mayoral positions in many municipalities nationwide, and in the center-leftist opposition party, the Sandinista Renovationist Movement (MRS). For initial discussion of alternative Sandinista leadership, see Anderson and Dodd (2007; 2008; 2009).

had begun in Nicaragua with Augusto Sandino's 1920s peasant movement and continued with the Sandinista revolution in the 1980s. The importance of any specific leader paled in comparison with the importance of Nicaragua's domestic struggle as part of that broader effort.

Let us explore the relationship between the revolution and the earlier peasant movement. Sandino's movement was separated from the Sandinista revolutionary movement by thirty years – Sandino, in fact, had died more than forty years before the Sandinista revolution was launched. But the revolution took his name and adopted many of his goals, including resistance to imperialism, national self-determination, and domestic social justice. But even if Sandino was not involved in the Sandinista revolution, he was responsible for the international perspective that defined both his movement and the subsequent revolutionary struggle. His thinking was influenced by ideas from Mexico and elsewhere. Explaining his decision to take up arms against the United States, Sandino said that he had worked in Mexico for a "Yankee" oil company, and that the experience caused him to decide in 1925 to return to Nicaragua to fight "for our sovereignty that had been placed in danger by the same Yankee imperialism" that he had encountered in Mexico.[6] Disgusted by the United States' meddling in Nicaragua's domestic affairs and by rural poverty, peasant landlessness, and elite land concentration, Sandino mustered an army of peasants in northeastern Nicaragua.

Nicaragua's politics at that time were divided between two non-electoral parties of notables, the Liberals and Conservatives, who represented different interests within the upper class.[7] These had controlled domestic politics throughout the nineteenth century and had allowed no room for popular participation. Sandino joined his peasant army with the Liberal general, Moncada, in an effort to roust the ruling Conservatives and their U.S. allies. Supported by Sandino's military strength, Moncada defeated the Conservatives and convinced the United States to support a new Liberal government under the leadership of a non-elected president, Juan Sacasa. Although Moncada had been willing to accept Sandino's military support in battle, he did not share Sandino's second goal, the ouster of the U.S. Marines and U.S. political influence from Nicaragua. In fact, Moncada and the Liberals were counting on U.S.

---

[6] "El Regreso a Nicaragua," 1926, reprinted in Sandino (1981); Torres (1984, esp. chap. 2). Unless otherwise noted, all translations are my own.

[7] Sartori (1976); Germani (1978); Mainwaring and Scully (1995); Mainwaring (1993). A pattern of taking power militarily and holding it until defeated by a rival party was common in Latin America in the nineteenth century. Negretto and Aguilar-Rivera argue that a two-party non-electoral regime was designed to promote economic liberalism and to avoid (render unnecessary) electoral competition by using non-electoral circulation in power. This legacy is one of the greatest problems facing modern democratizing Latin American countries. See Negretto and Aguilar-Rivera (2000). While Nicaragua's two elite parties were not electoral parties at the time of Sandino's struggle, they would eventually become foundational parties for the electoral system in ways that fit many of the theoretical constructs widely considered necessary for democratic electoral development. Anderson (2004).

support to keep the new Liberal government in power. Once the Conservatives were defeated, Moncada called for a truce and a return to pseudo-military control, this time by the Liberal Party.

Moncada unified his forces in the interior city of Boaco and called Sandino to participate in the signing of the truce. But Moncada's decision to cease fighting while U.S. Marines remained present in many areas of Nicaragua caused a rift between him and Sandino. Sandino publicly criticized Moncada and the Liberal Party elite for having "sold their country to foreigners.... They are fighting for a presidency that is based on foreign supervision.... We cannot permit this.... Nicaragua will be liberated only by bullets and at the cost of our own blood."[8] Sandino defied Moncada and left Boaco, taking his troops with him. "I don't care if the whole world comes down on top of us but we must fulfill our sacred duty. Against [the treaty] I will protest alone if I have to, if there is no one who will second me."[9] Four days later, in a circular given to the local authorities in every department (state) Sandino declared, "My resolution is this: I am not prepared to turn over my arms even if all [the other armies] do so. I will die with the few who accompany me because it is preferable that we die as rebels than that we live as slaves.[10] Writing directly to Moncada, whom he now rejected as Commander-in-Chief, Sandino responded, "I don't know why you presume to give me orders now. I remember that you always had a bad opinion of me when you were the Commander-in-Chief. ...Now you want me to disarm. I am at my post and I am waiting for you. *I will not sell out and I will not give up*: you will have to conquer me. I plan to fulfill my duty and my protest will remain for the future written in blood."[11]

Sandino and his peasant army went on fighting, using guerrilla tactics in the northeastern jungles against the U.S. soldiers sent to fight there. When Captain Hatfield of the U.S. Marines tried to communicate with Sandino to ask him to surrender, Sandino replied, "I received your communication yesterday.... I will not surrender and I wait for you here. I want a free country or to die. I am not afraid of you; I count on the ardor and patriotism of those who accompany me."[12]

While he came from humble beginnings and led a peasant army, Sandino's foreign travels helped him to cast his appeal in a universal language and to bring his struggle to international visibility. As the fighting wore on,

---

[8] "Regreso a Nicaragua," (1926). Reprinted in Sandino (1981, Vol. 1, pp. 79–80).

[9] Circular to the departmental authorities, Department of the Segovias, May 19 (1927); Sandino (1981, Vol. 1, pp 105–106).

[10] Circular to All Departmental Authorities, May 23, 1927; (Sandino, 1981, Vol. 1, pp. 107–109).

[11] Letter to Jose Maria Moncada, May 24, 1927. (Sandino, 1981, Vol. 1, p. 111). Italics in the reprinted version. For discussion of the military battle against Sandino, see Torres (1984, chap. 5). The phrase in Spanish Sandino used, "Ni me vendo, ni me rindo," became a battle cry for the Sandinista revolutionaries a generation later.

[12] Letter to Captain G.D. Hatfield, El Ocotal, July 27, 1927. Reprinted in Sandino (1981, Vol. 1, p. 121).

Sandino increased the international visibility of his domestic struggle by appealing for support to the other Central American nations, the President of Mexico, and Europe. He wrote for support to the Panamerican Congress being held in Havana, Cuba, on January 17, 1928,[13] to the presidents of the Central American nations in a letter of March 12, 1929,[14] and to Mexican President Emilio Portes Gil in January, 1929.[15] Later that year, in July, he sent a delegate, Jose Constantino Gonzalez, to the Second World Congress of Anti-imperialism being held in Frankfurt, Germany. In his speech to the delegates, read by Gonzalez, Sandino condemned "the abominable deeds carried out by the imperialist policies of the United States of North America in Nicaragua." He also condemned U.S. efforts to build a canal across Nicaragua, criticized Moncada's collusion with "Yankee imperialism," and proclaimed the sovereignty of the Latin American nations over their internal affairs. In response to Sandino's plea, the Congress passed a resolution in his support and in support of the twenty other delegates from Latin America. That resolution was worded as follows: The World Congress, "considering the armed intervention of the United States in Nicaragua, apart from being a brutal attempt against the autonomy and independence of a small people, is violating the most elementary human rights [of a small nation and its people] with the destruction of defenseless villages. [The Congress]...energetically condemned these barbarian acts carried out by the armed forces of the United States in the service of imperialism in Nicaragua...and extended its...support to the Army, under the command of General Augusto Cesar Sandino, for the Defense of the National Sovereignty of Nicaragua."[16]

Yet nationalistic struggle against U.S. military domination was only one part of Sandino's overall agenda. He also sought social justice, self-governance, and resource redistribution for Nicaragua's citizens, most of whom were peasants. Sandino's vision of social justice grew directly out of his nationalism and his harsh labor experience working for the U.S. oil company in Mexico. One of his central solutions to labor exploitation was self-organization. In an open letter to Nicaraguan workers and peasants, Sandino declared, "The working class in all of Latin America today suffers a double exploitation: that of Imperialism, principally Yankee and that of the native bourgeoisie or the national capitalists and exploiters...*Nicaraguan comrades* [sic]: organize yourselves. Your place is in the columns of the Latin American Labor Confederation, the only labor organization that defends the interests of the working class."[17]

---

[13] Sandino (1981, p. 223).
[14] Sandino (1981, p. 332).
[15] Sandino (1981, p. 304).
[16] The full text of Sandino's speech to the delegates of the World Congress and of the Congress resolution in response to his appeal are reprinted in Sandino (1981, Vol. 1, pp. 367–372).
[17] Dated February 26, 1930 (Sandino, 1981, Vol. 2, pp. 69–72).

As Sandino fought to wrest control of Nicaraguan territory from the Marines, he grounded his military strategy in his long-term vision of social justice. He aimed first to capture and hold rural areas so that his troops could feed themselves or be fed by the rural inhabitants who supported the army. We will capture the cities, he wrote, "when we decide it is convenient, but the land belongs to all of us."[18] When he had gained military control over several regions, Sandino established a system of regional authority that would address rural poverty, redistribute land back to the peasantry, and improve the living standard of rural people in territories protected by his army, along with a system of agricultural cooperatives owned by the poor. In an open circular to the authorities of the northern Segovia region, he explained his national goals: "Our army is preparing itself to take the reins of national power so as to proceed with the organization of large cooperatives of Nicaraguan workers and peasants. These will exploit our own natural riches for the benefit of the Nicaraguan family in general."[19]

While the rhetoric of orthodox Marxism was mostly absent from Sandino's writings and communications, the political ideals he had brought from Mexico and had now established in northeastern Nicaragua shared much in common with revolutionary ideas elsewhere. The appeal of these ideas helped create continuity across leaders and from one generation to the next. These ideas included resource redistribution according to need; communal control of the means of production in the form of land cooperatives; and a strong undercurrent of nationalism, sovereignty, and self-determination. Moreover, there were times in his correspondence, open letters, and announcements to regional authorities that Sandino used words like "revolution" to describe his movement and "capitalists" to describe his adversaries. In a letter to Humberto Barahona, a friend and supporter located in Costa Rica, Sandino called himself a "rational communist."[20]

These political declarations made it natural for a later generation of rebels, revolutionaries, and nationalists to find support and encouragement in the history of Sandino's struggle. Sandino was not middle or upper class and was not a university man – nor an artist, nor an intellectual. He called himself an "artisan" of "humble" origins. But he substituted travel for formal education, and became a savvy and effective communicator, thinker, and writer, fully in touch with currents of world thinking and international resistance to domination. As the self-confident leader that he was, he traveled abroad to appeal for international support for his cause. All of these qualities would later be inherited by the revolutionary movement that reinitiated his struggle a generation after his death.

In the end, Sandino achieved his main goal and the U.S. Marines departed, leaving the new Liberal Party government and President Sacasa supported by the

---

[18] Dated August 20, 1931 (Sandino, 1981, Vol. 2, p. 194).
[19] Dated August 27, 1932 (Sandino, 1981, Vol. 2, p. 245).
[20] Dated May 27, 1933 (Sandino, 1981, Vol. 2, p. 337).

National Guard under the control of Anastasio Somoza Garcia. Both Somoza and the Guard had been armed and trained by the United States. Sandino then laid down his arms, signed a truce, and visited Managua to celebrate with Sacasa. Accompanied by his two most competent generals, Francisco Estrada and Juan Pablo Umanzor, the three rebel generals left Sacasa's residence on the evening of February 21, 1934, and were murdered by members of the National Guard as they returned to their homes. Subsequently, on March 3, 1934, the National Guard attacked Sandino's cooperative in Wiwili, killing many peasants. On June 3, 1934, Somoza Garcia took responsibility for Sandino's murder, and on August 25, 1934, the unelected National Congress voted to grant amnesty to anyone who had been involved in Sandino's death or the attack in Wiwili.[21]

The story of Sandino's struggle is one of courage and defiance: the bravery of the underdog standing up against the might of an international giant, the domestic elites, and their military forces. Sandino and his supporters showed a self-reliance and independent initiative that not only developed without Moncada's or Sacasa's direction but, indeed, in direct defiance of Moncada's orders. Sandino was willing to oppose or disobey his social and military "superiors," who were wealthier and better armed. Moreover, he placed the conflict within an international dialogue of resistance to domination, national independence and sovereignty, and international political and social justice. In his struggle, Sandino received sympathy from like-minded thinkers abroad. The next generation of revolutionaries would wed their own ideas with those of Sandino to create a strong basis for a revolutionary movement that reached far beyond the personal appeal or lifetime of any single leader alone.

When the revolutionary movement began in the 1960s, Sandino's early stand in favor of the poor and in support of national self-determination struck a sympathetic chord among the new generation of revolutionary leaders and supporters. This group responded to the fact that the nation was still repressed under the dictatorship of the same Somoza family that had murdered Sandino, a family dictatorship still supported by the United States. When the guerrilla movement that would later become the Nicaraguan revolution first established itself, it adopted both the location and the name of Sandino's movement. By calling itself the Sandinista National Liberation Front (*Frente Sandinista de Liberación Nacional*, FSLN), the new guerrilla movement underscored its loyalty to a leader who was no longer alive but whose ideas and political symbolism offered a more unifying and inspiring power than any leader living at the time could have. It was a choice that revealed a great deal about the Sandinista revolutionary movement and about the kinds of social relations it would inspire.

Yet the early FSLN was not without strong, inspiring leadership among the living as well. The original core of revolutionary leadership consisted of three university students: Carlos Fonseca, Tomas Borge, and Silvio Mayorga.[22]

---

[21] For a broad history of U.S. intervention in Nicaragua see Selser (1984).
[22] Vanden (1982, p. 49); Ruchwarger, (1987).

Fonseca, in particular, had closely studied the life and writings of Sandino and tried to make these accessible to the Nicaraguan people.[23] These leaders set out in the 1960s on a long political struggle that would last nearly twenty years until it ousted the dictator they all opposed in 1979. In the process, the revolutionaries and their followers would be subjected to severe and prolonged political repression at the hands of Somoza's National Guard. Over the course of revolutionary struggle, two of the original leaders were killed, Mayorga in 1967 and Fonseca in 1976; on the day of victory, July 19, 1979, only Thomas Borge survived.

In this story of the loss of revolutionary leaders, the death of Carlos Fonseca on November 7, 1976, warrants particular consideration because of what it says about the evolving nature of leadership in the Nicaraguan revolution. Fonseca was the most important revolutionary leader and Somoza assumed that killing him would end the movement. Somoza instructed the National Guard to kill Fonseca and bring him the leader's head, as he would not be satisfied with mere word of Fonseca's death. The newspaper photographs of the National Guard soldier who arrived holding Fonseca's head by its hair appear to belong to some horrific Greek tragedy rather than to the behavior of a modern United States ally. That day marked a dismal low point for the Sandinista revolution. Somoza may have thought he was beheading the revolutionary movement itself in capturing, killing, and beheading Fonseca. But this was an assumption that betrayed a lack of comprehension that the FSLN was centered around a set of ideas instead of around the personality of any particular leader. Fonseca's death was a cause of deep grief among the revolutionaries because he was revered and admired, second only to Sandino himself. But the murder of Fonseca did not stop the revolutionary movement and new leaders soon stepped forward to take his place while still espousing the same fundamental ideals.

The ability to interchange leadership was a key factor that allowed the FSLN to survive more than a decade of deadly battle against the dictatorship and still emerge victorious in 1979 with youthful, energetic leaders committed to the original set of ideas. When leaders were killed, others remained and gradually assumed their places. The dictatorship was never able to eliminate all of the leaders. Many of those who headed the revolution in 1979 when it finally assumed power were not among those who had originally gone to the mountains and founded Sandinismo. Later leaders who emerged during the insurrectionary years included the Ortega brothers – Camilo, Daniel, and Humberto. Only Daniel and Humberto survived the insurrection and lived to become part of the new revolutionary government. New leaders also included Edén Pastora, Dora Maria Tellez, Carlos Nuñez, Sergio Ramirez, Jaime

---

[23] Fonseca (1984). For an excellent biography of Fonseca, including information on his political formation by Sandino's example, see Zimmermann (2000, pp. 8–9, 27). Zimmerman's chapter 7 deals with Fonseca's effort to make Sandino's story accessible and relevant to the Nicaraguan people.

Wheelock and Leticia Herrera. Among these, of course, some individuals were more inclined toward personalistic politics than others.[24] Yet in comparison with many other revolutionary movements, and particularly in contrast with Peronism, which we will study in the next chapter, Sandinismo had a low level of personalism.

In the final months of the insurrection, this cooperation among multiple, powerful leaders proved essential in the military conquest of Nicaragua, just as any successful, military operation relies upon many generals working together. The final revolutionary insurrection that defeated the dictatorship and caused Somoza to flee Nicaragua was a four-pronged military attack merging upon Managua from north, south, east, and west. Each prong, or "front," as the revolutionaries called them, was led by some of Sandinismo's most idealistic and committed young leaders. These would then become central figures in the creation of the new government.

From start to finish, the Sandinista revolution was a movement of many leaders, all contributing to the same goal. This leadership style created a sense of camaraderie and togetherness among the movement's leadership, a "we" of the revolution and of the revolutionary leadership. Caught up in a struggle for years before seeing victory, the revolutionary leaders developed a sense of togetherness that allowed them to continue even as so many among them died and the dictatorship endured. Leaders were forced to develop a belief in their ideas since these appeared more likely to transcend time and to survive than any particular individual. Indeed, these same ideas, coming as they did from Sandino, were already older than the guerrilla revolutionary movement itself. The creation of cooperation and mutual support around a set of revolutionary ideas transferred itself to the grassroots level, where it fostered the involvement and initiative that gave the revolution substance.

IDEAS OVER PERSONALITY: SANDINISMO AS MODERATED SOCIALISM

Just as Sandino had been influenced by political ideas from outside Nicaragua, benefiting from his nation's proximity to Mexico, Costa Rica, and the northern capitals of South America, geographical proximity also brought international political ideas to the next generation of Sandinista leaders. Even before they became engaged in political activism, Sandinismo's leaders were students, writers, poets, and thinkers. They were accustomed to reading great fiction and drama, as well as politics. This educational background allowed them to use ideas to understand the world. Carlos Fonseca, Silvio Mayorga,

---

[24] One of the most personalistic and non-ideological of the revolutionary leaders was Eden Pastora, the leader of the southern front that converged on Managua from the south and took hostage all members of the National Assembly. After the 1979 triumph, Pastora's personalism caused him to become increasingly marginalized within the FSLN leadership circles. Bardina (1984).

and Tomas Borge were all influenced by high school training in the northern Nicaraguan city of Matagalpa and then went on to acquire university education in Managua. Fonseca, for example, had read Cervantes, Pablo Neruda, and Rubén Darío, and had tried his hand at poetry and creative writing long before he began reading about political ideas from abroad. The world of education and learning from which these leaders emerged proved essential in determining the centrality of ideas within Sandinismo as a movement.[25]

Sandinismo developed at a time when leftist revolutionary ideas were well established in Western Europe, widely understood in the United States, and had already had an important impact in Latin America. Sandinismo followed not only the Russian Revolution, but also revolutionary movements in Mexico, China, and Cuba. Carlos Fonseca and other original leaders of the Nicaraguan revolutionary movement were strongly influenced by Cuba and by its version of leftist revolution, which had succeeded shortly before the Sandinista movement began in the early 1960s.[26] Unlike orthodox Marxism, but instead following the Chinese example, Cuban Marxism stressed a central role for the peasantry and proved that leftist social revolution was possible in a poor, underdeveloped, agrarian, nation. China and Cuba, both peasant nations, offered living evidence of this possibility. Nicaragua, also an agrarian nation whose poor were primarily peasants, fit the model that Cuba provided, even if it did not fit Marx's original call for industrialization and a working class.

What were the ideas that inspired Sandino? As we saw in the section above, Sandinismo was not the first Nicaraguan resistance movement to be influenced by events abroad – in this sense, the movement emulated Sandino as much as it did foreign revolutionaries. Sandino was born in 1895 in the mountainous, rural, northern province of Las Segovias. His mother did day labor under the debt bondage arrangement of that time. When he was old enough to work, Sandino also did day labor and worked as a mule merchant and mechanic. At twenty-five he left Nicaragua, working first for the United Fruit Company in Honduras and then for the Tampico Petroleum Company in Mexico. Arriving in Mexico soon after the Mexican Revolution, which had begun in 1910, Sandino was impressed by the ideas of resistance and reform generated by the revolution. He was particularly influenced by the example of the Mexican revolutionary, Emiliano Zapata, whose peasant movement had demanded a return of land to the peasantry. He was also affected by the Mexican Revolution's nationalist ideas of resistance to United States intervention and by the Russian Revolution of 1917.[27]

When Sandino returned to Nicaragua, he brought with him these ideas of nationalism and a vision of rural social reform. When battle again broke out

---

[25] For a discussion of the educational background of Carlos Fonseca, with some reference to that of the other original Sandinista leaders, see Zimmerman (2000, esp. chaps 2 and 3).
[26] Vanden (1979, pp. 41–62).
[27] Zimmerman (2000, p. 51); Booth (1985, pp. 41–42).

between the Liberals and Conservatives, Sandino found he could create an opportunity to put these ideas into practice. As we discussed earlier, he then joined Moncada's forces, but brought his own army and his own agenda with him. That agenda would eventually cause him to break away from Moncada and to go on waging his own battle against the U.S. Marines even after Moncada had signed a peace treaty.

While still engaged in his military struggle against the U.S. Marines, Sandino and his followers simultaneously installed a new administration in the mountains of Nueva Segovia and other departments protected by his army. Within that area, Sandino conducted a land reform. He established peasant cooperatives where land was owned in common and peasant families had access to enough land to support themselves. His goal was to build cooperatives anywhere that peasant families lacked access to land for self-support. This communal vision, combined with the goal of ousting U.S. control, constituted Sandino's promise for the future. This promise was part of the reason he was able to attract a large peasant following and form his "Crazy Little Army."[28] While Sandino's ideas of rural reform were not couched in a Marxist rhetoric, they prioritized community, communal ownership of property, and human need, visions that fit easily with the ideals of Marxism. Like those of Marxists, Sandino's ideas stated that property should be used to guarantee support and subsistence to the national population. Concentration of wealth and private property should not take precedent over human need.[29] The common threads between Sandino's ideas and those of Marxism were evident once a later generation of Sandinista revolutionaries learned them both and used them to create a revolution.

We see, then, that there was a close affinity between the ideas of leftist revolution in other parts of the world, the ideas of Sandino, and the ideas behind Sandinismo. By the time they were incorporated into the bedrock of a revolution, these ideas had been clarified and made specific to the Nicaraguan context. The most important elements in Sandinista ideology were: (1) Marxism revised to fit an agrarian context; (2) nationalism, sovereignty, and national self-determination; and (3) reformist Catholicism. As we saw earlier, ideas related to the first two had already been evident in Sandino's original movement of the late 1920s. "Liberation theology," which we will discuss later, was another of the many cross-national influences on Sandinismo.[30] Later, we will explore how these three components were developed and adapted to context in order to create a revolution.

---

[28] "The Crazy Little Army" is the term used by many of the common people when referring to Sandino's armed following.

[29] The idea that human need should take precedence over private profit also explained the bread riots and underlay the moral economy of the English crowd who engaged in such riots. Thompson (1971).

[30] For a summary of how Vatican II and Medellin influenced Catholic thinking in Latin America see Berryman (1989).

The first component underlying Sandinismo was the connection between poverty and a Marxist, or revised Marxist, explanation for that poverty. While they were not wealthy, Sandinismo's founders had enough resources to attend university. But they were not insulated from the poverty in which most Nicaraguans lived. They were appalled by poverty and by the human rights violations of the Somoza regime.[31] Drawing upon their reading about other revolutionary movements, they articulated their objections in a partially Marxist manner but also drew upon Sandino's history of defiance. This group of revolutionary leaders would eventually leave the university community to take their message to the poor. They chose as their original base of operations the same northeastern jungle from which Sandino had launched his own challenge to the U.S. Marines in the 1920s. In talking to the peasantry they framed their resistance to tyranny and their vision of a future in Marxist and Sandinista terms, creating a version of Marxist-influenced revolution couched in national history.

In Nicaragua, as in previous revolutions in Cuba, China, and Russia, the original guidelines of Marxism had to be adapted to the immediate domestic context in order to make revolutionary ideals consistent. The first step toward adaptation was to explain, using Cuba and China as models, that class-based revolution could succeed in an underdeveloped agrarian country that lacked both an industrial complex and a working class.[32] The Sandinista revolutionary leaders argued that Nicaragua had an agrarian version of capitalist class exploitation. Somoza and his cronies were wealthy because of an unjust distribution of national wealth in which Nicaraguan (agrarian) laborers were paid only a fraction of the value of their labor, leaving them unable to feed their families. The Somocistas by contrast, grew wealthy on the agro-export crops of coffee, cotton, and cattle, in large part because the wages they paid were grossly inadequate. The solution, argued the revolutionaries, was to overturn the system, creating a workers' state that would prioritize the needs of the poor and distribute wealth according to need. The creation of such a state would entail Somoza's overthrow and the confiscation of the agrarian property that belonged to his family and friends. This property would then be redistributed to the agrarian laborers as farming cooperatives on land owned by the new (workers') state. Profits from these worker-run enterprises would then be directed toward alleviating the worst aspects of poverty in Nicaragua: inadequate food supply, poor health, illiteracy and poor education, and inadequate housing. It was a fairly simple and straightforward rendering of Marxism, revised to fit Nicaragua's agrarian context, and advocating an overthrow of the economic and political system responsible for exploitation and poverty.

---

[31] On the use of repression to enforce exploitation and poverty under the Somoza regime see Anderson (1994, esp. chap. 5).

[32] For the Chinese argument that peasants could become revolutionaries, see Mao Tse Tung (1927).

The second component underlying Sandinismo was the role of the United States in perpetuating poverty and exploitation in Nicaragua. A key aspect of the Sandinista argument was the rejection of United States support for the dictatorship.[33] The revolutionaries knew that the Somozas had done military training in the United States and still retained close ties with the State Department. They knew that the arms used by the National Guard to enforce the exploitative agro-export system had been purchased from the United States or simply given to the dictator free of charge. Revolutionary hostility to Somoza's dictatorship thus naturally included hostility to the powerful northern neighbor who had supported and praised the dictatorship for decades.

Hostility to the United States was a theme common to revolutionaries elsewhere. Condemnation of the United States because of its support for a repressive domestic dictator had also been essential in the Cuban revolution, and in this sense, the Sandinista's were following a path of rhetoric and argument that had already been blazed for them. Rejection of the United States had also been a theme of the Mexican and Russian revolutions.

In their embrace of a version of Marxism and in their antagonism to the United States, the Sandinista revolutionaries were following the path of previous revolutionaries in Latin America and elsewhere. But in deliberately connecting leftist revolution to religion, the Sandinista's took an original approach. The third component underlying Sandinismo was liberation theology. The decision to connect the revolution to religion gained the Sandinista struggle an additional element of support and justification, one that came from some members of the clergy and touched many religious Nicaraguans in a way that a Marxist or nationalist argument alone could not have done.[34] For its originality, the role of religion in Sandinismo deserves particular attention here.

When Pope Paul VI convened the Second Ecumenical Council or Vatican II in the early 1960s, he called for a new vision of Catholicism that some have compared with the Protestant Reformation, except that liberation theology's ideas were introduced within the Catholic Church rather than as a rejection of it.[35] Vatican II unleashed a flood of creative energy aimed at revitalizing the Catholic Church and orienting it to look more closely at human lives and progress.[36] But when that directive was taken to the primarily Catholic Latin American continent, the examination of everyday reality revealed poverty and human misery that were themselves no accident. They were the outcome of exploitation and dependence, the result of the capitalist system unconstrained by electoral democracy.[37] This economic system characterized virtually the

---

[33] Vilas argues that national sovereignty is a fundamental part of revolutions in third world countries because these revolutions take place in a context of capitalist dependency (1986, pp. 23–30).
[34] Dodson and Montgomery (1982).
[35] Berryman (1989, pp. 26–27).
[36] Berryman (1989, pp. 26–27).
[37] Berryman (1989, pp. 26–27).

entire continent at the time of the second Vatican Council. Since Vatican II had been the product of a European perspective on Catholicism, this surprise outcome to the Vatican II directives caused leadership within the Church to call for a more specifically Latin American perspective on the teachings and ideas of Vatican II. The result was a conference of bishops held in 1968 in Medellin, Colombia. This second influential meeting of reformist Catholicism came to be known as "Medellin."

Pope Paul set the tone of Medellin, that of bringing the Church to the people, by traveling to Medellin. He was the first Pope ever to visit Latin America. He inaugurated the meeting as follows: "We wish to personify the Christ of a poor and hungry people."[38] He then exhorted the Latin American clergy to make Catholic practice relate to everyday reality.[39] The resultant Catholic perspective came to be known as "liberation theology." It had roots as well in the work of German philosopher, Ernest Bloch and in the writing of Brazilian clerical thinker, Leonard Boff.[40] Liberation theology called for four fundamental changes in clerical practice. First, the clergy were to join the human and temporal spheres, and use spirituality to improve the human condition rather than use it to exhort passivity and a quiet willingness to await "the other world." Second, liberation theology admitted that the Church was neither above nor outside politics and, judging from its history, had never been apolitical. Therefore its political position should be in favor of social justice and in opposition to repression and exploitation. Third, liberation theology advised that some elements of the kingdom of heaven could and should be built on earth today, and that it was the duty of good Catholics to contribute to such efforts. Finally, liberation theology acknowledged that human relations had the potential for conflict, and that in the context of poverty, exploitation, and repression, such conflict could well become class conflict.

This application of liberation theology to the everyday practice of Catholicism had profound implications. Christ was seen as one of the poor, and in moving closer to Christ, clergy and lay Catholic leaders were asked to move closer to the poor, both in practice and in lifestyle. The Pope urged nuns and priests to take their sermons to the poor, to move their religious ceremonies and social services closer to the poor, and to think first of the poor as they performed their religious duties. As the Church turned its attention to the poor, the clergy became more aware of the causes of poverty in Latin America, including the lavish and exploitative lifestyle enjoyed by many of the continent's upper classes and wealthy elites. In some countries where it became particularly influential, liberation theology and its new form of Catholic practice caused the clergy to become more reformist and even radical in their social and political views. They often supported political movements

---

[38] Lernoux (1982, p. 37).
[39] Tourrain (1988, p. 109).
[40] Tourrain (1988, p. 111).

or parties aimed at correcting social injustice and improving the lives of the poor, especially in Brazil, Chile, El Salvador, and Nicaragua.[41]

In Nicaragua, where a small elitist oligarchy connected to the dictator had grown wealthy through the exploitation of the poor majority, liberation theology had a radicalizing effect on the clergy. Priests and nuns became more critical of the dictatorship and increasingly sympathetic to the revolutionaries who vowed to remove it and install a regime favorable to the poor. A key Nicaraguan event that brought liberation theology together with Sandinista revolutionary thought and action came after Vatican II but before Medellin. Beginning in January, 1966 Ernesto Cardenál decided to make Vatican II dictates a reality in Nicaragua by experimenting with establishing a Catholic community among the low-income peasants and fishermen of the archipelago of Solentiname on a small island in the south of Lake Nicaragua, not far north of the Costa Rican border. A priest, poet, and renowned Nicaraguan intellectual, Cardenál was following the directives the Pope had given by taking his preaching, practice, and lifestyle directly to the poor. Cardenál chose Solentiname for his experiment because its remote location left it somewhat protected from the tensions, danger, and repression of Nicaraguan society under Somoza.

In Solentiname, Cardenál ran many Bible-study sessions that addressed the problems of poverty villagers confronted and related these to the Bible. He kept careful records of the discussions. From this dialogue, over several months, one can see how the poor came to view their situation in religious terms and how that realization had a gradual radicalizing effect. For example, villagers began to compare the death of Sandino to the death of Christ since both had cared for the poor and both had been betrayed by people they trusted and murdered by those in power. From this comparison, villagers understood their own situation as resembling that of Sandino. Opposition to poverty and exploitation and to the regime that fostered these conditions increasingly began to seem like a Catholic duty and villagers reflected upon political opposition in that light. Solentiname encouraged participants to think about working together to solve problems, an approach that also encouraged them to see each other in relatively equal terms. As the Solentiname discussions unfolded, Cardenál himself reestablished contacts he had previously had with a group of Sandinista revolutionaries who were in hiding just the other side of the border in Costa Rica. Toward the end of the Solentiname experiment, some villagers came to believe that their Catholic duty required them to support the revolutionary movement and even to become involved in armed action. Several village youth joined the Sandinista guerrillas, and some lost their lives in an armed attack on a National Guard post in San Carlos, in southern Nicaragua.[42]

---

[41] On the connection between revolution and religion in El Salvador see Montgomery (1982), Peterson et al. (2001), and Vásquez and Friedmann (2003).

[42] Extensive discussion of the Solentiname experiment, including presentation of some of the dialogue of bible-study sessions among villagers appears in Berryman (1989, chap. 1). For another rendering of dialogue among Christian revolutionaries, see Randal (1983).

The Solentiname experiment is important because it shows how Sandinismo and Catholicism came to be connected through like-minded thinking. First, the dialogue on the Bible-study sessions established that there was nothing spontaneous or accidental about the support of the revolution by grassroots Catholic communities. This connection required deliberate action by clergy members who were following leadership directives from Rome. Second, when Bible teachings were applied to everyday reality in Nicaragua, radicalizing effects were easy to achieve. Timing was also important here, and liberation theology represented a unique window in time for the Nicaraguan revolution. The conferences of Vatican II and Medellin took place just as the organized revolutionary opposition to Somoza was beginning in Nicaragua.

Although the deliberate connection between revolution and religion was unusual, Nicaragua was not the first instance where reformation within Catholicism had coincided with and contributed to a growing popular willingness to resist oppression. In pre-revolutionary France, the Jansenist movement had also encouraged the clergy to take Catholicism to the people by preaching mass in French instead of Latin, by exhorting the clergy to *earn* the people's respect rather than trying to command it simply by virtue of their station, and by encouraging a strong independence of mind among Catholics who were invited to "listen to the voice within." The combined efforts of the Pope and the French king to suppress Jansenism and punish Jansenists caused a deep popular aversion to Rome and the monarchy and became an important element in solidifying French revolutionary opposition to the monarchy.[43] The difference between Jansenism and liberation theology was that Jansenism was a grassroots initiative within the Catholic Church, which the Pope immediately tried to suppress through his Bull, *Unigenitus*. By contrast, the impetus for liberation theology came directly from Pope Paul VI and would only be discouraged and ultimately undermined by the subsequent Pope, John Paul II.

History has shown that both Jansenism and liberation theology represented momentary windows of opportunity that would soon close. The Pope rejected Jansenism and excommunicated French Jansenist priests; similarly, the response of the John Paul II, the next Pope, to liberation theology was to discourage it and encourage a return to popular passivity and obedience. In the aftermath of Pope John Paul II's leadership, Latin Americans may be "carried away by [religious] belief; [but] they return to crisis, poverty, and an absence of [Catholic] perspectives and models for action."[44]

But Rome's rejection of social action was still in the future and, for the Sandinistas, the window of opportunity opened at just the right moment, and offered a chance to strengthen their revolution and widen its base of support. In the late 1960s and early 1970s, the Church temporarily provided a model for ameliorative action. Thus the effects of Vatican II and Medellin began

---

[43] On this topic, see Garrioch (2002, esp. chaps 6 and 7; pp. 149–151, 166–171, 178–183).
[44] Tourrain (1988, pp. 119–122).

to filter down into Nicaraguan society in the early 1970s, precisely at the time that Sandinista and other secular domestic opposition to the dictatorship was gaining momentum. Whether one examined the multiple injustices of Nicaraguan society from the perspective of Marxist theory or from the perspective of the new liberating Catholicism, many of the conclusions would be similar. For a second brief shining moment, there was an affinity between Catholicism and revolution that greatly facilitated an alliance between those who believed in revolution and those who considered themselves devout and faithful Catholics.[45]

Encouraged by Medellin and inspired by Cardenál, other Nicaraguan clerics integrated liberation theology into everyday practice. As in Solentiname, this effort often had a radicalizing effect, making both the clergy and their parishioners more sympathetic to and supportive of revolution. As the revolutionary movement gained momentum, Nicaraguan clergy helped and supported the revolutionaries. Bible-study sessions sprang up in many parts of rural Nicaragua. In some parishes, these practices created a new lay-level strata of community leaders called "Delegates of the Word," who were trained to interpret the Bible in a reformist manner. Many Delegates eventually led their communities to support the revolution. Such encouragement often caused rural Nicaraguans to become sympathetic to the revolution and even to leave home to join the revolutionaries in the mountains. As the revolution strengthened and the dictatorship became more repressive, even the cautious Nicaraguan Archbishop Miguel Obando y Bravo began to distance himself from Somoza, rejecting the dictator's gifts to him, such as a Mercedez-Benz.[46] Obando y Bravo was cautious not to alienate the rich with his public speeches but his attitude illustrated that even the more conservative Nicaraguan clergy had ceased to support the dictatorship. Eventually even the whole clerical hierarchy in Nicaragua broke with Somoza.[47]

Nicaragua is a small country but there are still regional differences within it. These differences are exacerbated by the nation's poverty because national and local governments lack the funds for good roads. As with regional differences everywhere, some areas of Nicaragua are more progressive and open to influence from the ideas found in urban centers like Managua. Other regions are more isolated and more socially and politically conservative.[48] The entrance of

---

[45] In an overview of liberation theology and the Catholic base communities it created, Daniel H. Levine (1992) writes that their long-term fate has depended upon the circumstances of their birth such that some Latin American societies provided a more hospitable environment for liberating versions of Catholicism than did other societies. Thus, timing in Nicaragua also helped reformers within the Church. Efforts to establish Christian base communities in a context already vibrant with calls for political liberation found Nicaragua in the 1970s a particularly hospitable environment for liberation theology.

[46] Lernoux (1982, p. 89).

[47] Williams (1989, chap. 2, esp. pp. 39–41).

[48] For a discussion of pre-revolutionary and revolutionary politics in more conservative regions of Nicaragua see Anderson (1994, esp. chaps 1 and 2).

the Catholic Church into the effort at reform opened parts of the country that would have otherwise been more resistant or closed to ideas about reform and change. In more socially conservative areas, the Church introduced Delegates of the Word who then used the Bible and liberation theology to bring progressive ideas into poor communities. Whether via the Church in more remote areas or via urban influence in more central regions, the Nicaraguan people had multiple avenues to promote liberating ideas of social progress, reform, and revolution. The Church and its practice of liberation theology served the critical purpose of bringing more remote areas on board with the growing currents of revolution.

Most successful Marxist revolutionary movements have not enjoyed such a close relationship with the domestic clergy or such affinity of thinking. Sandinista thinkers and liberation theology clerics applied their intellectual energy to resolving the apparent contradiction between a Marxist-inspired revolution and a devout religious movement within the Catholic Church. Such thinkers and authors resolved the conflict by relying on the teachings of liberation theology itself. Both liberation theology and Marxism, they argued, were causes that favored the poor, prioritized social justice, and rejected class exploitation. Insofar as both had the same goals, there was compatibility, not contradiction. Many deeply religious Catholics became Sandinista revolutionaries, and many Sandinista revolutionaries embraced or at least tolerated religion as a central part of their belief system.

Sandinismo took power in July 1979 on the basis of this broad conglomeration of ideas. Just as Sandinista leaders had been forced to find common ground among these various ideas in the insurrectionary stage, so they continued to seek compromise once they had gained national power. One such compromise was with the rural poor, the key sector of the low-income class for whom the revolution had been carried out. Orthodox Marxism, especially as seen in the Leninist model of the Soviet Union, demanded that property, including land, be collectively rather than privately owned. Application of this to land reform in Nicaragua would mean turning property confiscated from Somoza and his allies into state-owned cooperatives. The newly empowered Sandinistas attempted to distribute land in this manner, but some of the rural poor objected. Their landless status had been imposed upon them forcibly by the Somoza system. Now they wanted to return to being peasants. They had not supported the revolution in order to exchange one boss (Somoza) for another (the state).[49] Nicaragua's rural poor organized themselves to demand that land be redistributed in family-sized farms. The new state compromised, distributing some land in individual plots and other land in the form of state-run cooperatives. It was hardly an orthodox Marxist solution, but it was in keeping with the Sandinistas' own ideals of redistributing resources and providing the poor with a dignified way of earning a living.

[49] For a detailed exploration of peasant motivation in joining the Sandinista Revolution see Anderson (1994, esp. chaps 2 and 5).

Other compromises with orthodox Marxism soon became necessary as well. Nicaragua remained an agrarian society. The wealthy as well as the poor depended on the land for survival. While the Somoza dictatorship had enjoyed the support of many large landowners, there were others who had not supported the dictatorship and some who had even supported the revolution. When Somoza and his closest allies fled Nicaragua, many landowners of large and medium-sized farms stayed in Nicaragua, determined to continue farming and hoping to help shape the new political system as well. As we will see below, many of these land-owning elites had helped the revolution in small or large ways, so the revolutionary government was reluctant to ignore their position entirely. In addition, in the absence of U.S. aid, the new government soon discovered that private farms and agro-export enterprises were one of the state's most important sources of foreign exchange. As a result, the Sandinista government compromised again. The Nicaraguan landscape soon interspersed private export plantations with state-owned cooperatives and individual family farms. Again, the compromise was hardly an orthodox Marxist solution, yet it followed the Sandinistas' own goals of prioritizing the poor in a pragmatic fashion. The resources brought in from large private farms helped fund state-financed health care, education, and housing.

The Sandinista state made still other compromises as well, all of which lay beyond the bounds of traditional Marxism as it has appeared in other settings. The tolerant attitude of Sandinismo toward Catholicism continued, but part of the Nicaraguan clergy began to oppose Sandinismo. As a consequence, the clergy itself split into pro- and anti-Sandinista factions. Yet the Sandinista state still accepted priests in government positions. Eventually the Church and the FSLN government moved to a position of "practical collaboration."[50] The Sandinista state also made compromises with liberal democracy rarely found in a Marxist or socialist government. These included holding elections in 1984 and 1990, creating a national legislature for which deputies were elected beginning in 1984, establishing a written constitution in 1987, and maintaining a relatively free press. In these ways Sandinismo was and remained a moderate version of Marxism, striking multiple compromises that most Marxist regimes have been unwilling to entertain.[51]

Throughout the insurrection and its first eleven years in power, Sandinismo relied on ideas. Those came from a broad range of sources – from Marxism to nationalism to reformist Catholicism. If the ideas of Sandinismo gravitated gradually away from orthodox Marxism and toward a moderate version of state socialism, ideas nonetheless remained central in the movement. They became a kind of horizontal glue, holding together people of profoundly different backgrounds. These individuals ultimately concluded that there was room within Sandinismo for many of these ideas without necessarily subordinating

---

[50] For a discussion of the divisions within the Church over Sandinismo and the movement toward collaboration see Williams (1989, esp. chap. 4).
[51] Anderson and Dodd (2002b; 2005).

one of them to the others. The breadth of Sandinismo itself left considerable common ground for its supporters, regardless of which of its ideas had been most influential to them. Compatibility among its foundational ideas produced a clear consistency to Sandinismo, both in its revolutionary stage and in power. This consistency produced a set of policy decisions that came to characterize the new government: prioritization of the poor, orientation of state resources in that direction first, pragmatic compromises with capitalists and capitalism where these cooperated with the revolution and brought much-needed resources, resistance to United States domination, and acceptance of religion. Friends and enemies alike could trust Sandinismo to take consistent positions on many issues, and could define their own position in support of or opposed to the Sandinista position.

The centrality of ideas discussed in this section, combined with the multiplicity of leaders discussed in the previous section, resulted in a greater level of consistency than is normally present in regimes that are centered around one personality or that lack grounding in a set of ideas. Consistency enhanced trust among social actors and in each other's actions and positions. Such trust would eventually help create the foundation for democracy.

GRASSROOTS ACTIVISM AND INITIATIVE

Arguments about social capital emphasize that citizens' associational experience is central in allowing them to learn skills of cooperation and mutual support. Associational experience is particularly important for democracy when it unites individuals of diverse backgrounds. Populations that learn these skills in multiple civic associations and activities are then more likely to take civic and cooperative skills to their political involvement as well. This section will show that the Sandinista revolution offered citizens extensive opportunities for organization and cooperation. Yet, like other revolutions before it, it occurred in a pre-democratic political world where some organization and association had already occurred periodically. These previous experiences made the Nicaraguan population easier to organize and more responsive to efforts at political organization. Revolution then greatly enhanced and directed associational and cooperative skills that were already present in Nicaraguan society.[52]

---

[52] While the relationship between grassroots initiative and socialist revolution was clear in the Nicaraguan case and has also been evident in many other cases of revolution, socialism does not always enhance grassroots initiative. For example, the socialist revolution in Mozambique followed the Soviet and especially Eastern European models much more closely than the Nicaraguan revolution did. Accordingly, it was more driven by elite initiatives, produced a much harsher state, and, after its demise, was sometimes ridiculed by peasant small holders as the "down with everything" government. It is hard to imagine Nicaraguan peasants mocking the Sandinista government in such a fashion. On Mozambique, see Pitcher (2002, esp. chap. 3, p. 263).

This relation has made itself evident in other societies as well. Where citizens have already achieved a modest level of organization, revolution greatly increases citizen associations. For example, David Garrioch has argued that in the years immediately prior to the French Revolution, French society increasingly became characterized by organizations of tradesmen and skilled workers. These organizations periodically engaged in politics and offered members a place to express political opinions, learn political skills, and develop more informed opinions about matters of state.[53] This opportunity was unique in monarchist France, which otherwise offered no chance for average citizens to participate in politics. But with the advent of the French Revolution, associations and organized citizen involvement increased greatly and had a more specific purpose. Similarly, Theda Skocpol has demonstrated that civic organization, only modest beforehand, increased greatly after the American Revolution.[54]

In pre-revolutionary Nicaragua, even before the start of guerrilla warfare, important experiences with political organization had emerged. One of these was Sandino's struggle. Initially it united peasants of the northeastern region in common cause with one element of elite opinion, the Liberals, in support of President Sacasa. But once Moncada signed a truce with the Conservatives, Sandino's struggle became more an action of one class of Nicaraguans, although it still brought together peasants from widely disparate regions of Nicaragua.

For all of its initial cooperation with elites, Sandino's struggle nonetheless represented an instance of grassroots initiative in which the impetus to fight the Conservatives came from Sandino and his rural supporters, rather than from any effort by General Moncada to recruit peasants into the struggle. Sandino's decision to continue fighting after Moncada's truce represented not only grassroots initiative, but also grassroots defiance and a strongly independent ability among common citizens to make important political decisions. In this manner, non-elite Nicaraguans could look back on Sandino's struggle as an organizational example as well as a source of political ideas.[55]

Between Sandino's struggle of the 1920s and early 1930s and the FSLN guerrilla revolutionary struggle of the late 1960s and 1970s, Nicaraguans also organized themselves at the grassroots level several other times. Such organization was particularly prevalent among laborers and peasants in the

---

[53] Garrioch (2002, esp. chap. 3, pp. 67–69, 83).
[54] Skocpol (1999); Woloch (1994, pp. 91–92).
[55] Patterns of the power of grassroots citizens' organizations are also visible in non-revolutionary settings where citizens nonetheless seek to change the state. For example, the repressive apartheid government of South Africa deliberately tried to oppress or eliminate black citizen organizations even before these began to organize resistance to the white supremacist state. The South African government appears to have understood that the flourishing of citizen organizations not under its dominant control can enhance horizontal ties and grassroots initiative, both of which represented a danger to apartheid. Giliomee (2003, pp. 512, 520, 522–525).

northwestern provinces of Chinandega and Leon. Chinandega has one of the largest concentrations of workers in the country because Nicaragua's largest sugar mill and its famous rum producer, Flor de Caña, are all located in the Chinandega municipality of Chichigalpa. Sandino's influence from the 1920s created a growing chasm between the expectations of workers and the labor policies of the Liberal Party factory owners in Chichigalpa. With the Depression, economic and labor conditions worsened. Finally, in 1936, sugar workers responded with a strike that eventually gained the support of railroad workers, dock workers, and taxi drivers.[56] President Sacasa ordered the National Guard to shoot the workers, and Somoza Garcia complied.[57]

Repression of this labor strike weakened Sacasa's presidency, and soon thereafter Somoza Garcia was able to oust Sacasa and assume the presidency himself. Despite his role in repressing the Chichigalpa strike, Somoza Garcia gained the presidency with labor support because he promised labor reforms and land redistribution in the Chinandega region. His promises appeared to address many of the concerns that had caused the labor strike, and low-income Nicaraguans now hoped Somoza would address the problematic labor conditions Sacasa had ignored.

In his early years in power, Somoza Garcia tried to maximize support to his government by promising labor much-needed reforms while also assuring his elite supporters he would take a tough stand against labor. He was soon forced to choose between these contradictory positions, and he moved closer to the political expectations of agrarian elites in both the Liberal and Conservative parties. He tried to unify these elite interests by supporting a Conservative, Leonardo Arguello, in a presidential election in 1947.[58] However, extensive fraud was necessary to gain Arguello's victory because the anti-Somoza, Independent Liberal Party candidate, Enoc Aguado, would have won with labor support by a margin of three to one. Somoza's imposition of Arguello. combined with his repression of labor for its support of Aguado, ended any pretense that Somoza Garcia supported labor and also ended labor's illusions that the first Somoza presidency would bring labor reform.

A final pre-revolutionary effort to support reform came with the second Somoza dictator, Luis Somoza Debayle, Somoza Garcia's elder son.[59] Of the three Somozas, Luis was the one most inclined toward reform. He supported labor and agrarian reform and presidential elections. A 1963 election produced Nicaragua's first elected president, René Schick. But Schick's death in 1966 ended what might have been a process of gradual democratization.[60] Luis Somoza continued to pressure for reform, including agrarian reform, from

---

[56] The department (state) of Chinandega is also home to Corinto, Nicaragua's most important port and one of the main ports in Central America.
[57] Gould (1990).
[58] Gould (1990, pp. 52–58).
[59] Gould (1990, pp. 52–58).
[60] Gould (1990, p. 247).

outside the presidency but was opposed in these efforts by his own younger brother, Anastasio Somoza Debayle. Luis's own untimely death ended the brotherly disagreement in favor of anti-reform voices.

Events in northwestern Nicaragua between 1930 and 1966 essentially amounted to unfulfilled promises and repression by the Somozas and their allies in response to grassroots activism and demands for reform. The Somozas promised labor reform and never delivered it, initiated land reform but never carried it through, and even began a democratically elected presidency which also ultimately never removed the dictatorship. In the end, however, popular organizational efforts learned important lessons about failure and success. Gould has argued that promises unfulfilled actually helped create revolutionaries among Nicaragua's rural poor. Hopes for reform, once ignited, could not easily be extinguished by reversals in national policy. And the failure of land reform taught low-income Nicaraguans that real land reform would require both greater organization and ultimately the overturning of the state.[61]

When the clandestine guerrilla movement of the FSLN began in the late 1960s, the guerrillas initiated their struggle in the northeastern Segovia mountains of Nicaragua. Far removed from the northwestern provinces where labor strife had created tension and had been violently repressed, the northeast was more remote and less likely to attract immediate state repression. It provided more protection and a chance for the movement to grow. The FSLN also chose that region because it had been the location of Sandino's struggle, where he found popular support in the 1920s. The hope of the new revolutionary movement was that rural people in the northeast would support the material subsistence of the guerrillas and eventually join their political cause. As we know from other revolutionary movements that have chosen such tactics elsewhere, to approach a revolution trying to rely on rural people who may or may not support the movement is risky. Ché Guevara, for example, tried the same tactic in Bolivia and saw his movement fail for lack of support from the rural people around him.[62] Unlike Ché, however, the Sandinistas were successful in garnering rural support, and such support became a form of clandestine associational experience that came with the early stages of the revolution.

During the years of clandestine struggle, revolutionary ideas and popular resistance to the Somoza dictatorship spread slowly to most areas of rural Nicaragua and eventually to urban areas as well, bringing with them opportunities for popular cooperation and the chance to learn from such interaction. In some regions, like the northwest, rural Nicaraguans were already predisposed to resistance by virtue of unsuccessful organizational experience with labor reform. In other areas, revolutionary support came more slowly and only after it appeared more likely to succeed.[63] In each area, low-income Nicaraguans formed themselves into clandestine groups that engaged in various forms of

---

[61] Gould (1990, pp. 252, 261, 169).
[62] Saldaña (2001); Harris, (2000).
[63] Anderson (1994, esp. chaps 2 and 5).

resistance, organized attacks on Somoza targets, and undertook multiple support activities. To develop and later to fight, these unofficial organizations relied on extensive popular cooperation and mutual support within the population. These were essential for attacks against National Guard targets, communication and coordination, and allowing the revolutionaries to survive repression in between attacks.

Revolutionary activities would have been impossible without extensive cooperation, mutual support, and group self-protection within Nicaraguan communities. Villagers and communities who supported the revolution could only do so by relying on and helping each other. Revolutionary struggle became a group effort in which individuals gave what they had and participated in whatever manner they could. Only with such mutual support did participants have any chance of surviving, and it was through such broad participation that the movement became a mass revolution. Young men and some young women joined the guerrillas; other women cooked food for them and carried it into the mountains and forests after dark because it was too dangerous for the guerrillas to enter the villages.[64] Women selling nacatamales and sweets on foot in urban streets also ferried across town pistols, other small arms, and supplies buried beneath the food they carried in wide baskets on their heads. Children on bicycles carried crucial, secret messages from one village to the next, slipping through National Guard lines unnoticed and providing a vast communications network that traversed the countryside. Older men offered their homes or sheds for guerrilla training activities or the construction of arms and bombs. Sometimes they built underground tunnels out of these sheds so that the guerrillas could escape quickly. Often they stood guard while training activities were underway in case a soldier or Somoza-sympathizer should happen by.[65] For example, an elderly villager, too old to fight, would stand casually at the door of his hut, smoking a cigarette and watching for the National Guard while his adult sons and friends held a secret strategy meeting inside. If the Guard appeared, a signal from him would cause them to disappear through a 200-yard tunnel he had dug at night, leading from beneath the house into the forest beyond. An adult polio victim, unable to drill in military training, would stand guard while other villagers practiced military maneuvers in a clearing outside his village.[66]

The involvement of large numbers of supporters from multiple social sectors contributed to the success of the revolution because the defeat of Somocismo required a prolonged struggle against a superior military force. By the time the revolution was at full military strength, that struggle entailed multiple military actions from all corners of Nicaragua. As mentioned above,

---

[64] These stories of individual and community cooperation in revolutionary participation come from fieldwork in Nicaragua in the 1980s. Regions where these activities were typical included the provinces of Masaya, Boaco, and Carazo.

[65] For discussion of mass participation in the insurrection see Chavarria (1982).

[66] Anderson (1994, esp. chap. 3).

eventually the FSLN developed a substantial military ability of its own and formed four military fronts, one each from the north, south, east, and west of Managua. This military effort was needed because Somocismo controlled the nation militarily as well as politically. His National Guard had become an occupation force with bases dispersed throughout the national territory. Revolutionary victory required a combat defeat of Somocismo and its National Guard.

As the revolution gained momentum, the numbers of individuals and communities involved in revolutionary activities increased greatly. Once many members of a community had joined the revolution, it became increasingly difficult for the apparatus of repression to operate successfully. In the months prior to the fall of the dictatorship in July, 1979, much of the population was involved in revolutionary cooperative action. In some communities, nearly everyone had joined the revolution.[67] Popular support for the revolution had become so extensive that in many sectors of the economy the Sandinistas were able to organize entire revolutionary labor unions, including the Sandinista Workers Central (*Central Sandinista de Trabajadores*, CST) and the Association of Rural Workers (*Asociación de Trabajadores del Campo*. ATC). The CST represented much of the working class within industries and factories, while the ATC represented the landless and agrarian workers.[68] When the revolution triumphed in July 1979, these large Sandinista organizations were officially recognized by the new government as labor representative organizations. They were given seats in the new sectoral legislature, the Council of State, in accordance with their size, and were used as models for the organization of many other sectors of Nicaraguan society.[69] These groups had both a national and local presence and often affected policy through grassroots agitation and mobilization.[70]

One place where the value and learning experience of grassroots organization is most clear is in the story of the ATC and another rural organization, UNAG (National Union of Farmers and Ranchers). As we saw in the first section above, Nicaragua's rural poor have historically played a crucial role in the struggle against elitist and foreign domination. During the insurrectionary years, rural support was again critical. In 1978, that support was unified under one umbrella organization, the ATC, which included landless Nicaraguans and rural workers. When the revolution triumphed in 1979, the ATC was one of the strongest constituencies in support of the new government. As agrarian reform began, ATC members were the first beneficiaries of land redistribution.

---

[67] Anderson (1994, esp. chap. 3).
[68] For a discussion of the pre-revolutionary organization of low income members of Nicaraguan society see Ruchwarger (1987, esp. chap. 2).
[69] Serra (1982; 1985).
[70] Kaimowitz and Thome (1982).

During its first three years from 1978 to 1981, the ATC was an effective grassroots organization. It moved from being an illegal union under the Somoza regime to being a legally recognized representative of the rural poor under the Sandinistas. During that transition, the ATC greatly increased its rural membership and experienced increasing popularity in the countryside. It gained political representation for the rural poor in the Council of State and participated there in discussions about legislation introduced by other mass organizations. Most importantly, it played a central role in designing and implementing the agrarian reform.[71] As a grassroots organization, it moved from involvement in armed insurrection to agitation for legal reforms for their members to participation in the implementation of those reforms. In the process, members saw the results that could be achieved through grassroots organization and initiative, and they learned the value of cooperation.

Yet the ATC's very success would eventually become a problem for the organization. In the enthusiasm of its success, the ATC incorporated small farmers and peasants into the organization. The union of landless rural workers and landed small proprietors has caused problems elsewhere in Latin America, as these two groups often have competing interests. For example, peasant producers may need to emphasize price supports, transportation needs, and the cost of fertilizer, pesticides, and tools, while landless rural people may find such claims secondary in comparison to the primary need for land. This clash has appeared within rural unions in Costa Rica[72] and now proved to be the case in Nicaragua as well. New peasant members of the ATC had needs very different from those of the landless ATC members. As a result, peasant members left the rural union to form a separate organization, the UNAG, that could concentrate more on the interests of small landholders.

Between 1981 and 1990, the ATC became less effective in protecting the interests of the landless, although it did have some important successes. It achieved significant benefits for rural women and children. It also placed many formerly landless workers into cooperatives of collective land ownership, and it obtained financial support from international donors. But the ATC moved too close to the Sandinista government itself, often supporting state interests rather than defending the interests of members. UNAG, by contrast, proved more successful than the ATC at promoting the interests of its members. The contrast between these two organizations shows that grassroots associations can also vary in their success and effectiveness, and from their experience we can learn what types of tactics enhanced or limited organizational effectiveness.

Eventually it became clear that yet a third rural sector felt inadequately represented by either ATC or UNAG. Large-scale landowners and ranchers formed Union of Nicaraguan Agricultural Producers (*Unión de Productores Agropecuarios de Nicaragua*, UPANIC) and pressured for reforms that

---

[71] Luciak (1995, esp. chap. 2).
[72] Anderson (1991; 1993).

supported agro-industry. Some of these, such as wage caps or limits on benefits, were in direct opposition to the needs and demands of ATC members. As these organizations and the revolution itself aged, each of these associations pressed for laws that benefited members with greater or lesser levels of success. Yet the overall picture is one of a society in which grassroots initiative and organizations were a key part of national policy and themselves constituted classrooms of learning about the strengths and limits of cooperation.

Nicaraguans organized themselves in other ways as well. At the local level, peasants organized into cooperatives or cooperative ventures. Some of these were state-run farms where the land was owned by the state. But even where land ownership was distributed in small family plots, rural people often joined together in cooperatives to purchase farm machinery and vehicles, smaller hand-held farm tools, fertilizer, and pesticides. They also cooperated in bringing their crops to market, using one large vehicle to transport everybody's crops rather than having multiple individuals transport their own crops to the market. The state supported these efforts by making larger purchases of fertilizer or pesticides less expensive than individual purchases. In urban areas, Nicaraguans joined into neighborhood organizations that worked together on group projects such as sinking a communal water pump or digging run-off canals at the side of village streets.

This pattern of organization soon emerged in associations of university and high school students, teachers, university professors, women, taxi drivers, bus drivers and other public transport workers, market vendors, and street vendors. When these groups had organized at the national level, they were granted seats in the sectoral legislature, and members subsequently voted in an internal election to choose the delegates who would represent their organization in the legislature. As the power of these poor peoples' organizations became clear, middle- and high-income Nicaraguans also organized into local and then national unions. These included organizations of large landowners, cattle ranchers, coffee and cotton barons, businessmen, lawyers, doctors, and bankers.

Policies of the Sandinista government also enhanced horizontal ties among the population. For example, in his study of Nicaragua's literacy campaign, Luciano Baracco argues that even government policies that prioritized social justice or social services enhanced horizontal ties. He illustrates how the literacy campaign of 1979–80, originally organized to combat illiteracy among Nicaragua's poor, ultimately accomplished even more in terms of community-building than it did in terms of the reduction of illiteracy. Young citizens who went to the countryside to teach literacy and older citizens who became their pupils were drawn together in a nation-building project that shared a common vision and goals across the country.[73]

In ways that began before the revolutionary triumph and then continued afterward, Nicaragua became a highly organized society, boasting multiple

---

[73] Baracco (2004).

popular organizations of various sizes and purposes. Many Nicaraguans belonged to more than one organization – in the workplace, in the neighborhood, and in conjunction with other activities. Part II of this book looks at organizational memberships to see how these patterns have held up beyond the revolutionary years. But the history of the Nicaraguan revolution shows that the insurrection itself and the first eleven years of the revolutionary government necessitated and encouraged popular organization. Ruchwarger has called the mass organizations "schools of democracy."[74] I suggest that they were, more specifically, schools for the development of bridging social capital. Because of the revolution, both in its insurrectionary stage and after taking power, Nicaraguans gained multiple opportunities to learn the skills and the value of cooperation, tolerance, and mutual support. These are the skills needed for bridging social capital. The Nicaraguan experience illustrates that these could be attained in a speedy fashion, over about one generation, where a national political movement encouraged and relied upon such high levels of popular organization and involvement.

CROSS-CLASS TIES

A final element necessary for the creation of bridging social capital is the existence of diversity within social associations, so that the ties of cooperation among individuals also link them to persons who are unlike themselves in at least some respects. Many of the cooperative and organizational ventures described in the previous section involved individuals of different backgrounds. Neighborhoods, for example, were often comprised of very diverse individuals who cooperated for mutual support and protection. Even the revolution itself, including its earliest days of struggle, had relied on the support of Nicaraguans from many different social and economic situations for its success. Ultimately the overthrow of Somoza was due in part to a broad, cross-class coalition of opponents, including middle- and upper-class university students; many members of the Conservative party who held positions as lawyers, businessmen, accountants, and bankers in the capitalist economy; a few dissident members of Somoza's Liberal Party itself; many members of the clergy; and, of course, the poor.

The revolution was first and foremost a movement of the poor, in which Nicaragua's peasants, workers, and low-income urban dwellers constituted the main forces. The rural poor fed, sheltered, hid, and fought alongside the Sandinista revolutionaries in many parts of Nicaragua, and several years before the revolution gained an urban following. The military battle became urban long before the revolutionary triumph, and gunfire was exchanged between the National Guard and revolutionaries in many Nicaraguan cities. In the urban battle, the poor were again central as soldiers and fighters, and in providing safe houses and hiding places. They played particularly heroic roles

[74] Ruchwarger (1987, p. 116).

in battles in the northern city of Estelí, in the battle of Monimbó in Masaya, in Leon, and in Managua, particularly in the tactical fall back from Managua to Masaya out of the working class neighborhood of Bello Horizonte in 1979 (see Chapter 4).

Yet the poor were not the only Nicaraguans who took up arms or protected those who did. The cross-class nature of revolutionary support, evident in the background of various revolutionary leaders, has been written about extensively. One critical source of revolutionary leadership was the national universities and their middle-class students. Carlos Fonseca, Silvio Mayorga, and many of the founding members of the FSLN were sons of middle class and wealthy fathers who were large landowners or worked in professional, white-collar positions in urban business and professional communities. Other middle class leaders included Jaime Wheelock and Carlos Nuñez. Some revolutionary leaders came from more working-class backgrounds, including the Ortega brothers and Leticia Herrera.

When the Sandinista movement initiated its struggle against the dictatorship, it was primarily a guerrilla movement influenced by Marxism and peasant-oriented Sandinista nationalism. But by the time the movement assumed power in 1979, it was a broad, cross-class coalition informed by Catholicism and social democracy as well. Part of the reason for these cross-class ties stemmed from dynamics within the movement itself. As the guerrillas struggled with the decision about how to sustain long-term, broad-spread opposition, three alternative strategies presented themselves. One, led by Tomas Borge and Bayardo Arce, argued for a prolonged popular conflict, somewhat similar to the strategy pursued by the Viet Cong in Vietnam. It would rely primarily on the low-income sectors of society. A second option, known as the proletarian option and led by Jaime Wheelock and Carlos Nuñez, was strongly influenced by the Chilean model of electoral socialist revolution and by dependency theory. The third option, known by that name, ultimately came to dominate the Sandinista movement. Led by the Ortega brothers – Camilo, Daniel, and Humberto –, this option embraced both armed struggle and a broad, cross-class appeal.[75] It recommended modifying and moderating revolutionary goals to attract support from social democratic opinion worldwide. The third option gained the support of Costa Rican ex-president José Figueres as well as of European leaders Olaf Palme and Willy Brandt. The breadth of this third option made the Sandinista revolutionary movement more palatable to the non-Marxist left and to centrists, and eventually allowed Sandinismo to gain broad support in Nicaragua.[76]

One example of non-leftist opposition to the dictatorship was the Conservative Party. The first Somoza dictator, Anastasio Somoza Garcia, initially seized the reins of power at the expense of the Liberal president, Sacasa. In order to disguise his power grab, Somoza declared himself a Liberal, although

---

[75] Camilo Ortega died in the battle of Masaya before the revolutionary victory of July 1979.
[76] Tourrain (1988, p. 338).

some members of the Liberal Party rejected his forceful joining of their ranks. Somoza's move into the Liberal Party made the Conservative Party one logical source of opposition to him, although there were also periods when the Conservatives cooperated with the Somozas. When Somoza Garcia suggested elections, the Conservatives tried to run a candidate to oppose him – Leonardo Arguello, who sought the presidency in an election that Somoza initiated but then undermined with fraud, as discussed earlier in this chapter. When it became increasingly clear that the dictatorship would never be sidelined by en electoral outcome, the Conservatives began to oppose the dictatorship in non-electoral ways.

One of the most visible Conservative opponents of Somoza was Pedro Joaquin Chamorro. The son of a Conservative family whose ancestors had served as non-elected presidents in nineteenth century Nicaraguan history, Chamorro himself had presidential aspirations that the dictatorship thwarted. Pedro Joaquin Chamorro had a long history of public and internationally visible opposition to the Somoza regime, primarily due to his writing. The first example of his written opposition to the Somozas was his law thesis, presented to the Law School of the National University of Mexico in 1948 and entitled "Labor Law in Nicaragua."[77] It investigated the unfair nature of Nicaragua's system of labor laws under the dictatorship. Following the receipt of his law degree, Pedro Chamorro returned to Nicaragua, where he married Violeta Barríos in 1950. He became involved in the publication of the newspaper *La Prensa*, which had historically been associated with both his family and the Conservative Party.

Pedro Chamorro was arrested by the Somoza regime in September 1956, just hours after the first Somoza was assassinated by poet Rigoberto Lopez Perez. Already known for his opposition to the dictatorship, Chamorro was charged with having been involved with a conspiracy against Somoza Garcia's life.[78] He was tried by a military tribunal rather than by a civilian court, a juridical pattern that the dictatorship followed with respect to all opponents. Despite the venue, he was found not guilty of involvement in any assassination plot. Lopez Perez was later found to have been acting alone.

However, the military tribunal did find Chamorro guilty of "having known that there would be a rebellion against the government" and of having kept that information to himself. He was sentenced to forty months in jail and held in the San Carlos Guard Post in southern Nicaragua.[79] Pedro Chamorro

---

[77] Pedro Joaquín Chamorro Cardenál, "El Derecho del Trabajo," thesis presented to the National School of Jurisprudence and Social Sciences, National Autonomous University of México, México, D.F. (1948). In Spanish the word for "law" and for "right" are one and the same so that the title in Spanish is more controversial than appears from the English translation. The Spanish title can also be translated as "The Right of Work." (Chamorro, 1948)

[78] Chamorro (1981, p. 2).

[79] This was the same Guard Post that nearly ten years later would be stormed by the Sandinistas and recruits from Ernesto Cardenal's liberation theology experiment in the village of Solentiname.

escaped from San Carlos in March, 1957. He then fled, together with Violeta, to San Jose, Costa Rica, where he remained until March, 1959. During his period of exile, Pedro Chamorro wrote his first book, an exposé of the Somoza dictatorship entitled *Bloody Lineage: The Somozas*. The book was published in Mexico in 1957. *Bloody Lineage* made Chamorro his name as an international writer and visible opponent of Somocismo. It went through three editions in Mexico but was banned in Nicaragua until finally being published there in 1978. It was republished in Mexico in 1978 and 1980.[80]

In 1959, Pedro Chamorro returned to Nicaragua, where he became involved with other middle-class writers and intellectuals in an effort to organize an insurrection against the dictatorship. In 1959, he traveled to Cuba and Venezuela with author Reinaldo Antonio Téfel, known for his famous sociological study of poverty in Managua's shantytowns.[81] The two authors went to Cuba to dialogue with Fidel Castro and Ché Guevara in the hopes of receiving Cuban financial support for an insurrection in Nicaragua. The trip was unsuccessful. In Cuba, the two Nicaraguans found that their political differences with the Cuban revolutionaries were too great, and the Cubans refused them aid. The Venezuelans were also unwilling to support an armed insurrection in Nicaragua.

In 1962, during the reign of the second Somoza, Luis Somoza Debayle, Pedro Chamorro became involved in the campaign for René Schick, who was elected in 1963. But, as seen above, that election changed nothing and was soon followed by the deaths of Schick, first, and then Luis Somoza himself. Those two deaths brought to uncontested power the third of the three Somoza dictators, Anastasio Somoza Debayle, and initiated the darkest and most repressive period of the Somoza years. Seeing that the election had not brought change, Chamorro became involved with the Group of 27, a collection of writers and intellectuals who opposed the dictatorship. In 1974, he joined that group in signing the Document of the 27 entitled: "There is No One to Vote For." Subsequently he participated in the formation of the Democratic Union for Liberation (*Unión Democrática de Liberación*, UDEL) and was elected president of its National Council, where he served until December 1977.

The goal of UDEL and its supporters was the construction of a "democratic and pluralist society."[82] Pedro Chamorro stated his own political position publicly. He sought:

a) an instrument of civil participation for all sectors of national society
b) political, economic, and social reforms that would permit a greater level of social justice and equality in society

---

[80] Chamorro (1980). Others of Chamorro's writings include "Diario De Un Préso: Testimonia de la Cárcel" (1961) and "*Los Pies Descalzos de Nicaragua: Monografia Sobre la Frontera Sur y el Eje Hidrografico Gran Lago-Rio San Juan*" (1970). Each of these publications revealed human rights violations, corruption, and mismanagement under the Somoza regime.
[81] Téfel (1976)
[82] Chamorro (1981, p. XV).

c) alternation in public power
d) the struggle against corruption and illicit enrichment
e) protection of human rights, especially for the lowest-income members of society
f) an *alliance* in search of these ends with *all other political organizations in the country* (my italics)

Going on to speak for UDEL itself, Pedro Chamorro wrote that "democratic politics, economic and social justice, and external independence" were the three fundamental objectives of UDEL. "Pluralism and unity were the essential characteristics of UDEL" and would be the kind of government UDEL would establish once it had assumed national power.[83]

While being involved with organized, domestic opposition, Pedro Chamorro continued to edit Nicaragua's most visible newspaper, *La Prensa*. He used the newspaper to criticize and attack the dictatorship, increasing public awareness of his position by writing for the domestic audience as he had previously done internationally. In his sustained opposition to Somoza, Chamorro's motives were personal as well as social. He had always had presidential aspirations of his own and sought to follow the example of his ancestors who had been Nicaraguan presidents. Pedro Chamorro would certainly have launched a campaign for the presidency if elections had ever become possible. Yet he also genuinely opposed and abhorred the human rights violations, repression, and social injustice that the dictatorship perpetrated, and wanted elections to be more meaningful than they had been in the nineteenth century. In the final years of Somoza Debayle, Chamorro's voice rang out across Nicaragua, using his newspaper to condemn the dictatorship and the sufferings of the Nicaraguan people.

Chamorro's call for coalition and cooperation spoke explicitly of the cross-class alliance that eventually developed in support of the Sandinista revolution. Unfortunately, both for Pedro Chamorro and for Nicaragua, he did not live to see either the downfall of the dictatorship or the pluralistic elements of the Sandinista regime. Pedro Chamorro was assassinated by Somoza's henchmen on January 9, 1978. He thus became one of the non-Sandinist leaders who had led the opposition but died before the dictatorship was defeated. Chamorro's murder touched off massive spontaneous demonstrations nationwide, marking the beginning of the final insurrection and the downfall of the dictatorship.[84] Speaking of Pedro's murder and funeral, and symbolizing the cross-class unity he had desired, his widow, future Nicaraguan President, Violeta Chamorro said,

> For me the tragedy was even more cruel because I was not here [in Nicaragua]. I returned and that night I saw the sea of humanity that came through the streets bringing me his body, already a martyr.... When we were having the wake in [the

---

[83] La Prensa (1981, pp. 249–49).
[84] Chavarría (1983).

offices of] *La Prensa* the Guard and the Somocistas came throwing tear gas bombs and shooting bullets.... The next day I received Pedro draped in the flag of Nicaragua, the simplest, poorest flag of coarse cotton. I don't know who put it on him; it must have been the people, *his* Nicaraguan people (her italics)....Before throwing in the first shovel of dirt the man who had the shovel said "Take it, Madam, the flag." "No," I said, "Leave it on him please, on his coffin. Pedro needed to be buried with his flag. And he is still there with it."[85]

Apart from writers and intellectuals, another influential group within the cross-class alliance developing against Somoza was the business community. While some business owners had benefited from friendship networks with Somoza, by the end of the 1970s many members of the business community had become disgusted with the regime. In July 1979, as triumph loomed, the business community set aside its differences in favor of a relatively united position for Somoza's ouster. After the dictatorship had fallen, the association of business elites, the Superior Council of Private Enterprise (*Consejo Superior de la Empresa Privada*, COSEP), negotiated with the new government in favor of its constituents.[86]

As discussed earlier, further evidence of cross-class and cross-societal support for the revolution came from the Nicaraguan clergy. Both clerics and revolutionaries found compatibility between the teachings of liberation theology and the ideology and goals of Sandinismo. Priests contributed to increasing grassroots level support for the revolution by teaching liberation theology in their Bible-study groups and classes. Out of this movement came the Delegates of the Word, grassroots level community leaders who then spread the teachings of Christ and the revolution deeper into popular communities. Some Nicaraguan priests also provided tactical and logistical support for revolutionaries, hiding guerrillas, ferrying fighters across dangerous urban areas, concealing revolutionaries in churches and feeding them where possible or necessary. In the final months of the dictatorship, Managua's Archbishop Miguel Obando y Bravo lent his voice to the multiple calls for Somoza's resignation. The Archbishop's move to join the anti-dictator forces lent prestige and international respectability to the domestic efforts to oust Somoza.

Explanations about the development of social capital point toward the need for individuals to develop relationships and cooperative ties with persons unlike themselves. Indeed, this is the definition of bridging social capital, that is, the development of social ties that bridge social differences. The brutality and determination of the Somoza dictatorship forced Nicaraguans to develop and use such ties. As is evident from the long struggle of the Sandinistas and of Pedro Chamorro and also from the efforts of the clergy, no single one of these efforts against the dictatorship was sufficient. Instead, a combined effort was necessary to bring down the authoritarian regime. In the cross-class alliance of revolutionary forces, we see how the Nicaraguan

---

[85] La Prensa (1981, pp. XVI–XVII).
[86] Spalding (1994, chap. 2, esp. pp. 61–62).

revolution contributed to and required bridging social capital. No other event in the history of Nicaragua had drawn together individuals from such diverse backgrounds: the business community, [87] the urban and rural poor, middle-class intellectuals, and the clergy. Yet the revolution did just that, providing Nicaraguans with an opportunity to learn to work together and to witness the advantages of cooperation.

If the FSLN and its shock troops of poor Nicaraguans provided the insurrectionary power needed to fight the National Guard and ultimately outnumber its repressive apparatus, it was the efforts of the clergy and middle-class writers who gave the insurrection the international legitimacy and wide domestic support it had by the time it took power. Long before the insurrection got underway, much less became successful, the international visibility of authors like Chamorro and Téfel prepared the international community to understand why there would be revolution in Nicaragua. And the Church, including its internationally visible leaders like Obando y Bravo and Cardenál, gave the insurrection moral authority and the implicit acceptance of Rome – no small contribution in a deeply Catholic continent. Thus, a combination of strengths and talents lay behind the revolution and would continue into the first decade of Sandinista government. This cooperation, as we will see in the data analysis of Part II, produced bridging social capital in Nicaragua.

CONCLUSION

This chapter has shown that Sandinismo created multiple cooperative ties in Nicaraguan society, a "we" of struggle against the dictatorship. These ties emerged first within a grassroots-based movement that fostered horizontal cooperation and mutual esteem. While Sandinismo clearly relied on leadership, it used multiple leaders, and over the course of the movement many different commanders emerged while some of the original ones died. This style of oversight limited the development of extensive personal control by one person and encouraged the movement to learn to survive beyond any single leader. Turnover in leadership and horizontal ties encouraged Sandinistas to develop and sustain cooperation among themselves and inspired popular initiative within the movement. The danger of violence that Sandinismo faced in its struggle for popular liberation and national power played a role in fostering grassroots initiative and reliance on multiple leaders. In the face of physical danger and state repression, low-income revolutionaries could not always depend on having a leader present to tell them how to defend themselves or how to fight back. By the same token, deliberate state efforts to eliminate the movement's leaders forced Sandinismo to produce new ones repeatedly and to rely on them if the movement was to go forward. Sandinismo thus created and needed multiple horizontal ties within the movement, as well as a political style of cooperation and trust. These traits later characterized the revolution

---

[87] Spalding (1994, chap. 2).

when it held state power and helped create patterns of cooperation and faith in each other among Sandinistas.

But Sandinismo also created extensive ties with other social groups and classes. The movement emerged initially in response to poverty and as a struggle for and by the poor. But, as they battled for power, Sandinista leaders made a conscious decision to reach out to and incorporate other social classes and sectors. Again, this decision was born of the armed struggle the revolution required and of the magnitude of danger the revolutionaries faced. Other social sectors and classes who cooperated with Sandinismo included the Catholic Church (even its conservative hierarchy), the middle classes, professionals, intellectuals and academics, and, eventually, much of the business community. Although these groups and some members of these groups had differences with Sandinismo on certain aspects of policy and future orientation, in the revolution itself and in many of its core values, Sandinistas and non-Sandinistas shared many goals and priorities. This experience helped Sandinismo create patterns of cooperation and faith between Sandinistas and other social groups and parties.

A key reason behind many Sandinista choices, including those that enhanced mutuality and cooperation, was its reliance on a consistent set of ideas. Although those ideas came from several sources, the presence of intellectuals and thinkers within leadership positions ensured that Sandinismo strove to keep ideology consistent. The movement looked to ideology for explanations, understanding, solutions, and inspiration rather than to the leadership or charisma of a single individual. Part of Sandinista ideology was originally Marxist and remained influenced by Marxism. As such, it explained poverty as structural rather than personal and advocated solutions that changed society. It sought to alter the structures that caused poverty and exploitation rather than to punish those who benefited from those structures (the rich). Once structures were changed, there was room for former adversaries to accommodate themselves within the new system, if they so desired. Sandinismo also altered its use of Marxism to allow the multiple cross-class ties it needed. The changes it made included an accommodation of Marxism to religion, especially to liberation theology, as well as economic cooperation with private landowners and businessmen.

Democracy is an exercise in dialogue. In that exercise, cooperation, and mutual faith are resources that can be used to advance democracy. Mutual trust increases the probability that citizens and leaders will cooperate to play the political game by democratic rules. It requires the appearance of new and different leaders and mandates rotation in power. It necessitates that citizens have a minimum amount of faith in each other – including the trust among losers in any given political battle that they will not be destroyed by the winners. Citizens and leaders alike must believe that there will be another day, another political competition, and another possibility of victory.

Other scholars of revolution and democracy have also suggested that there is a connection between leftist or reformist revolution and the development of mutual cooperation and associations on the one hand, and democracy, on the other hand. David Garrioch illustrates that the French Revolution resulted in part from a gradual rise in popular associations and citizen involvement in politics. These trends helped build the impetus toward revolution. Likewise, Isser Woloch shows that the French Revolution then further enhanced popular cooperation and associations, which flourished in unprecedented numbers after 1789. Lynn Hunt shows that the post-revolutionary increase of organizations enhanced French popular government and contributed to the French transition toward democracy.[88] With respect to the United States, Alexis de Tocqueville has argued that the presence of extensive popular organizations contributed to the strength and depth of democracy in America. Theda Skocpol shows that the American revolution greatly increased the number of popular associations, which flourished in the nineteenth century, subsequent to the revolution.[89]

Studies of party systems in the United States and elsewhere suggest that the development of a clear left/right party system with coherent delineation on both ends of the ideological spectrum also contributes to the strengthening of democracy.[90] Where a party system displays a strong representation on both the left and the right, it is easier for citizens to understand their own interests, place them on the ideological spectrum, and find the party that most closely approximates their own values and interests. By providing a consistent leftist party, Sandinismo also contributed to strengthening and stabilizing a democratic system in Nicaragua. Other social sectors and classes could align themselves with that definitive position or against it, as supporters of the right. The overall outcome was to define Nicaraguan politics around ideas and ideology rather than around personality, charisma, or the leadership of a single individual.[91]

There are many elements of compatibility between Sandinismo and democracy. Sandinismo encouraged horizontal ties, mutual cooperation, and the associational life that helps democracy thrive. It helped delineate the political system in ways citizens could readily comprehend and it initiated democracy's institutions and procedures within Nicaragua. It would not be surprising to find, therefore, that the kind of bridging social capital that enhances democracy is widely present in Nicaragua, particularly among those most loyal to Sandinismo. When we turn to the empirical evidence of Chapters 4 through 6, we will find out whether this is true. There we will see the extent to which

---

[88] Hunt (1984).
[89] Skocpol (2003).
[90] Downs (1957); Duverger (1954).
[91] Elsewhere I have argued that the basics of party politics that are essential to electoral politics were offered by Nicaragua's political parties even before the start of democracy or an electoral calendar. These basics included political delineation along a left/right spectrum, consistency of positions, and simplification of ideas and policies in language easily recognized by voters. See Anderson (2004). For a discussion of the basics of party systems see Lipset and Rokkan (1967), Cavarozzi and Garretón (1989), and Sartori (1976).

Nicaraguans evidence trust toward each other in terms of formal and informal ties and cooperation, and how Sandinistas compare with non-Sandinistas within the Nicaraguan population.

Yet the revolutionary foundation of Nicaraguan democracy also brought with it certain disadvantages. No movement can do everything and no democratizing nation can attend simultaneously to all relevant tasks. In the story of the Sandinista revolution, a neglected task was that of building the national institutions of state. In fact, almost no effort at institutional building had been undertaken by previous governments either. Beyond creating parties of notables in the nineteenth century, Nicaragua's leaders did very little to develop formal institutions of state apart from the presidency which was, itself, unelected. Little effort was made to create either a national legislature or an independent judiciary. The Somoza dictatorship did have both but these were deeply subordinated to the dictatorial presidency and primarily were a facade. In the post-revolutionary context of the massive demands for income redistribution, poverty control, and the basics of health, education, and national survival, creating formal state institutions appeared of secondary concern. In neglecting the establishment of institutions, therefore, the Sandinistas were attending to other tasks and also following a national tradition that predated their own movement. Given the power they had proven to have via mobilized and insurrectionary action, the establishment of formal institutions seemed to be a more minor task. Over the first decade of Sandinista rule and particularly in the latter half of that decade the new government did establish a legislature and judiciary, thus taking initial steps toward the institutionalization of the new democracy. Yet these were small steps that left the nation's institutional capacity lagging behind its capacity for mobilized, direct popular action.[92] In Chapter 7 we will analyze the broader implications of Nicaragua's limited institutional capacities.

---

[92] For a discussion of the development of Nicaragua's legislature and its growing utility in curbing the abuse of power see Anderson (2006b).

3

Creating "Us" and "Them"
Peronism and Bonding Social Capital

> In the upper left-hand corner was a remote scene framed in a tiny window: an empty beach and a solitary woman looking at the sea. She was staring into the distance as if expecting something, perhaps some faint and faraway summons. In my mind that scene suggested the most wistful and absolute loneliness.
>
> *Ernesto Sabato, The Tunnel*[1]

> It is not enough just to teach doctrine. It must be inculcated.... It is not enough just to know what it says. One must understand and feel it. That is why it must be inculcated.
>
> *Juan Perón, second class* on Political Conduct, Peronist High School, March 29, 1951[2]

> Well look, let me say it once and for all. I didn't invent Perón...or Evita....They were born as a reaction to your bad governments...They were summoned as a defence by a people who you and yours submerged in a long path of misery. They were born of you, by you and for you.
>
> *Enrique Santos Discepolo*[3]

If one stands on Argentina's south Atlantic shore, one will immediately understand that the first scene above, written by one of Argentina's most renowned novelists, is alluding to Argentina, itself. The country lies literally at the end of the earth. As a colony it "was not only separated by huge distances from the mother-country, but it was also at the periphery of the Spanish Empire, so much so that the Spanish Crown did not even send corregidores to administer the area."[4] It is a developed, industrialized country with a strong European background, but further removed from Europe and the United States than nearly any other such nation. It is closer to the South Pole than to North America or Western Europe, and traveling there from the heart of Western civilization requires a trip almost halfway around the globe. Argentina's distance from the

---

[1] From E. Sábato (1988, p 10).
[2] From Perón (1973, p. 36).
[3] Cited in James (1988, p. 7).
[4] Calvert and Calvert (1989, p. 208).

North Atlantic community is still considerable today, in a time of electronic contact, and was even greater in the 1940s and 1950s when Peronism took hold. One of Argentina's strongest sources of European influences came with the immigrants who arrived on Argentine shores. Disproportionately, these came from Italy, Germany, Spain, and the Slavic countries, rather than from Britain, France, or Scandinavia. Argentina thus absorbed some European ideas by contact but was isolated from others by distance. It is impossible to understand Peronism, its development, or its behavior, without factoring in these two influences: (1) Argentina's distance from North Atlantic political ideas, specifically those of the American and French revolutions, and (2) the importation of a select subset of European ideas, particularly those from Germany, Italy, and Spain, which were among the late and more troubled European democratizers.[5]

Like Sandinismo, Peronism was born as a reaction to injustice and shared some characteristics with leftist revolutionary movements. These have given it some secondary compatibility with democracy, which I discuss below. Peronism was anti-imperialist and oriented itself toward Argentina's working class, addressing the disadvantaged and exploited position of that class.[6] It improved the economic status of its followers, but it simultaneously recognized that part of the disadvantage of the poor lay in the disrespect and disdain with which they were treated by society at large and by Argentina's upper classes in particular. This emotional recognition of Argentina's poor is an important part of the reason for the deep personal loyalty that many Peronist followers developed for the movement.

Historic timing, location, and Perón's personal background, however, caused Argentina's mass social movement against injustice to take a very different shape than what we saw in Nicaragua, with vastly different implications for the development of democracy today. Peronism became a social movement, not a revolution. It assumed state power non-violently; it did not overthrow the state via mass insurrection. It reflected relatively little influence from nations where the ideas of democracy, leftist social revolution, and citizen participation first emerged. It displayed confusion about revolutionary and democratic ideas and styles of citizen participation. Instead, it was influenced by European political ideas and styles that had been rejected and defeated in the North Atlantic zone but whose rejection had not yet reached Argentina in the late 1940s when Peronism emerged.

Vehemently anti-Marxist, Peronism differed from leftist Sandinismo in terms of interpersonal relations, the nature of leadership, the role of ideas, and the relationship between classes. This chapter scrutinizes four characteristics

---

[5] Habermas (1996).
[6] Although Radicalism and some other political parties had tried to appeal to Argentina's working class before the 1940s, upon the arrival of Peronism Argentine labor still appeared fundamentally unattached to any political party. This availability offered Peronism an opportunity to capture the loyalites of the nation's working class. Germani (1978, pp. 68–69).

of Peronism that contributed to the type of social capital that developed in Argentina. They are: (1) Peronism's leadership style, (2) the role of ideas in directing the movement, (3) clientelist, vertical control that undermined grassroots initiative, and (4) the types of relationships Peronism fostered with other classes and with major groups, sectors, and institutions in Argentine society. These key elements were discernible at the beginning of the movement and became more pronounced with time. They deeply influenced Argentine society both within and beyond Peronism. They spawned distrust within and toward Peronism and fostered suspicion and contempt. These undermined the ability to cooperate within the Peronist movement and between it and other groups and sectors in Argentine society.

ONE CLASS, ONE PARTY, ONE SAVIOR

Peronism was Argentina's first mass movement of national political appeal but it was not the nation's first poor people's movement. From independence in the early 1800s through 1852 Argentina had experienced twenty-five years of dictatorship followed by a constitution written in 1853. Thereafter Argentina became an elitist system governed by exclusive parties of notables.[7] Although it instituted formal elections, in practice, like Nicaragua, Argentine politics excluded popular participation until the twentieth century. Of the nineteenth century, Hilda Sabato writes, "Elections were controlled and manipulated from above; the vote was a prerogative of the privileged few; 'the people' had no access to the polls."[8] Such a situation left open space for a political party to step in and appeal for support from the working class and the poor. Beginning in the 1890s and having electoral effect after 1912, a new party, the Radical Civic Union, brought the nation's first experience with democracy and universal male suffrage.[9] This first period of elections ended with a military coup in 1930. Perón's personal appeal to the poor began while the nation was governed by a military dictatorship and while he was Minister of Labor assigned to that post by the dictatorship. Perón then instigated and won elections, ending the military dictatorship, and he assumed power as an elected president in 1946.

In contrast with Sandino, Perón framed his fight for social justice in a personalistic manner and relied on charisma to win and hold popular support.[10] While previous Argentine leaders like Radical President Yrigoyen and dictator Juan Manual de Rosas had also used personalism, Perón took it to new levels

---

[7] Germani (1978, p. 226).
[8] Sabato (1992); Mustapic (1984); Galitelli (1987); James (1988).
[9] From 1930 forward the Argentine military played a central and mostly failed role in national politics. Fitch (1998).
[10] Writing about a very different context – that of contemporary India – Atul Kohli (1990) argues that personalistic, charismatic leadership has also undermined party coherence and power, ultimately undermining the party system entirely, as in Argentina. The lack of a strong party system has contributed to making India nearly ungovernable.

in its capacity to mobilize and control. He created an entire movement and later a political party around himself. Perón did not ascribe the ideas or goals of his movement to any predecessor, but rather considered them original, his own. This personalism encouraged a predominance of verticalism and the use of hierarchical ties within Peronism as mechanisms of control. These would become even more evident after the movement had been in power for several years, and more visible still after Perón's second election in 1952 and during his exile in Spain.

Perón did not place his movement in an international context. His view of Peronism as a specifically Argentine struggle reflected the nation's geographical isolation and his own limited education. Peronism was a charismatic movement wherein the charisma of both Perón and his wife, Eva, were key elements in keeping the movement together and guiding its direction, even when internal positions of the movement did not coincide. Weber defined charisma as authority "resting on devotion to the specific and exceptional sanctity, heroism or exemplary character of an individual person and of the normative patterns or order revealed by him."[11] Perón's style of leadership and his relationship to his followers closely fit Weber's definition of charisma, and Peronism is often studied as an example of charisma.[12] Scholars have also noted that people who have been excluded are more susceptible to the appeal of personalism. Perón used personalism and charisma to appeal to Argentina's excluded and marginalized working class.[13]

Even before Perón, Argentina had a history of personalistic leadership. This made Perón's movement an easy fit within national patterns. Argentina's nation-building process after independence in the early nineteenth century depended upon the powerful personality of one caudillo, Juan Manual de Rosas. Rosas used the extensive personal loyalty he had cultivated among his gaucho followers as a power base from which to take and hold national power from 1828 to 1852, unifying the country into a single national entity for the first time. After the defeat of Rosas, Argentina wrote a constitution modeled on that of the United States, including three formal institutions of state, the president, a bicameral legislature, and a judiciary. Argentina then ignored its Constitution and instead established non-electoral parties that were closed, elitist clubs of notables, "essentially conservative organizations representing different sectors of the upper class – principally the large landowners of the interior provinces and the commercial and livestock elements of the city and province of Buenos Aires.... During this period of conservative rule the masses of the people were almost completely removed from the political process."[14]

---

[11] Weber (1947, p. 328).
[12] Madsen and Snow (1991); Butler (1969); Calvert and Calvert (1989, p. 93).
[13] Similarly, Juan Carlos Torre writes that Argentina's labor movement was quite weak prior to Perón's arrival, a weakness that contributed to labor's marginalization (1990, pp. 39–51 and chap. 3).
[14] Snow (1972, p. 3). Daniel James writes that economic policies before and during the second World War had resulted in an expanded and strengthened Argentine economy. Yet the

The parties did not run for election or appeal to the people through electoral campaigns. Instead, elections were decided in negotiations among party leaders away from public view. As in Nicaragua's nineteenth century party system, no party or leader represented the working and lower classes, and no electoral opportunity existed to change the de facto system. Many of the excluded majority were European immigrants whose position in Argentina was made more precarious by laws allowing immigrants to work but making citizenship and voting rights much harder to attain.

In response to this closed, elitist system, a new mass political party emerged in 1890: the Radical Civic Union (*Union Civica Radical*, UCR), owing its name to its radical demand for universal male suffrage. Many of the original UCR leaders were aware of and influenced by events in Europe, and the advent of Radicalism represented a key moment in Argentine history when leaders deliberately tried to introduce progressive European ideas. Leandro Além founded the UCR in 1890 but did not live to see the party reach national power. Other leaders shared and promoted the goal of free elections and mass democracy. On the basis of these ideas, Radicalism agitated for twenty-two years before the Saenz Peña law made male suffrage universal and voting mandatory in 1912. When national elections arrived four years later, Radicalism moved toward national power.[15] Hipolito Yrigoyen won Argentina's first democratic election in 1916 and became the nation's first democratically elected president. But Radicalism in power took a personalistic turn. Yrigoyen governed by relying on charisma rather than by cooperative interaction with Congress within the presidential system. The result was that Argentina's first democratically elected president did not behave like a democrat while in office.[16] Peronism was Argentina's second populist movement of personalistic leadership.

Radicalism had also prioritized many of the social and political problems Peronism would later emphasize, but the reform was left unfinished. Radicalism had emerged in response to poverty as well as to the social and political exclusion suffered by Argentina's low-income and immigrant sectors, particularly in Buenos Aires and other industrial centers. It was a quest for popular dignity, respect, and normal democratic participation as much as a call for economic redress. And while Radicalism won political power promising reform, it was eliminated from the political scene before many of the promised social reforms had been completed. A coup that overthrew the Radical government in 1930 also ended Argentina's first democratic experiment. The Radical decade gave Argentines a taste of democracy, but then left them deprived of continued democratic involvement and disillusioned by Radicalism's failure to stay in the political game or fulfill its promises. The coup left a set of unmet

---

military government during this period ensured that benefits of prosperity went to the agricultural sector without sharing them with the working class (1988, chap. 1).
[15] For a study of Radicalism's successful appeal to working class electoral support in the Argentine city of Rosario just after the arrival of universal male suffrage see Karush (1999).
[16] Mustapic (1984); Peruzzotti (1997).

social and political needs and expectations that Peronism would only address sixteen years later.

Peronism picked up where Radicalism left off and began addressing the needs of the urban poor even before elections returned to Argentina. As a colonel in the army during the military regime that succeeded Yrigoyen, Perón was assigned to the Ministry of Labor. He used that post to improve working-class lives. His sympathy for the poor came partly from his own background. Raised in a lower middle class, military family, Perón's upbringing gave him limited economic opportunities, relative educational isolation (including from enlightened ideas about democracy), and a hierarchical view of the world. He was raised in southern Argentina, a region even more remote than the cities to the north. His father was a military officer, and as a boy Perón learned an ethic of vertical command. Typical among many military families, Perón's background did not emphasize education. He was not exposed to the world of the university, higher education, free thought, or the exchange of ideas among equals. Perón, instead, was encouraged to enter the military, a career path that would yield success through obedience to authority rather than through independent thinking. Although Perón never reached the very top of the military command, his considerable success in displaying vertical loyalty and obeying orders resulted in his rise, first, to the status of a colonel, and then to the position of Minister of Labor under the military government of the 1940s.

The latter title allowed him to initiate his relationship with the workers from a position of power over them, as a benefactor. While that power certainly gave him considerable control over the working class, his first and most obvious acts were those of aid and succor, and he used his power to deliver substantial benefits and reform to workers, including laws to improve wages and working conditions, and laws constraining employers from arbitrary firing practices. Over time these legal changes had a profound impact on the lives of the working class, substantially improving working conditions and lives of workers. In response, Argentina's working class gave its loyalty to Perón, and Perón became the beloved leader of the laboring poor.

A scenario uniting a leader with the poor through a preestablished hierarchical relationship differs greatly from that of leftist movements where leaders and followers often begin from a position of more powerlessness and marginalization than Perón had. Whereas Sandino and Sandinismo's 1960s leaders were either laborers or university students, Perón began his work for the poor from a position of relative power. He was already Minister of Labor when he decided to help the working class. Perón and his followers did not need to struggle to attain state power from which to enact reforms. Moreover, from his powerful position, Perón was able to hand his reforms, favors, and improvements down to his followers/beneficiaries without their active involvement or participation. This pattern of using a hierarchical relationship to deliver benefits would powerfully shape future relations within Peronism as well as the social values instilled in its followers. The context lent itself to a hierarchical process of reform rather than one of struggle, mutual support, and close ties between reformists and revolutionaries. Although they were its beneficiaries, the recipients of reform efforts were simultaneously barred from active input into the nature of reforms. Argentina's working class was left with few options other than loyalty and fondness, both of which they gave generously to Perón.

The bond between a leader able and willing to enact sweeping labor reforms and a working class prepared by historical and immediate context to give heartfelt loyalty to that leader owes much to Argentina's geopolitical context. Perón's assignment to the Ministry of Labor coincided with World War II. Officially neutral, Argentina traded with both sides. This complex and difficult task engaged most of the attention of the military government and its commanders. Their preoccupation permitted Perón to carry out his reforms and to develop bonds with his followers unnoticed by the government. By the time Perón's commanding officers discovered what he had done, it was too late. Perón had become the most popular leader in Argentina, and he no longer needed to follow orders or display obedience to his military superiors. He stepped out of the military chain of command and into political power based upon his ability to deliver reforms from above to his loyal followers below. Recognizing that he would not be permitted to continue with his reforms from within the military government, Perón called for an election, which he won easily based on his labor following. After a period of resistance from the military, during which time he was first arrested and then released, Perón was allowed to assume the presidency. Once in power, he continued his reforms on a national scale that soon involved rural areas and far-flung provinces as well as the urban centers.[17]

In the story of Perón's rise to power, there is no chapter about political struggle, popular armed resistance, group effort, mutual support against dangerous odds, or association among peers. Perón's rise to power is a story of hierarchy and peaceful movement into power supported by devoted followers. Perón achieved power by working within a chain of military command until he held enough power to step outside that chain of command. He assumed power based upon upward loyalty from grateful followers, and, beyond elections themselves, dependency primarily went upward, from his followers to himself. It was a model that relied on and encouraged vertical ties, simultaneously making unnecessary any horizontal ties of support and mutuality among followers. Peronists did not need to struggle together to achieve reforms. Instead they needed to show loyalty to a leader and, in displaying that loyalty, their movement achieved state power. It was an easy, non-conflictual route to success, but in its ease, Peronists were also denied the bonds of mutuality that we now know facilitate democracy.

Hierarchy and personal loyalty were not, however, only pragmatic tools in Perón's rise to power. They were permanent aspects of the movement. Perón encouraged them throughout his lifetime. Toward the end of his life, when

[17] Germani (1980); Llorente (1980); Mora y Araujo (1980).

asked in an interview to define a Peronist, he did so entirely in terms of personal loyalty: "For me, as leader of the movement, a Peronist is anyone who follows Peronist ideology and doctrine."[18] He saw himself as personally responsible for the achievements of Peronism and spoke of those accomplishments in the first person.

> I have worked with loyalty and sincerity and I have worked tirelessly to favor those who have been economically submerged and beaten down for one hundred years. Today they have better salaries, they dress, eat, and live better. They feel that they have gained dignity.... I have raised the flag of workers' dignity because this country needs the working man and the supreme dignity of work is what I am creating.[19]

Throughout his life, Perón worked tirelessly but not only for the dignity of labor. He also worked to ensure that no alternative leadership ever emerged from within Peronism.[20] Indeed, Perón's original intention was not to create a political party at all but rather to keep his organization a social movement. He never trusted political parties and recognized that one of their dangers was that they could become vehicles toward power for other leaders and competitors. Perón realized, however, that he needed elections to gain any kind of legitimacy and therefore he allowed Peronism to become a party so that he could consolidate his power through electoral means.[21] It was a personalistic, pragmatic choice rather than one based upon ideals.

Through a careful study of the internal dynamics of Peronism, McGuire has illustrated how Perón systematically undermined the development of any leaders who might become strong enough to challenge his own leadership.[22] He did this by watching new leaders as they first gained popularity. As one began to pull ahead of the others in popularity and power, he would throw his own weight behind a weaker leader, thus temporarily making the weaker man more powerful. But Perón would also reverse his support as soon as the person he was supporting appeared to gain more popularity. In this way potential challengers were always undermined from within Peronism

---

[18] Perón (1971, p. 2).

[19] Perón (1973, p. 41).

[20] One of the most poignant stories of Perón's systematic and deliberate destruction of an alternative leader was his treatment of Juan Atilio Bramuglia. Bramuglia was a loyal supporter of Perón and remained so his entire life. He also would have taken Peronism forward toward the strength of a political party competing within a democratic system if he had been allowed to do so. Instead he found himself undermined by Perón right up to the very end of his life. Other secondary leaders within the movement who appeared to be attracting an independent base of popularity in their own right met the same fate. Apart from Bramuglia, these included Domingo Mercante, Perón's own Vice-Presidential candidate in 1952, and Angel Borlenghi, Peron's Minister of the Interior. Borlenghi, who facilitated Perón's capacity to take over the non-Peronist labor unions, nonetheless labored under an implicit, permanant threat of dismissal. See Rein (2008). On Borlenghi, see Rein (2008, pp. 22, 33). On Mercante, see Rein (2008, p. 46).

[21] Page (1983, p. 273).

[22] McGuire (1997, esp. chaps 4 and 5).

long before they even approached having enough power to challenge Perón himself. This pattern left a legacy of divisiveness and distrustfulness within Peronism and among its leaders so that they were often each other's worst enemies and demonstrated a limited ability to work together. As we will see below, Peronism's style eventually contributed to Perón's ouster and his 1955–1973 exile in Spain. McGuire also writes that Perón still engaged in this erratic favoritism throughout his years in exile. Indeed, it became so common that Peronists within Argentina even developed an expression for it. To be "burned" was to have suddenly lost Perón's favor; leaders who fell from grace in this way had "been burned."[23]

Perón's effort while in exile to retain personal control and undermine competition for the leadership of Peronism ultimately succeeded. But he did sustain a serious challenge from Augusto Vandor. Vandor had been active in the ineffective resistance that emerged after Perón's ouster in 1955.[24] He remained active during two elections which the Radicals won because Peronism was proscribed. During the administrations of Frondizi and Illia from 1959 to 1966, Vandor emerged as an energetic, skilled labor leader from within the metal workers' union, one of the largest and most politically powerful of all the labor unions. The liberalization of the political climate under the two Radical presidents made it possible for Peronism to begin to revitalize itself. Vandor realized that he could never win by challenging Perón's leadership directly. Instead he swore his own personal loyalty to Perón while also working within the labor movement to gain personal support and popularity there. Perón eventually realized that Vandor's popularity had begun to represent a challenge to his own leadership. He moved to elevate another labor leader, José Alonso, in the effort to undermine Vandor. His directives to Alonso reveal Perón's attitude toward other leaders: "In this fight...the principal enemy is Vandor and his clique.... It is necessary to go after them with everything and to aim for the head.... There has to be a definitive resolution.... That is my word and you know the saying that 'Perón keeps his word.'"[25]

Finding that he could not defeat Perón by gaining party leadership, Vandor supported the military coup of 1966 and the ascension of General Ongania to power. For a labor leader to support a military coup seems puzzling. It was another pragmatic choice rather than one based on ideas. But it was a miscalculation. Once in power, Ongania distanced himself from Vandor, causing the labor leader to lose support among workers.[26] Soon after the Ongania coup and at the height of labor unrest in his home city of Cordoba, Vandor was murdered. Those responsible for the act were never found, although accusations and suspicions abounded. In the end, no alternative national leader emerged in

---

[23] Page (1983, p. 366).
[24] McGuire (1997, p. 83).
[25] Pereyra (1973, chap. 3, p. 266, note 29). Cited in Page (1983, p. 394).
[26] Page (1983, pp. 401–406).

Argentina during Perón's exile to promote the movement as a national political force or to challenge Perón for its leadership.[27] While in exile, Perón employed three strategies to eliminate leadership opposition within Peronism: expulsion, playing leaders off against one another, and a perpetual threat of his own return.[28] When Perón did finally return to Argentina in 1972, he took steps to ensure that Peronism presented a "monolithic front" and that no challenge to his power appeared from within the movement.[29]

An important part of the worshipful character of Peronism came with the role of Eva, Perón's second wife. Eva offered no challenge to Perón's absolute leadership and authority but only affirmed and increased his power. She publicly declared her unconditional loyalty and subservience to Perón and said that she was only acting for him and he through her. She even gave him credit for the Eva Perón Foundation, the beneficent organization she founded, and for all of its accomplishments. In her public speeches she asked Peronists to follow Perón in an unquestioning fashion. When speaking of Eva, Perón said "Evita adopted my political and social ideas, imbuing them with a feminine sensibility, to the point of creating within herself a second 'I.'"[30]

Eva shared Perón's commitment to improving the social and economic condition of Argentina's poor, particularly the workers. Working together toward this common goal was central to their relationship. After Perón was elected in 1946 and Peronism had achieved control over the state, Eva set up the Eva Perón Foundation from which she administered private charity to needy beneficiaries who asked the Foundation for help. In its relationship to the poor, the Eva Perón Foundation was characterized by vertical, clientelistic relations. The poor appealed directly to Eva for help and she handed down gifts in a gracious fashion. But the Eva Perón Foundation never encouraged the poor to mobilize and work together toward mutually beneficial goals. Rather than encouraging horizontal ties and mutual cooperation among the poor, the Foundation demonstrated that vertical ties directly to a leader were the best way for individuals to address their own poverty and improve their own individual circumstances.

Perón's early success with labor was owing to a system in which he permitted limited local union autonomy within a broader framework of firm government control at the top.[31] Yet with time, and particularly after he gained state power, Perón began talking about the need to "inculcate doctrine" into his followers as a way of "educating the masses" to his ideas. This approach would enhance and strengthen the worship of a single leader and the personalism

---

[27] One leader who tried valiantly to unite Peronism under an alternative leader, himself, was Juan Atilio Bramuglia who envisioned a more democratic Peronism than Perón wanted and a movement that would subject itself to electoral rules. Had Bramuglia succeeded, modern-day Peronism would be a very different political party. Rein (2008).

[28] Butler (1969, esp. p. 438).

[29] Page (1983, p. 428).

[30] Luca de Tema et al. (1976, pp. 54–55).

[31] Crassweller (1987, p. 19).

that increasingly characterized the movement. Educating and inculcating followers to think in a certain way also encouraged vertical ties from followers to the leader, and discouraged independent thinking or separate discussion in horizontal ways among equals. In 1948, within two years of being elected, Perón outlined this method of leadership in a meeting with Peronist legislators, directors, and leaders: "To guide the masses you have to instruct and educate them. That can be done in meetings, political conferences in our centers...not to get them to vote for us...but to talk to the citizens about their obligations."[32] This comment betrays a scant regard for the independent capacity of average citizens to think or act for themselves. It even suggests a cautious wariness about any conclusions they might reach on their own. It specifically shows little confidence that citizens acting independently can contribute to the progress of Peronism. By 1951, still within his first presidential administration, Perón established a high school for the purpose of inculcating Peronist doctrine into his followers. In the inaugural ceremony for the new school, Perón said,

> Doctrine must be inculcated in order for it to inform action. That is the fundamental reason for the existence of a school. This cannot be left free to heterogeneous interpretations of different men nor to the analytical examination of each one. Rather, in order to achieve conformity to this doctrine it is necessary to establish a center where each concept of doctrine is developed and presented for practical, rational execution. This is the basis, the reason for being and the need for a Peronist High School.[33]

For all the power of the unions that Peronism elicited, it never established an unassailable place for workers because it never institutionalized the union movement. Just as Perón's personalism resisted the creation of a political party, so he also resisted institutionalizing the unions. The ambiguous position of Argentina's unions contrasts with that of British unions, another nation where labor unions have achieved national political influence. In comparing the power of the trade unions in Britain and Argentina, Daniel James writes:

> For all its talks with generals, its open-shirted bonhomie with presidents, the Peronist unions' influence on the nation's councils was grudgingly recognized and strictly limited by the restricted tolerance for all things Peronist and working class. A scotch with the Secretary of Labor was, ultimately, a poor substitute for genuine institutions of integration.... the union leadership's power and position was thus both a source of strength, but also, ultimately, a source of weakness and frustration.[34]

---

[32] In a speech to meeting of legislators, political leaders, and directors of Peronist Party, June 18, 1948 (Perón, 1973, pp. 35–36).

[33] Juan Perón, Inaugural Ceremony of Peronist High School, March 1, 1951 (Perón, 1973, pp. 45–46). Italian fascism also went to considerable lengths to gain youth support by using the schools for indoctrination. It won youth support in part by promising that fascism was a "revolution," a birth of something clean and new. Yet, writes Germani, "Because of these promises many believed themselves fascists, only to discover later that 'their fascism' did not really exist." Much the same can be said of progressives and idealists who supported Peronism. Germani (1978, pp. 248–251, 253, 255).

[34] James (1988; 1978).

Creating "Us" and "Them" 79

Perón's leadership style created competition and distrust among leaders. Each secondary leader learned that his own interests were better served by catering to Perón than by engaging in cooperation with other leaders. In fact, by first supporting and then betraying leaders, Perón taught secondary leaders that betrayal and non-cooperation were accepted, expected, and personally advantageous. As a result, Peronist leaders lacked any capacity for cooperation and mutual support. The use of personalism and charisma rather than ideas to hold the movement together and the betrayal of each other by leaders left Peronism vulnerable to a successor who could master the arts of verticalism, betrayal, charisma, and personalism but who did not necessarily share Perón's dedication to social reform.

INCONSISTENT IDEAS: PERONISM AS AN AUTHORITARIAN POPULISM OF FASCIST TENDENCIES

Peronism was unlike any other mass movement in Latin America,[35] but like Sandinismo it was not unique in the world. The best comparative understanding of Peronism comes from considering it in comparison with non-leftist, hierarchical populist movements in Europe in the early twentieth century. In his careful study comparing Peronism with European fascism, Gino Germani writes that Peronism was an authoritarian populism that "was initiated and led by a group of fascist or nazi [sic] oriented generals."[36] According to Germani, Perón's "ideological leaning was fascist,"[37] and once he was in power he "continued to avail himself of [the support of] fascists,"[38] meaning elites who had sympathized with the European Axis powers and who shared interests with fascism's supporters in Europe. In addition, writes Germani, "It is from its nationalist and military origin that Peronism acquired its fascist character. Some of the regime's institutions were designed after the Italian fascist examples...."[39]

---

[35] This was true up until the time of Peronism and for many decades thereafter. Instead, movements that were like Peronism were primarily found in Europe. Now, very recently, another personalistic movement in Latin America is reminiscent of Peronism and that is the charismatic movement that Hugo Chavez has tried to create in Venezuela. Even there the similarity is limited. Peronism was never subjected to any true electoral competition but Chavez has been forced to submit himself to a popular referendum. Asked in December, 2007, if they would vote to keep Chavez in power until 2020, Venezuelan citizens voted against him.

[36] Germani (1978, p. 116).

[37] Germani (1978, p. 173).

[38] Germani (1978, p. 181). Apart from elites, an openly fascist popular group that supported Peron was the youth group, Alianza de la Juventude Nacionalista. Klein (2001) writes that the Alianza emerged during World War II, embraced the fuhrerprinzip and valued violence as an end in and of itself, as well as as a means toward other ends. It elevated rural workers as the solution to Argentina's problems, was pro-labor, and anti-Semitic.

[39] Germani (1978, p. 202). Germani ultimately concludes that Peronism was not a pure form of fascism because it relied on the mobilization of Argentina's working class while European fascism drew largely on the middle classes. He also concludes that Peronism also differed from European fascism in that it did not demobilize the working class. In this last observation,

I follow Germani in viewing Peronism as an authoritarian populism with fascist characteristics because merely classifying Peronism as populism leaves its understanding too vague. "Populism" includes so many dissimilar movements that its utility for theoretical analysis is limited, particularly when attempting to understand the kind of social capital generated through the movement.[40] Instead, I suggest that Peronist populism shared key analytical characteristics with the fascist mass movements that developed in new European democracies in the early twentieth century. Although Peronism was milder than many fascist movements, it nevertheless, falls within fascism's "magnetic field."[41] Characteristics that Peronism shared with fascism were the use of charisma and emotional bonding, a confusing combination of leftist and rightist rhetoric and policies, disingenuous electoralism, and oppression of the opposition. While many of the characteristics shared with fascism emerged more clearly after the movement attained power, they were present, although in more subtle form, from the beginning.[42]

Germani's understanding of Peronism is now outdated by events that have occurred within contemporary Peronism under Menem in the 1990s, after Germani's lifetime. Leclau also compares Peronism and the European fascisms, finding them quite similar, with both flourishing in severe economic crisis and drawing upon popular emotion (1979, esp. chap. 4 and pp. 176, 152). In the 1990s Peronism went a considerable distance toward demobilizing Argentina's working class and its own followers through the use of clientelism, a development that Germani suspected could happen. But he did not live long enough to see it develop as fully as it did under Menem. On Peronism's potential for "Machiavellian manipulation" of the masses by elites, see Germani (1978, p. 93). On the extensive use of clientelism to demobilize and disempower Argentina's working class and Peronism's own followers, see the careful study of Peronist political networks by Auyero (2001).

[40] "Populism" is understood to include movements as diverse as Peronism, the European fascisms between the world wars, the early twentieth century agrarian movement in the southwestern United States, the Quebec separatist movement, Ataturk's movement of the 1920s in Turkey, Tony Blair's political style in Britain in the early twenty-first century, and several personalist movements in the Middle East. Some of these populisms, particularly the fascist populisms, are deeply at odds with democracy, while others, such as the Quebec separatist movement, are fully compatible with democratic values, processes, and institutions. For an early analysis of populism and its variants, see Tella (1970). For a more recent and quite extensive work on populism in all its many forms see Hermet (2001). On the agrarian movement in the American southwest see Green (1978). For a consideration of classifications of Latin American populism see Weyland (2001). For a recent overview of populism in Latin America see Cammack (2000) and Szusterman (2000).

[41] Burrin (1984); Griffin (1995).

[42] Many scholars have accepted the placement of Peronism within a category of populism. However, such categorization is too indistinct and does not go far enough in helping us understand Peronism or the kind of social capital it created. First, the term "populism" has an innocuous and benign connotation to it that entirely fails to capture the aggressiveness, anger, and visceral hostility to non-Peronists that Peronism displayed. Such aggression and hostility were found in European fascist movements. Second, the term fascism captures the mass, society-wide appeal of Peronism and was also found in the fascist movements of Germany, Italy, and Spain. By contrast, populism is so broad a category that it can include very small movements that appeal to only small segments of society, such as the Quebec separatist movement, the agrarian movement in Kansas, or Le Pen's appeal in France. However, both populism

The point of a comparison between Peronism and fascism is not to insinuate that Peronism was as extreme as fascism. It was not. The purpose of the comparison is to explore the popular values that Peronism engendered, demonstrating how these affected trust and, with it, the development of bridging social capital. By imitating many aspects of fascist thinking and behavior, Peronism embraced contradictory ideas and positions.[43] This behavior undermined trust among average Peronists, between lesser leaders and Perón himself, among secondary leaders, and between Peronism and its non-Peronist opponents in the wider society. As European fascist movements struggled to gain and hold power and impose their agenda on society, they and their leaders were not concerned that they were undermining trust, betraying the faith of friends and enemies alike, and destroying democratic institutions and procedures because they did not believe in democracy and because their goal was to take and hold power *by any means necessary*. As an authoritarian populism with multiple fascist traits, much the same can be said of Peronism in its first nine years.

In contrast to the European fascist movements, the relationship between Peronism and democracy matters a great deal. In Europe fascism was defeated by either foreign or domestic actors before democratization began. By contrast, Argentina today is democratizing with Peronism at the heart of that process. Since trust and bridging social capital are central to democracy, the relationship between Peronism and trust or bridging social capital is crucial to the issues of this book. Social capital theory argues that a nation needs social capital – and therefore trust – in order to democratize successfully. For that reason, the extent to which Peronism undermined trust by emulating fascism is key to understand social capital in Argentina today and the difficulties it faces as it seeks to democratize with Peronism at the center of its democratic process.

Many populist movements, authoritarian and otherwise, utilize a surreal, mystic bond between followers and a charismatic leader. Studies of charismatic leadership and plebiscitary mass movements have argued that where ideology is absent, personal loyalty and emotional attachment to a leader will substitute as a means of holding the masses together. However, when emotional loyalty replaces ideological coherence, the movement may combine ideas from several ideologies, even when these are contradictory.[44] Hermet underscores the idea that populisms of all kinds rely on emotion and unreason as a bond

---

and fascism share a reliance on emotion and unreason as modes of binding followers to the movement. Hermet (2001).

[43] Of course, leftist movements and leaders may also engage in self-contradiction and, once in power, all movements take steps to perpetuate their own hold on power. My point here is that Peronism, fascism, and authoritarian populisms in general made contradiction part of their own standard fare so that inconsistency was much more pronounced than it has generally been in leftist revolutionary movements. Studying fascist movements across Europe, Michael Mann likewise argues that, unlike socialism, fascism had "no systematic theory." (2004, p. 10).

[44] Habermas (1996); Madsen and Snow (1991).

holding the movement together. I suggest that such emotion and unreason make it possible to hold together a powerful movement in the absence of a consistent set of ideas.[45]

Italian fascism revolved around the personality of Mussolini, a charismatic leader and gifted orator. Similarly, Hitler defined himself as the savior/leader who would lead Germany out of its dark times. A powerful orator and charismatic figure, Hitler organized a movement based strongly upon emotional mass bonding to himself and loyalty to his leadership. Spanish fascism revolved for forty years around the person of Francisco Franco.

Likewise, Perón offered his personal charisma instead of leftist ideology as a solution for working-class poverty. In the Argentine context of the early 1940s, Perón could easily have offered a class-based explanation and solution for poverty. In fact, the presence of a large, exploited working class meant that Argentina fit the orthodox Marxist model much more closely than did Nicaragua. But Perón, who had no university education and no exposure to intellectual ideas about poverty and revolution, appears not to have understood Marxism or any consistent, leftist ideology that would have helped explain Argentina's poverty or offered a solution. Instead, Perón said he was anti-Marxist and anti-socialist. Perón sometimes drew on the rhetoric of socialist leaders, but did so in a way that betrayed scant understanding of their ideas. For example, Perón said, "As Mao says, 'The first thing that one must discern as a leader is to establish, clearly, who are your friends and who are your enemies' Now that is what I am saying."[46] Perón thought he was quoting socialist ideology; instead he was drawing upon personalistic and even non-socialist aspects of Mao's leadership style, which had fundamentally been grounded in socialism. But as we saw in the previous section, personalism was something Perón understood and used. His military background enabled him to comprehend hierarchical command and control, loyalty and obedience, and the centrality of a single leader.

Charisma is a problematic basis for a movement and one that lends itself to confusion and contradictory signals, such as those that may emanate from any individual personality with its quirks, moods, and inconsistencies. These undermine trust in that movement and its leader. In fact, Max Weber argues that charisma alone cannot sustain leadership over the long run because eventually the emotional tie fades. Weber says, "New forms of hierarchical obedience would have to emerge if the great leader's vision was to have a lasting impact on politics."[47] Perón relied on charisma and tried to instill obedience with indoctrination. Yet obedience will be greater if subordinates share a common set of values based upon a consistent theme and charisma is replaced, or at least enhanced, by a more permanent bond. We saw in the previous chapter that a soft version of socialism – but an ideologically consistent set of

---

[45] Hermet (2001).
[46] Perón (1971, p. 3).
[47] Paraphrased in Butler (1969, pp. 423–425).

ideas – held Sandinismo together as a movement even across generations and as leaders died. Peronism, in contrast, relied primarily on charisma and failed to develop a consistent set of ideas. This is a common failing in charismatic movements. The result was an internally divided movement that became even more so after Perón's death in 1973.

European fascism deliberately used spectacle and emotion, combined with dependence upon one central leader, to enhance charismatic power.[48] Nazism became expert at creating visual images that entertained, influenced, and convinced while simultaneously creating an inner group of supporters united against those who did not partake in the spectacle or believe in Nazism.[49] Hitler gathered and addressed large crowds in efforts to arouse patriotism and support. He even directed his personal architect to create visual images as part of mass staged events.[50] Mussolini's famous March on Rome was a spectacle that became his final step in gaining national power. On a smaller scale, the French fascist Henrí Dorgeres created a visual spectacle on his market day appearances, giving an impression of menace and virile vigor as well as threatening violence and frightening the targets of peasant anger and scapegoats.[51]

When Perón was jailed by the military before being allowed to take power, large crowds gathered to demand his release. This inadvertent display taught him the power of crowds. After becoming president, Perón created public spectacles by gathering huge crowds of supporters outside the presidential palace. As a result of his popularity, Perón found himself faced initially with little opposition, and the more authoritarian side of the movement did not appear in these early stages. After Perón had won the presidency in 1946, he began to broaden his support base by taking his charismatic appeal outside of Buenos Aires to the low-income residents of the rural provinces. Each visit was carefully choreographed to produce a lasting memory among spectators. Perón and Eva arrived by train, waved and threw coins or small gifts into the large crowds of cheering loyalists. Decades later, provincial residents still had starry-eyed memories of Perón's visit to their province and his generosity to the crowds.

Charisma and spectacle relegated ideas and consistent ideology to a secondary place in European fascist movements. The use of ideas as a kind of glue that keeps people together within one movement, as we saw in Nicaragua, was less necessary when everyone's membership revolved around loyalty to a single personality. In Europe, fascism distinguished itself by its lack of clarity with respect to ideas. It often proclaimed both leftist and rightist ideas, depending upon the moment and the audience and relying upon emotion and

---

[48] The creation of spectacle is by no means confined to fascist or populist authoritarian parties. In India, "rule by theatrics rather than by the painstaking, mundane tasks of building party cells" has weakened democracy there. Kohli (1990, p. 191).

[49] Speer (1970); Bullock (1971).

[50] Speer (1970). For an overview of patterns of anger and blame in fascist popular movements see Anderson (2006a).

[51] Paxton (1997).

double speak to disguise inconsistencies. Fascism in Europe began its ascent by reaching out to the poor with leftist rhetoric but enacted policies friendly to capital, big business, and other traditional elements of the right once in power.[52] This contradiction generated confusion and distrust and its followers were often uncertain about where fascism stood on the ideological spectrum.[53] For example, Italian fascism made many promises, particularly to the rural poor, and even delivered land, higher salaries, and other reforms while it was still trying to gain popularity and power. But as it gained the upper hand in specific areas and later when it held national power, it withdrew its support for the peasantry and instead supported the landlords. Likewise, Hitler had a habit of reversing his own position between left and right, depending upon which audience he was addressing or his position in power.[54]

In Argentina, Perón began his effort to win the poor while he was still the Minister of Labor. Argentina's working class had not suffered a downturn in its fortunes similar to that experienced in Germany after World War I, or in northern France as peasants gravitated toward Henrí Dorgeres.[55] Instead, poverty and economic despair in Argentina were endemic and the result of policies depriving workers of improvements that came with economic prosperity.[56] Yet the same general economic deprivation that had moved peasants in Europe toward fascism drew workers in Argentina toward Perón. In power Perón delivered more reformist policies than the European fascists, but he also enacted policies supporting capitalism, a conservative Catholic Church, and other elements of the traditional right.[57]

Perón and his followers made a more careful effort than the European fascists to define Peronism's position with respect to the left and the right. While in the presidency, Perón published a pamphlet designed to clarify his "third position." It began with the assertion "Neither Yankees nor Marxists: Peronists." According to the President, this position represented "an entirely original alternative...[t]he Justicialist doctrine, the doctrine of General Perón." Perón criticized the inhumaneness of international capital, "which is nothing other than the economic phase of the liberal system...publicly launched with the French Revolution which, with the call for 'liberty, equality, fraternity' destroyed all

---

[52] Payne (1995). Likewise, Cesar Tcach argues that Peronism was essentially a conservative force in its relationship with Argentina's working class (1991, esp. pp. 277–282).

[53] For example, in Spain, intellectuals themselves exhibited some confusion about the contradictory positions espoused by fascism. Payne (1999, esp. chap. 3; 1987, esp. chap. 4).

[54] Farquharson (1976; 1986).

[55] Paxton (1997).

[56] These years brought increasing labor resistance and even violence, reaching their height in a large series of strikes in the internal city of Cordoba. These were violently repressed in a brief period that came to be known as the Cordobazo. For a history of the labor movement in the city of Cordoba, covering the role of both Radicalism and Peronism. Tcach (1991).

[57] In fact, Perón's charisma was such that he was not actually forced to choose between left and right until after his return to Argentina in 1974. At his May Day speech that year, May 1, 1974, Perón faced both rightist and leftist supporters in the plaza before him. He chose the right and the "left marched out of the Plaza de Mayo." Calvert and Calvert (1989, p. 130).

forms of association and delivered the workers to the inhumane game of supply and demand."[58] Perón criticized capitalism as a cold, international accumulative face without country or heart."[59] Perón was equally critical of dogmatic, international Marxism and the class struggle.[60] "Justicialism," he proposed, "sought to overcome the class struggle and supplant it with an agreement between workers and bosses with the support for justice that emanates from the state."[61] The third position was anti-imperialist, in support of political sovereignty and independence. It addressed social justice, the organization of the community, and the dignity of the family. It was based in labor unions and guaranteed that property have a social function.[62] Of his own movement, Perón said, "It is an ideological combination that is on the center, the left, or the right, according to circumstances."[63]

In fact, there were times that Perón's political position seemed so confused that one doubts if he even knew the differences among democracy, capitalism, and socialism. As he established his first presidential administration, Perón declared, "When liberal democracy has separated the working man from his instrument of work, it has not calculated his problems and has not counted on him."[64] Perón's sentence makes no sense, given that liberal democracy is not an economic system and had not even existed in Argentina since Yrigoyen's ouster in 1930. Capitalism, however, had certainly existed under the military dictatorship and a particularly harsh version of it, at that. One suspects that Perón may have been referring to "capitalism" rather than to liberal democracy, and may not have understood the difference between the two. His rhetoric was rife with such confusion.

We know, of course, that Perón did not establish an original third position. In fact, Argentina was as capitalist as ever under Perón, and he made no effort to redistribute property or to make property have a "social function," despite promises to that effect. There were, however, elements of a political and economic position that embraced neither Marxism nor liberal democracy and capitalism. Perón's system wedded workers and capitalist factory owners together in a corporatist relationship. Corporatism often results with workers bound into a subordinate position but lacking mechanisms of autonomous resistance outside the structure of the corporatist configuration. The arrangement fit nicely with Perón's own goals of control and his use of labor organizations as means toward that end. This position, however, was not novel and resembled the fascist movements of Europe. In the 1970s, an Argentine author, Salvador Ferla, recognized and embraced this similarity between Peronism and fascism. Ferla identified himself as a Peronist and fascist, and he considered the

[58] Perón (n.d., p. 5).
[59] Perón (n.d., p. 6).
[60] Perón (n.d., p. 8).
[61] Perón (n.d., p. 9).
[62] Perón (n.d., p. 10).
[63] Speech to Confederation of Intellectuals, September 5, 1950, See Perón (1973, p. 26).
[64] Speech before the Constituent Assembly, January 27, 1949, See Perón (1973, p. 143).

fate of Peronism in conjunction with that of fascism in Europe. Ferla's writing is actually clearer than Perón's own words, and it is worth quoting Ferla at length in order to understand both the relationship between Peronism and fascism and to see how Peronists understood the "third position."

[T]he "third position" is undoubtedly a socialism which was originally presented in 1946 as a "harmony between capital and labor" or a "humanicization of capital." "[T]hird position socialism" rejects Marxism for its inability to value the phenomenon of religion and for its rejection of all that is essential and its elevation of the absurd.[65] [The third position] sustains a double rejection: of capitalist liberal democracy and of the totalitarian state. It has an ultimately different objective. In liberalism the objective is the ascension of society through the success of the most talented individuals. In totalitarian socialism [the ascension of society] is through the development of an integrated economy. In the "third position" the objective is the happiness of man, as an individual, as a family, as a community.[66]

Identifying himself as a fascist, revolutionary and Peronist, Ferla argued that

[T]he best solution had been found by Italy, Germany, and Spain, "the proletarian nations" that had managed to liberate themselves without breaking brusquely with their own past. Through fascism they had managed to liberate themselves from international financial imperialism... For this reason we defined ourselves as "neither left nor right but anti-party."[67] "....We were also antisemites... [which derived from the fact] that most of the heads of the great monopoly businesses and of international and national financial capital... were Jews."[68]

Ferla says that the third position "... refuted liberal, constitutional democracy in favor of a corporatist project that used representation in the state through a professional path."[69] Ferla laments the outcome of World War II and the "death of fascism in Berlin" and concludes that the world has turned left.[70] "For those of us who did not want to die this way, we were together on the 17th of October, 1945 in the Plaza de Mayo with the descamisados, acclaiming and demanding Perón."[71] (This was the occasion on which Perón and his mass followers demanded the elections that would give him victory in 1946.) Ferla goes on to write,

[The year] 1955 surprised Peronism with a grave problem: ideological infiltration. There was an attempt to organize in the country [Argentina] a Christian Democratic Party with the idea of repeating here [in Argentina] the success obtained in Germany and Italy after the collapse of the war ..."[72] It remained incumbent upon Peronism

---

[65] Ferla (1974, pp. 17–18)
[66] Ferla (1974, p. 20).
[67] Ferla (1974, pp. 3–4).
[68] Ferla (1974, p. 4).
[69] Ferla (1974, p. 4).
[70] Ferla (1974, pp. 6–10).
[71] Ferla (1974, p. 6).
[72] Ferla (1974, p. 59).

then to resurrect "verticalism" and to carry forward the "Liberating Revolution" to liberate the Peronist bases to a "disciplined verticalism."[73]

Seen from this perspective, which Ferla clearly meant as sympathetic and supportive, Peronism was the natural and obvious heir to the European fascist movements. It represented an opportunity to establish in Latin America the fascist state that had been defeated in Western Europe. According to Ferla, that opportunity was worth fighting for. The effort to defeat Peronism was the same effort that had defeated fascism. Committed Peronists needed to fight for Peronism just as fascists had defended fascism.

Far from rejecting the authoritarianism of socialism and the capitalism of the liberal democratic west, Peronism embraced both. His government was a capitalist system that delivered some of the goods that socialism provides to society's poor but denied any institutionalized worker participation, either through representative democracy or through worker soviets. Under his leadership, the state nationalized most public services and then began delivering them to the population at subsidized prices. Perón advocated corporatist solutions that placed the state at the center in a paternalistic and ultimately authoritarian relationship to the population.

Both the European fascisms and Peronism shared a distaste for democracy with a disingenuous electoralism. They were willing to use elections to gain or keep power, if that seemed necessary, but they did not believe in democracy or in fair electoral competition for power. In each case, electoralism was a pragmatic choice to utilize any means of attaining power. When Hitler's efforts to operate outside of electoral channels got him arrested, he began competing in national elections, gradually increasing his popular support. Yet no one imagines that Hitler believed in electoral democracy. Once in power, Nazism ended democracy. Similarly, Italian fascism competed in local elections until it had gained national power and then eliminated elections entirely.

Operating in the Western Hemisphere under United States observation and coming after the defeat of European fascism, Perón was more constrained than Hitler or Mussolini had been. His disingenuous electoralism consisted in holding elections but violating many rules of electoral democracy during and after the campaigns. He held a first election in 1946, several midterm elections, and another presidential election in 1952. Peronism could be seen as milder than European fascism because it allowed elections. However, like Hitler and Mussolini, Perón never believed in democracy or elections as legitimate mechanisms for selecting leaders and did not want the alternation of leaders in power.

One reason why Perón was more willing than the European fascists to hold repeated elections was that, unlike them, he faced very little electoral competition among the poor voters, and thus for him elections held less risk. When Perón demanded an election in 1946, he faced no electoral competition since

---

[73] Ferla (1974, pp. 60–63).

the opposition parties had been caught by surprise. The lack of competition allowed Perón to emphasize the positive incentives his movement offered. Its more coercive side would not appear until later when Peronism faced actual opposition. While building a popular base and first seeking the presidency, Perón appealed to the urban working class. It was a narrow electoral base and a limited set of goals, but in the restricted democratic space that Argentina had after nearly fifteen years of dictatorship, it was enough to win the presidency. After winning in 1946, Perón increased his popularity in rural areas and enacted female suffrage, changes made with the 1952 election in mind. One result of Perón's electoralism was the election of a Congress in 1946. This event had profound implications for Argentine democracy which we will explore in Chapter 7.

A final characteristic that early Peronism shared with European fascist movements was the oppression of the opposition. Italian fascism displayed an innocuous demeanor in its earliest phases and while still seeking popular support. It became, however, increasingly violent and coercive as it gained political power. Peasants who joined fascist unions before fascism took national power received economic goods, but those who remained non-fascist were excluded from rewards. Later, rural dwellers were subjected to pressure to join the fascist unions if they wanted economic benefits. And still later, non-fascists and the opposition more generally became targets of threat, intimidation, and eventually violence. As Italian fascism gained more power, it became more coercive and less inviting, eventually holding its peasant following by intimidation, and violently punishing those who refused to become fascists.[74] Likewise, Nazism began by appealing to the poor, offering economic support, and proclaiming respect for the dignity of the working class. But in power it became even more oppressive than Italian fascism and used violence or the threat of it to intimidate opponents throughout its years in power.[75]

As with disingenuous electoralism, Peronism was milder than the European fascisms in its oppression of the opposition. Unlike Italian fascism, Peronism did not need to use violence to gain power and did not share Hitler's domestic or international extremes of violence. Rather, Peronist oppression and intimidation appeared after the movement took national power and began to encounter opposition. At the time of the 1950 midterm election during Perón's first presidency, opposition began to solidify, especially from the Radical Party. As a result, the Radical leader, Ricardo Balbín, was expelled from the lower chamber of Congress by the Peronist majority. Since the expulsion was illegal, the Peronists cloaked it in legality by claiming that

---

[74] Snowden (1989); Cardoza (1982); Corner (1975).
[75] For a fictionalized rendition of civilian life in Berlin under the Nazis and the extent to which intimidation and the threat of violence were pervasive, ubiquitous and subtle, see Fallada (2002). This novel is not intended to provide historic fact but to create in literary terms the sense of what life was like. It is written under a pseudonym. The author lived in Berlin throughout the Nazi years.

Creating "Us" and "Them"

Balbín had used disrespectful language in a campaign speech in the city of Rosario. Balbín still managed to campaign for the election by appearing, making a speech, and then slipping away into hiding. He was arrested on election day in 1950 when he went to vote and he remained behind bars until January, 1951.[76]

If Peronism's electoralism was disingenuous, it was not without long-term implications. While Perón did not believe in liberal democracy, he allowed some democratic institutions and procedures. This opened space for a greater compatibility with democracy than was ever the case in European fascism. When some democratic institutions or procedures are permitted even in an extremely constrained form, their mere existence opens the possibility of their utilization in a more fully democratic manner in the future.[77] In the case of Peronism, its periodic leftism and its use of a legislature offer two dimensions along which it may be made more compatible with democracy. I discuss the democratic potential of leftist Peronism at the end of this chapter; Chapter 7 considers the democratic contribution of Argentina's legislature.

After the 1952 election, in which Peronism retained the presidency and a majority in Congress, the movement faced rising domestic opposition from the other parties and the press. Peronists became increasingly intolerant of such dissent and turned to intimidation and street violence.[78] Peronist thugs had already burned or wrecked the offices of opposition newspapers *La Prensa* and *La Vanguardia* when Perón addressed a massive audience in the Plaza de Mayo. To his followers, Perón said "This thing about punishment [of the opposition] you are telling me to do. Why don't you do it?" In response,

One group headed for the Casa del Pueblo (People's House), headquarters of the Socialist Party and its now-silenced newspaper, *La Vanguardia*. "Jews! Go back to Moscow!," they screamed, throwing stones at the building.[79] There were sixty people inside. The response [the Socialists] received when they phoned the police for help was that no units were available due to the events in the Plaza de Mayo. Soon pieces of burning paper began to float through holes in the windows. The besieged Socialists barely managed to escape before a truck battered down the steel entrance and the edifice was put to a torch. Gasoline-fed flames destroyed the Juan B. Justo Workers Library, which housed a priceless collection of books, newspapers and pamphlets dealing with the labor movement in Argentina. The firemen who arrived belatedly on the scene merely kept the blaze from spreading.

...Other groups attacked the Casa Radical (Radical House) and the headquarters of the conservative National Democratic Party. Again the police and firefighting units remained impassive...[then] they decided to strike at the heart of the oligarchy: the Jockey Club on Florida Street.

---

[76] Page (1983, pp. 228–229).
[77] O'Donnell and Philippe Schmitter (1986).
[78] A government commission that Perón created had closed more that one hundred and fifty newspapers nationwide by 1950. *The Economist* (May 27, 1950, p. 895).
[79] Byron and Vacua (1968, p. 48).

> ...Several men with hatchets went upstairs to the main hall and hacked original paintings by Goya and Velasquez out of their frames. They piled them on the floor and started a bonfire...
> ...When foreign eyewitnesses returned in the early hours of the morning for a second look at the wreckage.... Fire had completely gutted the building.[80]

While Perón was not on the street leading these attacks on the opposition party headquarters and did not specifically order his followers to set fires, his involvement in the violence and intimidation is implicit, and his responsibility is complex and indirect, as was Mussolini's for fascist thug violence in Italy. This style of lawlessness would continue after Perón was ousted and would become associated with Peronism as a movement, whether or not Perón himself was present.[81] After the 1955 coup ousting Perón, for example, Augusto Vandor and Vandor's supporters "organized gangs of street toughs in exchange for a meal, a few drinks, and a night of camaraderie." In an even more sinister vein, Vandor recruited an "apparatus" of bodyguards and enforcers, including individuals on the edge of the law.[82]

As an authoritarian populism embracing many fascist traits, Peronism separated itself from the predominant currents of political thought in the North Atlantic democracies and the Soviet Union. But it did not develop a unique path. Instead, it followed a set of pariah political ideas from Germany, Italy, and Spain that the Western democracies and the Soviet Union had repudiated and defeated. These ideas were counterrevolutionary, anti-democratic, and inconsistent. Perón's personal lack of sophisticated education and Argentina's geographical isolation help explain this attachment to political thinking that had become outmoded elsewhere.

But Perón's unprincipled drive for power – another characteristic he shared with the European fascists – is another reason for his rejection of ideological consistency. Peronism prioritized the drive for power over all other considerations, including principles, policy consistency, and good leadership. By indulging itself with inconsistency and allowing itself to use leftist and rightist ideas to gain support, depending upon the audience and circumstance, Peronism called itself "pragmatic." But "pragmatic" is a gentle and apologetic term for something that was much more sinister and debilitating. While all political parties must have some degree of pragmatism and some ability to compromise in order to survive, the extreme inconsistency in Peronism's "pragmatic" drive for power created not only confusion but also distrust toward Perón, toward his movement, and among his followers. Most political parties view pragmatic compromises with the opposition that deviate from previous policy

---

[80] Page (1983, p. 272). Page's account is based on primary sources kept in the archives of the parties who were the object of Peronist violence and on eyewitness accounts from individuals who saw the violence.

[81] Similarly, Kohli also notes that "ruffians" and thugs have emerged in the face of state weakness in India. He notes, "... as more ruffians and corrupt individuals join a party, the weaker the party will be as a coherent organization." (1990, p. 58).

[82] James (1979); Walsh (1969, p. 146).

to be undesirable but necessary measures that break impasse. However, by making power its first goal and subordinating all other considerations to that primary concern, by always being willing to compromise with anyone over anything, Perón sent out a message that appeared to say that he essentially believed in nothing as much as in power itself. This message sowed deep caution and distrust in Argentine society. In the end, such behavior also showed that Peronism was a tool that could be used by any subsequent power broker, no matter what the message or goal was, nor how inconsistent that goal was with workers' interests.

THE LACK OF GRASSROOTS ACTIVISM AND INITIATIVE

The history of popular organization in Argentina before and during the Peronist social movement is very different from the Nicaraguan story before and during revolution. Argentines had very little history of popular organization or grassroots initiative. Perón then deliberately discouraged independent popular organization. His style of clientelist, vertical control over popular sectors fit well with previous national patterns, but went further than previous leaders in undermining the popular capacity to form organizations and associate independently. Thus, the Peronist movement undermined the bridging capital that is necessary for democracy.[83] Modern-day Peronism has refined clientelistic control over followers – it controls them even more fully than Peronism in the 1940s[84] – and continues to utilize populism to attract a popular following.[85]

In Argentina's history two dynamics operated: first, state building activities deliberately excluded popular participation or incorporated it only in a controlled fashion; second, unlike the Nicaraguans, popular sectors of Argentine society acquiesced in such top-down control and did not undertake extensive grassroots initiatives comparable to Sandino's war or the Sandinista revolution.

Argentina's first ruler was a brutal dictator, Juan Manuel de Rosas. He took power supported by an army of gauchos. But in power he repressed the population and all opposition. He was a caudillo who directed popular power and used it in his own drive for power. Nothing before or during Rosa's

---

[83] Other authors have presented views of clientelism that see clientelism as having a more democratic influence than I suggest here. For example, Sian Lazar (2004) argues that clientelism is democratic because it yields concrete material rewards to clients. Javier Auyero (2000; 2001) likewise emphasizes the material benefits of Peronist clientelism. While I do not deny that Peronism and other forms of clientelism may well yield concrete material benefits to followers, my argument rests more on the residue of personal disempowerment that results from such conveyor-belt reward systems. Citizens may receive material benefits in the moment when they need those, but they do not learn to act for themselves over the long term. The latter is a non-tangible benefit that could outlast the material claims of the moment.
[84] Auyero (2001).
[85] Szusterman (2000).

reign represented grassroots activism or initiative.[86] Similarly, the history of state building in the late nineteenth and early twentieth centuries is a story of elite-directed political development while popular initiative was conspicuously absent. Argentina enacted laws that allowed immigrants to work, but prohibited them from voting and attaining citizenship. They were not regular participants in the life of the nation.

The interlude of democracy instigated by Radical Party agitation deviated temporarily from this pattern of low levels of citizen participation. The Radicals elicited popular demonstrations, used them to demand universal male suffrage and competitive elections, and then won the presidency based on the popular vote. But even this brief period of popular involvement in politics was not characterized by grassroots initiative, much less by determined popular cooperation or resistance to oppression. Instead, the initiative toward democracy came from elite leadership within a new party that called on the people to vote but not necessarily to organize themselves.

In avoiding popular initiative or resistance to oppression and in accepting hierarchical authority, Argentina's lower classes resembled their counterparts in Italy and Spain more than they did the Nicaraguans. In Italy, hierarchical control increased with Mussolini's fascist movement.[87] But vertical ties and popular obedience and quiescence greatly predate Italian fascism, particularly in southern Italy where Robert Putnam found that democracy worked poorly. In Spain, citizen quiescence allowed hierarchical leadership and institutions to capture the loyalties of low-income citizens and thereby control their social behavior and political loyalties. This created a popular predisposition toward the kind of political control fascism would later establish. Victor Pérez-Díaz writes, "in general, its [fascism's] politics corresponded in large measure with the political attitudes of the peasants (centralization, authoritarianism, clericalism, control over social conflicts); [fascism] simply channeled the anticapitalist sentiments of the peasantry."[88] There is a sense, then, in which the political attitudes of Spain's poor "fit" with fascism. Much the same was true in Argentina, and this helps explain the ease with which Peronism found so loyal a following and with which Argentina's poor embraced Peronism. When Perón arrived on Argentina's political scene he likewise faced a history lacking in grassroots initiative. Even reformist initiatives had traditionally come from political leaders rather than from the grassroot level. Those political leaders had frequently directed and controlled popular political participation (as with Rosas and the Radicals), or discouraged and repressed it (as with the military dictatorships).

This pattern of top-down directorship and a lack of grassroots initiative fit nicely with Perón's own political style, which relied on vertical control and

---

[86] For an exploration of the fit of the Rosas dictatorship within Argentine political culture see Anderson (2002, pp. 99–132).
[87] Snowden (1989); Corner (1975).
[88] Pérez-Díaz (1973), my translation.

hierarchical political relations. Average citizens responded well to Perón's style of leadership since it was similar to previous leadership patterns in many ways. Just as historical patterns of popular political activism supported and encouraged the rise of a revolution in Nicaragua, so a long history of vertical political relations in Argentina allowed compatibility between Perón's leadership style and popular politics in Argentina.

Social capital theory argues that democracy will grow more naturally and work more smoothly where citizens have established horizontal ties among themselves and learned to associate cooperatively with each other. Such horizontal ties and associational experience were already in short supply in Argentina before the advent of Peronism. But vertical relations within Peronism further limited grassroots initiative and horizontal attachments in a purposeful manner not seen previously. When grassroots initiatives did appear, Perón maneuvered to ruin them. Thus, Argentine citizens who joined the Peronist movement came less experienced in associations and cooperation than their Sandinista counterparts in Nicaragua. Their political experience with Peronism further weakened their capacity for independent initiative by providing few chances for horizontal ties and positive associational experiences within the Peronist movement itself.

As in his relationship with ideas and policies, Perón's position on grassroots initiative was confusing and contradictory: the rhetoric he spoke did not correspond to the actions he took. In some of his speeches, Perón stressed the benefits of popular organization and particularly the organization of labor. "The poor should seek in the association [with each other] and in the strength of the organizations of the State the protection of the right to live with dignity."[89] "I want Argentines to have an organization that forever guarantees them their own dignity, their own liberty and their own life."[90] But, although Perón called for popular organization, his public speeches indicate that he saw the benefit of organization accruing to himself and his leadership as much as to the workers themselves. Perón said: "The popular organizations should organize themselves for themselves and in the manner that they wish."[91] But also: "When my comrades, in a little bit of a hurry, came to tell me, 'My general, we have to get organized, we have to bring the people together,' I answered 'Don't be in such a hurry; all the time that we have spent in indoctrination, we will save that time later when we go to organize. The most important is doctrine, organize the spirits, the comprehension and the intelligence of the men. Once we have accomplished that it is easy and rapid to bring them together."[92] The first statement emphasizes the freedom of the people to organize themselves for themselves. The second statement says nothing about self-organization and even places organization itself in

---

[89] October 15, 1944 (Anonymous, 1971, p. 17).
[90] February 19, 1952 (Anonymous, 1971, p. 23).
[91] June 1, 1953 (Anonymous, 1971, p. 28).
[92] October 25, 1953 (Anonymous, 1971, p. 31).

a secondary place to indoctrination. In fact, this last statement appears to emphasize control of the masses, and suggests that indoctrination will permit such control. Once indoctrination is complete, bringing the people together – while also keeping them under control – will be easy. Perón saw himself, and not the people, as responsible for Argentina's working-class organizations. He believed that without him they would never have emerged: "Everything that has been done in the country for the free organization of the people is a product of having awakened their social conscience."[93] Given the lack of grassroots initiative in Argentina up to that time, Perón may well have been correct.

Both the theme of self-organization and the theme of indoctrination run through Perón's public discussion of popular organization. But it is the latter theme – organization as a means of control – that is the more predominant. Perón said: "Experience shows that the better-organized working masses are the ones that can be directed and better managed [with respect to] all orders."[94] Perón disguised his orientation toward control by maintaining that he was enacting an original third position which was for the benefit of the workers: "We do not divide the country into classes to throw them into a struggle of one against the other. Instead we try to organize them so that they will collaborate for the greater good of the Nation."[95] But as we saw in the previous section, the third position was neither original nor democratic. Peronism was initially successful because it appealed to workers excluded from the political system. Buoyed by attacks on domestic elites and foreign economic imperialism,[96] Perón temporarily gained strength "by nationalizing industries and by constantly harping upon the massive forces against which he must struggle."[97] But as the movement succeeded and the working class became more integrated into Argentine society, workers gained efficacy and an ability to judge for themselves the performance of their leaders.[98] Peronism then needed to respond to its own constituency by allowing independent development, greater grassroots initiative, and the rise of secondary leaders. Perón's personality, however, as we have seen previously, was incompatible with those new needs. Instead, Perón continued to lead by placing his own ideas front and center, working to indoctrinate followers into the absolute correctness of his own thinking, and undermining any new leadership within the movement.

In fact, this effort at control showed itself even in Perón's very earliest days in power. Even among labor unions and leaders, Perón could not permit competition. "By 1946 Perón had destroyed the [alternative] labor party of Luis Gay and Cipriano Reyes...and had its principal leaders confined and

[93] September 24, 1951 (Anonymous, 1971, p. 23).
[94] August 25, 1944 (Anonymous, 1971, p. 17).
[95] August 11, 1944 (Anonymous, pp. 1971, 17).
[96] Butler (1969, p. 429).
[97] Butler (1969, p. 429).
[98] Butler (1969, pp. 426, 429).

tortured."[99] He did this despite the fact that Gay and Reyes had used their organization to help obtain Perón's release from prison prior to the 1946 election. This is another instance of Perón betraying other leaders who had been strong allies. As Perón established his new government with the support of Argentine workers, his control tool was a law of professional associations put in place while he was Minister of Labor in 1945. It allowed only one union per industry, and that single union had to have formal approval from the Labor Ministry.

David Butler suggests that charisma can provide emotional support to discontented people by giving them propaganda instead of immediately improving their lives.[100] Over the long term, however, a movement must provide more, and Peronism's long-term prospects were curtailed by its leadership's negative attitude toward grassroots initiative. In the end, lack of flexibility in a stagnant organization limited Peronism's ability to change and adapt, and perpetual divisiveness among leaders limited his own control of the movement, even though it also protected him from challengers.[101] In this way, Perón himself set in motion the factors that would cause long-term trouble for the movement. Daniel James writes that Perón was "unwilling to tolerate much independence among his subordinates." With that "he lost the capacity to build a flexible organization that could someday achieve...accommodation with the rest of society."[102] Perón feared being supplanted as leader more than he valued the continued strength and survival of his movement. Moving always to protect himself, "he continuously purged the labor movement" and in doing so undermined its capacity for grassroots initiative and action independent of himself.[103] The results "fostered rank-and-file passivity" as well as apathy and acquiescence.[104]

Social capital theory describes the need for horizontal associational relationships among citizens in order for social capital to develop. Perón's deliberate efforts to control his followers, to tie them individually and vertically to himself through indoctrination and patronage, limited and undermined the horizontal relationships needed for bridging social capital. Hence, the leadership directives and the style of the movement itself mitigated the development of positive social capital. Yet Perón's personal attitude toward the autonomy of his followers was only one of the forces opposing the creation of bridging social capital. Just as "[t]he example of corrupt or self-interested leaders reinforces selfishness and egoism that undermine efforts at collective action,"[105] Perón's personality was so strong and influential that the movement

---

[99] Butler (1969, p. 432). Perón's ability to intervene the non-Peronist unions was greatly facilitated by his Minister of the Interior, Angel Borlenghi. Rein (2008, p. 42).
[100] Calvert and Calvert (1989, p. 112, pp. 122–25); Butler (1969, p. 432).
[101] Butler (1969, p. 437).
[102] Butler (1969, p. 430).
[103] Butler (1969, p. 430).
[104] James (1988, p. 258).
[105] Levine (1992, p. 195).

imprinted his personality on itself and on the dynamics among other leaders. Peronism developed internal mechanisms hostile to mutual cooperation and grassroots initiative. Among secondary leaders, an attitude of mutual hostility prevailed, even in Perón's absence. Thus Vandor, for instance, worked in hostile competition with other leaders rather than working with them toward a common goal.[106] Other leaders also responded antagonistically to grassroots initiative from within the unions.

If Perón's heavy-handed style of control characterized the movement between 1946 and 1955, it might have decreased after 1955 while Perón was in exile. Instead such patterns continued beyond the first Peronist presidencies. Perón was particularly concerned not to lose control of Peronism while in exile. In 1956, he remarked, "My anxiety was that some clever man would have taken over." Finding himself out of power, Perón's first concern was about his own power and not about the fate and welfare of his followers. His concern for his own power first and foremost was infectious within the movement.[107] Of Perón's exile, when the movement might have been cooperating to accomplish his return, Daniel James writes: "[T]he union leaders became, ironically, the chief exponents of verticalism – the campaign for unquestioning respect for hierarchical authority within the movement. By late 1974 they had driven their young opponents from the mainstream of the movement."[108] There were, in fact, some spontaneous strikes and struggles among workers following Perón's ouster, but Perón's efforts to undermine grassroots autonomy were effective, and the workers' efforts never had any long-term effect.

In a different context and examining a very different social institution, Daniel Levine finds that social progress conducted within an hierarchical context, even when done for the best of intentions, will have limited long-term effect if it fails to create an autonomous popular capacity for independent initiative and self-direction. In studying the social progress conducted with

---

[106] James (1988, esp. chaps 7 and 8).
[107] Calvert and Calvert (1989, p. 126).
[108] James (1988, p. 245). James also observes that the principal victims of this verticalism tended to be the more progressive Peronists. Recognizing that during his exile Peronism was getting divided, Perón assigned the leadership of "the conservative currents" to Vandor and that of the "revolutionary wing" to Framini (1988, p. 161) But the more powerful, conservative leaders were unwilling to tolerate competition. Thus, the [conservative] union leadership "had also, with the aid of the emerging extreme right of Peronism, succeeded in removing all of the figures of political Peronism who had shown sympathy for the radical sectors. Even before Perón's death the governors of Buenos Aires, Cordoba, and Mendoza had been forced to resign. In Buenos Aires the new governor was Victor Caliber, a leader of the metal workers. Between July and October, 1974 the union bureaucracy also settled their scores with the *closest* [class oriented] union opposition. They made use of the greatly enhanced powers granted them by a new Law of Professional Associations passed in November 1973 and semi-official terrorism directed at these unions. The militant leadership of SMUT Cordoba, the Buenos Aires print workers, and finally the Cordoba light and power workers were in rapid succession legally removed from their posts and then declared to be outlaws." James (1988, p. 245).

pastoral oversight in the hierarchical Colombian Catholic Church and comparing it with the more participatory Venezuelan Church, Levine writes of the former:

> If and when the "good" father or sister leaves, what will sustain action and conviction if no autonomous capacity for setting directions and managing events has been developed? While a sympathetic bishop or religious order can sustain and shield groups with human, material and symbolic resources, by the same token, hostile church structures can scuttle the strongest groups or keep them from appearing in the first place.[109]

Much the same can be said for Peronism. If Perón was a sympathetic figure with genuine concern for Argentina's poor, his insistence upon a vertical structure and hierarchical control ultimately undermined their capacity to carry on for themselves. When he was ousted from power they were powerless to bring him back on their own initiative. After his death, the entire movement was left vulnerable to another charismatic leader who could seize the reins of vertical control but use them for a very different purpose, perhaps even undermining the very reforms Perón had conducted using those same mechanisms of control.

This exploration of grassroots initiative – or rather the lack of it – is important for its value as a direct comparison with Sandinismo, which actually fostered grassroots initiative. Yet it is important to note that Argentine society did generate several instances of grassroots activism during the Peronist years. These, however, came from outside Peronism and were thoroughly crushed by Perón's authority and his directives to the police. As we have seen before, one such example was the organizational initiative of the non-Peronist labor unions that continued to exist and agitate immediately after Perón's 1946 election. Perón responded to such initiative by jailing its leaders. Direct repression was then followed by official and legal control, prohibiting the development of independent unions after the earlier non-Peronist unions had been crushed. A similar but more geographically dispersed grassroots initiative emerged in 1946, when nationwide strikes marked the students' response to Peronism's intervention in the universities. As we will see in the next section of this chapter, Perón responded by expelling the students from their universities or violently repressing their strikes.[110] As with the workers, repression was subsequently followed by unionization of the students whom Perón expected to control through syndicalist structures as he did the workers.

This exploration of Peronism in relation to grassroots initiative is fundamental to our consideration of Peronism as a democratic precursor. Peronism's

---

[109] Levine (1992, p. 52).
[110] For a history of university student resistance to repression in Argentina, including Peronist repression, see Polak and Gorbier (1994), El Movimiento Estudiantil Argentino (Fringe Myriad, 1976–1986). Polak and Gorbier point out that student resistance to Peronism was due not only to Peronist repression but also to the fact that many Argentine university students were sympathetic to aspects of Marxism, which Peronism vehemently opposed. Polak and Gorbier (1994, esp. chap. 1).

style of associational relationships, both at the grassroots level and between leaders and followers, encouraged vertical ties of loyalty and discouraged horizontal ties of mutuality. Both in its movement toward power and after assuming power, Peronism provided neither need nor opportunity for people to associate with each other, work together, support each other, and learn cooperation and tolerance through engaging in a common struggle or endeavor.

CLASS HOSTILITY, ENEMIES, SCAPEGOATS

Bridging social capital requires that individuals join with people unlike themselves in at least some ways and for some cooperative purposes. By contrast, bonding social capital inhibits bridging ties, undermines relationships or cooperation with others who are different, and promotes cooperation only within a given group and only by binding those inside the group together *against* outsiders and enemies. In the attitudes Peronism brought to its view of non-Peronists, bonding social capital is the best description of the kind of tie Peronism created among followers. Peronism did not create cross-class bridging social capital.[111]

In the first section of this chapter we considered Perón's hostile attitude toward all alternative leaders and any who would eventually replace his leadership or share in the leadership role. Given its antagonism to alternative leaders and ideas, it is not surprising that Peronism also directed considerable hostility to anyone outside the movement. In fact, whipping up anger towards non-Peronists was a key part of Perón's emotional, charismatic appeal. In doing so, Perón encouraged cohesion among his followers and loyalty to himself by persuading workers to look for enemies all around and to view the world as a conspiracy against Peronism.[112] There is irony in this perspective: Sandinismo, which indeed faced violent repression, did not develop a conspiratorial view of the world; Peronism, which had been allowed to take power by election, saw conspiracy everywhere. This attitude caused Peronists to bond with each other and to search for social and political relationships with persons like themselves, the very definition of bonding social capital. Viewing the world as a conspiracy against Peronists likewise discouraged any efforts at cross-class ties or mutual cooperation across social groups or sectors.

This hostile view of other classes and social groups served a political purpose in a personalistic, charismatic social movement. Finding and targeting

---

[111] Nicolas Shumway (1991) argues that the foundational culture and "guiding fictions" of Argentina included attitudes of deep hostility toward those unlike oneself. Argentina's original leaders saw the world around them as dangerous and fearful. In response they advocated freedom by repressing or killing those who were on the "wrong" side, namely those who disagreed with themselves. In the United States the founding myth was that the struggle for national independence was a unifying experience while, in Argentina, the struggle to define "nation" was divisive.

[112] The tendency to perceive enemies is part of fascism's pattern where ever it emerges. Anderson (2006)

enemies serves to whip up emotional frenzy in support of the leader and his movement. It directs that frenzy toward specific targets who can then be blamed if the movement does not deliver as much change as quickly as it promised. Class enemies and wealthy Argentines were the object of Perón's demagogic harangue, which bought him time from his angry followers while he worked to enact real change. Anger was part of the glue that bonded Peronists together.[113] If one was a victim – and Peronists felt they were – then someone must be to blame. As Perón and his followers looked around, they saw many enemies. Susan and Peter Calvert have argued that the tendency to see enemies within society "may reflect the absence of a more tangible enemy,"[114] itself another product of Argentina's distant geographic location.

Here again, Peronism especially resembled Italian fascism, whose favorite enemy and scapegoat was socialism – specifically individual socialists. Italian fascism encouraged followers to use violence against socialists in the local area. Eventually fascism's followers included local thugs and criminals who simply enjoyed intimidating and bullying others. In Italy, violence became quite prevalent as socialists and fascists battled each other on street corners after dark.[115] Similarly, French fascism used emotional rhetoric and an explanation of crisis that encouraged anger, blame, and a perspective of victimization. The French peasant fascist leader, Henrí Dorgeres blamed the democratic state for its failure to support and protect farmers and agricultural prices. On market day he gathered followers into rallies, creating a spectacle and persuading onlookers. He directed hostility toward immediate representatives of the state in the local area, namely rural-school teachers.[116]

In contrast to Italian fascism, Peronism only became violent after it held national power and when it first faced potential electoral challenge from the other parties. Even then, the level of human rights violations was less in Peronism.[117] But even before it exercised violence, Peronism saw enemies.

---

[113] A view of the world that emphasizes divisions between "us" and "them" is not confined to Argentina and has sometimes also characterized United States social relations, particularly along lines of race and religion. L. Harris (2003) and Morone (2003). One moment in U.S. history when notions of "us" and "them" assumed deadly salience was during the Salem witch trials of 1692. For a meticulous examination of those trials and of suspicions enactments of world views of "us" and "them" see Norton (2002).

[114] Calvert and Calvert (1989, p. 210).

[115] The struggle for rural control eventually became very violent. Fascism violently targeted socialists – in rhetoric and in practice – as the scapegoats to blame for all that was wrong in Italy. Included among socialists who were blamed and targeted for violence were politicians, students, intellectuals, and members of the university community who sympathized with socialism. Violence against socialist scapegoats became momentarily visible at the national level when fascists murdered the socialist legislator, Matteotti, gunning him down on a street in Rome, shortly after he had given a speech in the legislature opposing the rise of fascism.

[116] Paxton (1997, p. 4, pp. 30–32).

[117] A fortuitous gap between a hostile, aggressive political rhetoric and a somewhat less repressive political regime in actual practice was not confined to Peronism. Mann has argued that fascism in Europe was more totalitarian in its aims than it was in its actual practice; (2004, pp. 14–15).

First and foremost among these were class enemies, both the wealthy and the middle class. Its antagonism toward the wealthy, especially toward those with ostentatious lifestyles, was one of the aspects of Peronism that caused its supporters and followers to mistake it for socialism. But in its hostility to the middle class, Peronism cut itself off from allies who have often gravitated toward the left, and sometimes even toward the socialist left, as we saw happened also in Nicaragua. Such allies might have included professionals, the educated, and the university community.

We saw in the previous chapter that Sandinismo also defined the wealthy, especially those connected to Somoza, as part of the problem to overcome in achieving a just society. Yet there is a distinction between seeing the wealthy as part of the problem because of their place and role in an economic system that itself must change, and defining the wealthy as enemies for who they are. Peronism, unlike Sandinismo, never offered a social and economic solution that would fundamentally change the capitalist system. Peronism talked about and achieved labor organization *within* capitalism. But Peronism never went further and never enacted basic structural reforms to change the system that had concentrated wealth. By seeking to change the system itself, and with it the exploitative land owning class, Sandinismo imagined a scenario in which its class adversaries could eventually change and be embraced. But Peronism, not seeking to change the system and not even defining it as problematic, did not offer a solution that incorporated the wealthy into a new and more just system. Moreover, as Peronism split into right- and left-leaning elements during Perón's exile, it was the conservative and right-leaning elements who prevailed in the internal struggle, while the left was soundly beaten and driven out.

If the reasons for worker antagonism toward the upper class were obvious, the logic for placing the middle class on Peronism's list of enemies was less clear. But the reasoning again fit with a charismatic movement searching for ways to bind its followers together emotionally. Argentina's middle class was Peronism's enemy not because of who they were but because of who they were *not*. They were not workers and therefore did not belong to the group of insiders who constituted Peronism. Middle-class Argentines were part of "them," not part of "us." The middle class had been included in an exclusionary society that historically had not permitted a place for the working class. Children of the middle class went to schools. Middle-class employees had reasonable salaries. Many had attended university and through that venue moved out into social respectability. The middle class symbolized the inclusion that workers had been denied. They were enemies because of what they symbolized for the workers, not because of any specific thing they had done to the workers.

Here we find another group who would be unable to change their position vis-à-vis Peronism. Because they were enemies by virtue of who they were and what they symbolized, not because of what they had done, middle-class citizens could do little to change their fundamentally wrong position in the worldview of Peronism. Establishing a list of enemies without providing a logic through which they could achieve accommodation with Peronism also provided the movement with a set of permanent scapegoats and a reason for permanent anger. Like the upper class, the symbolism of the middle class as enemies also gave Peronists a reason for angry bonding with each other and against someone else.

Hostility toward the middle and upper classes brought with it hostility to several institutions in Argentine society. One such institution was the other political parties; another was the national universities. Peronism declared both on its list of enemies. Perón was hostile to all political parties, even to a Peronist political party. He did not want a Peronist party because it might get beyond his personal control and give rise to other leaders with their own bases of popular support. As we mentioned earlier, Perón only allowed his movement to become a political party as the 1952 elections approached and he realized that he would need electoral legitimacy to stay in power. Elections themselves then crystallized Perón's hostility to the other political parties precisely because they represented alternative contenders for power. By the 1950 midterm election, as mentioned earlier, Peronists in Congress had ejected Radical Deputy Ricardo Balbín from the legislature and Perón himself had issued an arrest warrant for the opposition leader. Likewise, in the 1952 May Day Plaza speech, Perón suggested that his followers seek their own revenge against "enemies." Immediately thereafter, Peronists attacked and burned the party headquarters of the Radical, Socialist, and Conservative Parties.

Like political parties, universities are institutions fundamental to democracy,[118] and in Argentina in the 1940s, they were also bastions of the upper and middle class. The exclusive system that Peronists understandably reviled permitted few opportunities for low-income students to enter the university system. Therefore the universities also symbolized another arena of society from which workers felt excluded.[119] Peronists articulated their hostility to the universities in several ways. One place for venting their antagonism was on the floor of the Congress, and their diatribes there are recorded in the transcripts of Congressional sessions. (We explore that venue in Chapter 7.) After 1946, Peronists held an absolute majority in both chambers of Congress and could pass any law over the opposition minority. But the opposition, primarily Radicals but also Socialists and other small parties, was represented by Deputies, many of whom came from the university communities or were highly educated professionals of the middle class (lawyers, writers, scientists). These legislators were treated with the utmost scorn and contempt, despite the fact that their opposition was only verbal and carried with it no possibility of outnumbering the Peronist majority. The words spoken, particularly inside

---

[118] Gutmann (1987).
[119] It is interesting to note here that historians have often pointed to Hitler's exclusion from the universities of Vienna in his twenties when he applied for entrance that marked the beginning of his angry, vengeful and blaming move toward political power. Hamann (1999, esp. chaps 1–3).

the lower chamber, serve as living testimony of the extent to which Peronists bonded to each other in a sense of solidarity among "us," while treating others with hostility and cruelty that denied "them," and Argentine society itself, any opportunity for adaptation and compromise.

Congress was only one place where Peronism attacked members of the educated and professional classes. Peronism also made control over the universities a part of official policy. As the nature of Peronism became more clearly evident in the months after the 1946 election, Peronism found itself faced with growing hostility from the university communities. Students and professors alike, seeking an atmosphere that encouraged free thought, responded negatively to Perón's increasing efforts to indoctrinate his followers and to establish schools that told people how to think. Students responded with protests and demonstrations. Professors responded by teaching students to think for themselves, even if that meant criticizing the new regime.

Perón reacted to such resistance with an official policy of intervention, a form of micro management designed to gain control of the universities and eliminate the opposition sheltered therein. In May 1946, Perón issued an executive decree that intervened all six state universities.[120] The decree was immediately repudiated by the Radical Party, the (conservative) National Democratic Party, the Socialist Party, and the Communist Party. In inaugurating the next session of Congress on June 26, 1946, Perón denounced the universities for "their absolute separation from the people and their total unfamiliarity with their needs and aspirations."[121] He then declared that all university education would be free of charge and assured Congress that the universities would retain their autonomy "insofar as they do not oppose popular sentiment and the interests of the nation." He declared that "the Executive Power has the full right to intervene in the government of the universities, because its criteria is that of the triumphant majority."[122]

Following this intervention decree, the new "interveners" began firing professors. One particularly visible professor, Amado Alonso of the Faculty of Letters at the University of Buenos Aires, was on leave and in residence at Harvard University at the time that he was fired for "abandoning his post." The American Academy of Arts and Sciences sent a letter of protest to Perón, to no avail. By the end of 1946, seven months after the decree, as many as 12,000 professors had been fired from the six universities nationwide, a figure that amounted to approximately one third of all university faculty in Argentina.[123]

---

[120] Calvert and Calvert (1989, p. 188).
[121] Bunk (2001, pp. 133–145).
[122] This is an interesting use of words and resembles using the executive electoral mandate as a kind of weapon against the democratic institutions of society. In fact, Yrigoyen had used almost the same words when justifying his determination to defy the checks and balances Congress tried to impose against him.
[123] Bunk (2001, p. 136).

As the universities then tried to continue functioning, they lacked the staff to administer exams, and, in some cases, students found that they were being tested and graded by administrators and clerical assistants. This provoked massive student protests; students understood that passing exams and receiving degrees under such circumstances rendered the degrees meaningless. As an example of grassroots initiative, these demonstrations erupted throughout the country and made Perón's policies inside the universities more publicly visible. In each case, the police were called onto the campuses to put down the protests. The Minister of Public Education then declared that all students who were on strike or demonstrating and therefore did not take their exams were expelled from the universities. The decision to expel striking students provoked further resignations by other professors who had not, to date, been fired. Within a year after Perón had taken power, Argentina's reputable and internationally famous university system was in shambles. Despite this turmoil, or perhaps because of it, in March of the following year, 1947, when Perón asked for Congressional approval of the decree intervening the universities, the Peronist-dominated Congress recorded seventy-five votes in favor of the decree and thirty-five votes against.

Following this effort to subjugate the universities and expel opposition, Perón threw open the doors of the nation's universities. Between 1947 and 1955 the number of students enrolled in Argentine universities grew from 51,272 to 143,542, nearly a three-fold increase.[124] To accommodate the increase, Perón's interveners inside the universities hired new faculty who were in agreement with Peronist policies to replace those who had been fired or had resigned. These newcomers had little professional standing or teaching experience and their presence in the faculty downgraded the universities considerably. Additionally, the presence of Peronist professors decreased the amount of free exchange of ideas that was possible under the new authoritarian university administration.

Perón, however, felt that he did not have enough control over the students. He "unionized" the students into official organizations overseen by the government and declared that these student unions should be at the service of the state. When a chemistry student at the University of Buenos Aires who was a member of the Communist Party, Ernesto Bravo, disappeared on May 19, 1951, more student strikes ensued. Julio V. Otaola, then Rector of the university, repressed the strikes on the grounds that they had been "political and communist." It is interesting to note that a few of the more progressive clergy voiced concerns about this conflict over the nation's universities, and about the absence of any intellectuals or intellectual leadership within Peronism.[125] Yet most of the clergy remained silent on the matter of the universities, and the Church took no steps to stop Perón's actions against Argentina's institutions of higher education.

[124] Bunk (2001, pp. 145–148).
[125] Bunk (2001, p. 141).

The fate of the University of Cordoba has attracted particular attention as an example of Perón's effect on Argentine universities. Cordoba was one of Argentina's oldest universities, dating its founding to the 1600s. The Perón-appointed intervener essentially became the governor of the university. He had final decision-making power over the university, thereby eliminating faculty and student governance. He enacted a number of policies designed to eradicate opposition to Peronism from within the institution. These policies affected the classes and majors students could choose, the content of material on the syllabi, the books students were allowed to read, and the subjects faculty and students were allowed to research. It was micro management down to the closest detail. Faculty members were fired at the will of the intervener, with those targeted inevitably being those who had voiced opposition to Perón or who now opposed any aspect of management of teaching and research inside the University of Cordoba. Subsequently the Intervener fired all faculty members over fifty-five and replaced them with younger professors. Ostensibly the argument was that Peronism wanted to inject new blood and new life into the university and eject those who represented old ways of thinking. The professors fired were among the most established in their fields, individually commanded the greatest respect and deference, and often had been the most outspoken against Peronism. New faculty brought in instead were devoted Peronists who were also less well-established in their fields and less likely to command respect independent of their Peronist identity. As the Peronist intervener gained more control over the University of Cordoba, eventually entire departments and programs were eliminated, in particular those of the social sciences and humanities since, unlike the hard sciences, these taught students to think critically on their own about their society. Students also became targets of Peronist repression inside the University of Cordoba. Those who had protested or otherwise demonstrated their opposition to Peronism found their funding cut and their educational subsidies eliminated. Eventually many students were expelled from the universities entirely for their opposition to Peronism.

Yet a third major institution with which Peronism came into conflict was the Catholic Church. Unlike with the parties or the universities, Perónism began its rule having a positive relationship to the Church. The relationship began on a positive note because, to the delight of the conservative clergy, Peronism reversed the secular progressivism that had characterized Argentina in the early twentieth century. In 1884, under the presidency of Julio Argentino Roca, Argentina had officially separated church and state and abolished religious education in public schools. In this action, it allowed itself to be momentarily influenced by enlightenment thinking from Europe and the North Atlantic nations. As the country began to gain a growing number of non-Catholic immigrants, this separation of church and state and the absence of religious instruction in public schools represented one of the more progressive and attractive aspects of Argentine public policy.

In the face of such progressive laws, the Argentine church itself remained politically and socially conservative. With the exception of a minority of more progressive "democratic Catholics," the Argentine church more closely resembled the Spanish Church than it did churches influenced by Liberation theology. Like the Spanish Church of the early twentieth century, the Argentine Church was generally negative about civilian government and about democracy itself.[126] According to its perspective, civilian governments had allowed the family to decline, permitted school instruction to deteriorate, aggravated class struggle, failed to support farmers, and allowed the expansion of "ominous" social doctrines.[127]

The Argentine Catholic Church embraced a decree issued by Perón on December 31, 1943, which again imposed Catholic education in public schools. When Perón then moved in 1946 toward elections, the church openly supported him and declared itself against any parties (most of the rest) that supported legalizing divorce. If one looks closely at published documents from the Catholic Church, including documents supporting religious education and calling for a corporate society of cooperation between capital and labor, one can see a pronounced affinity between the doctrine and policies espoused by the Church and official positions taken by Perón in power. Although some clergy were nervous about the growing power and ascendancy within Peronism of the unwashed "plebes,"[128] in these early days much of the clergy saw Perón as more positive than negative because he was a bulwark against communism and represented a vehicle through which the Church, itself, might increase its influence in society.[129]

After being elected, Perón sought to make his decree imposing religious education more legitimate. He proposed it for Congressional ratification in 1946. The imposition of mandatory religious education greatly enhanced the early alliance between Peronism and the Church but caused further conflict between Peronism and the other parties. The request for ratification evoked street demonstrations and a long, rancorous debate on the floor of the lower chamber. The discussion served only to heighten the visibility of and the conflict over a measure that was unnecessary in the first place and already a law in any event, thus adding insult to injury. It also did much to publicize Perón's alliance with a politically and socially conservative Church and to underscore the uselessness of vocal opposition and the subordinate position of Congress within the Peronist regime.

The imposition of religious instruction in public schools, especially in the face of opposition from the public and several political parties, not only alienated the other parties and the educated, but soon alienated lower- and middle-class Argentines who had begun to sympathize with Peronism but who were not Catholic. The outcry became so great that in 1954, Peronism itself

---

[126] Perez-Diaz (1973) argues that the Spanish Catholic Church was so socially and politically conservative and hierarchical that its teachings fit naturally with fascism.
[127] Bianchi (2001, p. 14).
[128] Bunk (2001, p. 60).
[129] Bunk (2001, pp. 60, 65).

passed a second law repealing the first law. In the process, however, Peronism had first alienated (further) the Radicals and middle class, then alienated some of its own supporters, and finally alienated the Catholic Church itself with the repeal of the original law. Where Perón might have created an ally in the Church,[130] he instead antagonized both the other parties and the Church. Moreover, his policy reversal showed that he could not be trusted to maintain a consistent position.

In fact, the conflict with the Church had begun before 1954. In acts of true progressivism, Peronism legalized divorce and prostitution, and granted legal rights and legitimacy to children born in common-law marriages even if these had not been sanctified by the Church. These laws alienated the Church, which gradually withdrew its support for Peronism. The repeal of the law imposing religious instruction then further alienated the Church. Eventually conflict became more overt. A religious demonstration in Buenos Aires took on political overtones, and subsequently two clergy, Auxiliary Bishop of Buenos Aires Manuel Tato and Father Ramon Novoa, were expelled from Argentina. In response to these expulsions, the Vatican responded as follows:

Since these [two clergymen]...suffered violence against their persons...and were impeded from exercising their duty and were expelled from Argentine territory...the Holy See declares all those who committed these crimes and all of their leaders of all levels...to be excommunicated *latae sententiae* according to the special powers of the Holy See.

Now Perón and many Peronists found themselves targeted by the Church's highest sanction and in a manner that went far beyond national conflicts and domestic attention. Their vengeance was swift. On the day of the excommunication, an angry mob attacked, burned and desecrated several churches in Buenos Aires. The mob was disguised, and their identity remained unknown. Several labor centers were accused, and Perón denied that workers had been involved, but it was clear that the mob had operated with complete impunity, and their attacks had been carried out without any fear of law enforcement.[131] In this context, the 1954 repeal of the law mandating religious instruction was one further step in the already deteriorated relations between Peronism and the Church. As a consequence, the Church assumed a stance of definitive opposition and ultimately supported the 1955 coup against Perón.

The story of Peronism's relationship with the Argentine Church reveals defining characteristics of the movement. First, it shows Peronism's ability simultaneously to support progressive and conservative positions (divorce and mandatory religious instruction). Second, it shows Peronism's willingness to take conservative positions that were at odds with the interests of its primary constituency, the working class. Third, it illustrates Peronism's willingness to take positions and reverse them in the interests of increasing

---

[130] Calvert and Calvert (1989, p. 28).
[131] Bianchi (2001, pp. 312–314).

or retaining its own power. Perón had originally supported religious instruction because such a position purchased conservative Catholic support in the first election. Later, he chose to reverse the law that imposed religious instruction in public schools because such an imposition was undermining support among workers.

Finally, the story shows the extent to which Peronism had a capacity to antagonize other sectors of society, often unnecessarily creating new adversaries where it might have had neutral observers or even allies. This practice widened and exacerbated divisions within Argentine society instead of building bridges and finding common ground among diverse groups. In fact, the conflict with the Catholic Church may well have become more rancorous precisely because Peronism had originally taken a position favoring the Church and then reversed it. The movement became a severe disappointment for the Argentine clergy. But unnecessary antagonism, as with the Church, never serves to increase trust in any society. As yet another example of the dangers of inconsistency, both the law on religious instruction and its repeal left other Argentines angry and alienated, further decreasing trust and making it more difficult for Peronism to reach common ground with the rest of society.

As we saw in the second section of this chapter, another "enemy" of Peronism was capitalism – a position that made it easy to confuse Peronism with socialism. With respect to capitalism, Peronism was again contradictory. Perón simultaneously declared that capitalists were the enemy but also vowed to bind together workers and the capitalist class. On the one hand, Perón declared that capitalism had imposed inhumane conditions on the working class and was, therefore, an enemy Peronism needed to overcome. On the other hand, he tolerated domestic capitalists and sustained the capitalist economy. At first, Perón resolved this contradiction by accusing foreign capitalists of causing the inhumane nature of Argentine capitalism. In contrast to foreign capital, domestic capitalism could be embraced through corporate bonds between workers and industrialists. But even this partial resolution was revealed as contradictory when Perón began to pursue foreign capital because his economic policies were ruining the economy. Throughout his reign of power, Perón maintained this contradictory position, rhetorically condemning capitalism while tolerating or embracing capitalists in policy.

According to Wynia, Perón's economic policy ultimately brought Argentina's economy to a standstill. Productivity fell. Exports dried up. The nation lacked the resources to fill the heightened welfare expectations of the working class and labor intransigence and strike activity only demanded more perks without recognizing that the economy was in shambles. Wynia concludes that Perón could have avoided economic disaster by reaching some level of cooperation with industrialists. But cooperation was not part of Perón's style. "He chose to be combative rather than conciliatory" when dealing with industrialists and non-workers who did not benefit from his new economic programs. Wynia also suggests that intransigence and aggression were, in fact, Perón's best, short-term strategy as he first took power, because it was by creating combat that he was able to build and hold together a working-class following.[132] In the end, however, by choosing to operate in a confrontational fashion, Perón was the greatest loser. Like reformist governments elsewhere, he could not destroy Argentina's economic elites. He antagonized them but could not render them powerless.[133]

The decision to declare foreign capital an enemy fit well with another Peronist position: anti-imperialism and hostility to all foreign intervention in Argentina, especially from the United States. Never mind that Perón himself would eventually seek foreign economic investment in Argentina, particularly from the United States. When that came about, Perón explained it as more pragmatism in response to the moment. For Perón, Yankee imperialism always remained one of the primary enemies of his movement, and he resented any U.S. efforts to influence domestic events. This position was another reason why Peronism was often wrongly taken for a form of socialism, which, as in Nicaragua, often included anti-imperialism as part of its position.

Anti-imperialism in Argentina in the late 1940s and 1950s, however, had less substance to it than anti-imperialism in Nicaragua from the 1920s onward. The United States had never intervened militarily into Argentina, had never backed one political party in a military struggle against another party, nor had it imposed and supported one dictator after another. The U.S. had even tolerated Argentina's mild enthusiasm for the Axis Powers during World War II and had suffered Argentina's refusals of requests for support for the Allied cause. Thus, in comparison with U.S. behavior in Nicaragua, U.S. policy toward Argentina had been considerably less intrusive. Nonetheless, anti-imperialism was a rhetoric that worked and Peronism needed enemies to strengthen the emotional bonds of solidarity among followers. It needed enemies against whom to direct anger while it waited for positive change. Yankee imperialism provided another convenient scapegoat.

In the final analysis, "enemies" included all those who disagreed with Perón and anyone within the movement who gained too much power. Before the end of Perón's life, the category of enemies had expanded to include not only the wealthy and middle classes and their parties and institutions, not only foreign capitalists and Yankee imperialism, but even some members of the working class. As discussed earlier, Perón moved swiftly, after taking power, to eliminate trade unions that were under the rubric of other political parties and to jail other working-class leaders. Similarly, by his ouster in 1955, another portion of the working class had moved away from Perón and no longer supported him.[134] They became the "enemies within," or the "virus" to which Perón referred upon his return to Argentina in the early 1970s. There is a sense in which Perón had made his search for enemies a self-fulfilling prophecy. Where

---

[132] Wynia (1978, p. 75).
[133] Wynia (1978, pp. 79, 80).
[134] Calvert and Calvert (1989, p. 109).

none had existed beforehand or where accommodation might have been possible, his rigidity, intransigence, aggression, and determination for personal control eventually produced enemies, even among the working class. This long list of enemies made Peronism a force against rather than for bridging social capital and a force that undermined cross-class ties when they developed outside of Peronism.

CONCLUSION

This chapter has demonstrated that Peronism did not create bridging social capital and, in many ways, acted in a way that deliberately undermined its ability to build bridges with other social sectors, find common ground with adversaries, and find common ground with the rest of society. In this way and others, it shared characteristics with the European fascisms, which themselves sought domination, not cooperation, within their own societies. We would hardly look to European fascist movements to find sources of the internal social relations that contribute to democracy because those movements were openly and avowedly anti-democratic, and did not seek to accommodate democracy and its institutions either domestically or abroad. In the end, it was the European fascisms that tried to destroy democracy in the North Atlantic region. Therefore it is hardly surprising to find fascism's Latin American cousin, Peronism, creating social relations within Argentina that were and are antithetical to democracy. These included the use of personalism and individual dominance over institutions, processes, and other leaders; the subjugation or destruction of grassroots initiative; and the creation of enemies and antagonists rather than common ground and cooperation. The similarities between Peronism and fascism help us understand that Peronism has made democracy more difficult in Argentina.

As we move beyond the historical consideration of social relations within Argentine society, it is important to remember that no previous democracy has ever attempted to develop while simultaneously achieving accommodation with a populist movement of historical fascist characteristics. In Europe, fascist movements ended (in France and Spain) or were destroyed (in Germany and Italy) by either domestic or international actors before democracy could flourish in those societies. Indeed, where fascism had taken hold nationally, no serious, long-term effort at democratization unfolded until fascism had been eliminated. This will be a key point to remember as we study the nature of social capital in Argentina and the development of democracy that has been affected by it. Precisely because the bonding social capital that fascism produced was so antithetical to democracy, European nations found they needed to end these movements and reduce these suspicious and exclusionary bonds before democracy could begin to take hold. What would European democracy look like today if powerful movements having fascist characteristics, extensive antagonism to non-members, and the concomitant bonding social capital such characteristics produce had remained alive and nationally influential? The Argentine story provides an answer to this question and indicates the kind of obstacles Argentine democracy confronts as it struggles to develop.[135]

We see in the form of organizational ties that Peronism advocated and created an example of bonding which creates a "we" and a "they." The "we" was the group of insiders that were workers and followers of Perón, those who believed in Perón, ascribed to his perspectives and his explanation for local and national problems, and agreed with his solutions and proposals for Argentina's future. This group of insiders was bonded together internally and equally bonded against those outside the group. Outsiders and enemies were many, and their numbers grew over time. This form of social cohesion exemplifies bonding social capital. It is not conducive to democracy and is antidemocratic both in its intent and in its result. As with the European fascisms and other populisms, the Peronist bond created in Argentina among Perón's followers and supporters was so antagonistic and aggressive that it eventually contributed to Perón's ouster in 1955. The incompatibility of bonding social capital and democracy rests in the fact that it emphasizes divisions within society rather than bridging differences among citizens and enhancing their ability to work together and respect each other. By relying on charismatic personalism and vertical ties; by undermining flexibility, dynamic internal leadership, and grassroots initiative; and by fostering hostility and divisiveness, especially among classes, Peronism fostered internal views of "us" (the Peronists) versus "them" (the non-workers, the capitalists, the elites, foreign imperialism, the Radicals, the intellectuals, the press, the universities, the Church, and so forth) that decreased society's ability to cooperate and make democracy work.

David Butler has suggested something even more startling about Peronism.[136] He argues that Peronism ultimately failed both as a movement and as a legitimate social actor even on its own terms, namely in support of labor interests. It failed for many of the same reasons that it created bonding social capital and was antithetical to democracy, because Peronism, by relying so heavily on charisma, ultimately pegged its long-term success to the excluded and marginalized position of labor in 1945. But as the Peronist movement succeeded and labor achieved material gains and greater social acceptance, Peronism needed to change in order to keep up with its own constituency. It failed to do this precisely because of Perón himself. In his determination to retain personal control over the movement, Perón destroyed any nascent political leaders and with them the flexibility, resilience, and dynamism that accompanies new blood. Deprived of the virtue displayed in Perón's own charisma, the demands of labor became increasingly calculative and less emotive. Perón could not

---

[135] In his study of the struggle to develop democracy in the aftermath of strong man, personalistic rule, Hartlyn (1998) also considers the legacy left by "neopatriomonialism" and its deleterious consequences for democratization.

[136] Butler (1969).

keep pace with such changes, and any new leaders who might have been able to do so were destroyed by Perón's internal maneuvers.

If the goal of Peronism was to create a flexible, dynamic, political representative of the labor movement that would successfully defend labor interests into the long-term future, then Butler is correct that Peronism failed. But scholars have continued to debate whether that was Perón's only goal in the first place. Some suggest that Perón was simply power-driven, like other populist authoritarians in Latin America and Europe both, and that the labor movement for him represented only a path toward power. If power was his goal, then Perón succeeded, and whatever happened to the labor movement in the aftermath is only secondary. Yet that debate goes to the nature of Perón as a man and depends upon whether one has a sympathetic or skeptical view of him. Was he the poor man's hero or a power-monger? Perhaps he was both. Perón was complex, both power-driven and self-promoting, but also genuinely interested in the welfare of the working class, with the dual nature of his personality explaining the contradictions of his personalistic movement. Yet we need not resolve that question here because even a sympathetic or charitable view of Perón reveals the incompatibility of Peronism and democracy.

Regardless of whether Peronism succeeded as a long-term labor representative, it certainly did succeed as a long-term social movement and as a source of identity for Argentina's working class. As such, it created, enhanced, and reinforced certain kinds of social relations, specific attitudes towards "the other," and distinct modes of action and activism. These caused Peronists to bond with each other in ways emotionally fulfilling to themselves but not necessarily conducive to cooperation or democratic process in the society at large or over the long run. In describing Peronism, Susan and Peter Calvert speak clearly: "democratic values have been flatly rejected. De facto violations of democratic procedure have been accepted."[137] As restrained fascism or as a failed labor movement that died on the altar of personalism and internal division, the original version of Peronism was incompatible with democracy and the respectful efforts at inclusiveness and building faith in each other that democracy entails.

Many studies of Peronism have pointed out that the movement did deliver material goods to the poor and it still does in contemporary Argentina. In circumstances of dire poverty, this is no small accomplishment and cannot be ignored. Moreover, when the poor are drawn to a movement that delivers food, a job, services or medication that allows them to survive, their attraction and loyalty to that movement are surely understandable. However, the fundamental problem with satisfying human needs via a clientelistic, vertical, and domineering organization is that it provides a short-term immediate solution at the very high cost of any real, long-term gains. Individuals who succumb on the basis of need to a clientelistic, non-democratic movement may gain food, medicine, water, and electric service in the short run. Yet they simultaneously

---

[137] Calvert and Calvert (1989).

lose any capacity to unite with others like themselves, mobilize on the basis of grassroots initiative, and exercise greater influence over politics from below.[138] Thus, while Peronism meets people's needs, it does so by disempowering them. Over the long run, such a movement can only thrive by perpetuating poverty and need because its clientelistic mechanisms of domination will become less influential if poverty decreases.[139]

Chapter 1 suggested that where democratic or bridging social capital is in short supply, the formal institutions of the democratic state can serve as an alternative resource upon which to build democracy. Peronism, like Sandinismo, relied on mass mobilization for political power without attending to institutional development. However, unlike Sandinismo, the values Peronism instilled in its followers were antithetical to rather than supportive of cooperation, mutual faith, and therefore democracy. Yet unlike Sandinismo, Peronism emerged upon a scene where political predecessors had already attended to the establishment of formal institutions. Indeed, the popular movement which preceded Peronism, Radicalism, had pursued its political agenda within those institutions, rather than jettisoning them entirely. Like Radicalism before it, Peronism took as its leader a man who had been fairly elected president and then reelected again in 1952. It also kept open the national Congress and filled it with elected Peronist Deputies and Senators. Although Perón's activities weakened and undermined Argentina's institutions, it did not destroy them and, by accomplishing some tasks through them, inadvertently granted them continuing legitimacy. Even where Perón made law by decree, as with imposing religious education, he later asked the Congress to legitimate the decree. Therefore, although Peronism undermined many aspects of Argentina's democratic institutions, it also worked within them and through them, acquiring in the process a more institutionalized status than Sandinismo achieved in Nicaragua. While neither popular movement aimed to institutionalize its power, by coming to power where relatively strong institutions already existed and working through them, Peronism inadvertently kept Argentina's tradition of relatively strong institutions, while Sandinismo neither had upon its onset nor created in its first decade institutions that were as strong as Argentina's. This difference in institutional history and development makes a difference for the kind of democracy that is developing in each nation today.

---

[138] For a study of clientelism as a systematic method for undermining popular initiative see Fox (1994).

[139] Alternative views of populism (its ability to meet human needs versus its disempowering, anti-democratic consequences) are common in the literature and do not confine themselves to discussions of Peronism. See, for example, Canovan (1999) and Arditi (2004). Arditi's view is closer to my own. He suggests that the costs in anti-democratic results of populism are greater than the gains made in material goods. He writes, "Populists get away with undemocratic behavior as long as their actions are perceived to represent the will of the people." (2004, p. 142). Needless to say, it is the right-wing populists themselves who make such claims.

PART II

AN EMPIRICAL EXAMINATION OF THE ARGUMENT

4

A Tale of Two Neighborhoods
Social Capital in Nicaragua and Argentina

> I watched a boy die here. He was lying just out of my reach on this street corner and the gunfire was too thick to go out after him. He kept calling to me. He bled to death. I have never forgotten that.
> *Sandinista revolutionary Managua, Nicaragua*

> Eva Perón gave my mother a sewing machine and that has made everything possible.
> *Peronist taxi driver Buenos Aires, Argentina*

It was late June, 1979, in Nicaragua. The southern column of FSLN guerrilla fighters had reached Managua and was engaged in hand-to-hand combat in the streets against Anastasio Somoza's National Guard. It was the beginning of the end, the start of the final battle for control of the capital city and, with it, the country and the state. The guerrillas were being hidden, sheltered, fed, and treated for battle wounds within one southern Managua neighborhood, Bello Horizonte. But in this early stage of the battle for Managua, the guerrillas were losing. The other three columns of guerrilla fighters converging on Managua from the north, west, and east had not yet arrived, so the FSLN leaders of this first column decided to fall back from Managua to the neighboring city of Masaya, less than twenty-five miles away and firmly under the control of the revolutionaries. From there they would wait for the other columns to arrive, and they would converge on Managua together.

The air force of Somoza's National Guard had discovered that Bello Horizonte was sheltering the guerrillas and, because his troops could not enter the neighborhood directly due to street blockades, had begun indiscriminate bombing of civilian homes. For the FSLN to fall back to Masaya and leave the civilian population of Bello Horizonte behind them would have meant leaving those who had protected them defenseless before the Guard, which made no distinction between civilians and guerrillas. The word went out: "No, the FSLN will not leave the population behind." On the night of June 25, 1979, the entire neighborhood of some twelve hundred households, including children and the elderly, gathered silently under the cover of darkness. Then the civilian population and the whole guerrilla column walked side by side all night long, covering the twenty-five miles to Masaya. By the next morning, they were safe in Masaya, and Bello Horizonte was deserted. It would remain that way until July 19, 1979, when all four guerrilla columns merged together on Managua and took the city successfully.[1]

La Matanza is one of the oldest neighborhoods in Buenos Aires. Its history goes back to the days when it was a quaint Spanish village, home in the nineteenth century to writers and artists and hard hit by a cholera epidemic in the mid-nineteenth century. But as Buenos Aires grew, La Matanza became a part of it, absorbed into the hustle and bustle of a huge modern city. As Argentina industrialized in the twentieth century, many key industries built factories on the outskirts of Buenos Aires so that towns and villages that had been outside the city were now closer to the new factories. La Matanza became an outlying neighborhood of the city and home to the growing number of Southern and Eastern European immigrants who came to Argentina in the early twentieth century to build a new life.

Workers in La Matanza found their new life to be harsh and cruel. Housing was old and dilapidated; water, heat, and sewage were inadequate; and education was poor. Workers labored long hours for very low pay and were not organized to defend themselves. Before 1916, they were allowed to work in Argentina but not permitted to participate in politics because "elections" were decided by an elite group of conservatives. Workers were subjects, not citizens. Between 1916 and 1930, La Matanza residents supported Radicalism, but even this brief opportunity for political participation was soon stifled by military dictatorship.

When Peronism arrived in Buenos Aires in the mid-1940s, La Matanza residents were overjoyed. Finally they had a leader who cared about them and was willing to alleviate their poverty. Perón and Eva visited La Matanza and were greeted by cheering, mesmerized crowds of workers and their families. When Perón was jailed in 1946, residents of La Matanza traveled en masse to the central Plaza de Mayo in downtown Buenos Aires to demand his release. From then on, La Matanza residents were among the most adoring and faithful of the Peronist crowds. As workers in Argentina's key electrical, metalwork, and slaughterhouse industries, La Matanza residents were important beneficiaries of Perón's reforms and largess. In return, they became Peronist loyalists. La Matanza's centrality to Peronism is exemplified by the number of local and national Peronist leaders it has produced. All of these leaders have successfully used the party machine on their path toward political power.[2] Most recently they include Alberto Balestrini, mayor of the township; Alberto Pierri, speaker of the Chamber of Deputies (lower house) during Menem's presidency; and presidential hopeful Carlos Ruckauf.

---

[1] Chavarria (1982, pp. 25–40, esp. pp. 36–37).
[2] For a more general consideration of machine politics in the Buenos Aires neighborhoods see Miguez (1995, pp. 91–106).

Tale of Two Neighborhoods

Although the story of each of these two neighborhoods is similar in that it is one of hardship and poverty, the popular response to such hardship is different. In Bello Horizonte residents pulled together as a community, fought back against oppressors, helped each other out, and moved forward as a group. In contrast, residents of La Matanza suffered and endured in silence, waiting passively for help. In La Matanza there is no story about community, much less of community action. Instead, there are stories of individual upward movement by means of personal loyalty. These descriptions fit with the images of popular action – or the lack thereof – that emerged in the first part of this book. The data analyzed in this chapter are drawn from the two neighborhoods of Bello Horizonte, in the outskirts of Managua, Nicaragua, and La Matanza, in the outskirts of Buenos Aires, Argentina. These neighborhoods were selected specifically because of their colorful histories and their close involvement with the mass popular movements in their respective nations. If the argument of this book is correct and popular history matters in shaping social values, then we should see the evidence in the public opinion and behavior of residents from Bello Horizonte and La Matanza. If Sandinismo and Peronism indeed left the social values I suggest they did, then there are few places where that legacy would be more apparent than in the two historic neighborhoods studied here. In addition, to the extent that individuals in these two neighborhoods identify with the mass movement under study here, the data collected from self-identifying Sandinistas and Peronists will facilitate statistical analysis.

The analysis of this chapter and the next two uses the political science understanding of social capital, namely that it is "embodied in horizontal networks of civic engagement."[3] Using questions that Putnam has applied in his own studies of social capital, the data analysis here scrutinizes several measures of horizontal ties among citizens in these two historic neighborhoods. It looks at these measures according to identification with Sandinismo or Peronism, and also with respect to several standard socioeconomic categories. The evidence falls into three broad categories: (1) organizational membership and level of activity, (2) democratic values, and (3) political participation and assessments of democratic institutions and procedures. This chapter considers category organizational membership and level of involvement, both indicators of social capital according to previous studies. Chapter 5 considers democratic values. Chapter 6 looks at participation and assessments of democratic institutions and procedures.

The approach used in this Chapter builds on Robert Putnam's studies in Italy and the United States. It draws as well on historical studies, such as Theda Skocpol's work on voluntary associations and association memberships, which are used here as one indicator of social capital among the residents of these two neighborhoods. The presence of bridging or democratic social capital as captured in these measures reflects the basic faith people have in other citizens around them. Indicators of social capital include questions

[3] Putnam (1993, p. 176).

about people's associational activities, membership across a variety of kinds of organizations, and how many associations they belong to. As examined here, social capital addresses empirically the question of how willing people are to join groups and work or play together as a group.

If my argument is correct, we should find that social capital is higher in Bello Horizonte than in La Matanza. This would be reflected in higher levels of associational memberships and activities in Nicaragua, and in lower such levels in Argentina. Of additional relevance is whether we will find differences inside these two neighborhoods as well as across them. If the historical argument about popular politics in these two nations is correct, then we should find that in Bello Horizonte social capital is higher among Sandinistas than among non-Sandinistas, whereas in La Matanza social capital is higher among non-Peronists than among Peronists. We would also expect these findings to be true about both social and political capital. Whereas levels of social capital are indicative of the quality of generalized social relations, levels of political capital are directly relevant to the strength of democracy and the extent to which it is supported by its own citizens. Chapters 5 and 6 look at Political Capital.

Before proceeding with this analysis, a word is in order about the fundamental divisions studied here. One way to evaluate the argument and the historical evidence is to focus on differences in social capital between partisans. This means between the Nicaraguan respondents who call themselves Sandinistas and those who do not, and between the Argentine respondents who call themselves Peronists and those who do not. This task is made easier by the fact that these two mass movements have today become national, electoral parties that tend to attract the votes of those who identify themselves with each party. Another reason to centralize party identification in this study is Mark Hulliung's suggestion that parties are the most important receptacle for civic life in modern democracies. He argues that, where parties are in decline, as in the United States, civic life is also in decline.[4] If Hulliung is correct that parties are crucial to the survival of civic life in modern democracies, then any understanding of civic life and democracy in Nicaragua and Argentina requires paying attention to the relationship between parties and civic values. We can direct our attention to parties and civic values by scrutinizing the relationship between party identification and individual values among party self-identifiers.

But earlier studies of social capital have also looked at other key popular divisions such as gender, age, education, and income and have studied the relationship between these categories and social capital. We also examine socioeconomic and demographic divisions here. Such analysis allows us to check the partisan findings to ascertain the extent to which differences in social capital follow social divisions separate from partisanship. In addition, the examination of demographic and socioeconomic differences allows us to review the policy implications of these findings.

[4] (2002, pp. 86–87.)

The empirical analysis for this chapter rests on two neighborhood databases and two national samples. The neighborhood databases are drawn from the two colorful neighborhoods of Bello Horizonte and La Matanza. Bello Horizonte is a small community, whereas La Matanza is huge. The two databases reflect these size differences: The Bello Horizonte database contains slightly more than 400 respondents; the La Matanza database contains 1,200. These samples comprise .04% of Managua's population and .012% of the Buenos Aires population.[5] The national samples are from the Latinobarometer study for 2007 and are available for both Nicaragua and Argentina. In the Latinobarometer, the Nicaraguan national sample is 1,000 respondents; the Argentine national sample is 1,200.

ORGANIZATIONAL MEMBERSHIP IN THE TWO NEIGHBORHOODS

We make our comparison of social capital in Bello Horizonte, Nicaragua, and La Matanza, Argentina, by looking first at formal associational memberships. It is important to note that these are original data on social capital in two developing democracies and, as such, constitute a unique and original first step toward comparing how the national histories explored in Part I have affected patterns of social relations and association in these two nations. These samples are precisely the kind of data we need to explore the validity of the argument here. They point toward possible trends in the general population of each nation.

In each case and for each sample, we are surveying low-income, working-class respondents. Because both Sandinismo and Peronism were movements of the poor, aimed at addressing poverty and injustice among their adherents, these citizens are precisely the kinds of respondents for whom the politics of

---

[5] Unlike public opinion surveys that are voting studies, public opinion surveys designed to uncover levels of social capital in society are still quite new in Latin American societies. Accordingly, although citizens might readily respond to questions about vote choice, candidate preference, and various kinds of evaluations of candidates, we are breaking new research ground when we ask about membership organizations. With respect to the collection of data, this meant that respondents often did not understand, at first, what was being asked of them. When asked if they belonged to organizations, they often did not bring to mind which organizations they did engage with. This discovery was made in both Nicaragua and Argentina when the pilot studies in each nation were launched.

In response to this discovery, I worked closely with pollsters in each nation to develop survey instruments that would uncover associational memberships. This meant, in essence, using multiple probes after the first question was posed in order to uncover the full extent of organizational memberships. The survey instruments also gave examples, along with the questions, so as to make it clear to respondents what kinds of answers we were soliciting. Thus a question went as follows: "Do you belong to any neighborhood organizations? For example, do you belong to an organization such as an organization concerned with the local schools, the local water supply, the condition of the neighborhood streets, or the public transport availability? What about an organization that concerns itself with neighborhood crime?" Probes like these would eventually uncover the full extent of organizational memberships. In addition, in each nation the pollsters asked final probes like, "Are there any other organizations you belong to?" "And any others?"

Note: ( ) = Raw numbers.
Totals may not equal 100% because of rounding.
Source: Urban Samples: Bello Horizonte, Nicaragua, 2002 (*N* = 403); La Matanza, Argentina, 2002 (*N* =1200).

FIGURE 4.1. Nicaragua and Argentina: Levels of organizational memberships, simple frequencies by percentage.

these movements was most relevant and most salient.[6] In Managua, these were the kinds of citizens Sandinismo aimed to recruit; in Buenos Aires, these were workers and workers families who were the most important supporters of Peronism. If, in fact, the influence of these two movements was real and lasting in the way I have suggested, then it is precisely among these citizens that we should find evidence of the long-term social influence of these movements.[7]

Figure 4.1 provides an initial overview of associational memberships in these two neighborhoods. In each neighborhood respondents were asked whether they belonged to a series of different organizations. These included organizations within the neighborhood itself, and also larger organizations

---

[6] Although the focus here is on levels of social capital among individuals, other students of social capital have shown that it can also accrue to organizations themselves, allowing the latter to deal more easily with other organizations because they have built a basis of trust among one another. Smith et al. (2004, Vol 52, # 3, pp. 508–530).

[7] Although my data focus on the poor in each nation, another recent study of trust in Argentina and Mexico has underscored regional variation. In their new study, Matthew Cleary and Susan Stokes (2006) find that social trust is lower in regions of Argentina were Peronism is more predominant.

that extended beyond their immediate neighborhoods such as labor unions, sports organizations or clubs, social clubs, political groups, and any other type of associations. These questions drew upon a series of probes in which respondents were asked about memberships in specific types of associations or voluntary organizations, and then probed again about any other memberships in such organizations. The different kinds of organizational memberships are explored at greater length below. Let us begin by combining all organizational memberships. The results in Figure 4.1 show citizen memberships in all voluntary organizations or associations of any kind.

Figure 4.1 reflects the size of the two neighborhood samples and illustrates, within each, the levels of organizational membership of the respondents. The figure shows that the Nicaraguans joined voluntary organizations in a higher proportion than did the Argentines. In Bello Horizonte, more than half of the respondents (57.1%) did not belong to any organization, but 43% of respondents did belong to at least one organization. By contrast, in La Matanza, 83% of respondents belonged to no organizations, and only 17% belonged to any organization at all. The reader will remember that in both of these neighborhoods the respondents were poor citizens, folks who spent long hours working at poorly paid jobs, who might have worked a second job in order to make ends meet, and who could afford little or no household help to assist with daily chores. Such citizens would also have very limited time and resources to spend in voluntary associations or on organizational dues. Given those social circumstances, 43% of Nicaraguans who belong to at least one organization is a fairly high number. Despite poverty, limited time and money, and low education, these Nicaraguans are members of voluntary organizations, whereas the Argentines appear much more reluctant to join them.

We continue by scrutinizing different kinds of organizational memberships. In both neighborhoods respondents were asked if they belonged to a neighborhood organization, to a labor union or trade union, to a social club of any kind, and to a religious club (such as a Bible study group, a church singing group, or a social club associated with one specific church). Church attendance and activity were explored separately. The answers to these questions provide a simple comparison of types of organizational memberships across the two urban samples. Figure 4.2 gives the simple additive advantage that goes to the population with higher membership levels. For each type of organization, a larger percentage of Nicaraguans than Argentines said that they belonged to that kind of organization.[8]

---

[8] In an effort to test Putnam's theory with data from six Central American countries, Amber L. Seligson finds that only membership in a "community improvement association" is associated with higher social capital, which she measures as higher "demand making." The category here that most closely corresponds with A. Seligson's "community improvement association" is "neighborhood association." In contrast with A. Seligson's findings, this chapter shows that membership in all kinds of non-religious organizations is associated with higher bridging social capital. Seligson (1999, Vol 32, # 3, pp. 342–362).

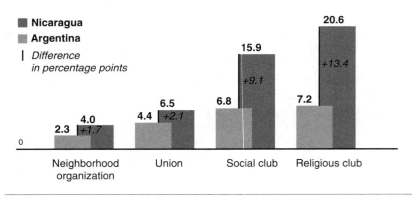

Source: Urban Samples: Bello Horizonte, Nicaragua, 2002 (N = 403); La Matanza, Argentina, 2002 (N = 1,200).
FIGURE 4.2. Percentage membership in four different types of organizations: Bello Horizonte, Nicaragua and La Matanza, Argentina.

The last bar of Figure 4.2 is interesting. The reader will remember that religion has played a key role in Nicaraguan politics. It was one of several factors that helped Nicaraguans join with each other across social divisions in order to oust the Somoza dictatorship and establish the Sandinista revolution. It was one of the elements that contributed to bridging social capital in Nicaragua. By contrast, the Argentine Catholic Church was another source of vertical authority and social control, and it has fostered few horizontal links in the national population. Here we see empirical evidence of the role of religion in fostering horizontal ties and associational memberships among these two populations. Nicaraguans were far more likely than Argentines to belong to a religious club of some kind. Moreover, the Nicaraguan advantage is much greater – a difference of more than 13% – with respect to this type of organization. The difference in styles between the hierarchical, socially conservative Argentine Catholic Church and the more participatory Nicaraguan church has meant that, at least in these two neighborhoods, Nicaraguans are nearly three times more likely to belong to a religious club than are Argentines.

Organizational Membership Across Parties

Our next step is to determine whether there are differences within these two neighborhoods between party affiliates with respect to organizational memberships. If one asks today whether respondents are Sandinistas or Peronists, one finds a floor of support in each nation for the parties that are the heirs to each of these two movements. Let us see how these two groups compare in their organizational memberships to citizens from their own societies who do not identify with or support Sandinismo in Nicaragua or Peronism in Argentina. Two different hypotheses present themselves: If the overall mentality of Sandinismo and Peronism has penetrated their respective societies, we

TABLE 4.1. *Bello Horizonte, Nicaragua: Types of Organizational Membership, Significance Levels with Respect to Party Identification – Sandinistas versus Non-Sandinistas*

	Level of Statistical Significance
Sandinistas more likely to belong to...	
...a neighborhood club	0.030
...a union	0.221
...a social club	0.022
...any type of non-religious club or organization	0.010
Sandinistas less likely to belong to...	
...a religious club or organization	0.172

Source: Urban Sample: Bello Horizonte, Nicaragua, 2002 (*N*=403).

might not find any further differences than what we have already discovered in the previous discussion. On the other hand, if there is a differential influence of Sandinismo and Peronism within their respective societies, then we should find differences in organizational participation between Sandinistas and non-Sandinistas in Nicaragua and between Peronists and non-Peronists in Argentina. The alternative perspective to this line of argument, also known as the "null hypothesis" in statistical language, is that neither social movement influenced social capital at all. In that case we will see no differences in membership and organizational activities between Nicaraguans and Argentines. We also will not see differences between Sandinistas and non-Sandinistas, or between Peronists and non-Peronists.

Let us begin by examining the Nicaraguan data in Table 4.1. The reader will recall that the urban respondents answered questions about four different kinds of organizations: neighborhood organizations, unions, social clubs, and religious clubs. With respect to the first three, being a Sandinista meant a higher level of membership, and the bivariate relationship was significant with respect to the first two: a neighborhood organization and a social club. Sandinistas were also more likely to be union members, but enough non-Sandinistas were also union members to make that relationship insignificant in a simple bivariate test.

Party identification as a Sandinista had the reverse effect with respect to religious clubs. Non-Sandinistas were more likely to be members of a religious club or organization – not counting the Catholic Church itself, of which nearly everyone is a member. Again, however, enough Sandinistas also belonged to religious clubs that this relationship was not statistically significant. The finding with respect to religious organizations other than church membership itself is interesting because Putnam has found that religiosity is negatively correlated with civic engagement. This finding bears further investigation in a larger data set in which levels of statistical significance would be easier to achieve than they are with the small Bello Horizonte sample. Chapter 2 argued that Sandinistas were more likely to have higher levels of trust toward others and consequently were more likely to engage in horizontal ties with others via organizational memberships. This initial analysis shows that argument to be true only with respect to non-religious organizations.

An examination of overall organizational memberships in Bello Horizonte revealed that Sandinistas were more likely to belong to one or more non-religious organizations, whereas non-Sandinistas were less likely to belong to any non-religious organization. This relationship was statistically significant at the .01 level and was particularly strong because the adjusted standardized residuals were above 2.0 (2.6) inside the individual cells.[9] Those residuals are not shown here because this bivariate relationship and the others discussed previously, for reasons of space, are summarized in Table 4.1, with their statistical significance levels only.

We can view the findings of Table 4.1 more succinctly by creating an index of associational membership. This index combines consideration of all these various organizational types by using a measure of membership in any and all types of organizations and voluntary associations except for religious clubs. Religious clubs are excluded here because membership in them has a reverse relationship to the party identification that the other types of memberships have. An index of non-religious organizational memberships demonstrates a clear relationship between being a Sandinista and belonging to a (non-religious) organization. In Figure 4.3, the column on the far right summarizes the total number and percentage of memberships in non-religious organizations for the Bello Horizonte sample. The reader will remember that, for non-Sandinistas, the most common type of associational membership was religious club membership.

We turn now to the Argentine data to discern whether there are differences within La Matanza between Peronists and non-Peronists with respect to organizational memberships. We find that the Argentine data are less complex and rich than the Nicaraguan data because so few Argentines belong to any organization at all. In fact, among the Argentines of La Matanza, only slightly more than 12% of our sample actually belonged to any organization at all. This tiny percentage by its very nature means that there will not be statistically significant differences between the various subcategories of organizational type listed in Figure 4.3. If we combine all the types of organizations probed in the Argentine sample, though, we find that there is a pattern and that it is in the expected direction. Peronists are less likely to belong to any organization at all than are non-Peronists. However, even there, the relationship was not statistically significant.

The relationship between partisanship and organizational membership in Argentina is statistically insignificant because so few Argentines in this sample had any organizational memberships at all. The fact of statistical

---

[9] On the use of residuals as an indicator of statistical significance, see Agresti (1996, pp. 38–39), Agresti (2002, pp. 80–82, 585–589) and Haberman (1978, *Vol 1*).

Tale of Two Neighborhoods

FIGURE 4.3. Bello Horizonte, Nicaragua: Index of all organizational memberships (non-religious) by party id percentages.

insignificance between the two groups is discouraging for Argentine associational life because it illustrates the extent to which non-Peronists as well as Peronists are reluctant to join organizations. I have suggested that Peronism encouraged vertical ties and upward loyalties to a leader, but not horizontal ties among peers in a way that would enable popular action or encourage democracy. Within this sample, those who call themselves Peronists have been influenced by those values, and nearly 90% of them have not joined an organization, voluntary association, or social club of any kind. Yet the truly discouraging part of these results for democracy in Argentina is that such anti-organizational dynamics and such lack of horizontal ties have also spread beyond the Peronists to affect even those who do not consider themselves Peronists. Among non-Peronists, 86% also have not joined any organization.

Organizational Memberships: Other Influences
The analysis from these neighborhoods supports the argument of this book. Within these two localities, Nicaraguans have stronger organizational relations than do Argentines. Moreover, among these Nicaraguans, Sandinistas are more likely to join associations and organizations than are non-Sandinistas. The patterns between party groups are more complex, however, with respect to the Argentines. While there is evidence that Peronists are even less likely to belong to organizations of any kind than are non-Peronists, Argentines in general are reluctant to join any organizations at all. This reluctance is evident across the party groups. While these results support our argument, they bode poorly for the future of Argentine democracy. Despite more than thirty years since Perón's death and nearly twenty-five years of democracy that had passed when these data were collected, the cold, suspicious, uncooperative breath of Peronism still blew over La Matanza, making most of these Argentines reluctant to engage with others in organizational interaction.

I have suggested that the history of popular politics and the deep emotional experiences that accompanied the social movements of Peronism and Sandinismo are powerful influences that have shaped popular attitudes in ways that affect social capital. I illustrated why Peronism created suspicion and a disinclination to cooperate while Sandinismo encouraged cooperation and trust within and across social groups. But are there influences other than popular political history that might also create bridging social capital? Answers to such a question would indicate whether there is anything Argentine society can do to enhance social relations among citizens, given its history of Peronism and the continuing influence of that social movement. We can explore these questions statistically.

One way to begin that exploration is by separating out other potential sources of positive social capital. This section addresses four standard socioeconomic categories in relation to associational memberships: age, gender, education, and income. Do members of some social or demographic categories have more faith in others, and exhibit a greater tendency to join organizations? These four sets of categories offer an important initial step toward exploring social capital apart from popular history. This is because all of these categories can be affected by social and political policies, and therefore by human agency within any developing democracy that is determined to enhance democratic social capital and understands how to do so.

For example, if we find that one age group is more inclined to join organizations, then we can look at the cohort experience of that group to determine what might have caused the difference. Policy makers can then replicate the positive experience among one age group and apply it to the others. Similarly, if one gender is more inclined than the other to join organizations, then policy makers can try to replicate the more positive inclinations with the other gender. Education, of course, is possibly the most easily addressed difference in social experiences, and if we find that the more educated are more inclined to join organizations then education is an obvious way to create positive social capital. Finally, income is a social difference that can be addressed with policy changes. Studies in developed societies have already found that more affluent citizens are more likely to join organizations. Is the same true in new democracies? If so, development policy that enhances the income level of all citizens will also positively affect social capital. Let us consider how these four socioeconomic and demographic categories relate to organizational memberships.

In both nations, men were more likely to belong to one or more organizations than were women. Among the Nicaraguans, 23.6% of men but only 18.5% of women belonged to one or more organizations. Among the Argentines, 18.3% of men but only 14.8% of women belonged to one or more organizations. The Chi Square statistics in Figure 4.4 show that the relationship between gender and organizational memberships was statistically significant in both nations. In developing societies, particularly those characterized by machista relations between genders, women are frequently isolated as homemakers and remain alone nearly all day long, rather than associating with others as in the working world. In addition, they are often responsible for child care in a manner that keeps them at home. The finding that women are less likely to join associations may be the result of these gender dynamics and of the social, political, and financial disadvantages women face. If isolation or discrimination or both are reasons for lower levels of associational memberships among women, this is a circumstance that can be addressed, and ameliorated, by social policy.

In contrast with gender, there was no relationship between age and organizational memberships in either neighborhood. Differences in cohort experiences across the age groups do not produce differences in tendencies to join organizations, at least as seen in the samples tested here. The finding might well indicate that, with respect to social capital, democracy is a dependent variable rather than a causal variable, itself benefiting positively from influences that enhance bridging social capital but not necessarily able to influence citizens to join organizations. At the very least, the influence of democracy on creating a greater propensity to join organizations may well be diluted by other factors, such as income and education, or by policies. Putnam and Skocpol have found that the propensity to join organizations has very much declined in the United States over recent decades, and this is true despite the continuation of democracy.[10] Thus, it should not be surprising that thirty years of democracy in Nicaragua and Argentina has not, in and of itself, produced a greater willingness to join organizations among citizens who have primarily lived under democracy. While one would have hoped that the advent of democracy with respect for human rights and civil liberties would have encouraged younger citizens to become joiners, apparently this has not happened, at least not yet and not in these two samples.

Although age was not related to organizational memberships, in both samples education had a strong, positive relationship to the tendency to join organizations. In Argentina, the relationship between organizational memberships

[10] Putnam (2001); Skocpol (2003).

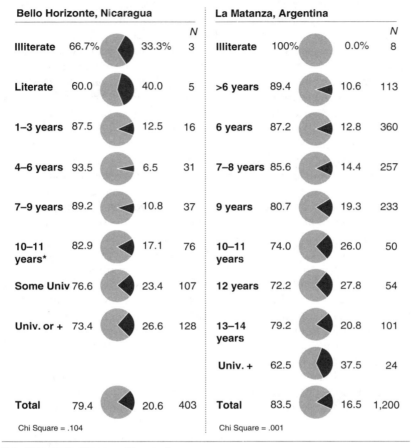

FIGURE 4.4. Organizational memberships by educational level, by percentage.

and education appeared at the division between no organizational memberships versus one or more such memberships. The relationship between education and organizational memberships was even stronger in Nicaragua. These relationships are listed in Figure 4.4, in which the numbers for both neighborhoods are statistically significant at .1 or better.

The data in Figure 4.4 tell an important story. First, the reader will note that the categories are slightly different for the two countries, reflecting the different histories of education in each nation. In Nicaragua, the category "literate," apart from any level of elementary education, exists for the Nicaraguan sample but not for the Argentine sample. A Nicaraguan respondent could respond that he or she was literate but had never completed even one year of elementary education. By contrast, no Argentine respondent gave this response. This difference exists because the Sandinista government, which took power in Nicaragua in 1979, launched a literacy crusade aimed at making adults who were beyond school age literate. This campaign was widely successful and resulted in large increases in the literacy rate among adult Nicaraguans. Adult students who participated in Nicaragua's literacy campaign became able to read simple materials, write simple sentences, and sign their name. In addition, an adult literacy program continues today in many Nicaraguan municipalities nationwide.[11] No such counterpart literacy campaign has ever been conducted in Argentina, including during the height of Peronist power. Therefore, Argentines generally have only one chance to become literate, and that chance comes when they are children of school age. To date, Argentine society has not given its citizens another mass opportunity to gain literacy if they miss becoming literate when they are children.

This is an important difference between the two societies since citizen willingness to participate in one or more organizations jumps significantly between the first and second educational categories in both sides of Figure 4.4. Within this sample, the Nicaraguans who were completely illiterate showed a 33.3% rate of joining organizations, while among those who had never attended elementary school but who were, nonetheless, literate, 40% said they belonged to one or more organizations. The sample itself is small, and further investigation of this pattern with a larger sample would determine whether it is widespread. Separating out the Nicaraguan data to include a category of literate adults who have not attended school allows us to uncover the potential importance of literacy, whenever it is acquired. That discovery could not have been made with the Argentine data alone. Becoming literate as an adult, after long years of illiteracy, may be an experience of empowerment for adult Nicaraguans. In this sample it clearly increased the willingness to join organizations. The Argentine sample also shows a jump in organizational memberships between the first and second category, from 0% to 10.6% who belong to one or more organizations. Even with a low level of education, Argentines who are literate are more likely than the illiterate to form horizontal ties with others in the form of organizational memberships. If the achievement of literacy is an empowering experience for an adult, then the absence of an adult literacy campaign has precluded that opportunity for empowerment in Argentina. It has also decreased the chance that adults will join organizations.

Beyond the first two pie graphs on both sides of Figure 4.4, we see a trend by educational level across both samples. As education level increased, respondents were more likely to belong to one or more organizations (as

---

[11] This program is called "Yo Si Puedo," translated "Yes, I Can." Most Nicaraguan mayors can give precise figures of how many adults over age 18 were certified as literate by the program in the last calendar year and how many adults are currently enrolled in the program.

shown in the dark wedge of each pie chart). That wedge grows in size from the top of the chart to the bottom on both sides of the figure. This finding is as important as the literacy finding discussed above. In both samples, exposing respondents to education appears to increase social trust and the willingness to form horizontal ties as expressed in organizational memberships. The data from both nations illustrate that investment in education will increase social involvement, organizational participation, and, with them, social capital.

There is a third important finding concerning education from the data in Figure 4.4. We can see that access to a university education or to some part of a university education is more prevalent in Nicaragua than in Argentina, despite the greater absolute level of poverty in Nicaragua and the nation's more scarce resources. Sandinismo has historically had a positive relationship with the nation's universities and the revolutionary movement encouraged its participants to go to university. By contrast, Peronism had a hostile, contemptuous attitude toward the nation's universities and involvement with Peronism discouraged any positive experience with the universities. Attention to university educational levels is important to our understanding of social trust and organizational membership: in both samples, respondents with some degree of university education were one of the groups most likely to belong to organizations. In the Argentine sample, they were the group with the highest absolute level of organizational membership.

Figure 4.4 shows a general upward trend in organizational membership associated with educational level. But if we scrutinize the two sides of the figure, we see a turning point in each database. Let us begin by looking at the left side of Figure 4.4. Ignore, for the moment, the first three pie graphs because they contain such a small number of respondents. Look instead at pie graph #4, (four–six years of education). Among this group, organizational membership is actually quite low. But organizational membership takes a dramatic jump at ten–eleven years of education (completed or nearly completed high school), and membership jumps again with having attained some university education. Thus, among the Nicaraguan sample, ten years of education is something of a benchmark. At that point, willingness to engage in organizational memberships grows dramatically. This finding is particularly important among a sample in which most individuals have reached the benchmark and attained at least ten years of education.

The ten-year educational benchmark in Nicaragua has a counterpart in the Argentine data. If we look at the right side of Figure 4.4, we find a similar turning point at a comparable educational level. In the first three pie graphs on the right side of Figure 4.4, organizational memberships are low – between zero and 12.8% of each subgroup. Membership increases to 19.3% with nine years of education and, from that point onward, remains above that level for each subgroup. While absolute levels of membership in the Argentine sample are still quite small compared with those among the Nicaraguans, we can still detect a turning point in the Argentine sample at nine years of education, the point at which organizational membership levels increase markedly. This point is roughly comparable with the ten-year benchmark in Nicaragua.

These data indicate that a crucial level of social trust is reached at about nine to ten years of education. This finding is doubly important since it holds true across both databases. Many societies have underscored the importance of primary education and the completion of six years of basic education. But fewer societies have placed equal emphasis on a high school education. Even in the United States, only eight years of education are legally mandatory; and high school, which begins in year nine, is not compulsory. In less-developed nations of low affluence levels and in new democracies, this neglect of high school education is even more pronounced. In both Nicaragua and Argentina, the law requires only an elementary school education. Yet these data show a clear connection between some level of *high school* education and organizational memberships. In both samples, citizens were far more likely to belong to an organization if they had completed primary and two school and at least one year of high school (grades 1–8).

If basic education is important for social involvement – and the Nicaraguan literacy category underscores that importance – then both data sets show that more education is even more important for social involvement. If societies can increase organizational memberships by providing access to education, they can increase social interaction even more by providing access to more education, in particular, access to high school education. National-level samples in both nations would reveal whether this trend is widespread in both societies. If so, investment in education seems to be one obvious way that newly democratic societies can increase social involvement and social trust.

Given that educational levels are higher in the Nicaraguan sample, and that social trust is higher as well, there appears to be an interactive and mutually reinforcing relationship among Sandinismo, education, and higher social involvement. The effect of Sandinismo is twofold, one direct, one indirect. Identification with the political party and political movement of Sandinismo enhances organizational memberships and horizontal ties, and, with them, mutual faith and social trust. Being Sandinista as an individual has a direct effect on higher organizational memberships. But Sandinismo in power and in control of national educational policy had an additional, indirect effect on organizational memberships as well. By having created national policy to increase fairly dramatically the base educational level of the population, Sandinismo has increased organizational memberships that way as well. At the level of adult literacy, and in high school and university access, this effect is visible, since all three are associated with a greater propensity to form organizational ties with others. Both high school and university were free and widely accessible during the Sandinista years. High school is still free today in Nicaragua and Argentina.

Likewise, the effect of Peronism is twofold and interactive, with both influences undermining social involvement. We saw from the movement's history that Peronism did not value education as highly as did Sandinismo. While in power, Peronism used primary school education as an important forum for indoctrination but did not initiate a literacy campaign. In the state-funded primary schools, prostheletization in favor of Catholicism was made an official national policy and that law remained in effect until the last months of Perón's first nine years in power. Similarly, Peronist high schools were set up primarily as fora of indoctrination, as Perón's own speeches indicate. Finally, Peronism lived in long-term conflict with the universities, a conflict that derived in large part from Perón's determination to use the universities as additional fora for indoctrination. Indoctrination, of course, is not the purpose of education. Perón's emphasis on top-down vertical control undermined citizen propensity to join horizontal organizations. That emphasis then interacted with a tendency to devalue education, which has a low priority in contemporary Argentine society. Even the university reforms that Peronism did institute served only to cheapen the value of the education attained by drastically undercutting university quality, autonomy and function. Both the influence of Peronism itself and its policies undercutting education now mitigate citizen membership in organizations, as well as the social trust reflected by and increased through such memberships. Public universities in Argentina are still officially free, including to workers, but the cultural tension between workers and universities makes it less likely that workers will attend university than is the case in Nicaragua.

Despite the negative connection among Peronism, education, and social trust, the relationships in Figure 4.4 are potentially exciting and positive with respect to the development of social capital in Argentina. The data show a point where policy makers can intervene into the public experience in ways that enhance human relations and inspire bridging social capital. Nations need not be helpless pawns before their own past, permanently out of luck if history has undermined social capital. In both samples, higher levels of education were associated with higher levels of organizational memberships. The fact that this relationship holds true across two very different data sets from two very different societies gives us greater confidence about the relationship found here. Education appears to be related to greater faith in others, at least as measured by the willingness to join organizations and to interact with others through those organizations. Education is a social good that societies can provide in greater abundance to more citizens, enhancing social trust today through social policy.

As these data indicate, Nicaraguans have already found a powerful influence toward social trust in Sandinismo, itself. Yet Nicaraguans are not utterly reliant on the effect of a positive popular political history. Nor are they condemned to a declining influence toward bridging social capital while Sandinismo is out of power. Quite apart from the influence of the Sandinista revolution, today Nicaraguans can continue to enhance mutual trust through educational policy. Moreover, there are many reasons to provide access to public education, quite apart from the creation of positive social capital and the enhancement of democracy, particularly given Nicaragua's poverty.

Educational levels in Argentina are low relative to the nation's wealth, and, among these two samples, more Argentines than Nicaraguans have lower educational levels. Of the Nicaraguan sample, 22% had nine years or less of education. The comparable statistic for the Argentine sample is 81%. When one moves outside the working class, Argentines are a more highly educated population. Yet Argentine workers could benefit from more education. The Argentines in this sample, like their Nicaraguan counterparts, appear more likely to join organizations when they have higher levels of education, and particularly when they have finished at least some years of high school. Here is a discovery that could bode well for the enhancement of bridging social capital in Argentina. Even where Peronism has had a powerful influence, even among low-income citizens, introducing education into the picture will raise levels of social trust, as illustrated in organizational memberships. The anomie and suspicion Peronism generated, the inability to work together or relate to each other in horizontal ties that Peronism's history exemplified, could, conceivably, be gradually overturned by educating the population, particularly the working class. As in Nicaragua, education is something that a society can elect to provide to citizens as a deliberate policy. Insofar as organizational memberships reflect and enhance bridging social capital, Figure 4.4 illustrates that doing so will enhance democracy in Argentina.

We turn our attention now to the relationship between organizational memberships and income. Given the relationships we have found between education and organizational memberships and the fact that education is usually positively associated with income, we might expect organizational memberships to be greater in number as income increases. The relationship between income and number of organizational memberships showed that organizational involvement increased with income. The relationship was statistically significant in the Argentine sample ($p = .000$) but not in the Nicaraguan sample ($p = .272$). In both neighborhoods, organizational memberships were quite low for the lowest income category so that, to some extent, poverty itself is responsible for low levels of organizational membership. But this was more true in Argentina than in Nicaragua.

Both education and income were positively related to organizational memberships. But in a new democracy, educational levels may be something that governments can influence more easily than they can income. Moreover, the relationship between education and organizational involvement is more clear and more linear than is the relationship to income. Thus governments wishing to create higher propensities toward social involvement through organizations might find it constructive to invest in education, rather than in direct income distribution. Investment either in adult literacy or in high school education appears particularly useful. For Nicaragua, investment in education is already a national priority and significant strides toward a more educated population have already been taken. In part this is due to a set of national patterns that became well established during the Sandinista years. Even beyond the Sandinista defeat in 1990, popular demands have kept education high on the list of priorities in many municipalities nationwide. And with the Sandinista sweep of municipal governments in 2000, 2004, and 2008, a party that prioritizes education can use municipal government to enhance education whether or not it is in control of the presidency.[12]

In Argentina, however, the positive benefits of education toward which these findings point are more difficult to achieve. If the findings above on education were to hold true nationwide, then one of the most important contributions one could make to Argentine democracy today would be to become a K-12 teacher. And yet, teachers and education are a low priority in Argentina. In the 1990s teachers and university professors could not even make a living on the salary they earned and were forced to work a second job or leave their chosen profession entirely. When, in the early 1990s, Argentina's teachers went on strike to increase their salaries, then-president Menem labeled them "subversives" and teachers' salaries remained very low. In the 2000s, teachers' and professors' salaries have improved but are still dismal, particularly in public schools and universities. In contrast to the Peronists, the Radicals have a positive relationship with the nation's schools and universities but the Radicals are extremely weak and growing more so. The Radical party has held the presidency for only about seven years of the last twenty-six and they have never controlled both chambers of the Congress since the return to democracy in 1983. In the 1990s the Menem government established several new universities and made other quite controversial changes to primary and secondary education. The effect of these reforms is becoming more evident now but it is not clear how or whether they have affected social capital. Yet education may help decide the future of Argentina's democracy and attention to it would make for good public policy regardless of which party is in power.

NATIONAL ASSESSMENTS OF ORGANIZATIONAL MEMBERSHIP

Before leaving this study of organizational memberships in the two neighborhoods, let us see what we can learn about organizational memberships in national samples from both countries. We draw here upon the Latinobarometer data from 2007. In that year the Latinobarometer study asked Latin Americans about membership in various types of organizations. These included activism in (1) a political party, (2) a union, professional association or business organization, (3) a religious organization, (4) a sports organization, and (5) any other type of organization not covered by the previous four categories. Respondents were asked to categorize the level of their

---

[12] During the presidency of Arnoldo Alemán, the electoral calendar was changed to separate municipal elections from national elections when previously the two had always been simultaneous. In the first separate municipal election in 2000, the Sandinistas won a nationwide landslide, and they have dominated municipal elections ever since. The Sandinistas currently hold the majority of all mayoral offices in the nation. See Anderson and Dodd, *Learning Democracy*, esp. chaps 8 and 9. For a discussion of the 2008 Nicaraguan municipal elections, see Anderson and Dodd, (2009, Vol 20, # 3, pp. 152–167).

participation across four categories of activism as follows: (1) belong and participate actively, (2) belong but do not participate actively, (3) belonged previously, and (4) have never belonged.

In 2007 the Latinobarometer data showed the same results found in the findings from the two neighborhood samples. With respect to every kind of organization listed above, Nicaraguans were always more likely to belong than were Argentines and the difference was always statistically significant. This difference was particularly pronounced with respect to the question about political parties, a finding that provides continuing evidence of the horizontal nature of political parties in Nicaragua, including the Sandinista party. Nicaraguans were more likely than Argentines to belong and participate actively in a political party and more likely to belong without participating actively ($p = .000$). Argentines, by contrast, were more likely never to have belonged to any political party ($p = .000$).

The 2007 data are also particularly interesting with respect to the question about union, professional or business organizational membership. Given the high level of union activity and membership in Argentina, one might expect this finding to favor Argentina but it does not. Despite the high level of union membership in Argentina, Nicaraguans were still more likely to belong and participate actively or simply to belong to a union, professional or business association ($p = .039$).[13] Likewise, Nicaraguans were more likely to belong and participate actively or simply to belong to a religious organization ($p = .000$) to a sports organization ($p = .000$) or to any other type of association not covered by the previous four categories ($p = .000$).

CONCLUSION

Part I of this book explained why social capital would be high in Nicaragua and low in Argentina. The data analysis presented in this chapter shows how the differences in social capital in the two nations under study here manifest themselves with respect to organizational activity. Within the neighborhood and national samples considered here, we have found important and significant differences in organizational memberships. We also found differences within the two neighborhoods along lines of partisan preference. The differences between nations and between partisan groups support the theoretical argument of this book. In national samples Nicaraguans were more likely to be organizational members and organizational activists. In the two neighborhood samples, Sandinistas were more involved in formal organizations while Peronists were less inclined to belong to formal organizations than were non-Peronists. These findings are in keeping with the argument of Part I that Sandinismo fostered horizontal ties, mutual faith among citizens, and greater associational interaction. Peronism, by contrast, undermined horizontal ties and citizen mutual faith. It left Argentine society in general and Peronist

---

[13] On the widespread nature of union membership in Argentina see Ranis (1995).

partisans in particular with a lower capacity for associational interaction than otherwise might have been the case.

These findings challenge other theories about development and democracy. Modernization theory, for example, always advantages more wealthy, industrialized and cosmopolitan societies, suggesting that democracy will develop more readily there. The arguments of the world values study likewise favor less traditional societies over more traditional ones, suggesting that democracy will develop more readily in less traditional contexts. Argentina is clearly a more wealthy and industrial society and, in that regard, would be favored by modernization theory. Yet the social capital data here advantage Nicaragua. Likewise, world values conclusions would label Nicaragua the more traditional society and the one less likely to democratize. Yet the social capital data here offer the opposite conclusion. We will revisit the contrast between the findings here and other theories about democratization in the Conclusion to the book. While the bulk of the analysis of this chapter rests upon neighborhood samples, recent national data confirm the neighborhood findings at the national level: Nicaraguans are still organizational joiners and activists; Argentines are not.

These empirical findings offer support for the argument of this book at the local and national levels. Yet they are also limited in what they say about the development of democracy. The limits of the findings here are also the limits of social capital theories more generally. Both Tocqueville and subsequent social capital scholars require us to make a leap of faith. Where social relations are strong, they tell us, democracy works better. Certainly the macro picture of democracy in Nicaragua and Argentina confirms this argument and the micro-level story of these two neighborhoods does the same. In the contemporary news media, we have already heard distinctly different reports about the development of democracy in Nicaragua and Argentina. A poor nation with almost no industrial development, reliant on a few agricultural cash crops, and deeply dependent on exports, Nicaragua's democratic transition appears to move forward gradually but steadily.[14] By contrast, a wealthy, industrialized nation with a diverse economy and considerably less export dependence, Argentina has been very much in crisis as presidents resigned, electoral candidates withdrew, and the economy appeared in free fall.

From the data in this chapter, we see an initial explanation for that difference. Despite its economic and industrial disadvantages, Nicaragua has a strong advantage in social capital. Nicaraguans trust each other, at least enough to join voluntary associations and participate in organizations. Argentines represent the reverse scenario. Despite its advantages of size, industrial development, and relative export independence, citizens in Argentina lack social capital. Argentines do not trust each other enough to join organizations in high numbers or participate actively. This explanation suggests that Tocqueville was right: associations matter for democracy. Putnam and Skocol

---

[14] Anderson (2006); Anderson and Dodd (2009).

are correct that social capital does help make democracy work. Its presence is helping the new Nicaraguan democracy. Its absence leaves the Argentine democracy limping along in more difficulty than the nation's wealth would lead us to expect.

Nevertheless, this chapter and social capital studies more generally have not yet shown a direct empirical link between organizational memberships and democratic political action, participation, democratic values and confidence in democracy's institutions and processes. We can only trust in that link by making a leap of faith. I believe that we can do better than such a leap of faith in tracing the connection between social capital and support for democracy. Because this study has the advantage of standing on the shoulders of several previous studies of social capital, we can consider the associational picture presented here and also examine questions that specifically address political values, different kinds of political action and support for democratic institutions and procedures. The next two chapters take up that challenge.

5

Democracy and Its Competitors
Political Values in Nicaragua and Argentina

> Our political culture is different, our vision of democracy is distinct.
> *Peronist leader, speaking of his own party*[1]
>
> The political orientation of my Country should distance itself from all types of caudillismo...
> *Augusto C. Sandino, speaking to his people on the occasion of a proposed election, October 6, 1927*[2]

If we want to trace the empirical connection between social capital and support for democracy, one place to begin is with political values, themselves the basis of actions. Such an examination can ascertain how fully citizens support democracy as opposed to some other authoritarian or less than fully democratic regime. This chapter examines political values in these two nations, looking at liberal democratic, radical democratic, and non-democratic values in Nicaragua along with democratic, authoritarian, and clientelistic political values in Argentina.

The empirical bases for this chapter are several. First, we introduce two historical data bases which facilitate the study of political values at the national level. In each country we are fortunate to have a large data base of public opinion drawn from the late 1990s at a time when the memory of a previous, non-democratic regime was much more recent than it is today. In the late 1990s many Nicaraguans could easily remember the authoritarian Somoza dictatorship while many Argentines could likewise remember the brutal military dictatorship of 1976–1983. Asking questions about political values that draw upon data from that time period allows us to compare the loyalties of respondents to non-democratic regimes in a way that would be much more difficult today. The two historical data bases ask respondents about regime preferences across democratic and non-democratic regimes. The comparison allows us to see how the differences in social capital found in these two

[1] *Buenos Aires Herald*, December 22 (1985, p. 17).
[2] Pensamento vivo, Vol. 1, pp. 158–160, San Jose, Costa Rica, Educa, 1974, republished Editorial Neuva Nicaragua, Managua, Nicaragua, 1981.

nations translate into different political values and different evaluations of non-democratic regime alternatives. This chapter also draws data from the Latinobarometro 2007, the most recent available, to contrast political activism and values in each country in recent times. The use of this recent data base allows us to evaluate how the differences in social capital across Nicaragua and Argentina have caused different values and styles of activism as democracy has aged and memories of authoritarianism have faded.

POLITICAL VALUES: DEMOCRACY AND ITS COMPETITORS

The different kinds of political values scrutinized here are subtle and nuanced, reflecting the political history of each nation. These subtleties allow us to examine political values favoring radical democracy or clientelism, as well as the difference between support for democracy versus authoritarianism. For example, the Nicaraguan data set allows us to distinguish between citizen support for liberal democracy versus radical democracy. The first prioritizes formal institutions and procedures, while the latter combines these expectations with desires for income redistribution and some measure of economic democracy. Nicaragua's Sandinista history and the difference among regimes prior to 1996 allow us to scrutinize these preferences. Similarly, since Argentines have been exposed to the highly clientelistic Peronism as well as to authoritarianism, historical regime differences allow us to scrutinize clientelistic political values and preferences for democracy and authoritarianism in Argentina.[3]

Since the questions asked in these two national surveys speak specifically to the political circumstances of the two respective nations, the questions are not and should not be identical. Nonetheless, across the two nations these data address three broad categories of concern: (1) support for democracy versus authoritarianism, (2) support for radical democracy versus liberal democracy where appropriate (in Nicaragua), and (3) support for a clientelistic regime that is only partly democratic where appropriate (in Argentina).

I. Nicaragua

We begin with an historical perspective on political values in Nicaragua. The year 1996 was an ideal moment to ask Nicaraguans for this contrast in preferred regimes and the values behind individual choices. In 1979 Nicaragua went from a dictatorship to socialism; in 1990 the nation changed again, from socialism and radical economic democracy to capitalism and liberal democracy. In 1996, therefore, Nicaraguans had just seen six years of a

[3] In making this distinction between radical and liberal democratic political values, I am drawing on the work of political theorist Margaret Kohn (1999), who argues that a broader definition of democracy, expanded to include economic democracy and economic rights, is a version of democracy distinct from liberal democracy. This broader definition of democracy, of course, is the definition of democracy that the Sandinista government used but is also the definition of choice in other contexts, such as in France.

liberal democratic regime under Chamorro but many could also remember the Somoza dictatorship and the Sandinista years.[4] Like Ortega before her but unlike Somoza, Chamorro had been democratically elected.[5] More than Somoza, she had respected democratic process. But she had defined democracy more narrowly than had the Sandinistas. Democracy for Chamorro was limited to political rights and civil liberties but excluded economic rights that the Sandinistas had defined as part of democracy. Thus 1996 was the first point at which Nicaraguans could look backward over recent times and contrast living memories of an authoritarian regime, a liberal democratic regime, and a radical democratic regime.

To uncover the presence and level of democratic values in Nicaragua, respondents in this nationwide survey were asked which of these regimes they preferred. This question allowed respondents to choose among the political regimes that had governed the nation recently. They were asked, "Under which of the following three governments would you prefer to live? Somoza, the Sandinistas, or Chamorro?" Respondents who said that their preferred government was the Somoza regime are considered to have preferred an authoritarian government and to be displaying authoritarian political values. Those who said that their preferred government was Chamorro's are considered to have preferred a liberal democratic government and to be displaying liberal democratic values. Respondents who said that their preferred government was the Sandinista government are perceived as preferring a radical democratic regime and as displaying radical democratic values.

Figure 5.1 examines the relationship between party identification and democratic values. The size of the data set allows us to separate non-Sandinistas into three other party-identification categories: Liberals, Conservatives and Independents. The size of the pie graphs in Figure 5.1 reflect the size of each of these four groups. Figure 5.1 shows a strong relationship between the different partisan identities and democratic values with a Chi Square ≤ .01 and strong residuals within the cells in the expected direction. We will scrutinize the figure carefully. First, looking at the bracketed number for each pie graph, we see the percentage of each partisan group who prefer a democratic regime, either a liberal democratic regime or a radical democratic regime. At the bottom of the chart, that number is 64.9%, indicating that more than two-thirds of all respondents prefer democracy over authoritarianism.

Second, among those who identified themselves as Sandinistas, 87.8% preferred a radical democratic regime while an additional 5.3% preferred a liberal democratic regime. The figure in column 3, row 3 indicates that 93.1% of Sandinistas preferred some form of democratic regime. Among Sandinistas, only 6.9% said they preferred an authoritarian regime. Such a strong preference

---

[4] These kinds of data will be harder to collect in Nicaragua as the memory of the Somoza regime, in particular, fades into the past. For this reason, the 1996 data are particularly important for the study of democratic values in Nicaragua.

[5] Anderson and Dodd, (2005).

Democracy and Its Competitors

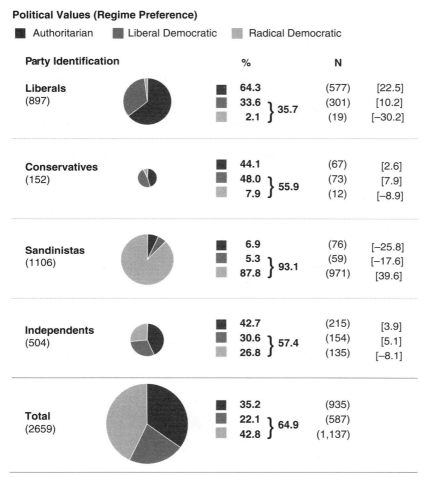

FIGURE 5.1. Political values in regime choice in Nicaragua by percentage and by party identification.

among Sandinistas for a democratic regime contrasts particularly strongly with political values among Liberals. Among Liberals (row 1), 64.3% said they preferred an authoritarian regime (the Somoza dictatorship), while only 35.7% preferred some form of democratic regime (33.6% preferred a liberal democracy, Chamorro's government, and 2.1% preferred a radical democracy, the Sandinista government). Conservatives and Independents fell in between these first two groups: among Conservatives 55.9% preferred democracy and 44.1% preferred authoritarianism; among Independents 57.4% preferred democracy and 42.7% preferred authoritarianism. Among these four groups, Sandinistas clearly showed the highest level of democratic values and the lowest level of preference for authoritarianism. Liberals, by contrast, exhibited the highest level of preference for authoritarianism and the lowest preference for any form of democracy. The Liberals also were outliers with respect to the population as a whole. Their group percentage preference of only 35.7% for democracy contrasts with the overall percentage of 64.9% preferring democracy for the respondent pool as a whole.

In order to explore further the strength of democratic and authoritarian political values in Nicaraguan society, we look next at the relationship between democratic values and several standard demographic categories: gender, age,

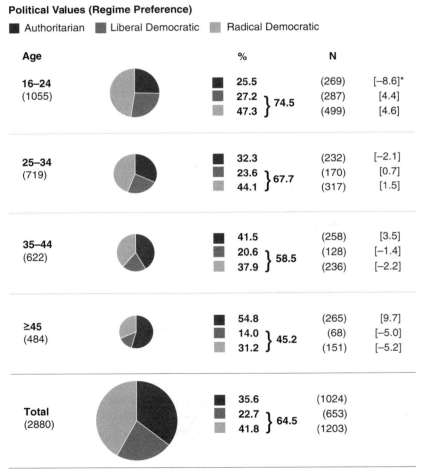

FIGURE 5.2. Political values in regime choice in Nicaragua by age.

Democracy and Its Competitors

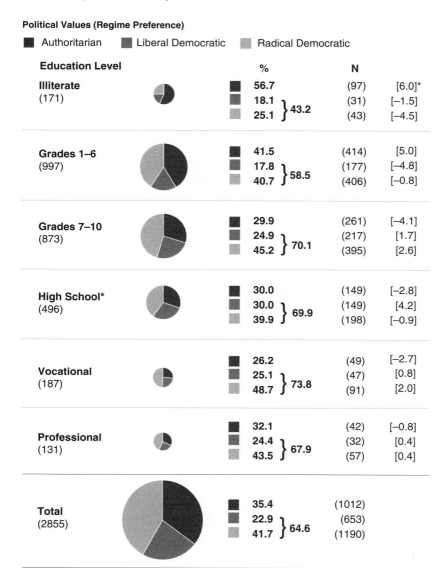

FIGURE 5.3. Political values in regime choice in Nicaragua by education.

and occupation. Among these, gender showed no statistically significant relationship to democratic values. The other two demographic categories showed a significant bivariate relationship to democratic values, with strong residuals indicating significant differences among the cells as well.

The analysis in Figures 5.2 and 5.3 reveals strong relationships between age and democratic values and between education level and democratic values. Among Nicaraguans, at least in the late 1990s, increasing age was clearly related to a greater propensity toward authoritarian political values. Each increasing age category had a higher percentage that preferred the authoritarian Somoza regime than the next younger age group. For both liberal democratic and radical democratic values, greater youth was significantly related to more democratic values and that relationship was linear, although the residuals were not always statistically significant at 2.0 or higher. Similarly, education was also significantly related to democratic values in the bivariate equation. A higher level of education was significantly related to a higher level of democratic values, either liberal democratic or radical democratic values, while lower educational levels were associated with greater authoritarianism. If we think back to the analysis in Chapter 4, the reader will recall that higher levels of education were also strongly related to higher levels of organizational membership. Now we find that more education is related to higher democratic values. We can conclude from these findings that education is a democratic influence in Nicaragua, contributing both to greater horizontal ties within society and to greater levels of democratic values in politics.

Since party identification, age, and education are all significant in bivariate relationships to democratic values, it is useful to consider them in a multivariate model so that we can see the relative strength of each variable. This analysis requires a multinomial logistic regression rather than a simple linear regression or binomial logistic regression because the dependent variable is neither linear nor dichotomous, but categorical. Multinomial regression does not provide predictive strength for the model as a whole, so we cannot know fully how these three independent variables determine political values. But we can know which of the three exerts the strongest influence.

The equation on p 146 excludes Independents since they declined to provide a partisan identification and this is an analysis testing the relationship between partisanship and democratic values. All other respondents are ordered from least conservative to most conservative, making the independent variable, "Partisanship" ordinal. From left to right, that order is Sandinistas, Conservatives, Liberals.[6] Also excluded are respondents who did not answer the question that is the dependent variable in this equation: "Under which regime would you prefer to live?" The age variable is the same one used in Figure 5.2 and has four categories; the education variable is the same used in Figure 5.3 and has six categories.

Multinomial regression analysis functions on the basis of probabilities. It compares the probability that individuals within each category of each

---

[6] In Nicaragua, those who call themselves "Liberal" stand to the right of those who call themselves "Conservative." This is confusing for readers from the United States who are accustomed to thinking of Liberals as standing to the left of Conservatives. The reasons for Nicaraguan Liberals being so far to the right are historical, based in the original interpretation of the word "liberal" as supporting laissez faire market economics. Anderson and Dodd (2005, chap. 2).

independent variable will have each of the political values under consideration. It takes the final category of the dependent variable and of each independent variable as a baseline, and compares that baseline to the probability of individuals in each of the other categories having the dependent variable value in question.

To determine the relative strength of each of the three independent variables – party identification, educational level, and age – we look down the second column (significance level). Variables at a .05 or higher level of significance were the strongest determinants of political values. From the analysis, we see that party identification was a significant indicator of democratic values, while the influence of education became insignificant. Age was significant among the younger cohorts. When we look at the top half of the figure, we are examining the propensity of respondents to hold authoritarian political values (to have preferred the Somoza regime) as opposed to radical democratic values (to have preferred the Sandinista government). Looking at column one in the top half of the figure, we see that Sandinistas were significantly less likely to prefer authoritarianism than were Liberals (the baseline) by a coefficient of −5.926. Similarly, Conservatives were less likely than Liberals to prefer authoritarianism by a coefficient of −1.822, although the gap between Conservatives and Liberals was much smaller than that between Sandinistas and Liberals. Both of these coefficients were statistically significant, although the coefficient for being a Sandinista was much larger. Sandinistas were even less likely than Conservatives to prefer an authoritarian regime.

When we look at the second half of Table 5.1 (liberal democracy) we are examining the propensity of respondents to hold liberal democratic values (and to have preferred the Chamorro government) as opposed to radical democratic values (the Sandinista government), which the statistical model uses as the baseline. We see that party identification also produced a significant difference in the preference for liberal versus radical democracy. Sandinistas were less likely than Liberals to prefer liberal democracy versus radical democracy by a coefficient of −5.540 (sig = .000). It is interesting to see that Conservatives were also less likely than Liberals to prefer liberal democracy over radical democracy by a coefficient of −.962. Self-identifying Conservatives were slightly more inclined toward radical democracy than Liberals.

The significance of age was uneven in the two halves of Table 5.1. Voting age in Nicaragua is 16, and the youngest cohort begins with that group. In the top half of the table, older respondents were much more likely to hold authoritarian political values than radical democratic political values. The youngest respondents (16–24) were significantly less likely than the oldest group to prefer authoritarianism by a coefficient of −1.186; the second youngest group (age 25–34) was significantly less likely than the oldest group to prefer authoritarianism by a coefficient of −.983. The differences in authoritarian values between the two older groups were significant at the .028 level. Thus age was always significant at .1 level or better with respect to present for authoritarianism. But age was not significant with respect to preference for liberal

TABLE 5.1. *Nicaragua: Multinomial Regression Analysis (Independents Excluded): Dependent Variable = Political Values*

Dependent Variable	Independent Variables	Beta coef	Sig Level	Exp(B)
Authoritarianism	Intercept	3.782	.000	
	Party Identification			
	Sandinista	−5.926	.000	2.670E-03
	Conservative	−1.822	.000	.162
	Liberal	0		
	Education Level			
	Illiterate	.880	.134	2.410
	Grades 1–6	.509	.273	1.664
	Grades 7–10	.253	.591	1.288
	High School	.366	.453	1.442
	Vocational	.290	.592	1.336
	Professional	0		
	Age			
	16–24	−1.186	.000	.306
	25–34	−.983	.000	.374
	35–44	−.606	.028	.545
	≥45	0		
Liberal Democracy	Intercept	2.722	.000	
	Party Identification			
	Sandinista	−5.540	.000	3.925E-03
	Conservative	−.962	.014	.382
	Liberal	0		
	Education Level			
	Illiterate	.151	.803	1.163
	Grades 1–6	−.175	.708	.839
	Grades 7–10	5.216E-02	.912	1.054
	High School	.205	.673	1.228
	Vocational	.337	.532	1.400
	Professional	0		
	Age			
	16–24	3.671E-02	.898	1.037
	25–34	−7.519E-02	.802	.928
	35–44	−9.54E-02	.758	.909
	≥45	0		

Note: Model Fit Information: −2 log likelihood; Sig level = .000.
Nagelkerke Pseudo R squared = .689.
Source: Nationwide surveys in Nicaragua taken in October and November, 1996, conducted by DOXA.

versus radical democracy. In the second half of Table 5.1, the age coefficients were insignificant, and age differences did not produce statistically significant differences in the preference for liberal versus radical democratic values. Younger respondents are less authoritarian in their political values, but as democrats they may be either liberal democrats or radical democrats. The difference between the two kinds of democratic values is not statistically significant among younger voters.

Education was generally not significant in this model. However, we know from the bivariate relationships examined earlier in this chapter and in the previous chapter that education is important in Nicaragua. It is related to more organizational activity and to higher social capital. Yet, in this model, higher levels of education were not related to higher democratic values. That conclusion seems hard to accept in light of what we already know about the relationship between education and organizational memberships and between organizational involvement and political participation. Further study of education and political values is needed to resolve this apparent contradiction. Most of these respondents had similar levels of education.[7]

Let us reconsider this same equation by including the Independents in the analysis. As the fourth-listed category on the independent variable, Independents were used as the baseline group, and the probability of authoritarian or liberal democratic values for party identifiers was compared with the probability of that value among Independents. Again, in this equation, respondents who did not answer the regime preference question (the dependent variable) are excluded from the equation. The independent variables used are the same as those used in Table 5.1.

Again, we see that education proved statistically insignificant, but both party identification and age produced significant differences in political values between the Independents and the party identifiers. Sandinistas were less inclined toward authoritarian political values (as opposed to radical democratic values) than the Independents were by a coefficient of −3.044 (sig = .000). Comparing this coefficient with its counterpart in Table 5.1 shows that there was a much greater difference between Sandinistas and Liberals than there was between Sandinistas and Independents; regardless, in either equation Sandinistas were the group less likely to prefer authoritarianism. However, in Table 5.2, both Liberals and Conservatives were more likely than Independents to prefer authoritarianism by coefficients of 2.894 and 1.083, respectively (sig = .001 and .000, respectively).

---

[7] Looking back to Figure 5.3, the reader will note that 2366 respondents out of a total of 2855 gave education levels in the middle three categories: grades 1–6, grades 7–10 and completed high school. A total of 82.8% of these respondents had between one and 11 years of education, leaving little variance at the low and high ends of the education scale. The other 17.2% of respondents distributed themselves across the lowest category (illiterates) and the two highest categories: vocational training and professional or graduate training. This is the lack of variation across the whole education variable to which I am referring.

TABLE 5.2. *Nicaragua: Multinomial Regression Analysis (Independents Included): Dependent Variable = Political Values*

Dependent Variable	Independent Variables	Beta coef	Sig Level	Exp(B)
Authoritarianism	Intercept	.940	.011	
	Party Identification			
	Sandinista	−3.044	.000	4.766E-02
	Conservative	1.083	.001	2.953
	Liberal	2.894	.000	18.063
	Independent	0		
	Education level			
	Illiterate	.567	.216	1.763
	Grades 1–6	.349	.302	1.418
	Grades 7–10	.228	.509	1.256
	High School	.526	.146	1.692
	Vocational	.290	.484	1.336
	Professional	0		
	Age			
	16–24	−1.283	.000	.277
	25–34	−.886	.000	.412
	35–44	−.512	.025	.599
	> 45	0		
Liberal Democracy	Intercept	−4.87E-02	.902	
	Party Identification			
	Sandinista	−2.993	.000	5.013E-02
	Conservative	1.629	.000	5.100
	Liberal	2.582	.000	13.221
	Independent	0		
	Education level			
	Illiterate	9.840E-02	.841	1.103
	Grades 1–6	−7.57E-02	.830	.927
	Grades 7–10	.290	.413	1.336
	High School	.662	.074	1.939
	Vocational	.633	.132	1.883
	Professional	0		
	Age			
	16–24	−8.22E-02	.735	.921
	25–34	−4.02E-02	.873	.961
	35–44	2.018E-02	.938	1.020
	> 45	0		

Note: Model fit information: −2 log likelihood = 2609.546; Sig level = .000. Nagelkerke Pseudo R squared = .619.
Source: Nationwide surveys in Nicaragua taken in October and November, 1996, conducted by DOXA.

Similarly, age differences produced significant differences between authoritarianism and radical democratic political values, but not between liberal and radical democratic values when the Independents were used as a baseline. Thus, within any age category, Independents were more likely than party identifiers to prefer authoritarianism, and those differences were statistically significant at .000 with respect to the younger two age groups and significant at .025 between the two older groups. The coefficients were −1.283, −.886, and −.512 respectively.

Looking at the second half of Table 5.2 (liberal democracy) we see that neither age nor education produced significant differences in liberal versus radical democratic values between Independents and party identifiers. However, party identification was again the strongest independent variable. Sandinistas were significantly less likely to prefer liberal democracy over radical democracy than were Independents by a coefficient of −2.993 (sig = .000), while both Conservatives and Liberals were more inclined than Independents to have liberal democratic versus radical democratic values.

The inclusion of this second equation using Independents as the baseline indicates that Independents, on the whole, were much more inclined toward authoritarianism than the Sandinistas (by a coefficient of 3.044) but less inclined toward authoritarianism than either the Conservatives or Liberals (by coefficients of 1.083 and 2.894 respectively). They were also more inclined toward liberal democratic values than Sandinistas (by a coefficient of 2.993) but less inclined toward radical democratic values than either Conservatives or Liberals (by coefficients of 1.629 and 2.582 respectively). In either equation, party identification was always the strongest indicator of political values, while age was significant for those 35 and under. As a group, Independents clearly stand in the middle of the population, being generally less authoritarian than the Liberals but more authoritarian than the Sandinistas. The Independents sometimes stand to one side of the Conservatives and sometimes to the other. Political values among Independents appeared to be the least predictable of the four groups, although they were probably more different from the Sandinistas than they were from the other two groups.

Party identification was the strongest indicator of democratic values, and identification with the bridging organization that was and is Sandinismo produces the highest level of democratic values and the lowest inclination toward authoritarianism. However, democratic values in Nicaragua will also increase with the natural aging process of Nicaragua's population. The connection between Sandinista partisanship and democratic values would seem to indicate that if the Sandinistas continue to have a strong base of popular support, then democracy will still have a strong following.[8] Similarly, if identification

---

[8] New work on Nicaragua indicates that the electoral support base for the Sandinista party in the most recent 2006 national election remained near the 40% it has been since 1990. It was 38% in 2006. However, the strength of the party can be seen more readily at the local level, specifically with respect to local elections for mayors: popular support for Sandinista mayors is stronger than the national support for Ortega (Anderson and Dodd, 2007; 2008; 2009).

with the non-Sandinista parties, particularly the Liberals, rises while they still demonstrate low democratic values, then support for democracy in Nicaragua could decline. For the time being, it appears that democratic values in Nicaragua are closely related to the fate of the Sandinista party.

Before closing this section on Nicaragua, a word is in order on the different kinds of democratic values we have found to exist there. The analysis indicates that there is a base of support in Nicaragua for a version of democracy that includes some measure of economic democracy as well as support for liberal democratic procedures. The foundation of this support lies in the Sandinista revolution. With regard to respect for human rights, the rule of law, and democratic procedure, it apparently doesn't matter whether democrats are radical or liberal in Nicaragua. Radical democrats stand with liberal democrats in support of these democratic basics. But the distinction between support for radical versus liberal democracy could matter a great deal with regard to electoral choices and policy construction in Nicaragua's future. While most Nicaraguans support democracy, some of them support a radical egalitarian version of democracy while others do not. This is a discussion and an argument that Nicaraguans will have to resolve for themselves. As scholars trying to understand democratic values in Nicaragua, we need to be aware of this important difference in expectations about democracy among Nicaraguan citizens.

II. Argentina

If the choice in Nicaragua has been between liberal or radical democracy on the one hand, and the legacy of sultanistic authoritarianism on the other, then authoritarianism provides the primary foil against which to measure the growth of democratic values in Nicaragua.[9] Argentina, by contrast, has a more complex non-democratic history. Argentina's current democracy emerged out of a ruthless military dictatorship that was at least as capable as was Somoza of human rights violations. Yet dictatorial authoritarianism has not been the only adversary against which democracy struggles to develop in Argentina. As Chapter 3 illustrated, the clientelistic, vertical ties inspired by Peronist patronage constitute a more subtle but equally difficult challenge for democracy. Democracy requires strong, healthy horizontal ties, bridging social capital, the rule of law, and transparency in order to thrive. Clientelism – with its invisible vertical lines of control, slavish dependence upon the powerful, induced passivity, and fatalism – constitutes an additional obstacle against which democracy is developing in Argentina and an alternative loyalty against which democratic values struggle to emerge today.

The empirical data on political values in Argentina will demonstrate that both of these non-democratic alternatives – dictatorship and clientelism – compete against democratic values, with reasonable or strong followings among

[9] Linz and Stepan (1996, esp. chap. 3).

Argentina's citizens. While the authoritarianism of the military years does not today enjoy an extensive following, the military Proceso government and its legacy still had some supporters in 1997. The more significant competitor to democracy, however, is clientelism, partly because of its much greater following and partly because of its insidious subtlety, its ability to disguise itself behind popular and electoral support, and its capacity to deliver real goods. Clientelism competes with democracy by undermining political institutions and processes that would otherwise allow problems to be solved in an open and transparent manner. It also encourages individualistic self-help responses to problems, rather than cooperative self-help mechanisms which foster bridging social capital.[10]

Political Values
Again, we begin with historical data. These were collected in 1997 during the Peronist government of Carlos Menem. That year is comparable to the year 1996 in Nicaragua: By 1997 Argentina had lived under democracy for fourteen years. The military government that ended in 1983 was a living memory for many of these respondents while the Radical government of 1983–1989 was also a recent recollection. As in Nicaragua, therefore, the data were collected at a point in time when three very different governments were part of the recent past and the current moment: military authoritarianism (1976–1983); a liberal democratic, Radical government (1983–1989); and clientelistic Peronism (from 1989 to the point at which the data were collected). Unfortunately, partisanship is not available for this survey.[11] However, a number of other angles on political values are available for analysis. One important variable is, occupational status which, in Argentina, is closely related to partisanship. Most workers are Peronists. This section explores a data set of 1000 respondents drawn from five major Argentine cities: Buenos Aires, Cordoba, Rosario, Mendoza, and Santa Fé, as well as from Buenos Aires province. These cities are among Argentina's largest and economically most important.

As in the Nicaraguan survey, Argentines were asked which of the nation's recent regimes they most preferred. The question revealed the extent to which

---

[10] Schonwalder and Gerd, (2002). The tension between clientelism and democracy has been explored extensively in the case of Mexico. Jonathan Fox (1994; 2008), for example, argues that clientelism undermines accountability which is a fundamental requirement of democracy. Similarly, Susan Eckstein (1989) has argued that clientelism was a fundamental pillar of the authoritarian system in Mexico. Where clientelism exists simultaneous with an electoral calendar, this is not evidence of any compatibility between clientelism and democracy. Rather, it is evidence of the incomplete, problematic, and developing nature of democracy or even of de-democratization. Tilly (2007).

[11] Partisanship is unavailable for analysis because most respondents declined to define themselves as identifying with or preferring either major party. Many Argentine respondents felt disgusted with both major parties at the time of the interview and responded to an initial question about partisan preference stating so. Such resistance can be overcome by constructing several probes and using them in the questionnaire. The use of probes uncovered partisanship in the La Matanza neighborhood survey analyzed earlier but was not done for the nationwide survey.

authoritarianism and clientelism compete with liberal democracy as the regime of choice. Respondents were specifically asked which government they preferred to live under. Their choices were five: a military regime, the Radical governments of Ilia and Frondizi, the Peronist government of 1973–1976, the Radical government of Alfonsin (1983–1989) or the then-current Peronist government of Carlos Menem (1989–1999). Responses were then grouped into three categories: a military government (authoritarianism), a Peronist government (clientelism), or a Radical government (liberal democracy).

These three categories are imperfect. A Peronist government operates with some aspects of liberal democracy, such as elections. By the same token, clientelism exists in some parts of Argentina's political system under any government. Some non-democratic practices existed under Radicalism. For example, Frondizi and Ilia were elected while Peronism was proscribed as a political party, although Peronists were allowed to vote. Proscription was not a liberal democratic circumstance. Despite these qualifications, these three categories offer a starting point from which to scrutinize political values in Argentina. We will see that there are significant differences in the categories of citizens who support these regimes and in the characteristics that they value in a government.

Across all respondents, 16.3% said they preferred a military regime, 49.2% preferred a Peronist regime, and 34.5% preferred a Radical regime. Nearly half of respondents preferred Peronism, despite the clientelism and disregard for democratic procedure that prevailed during both Perón's and Menem's presidencies. Equally disturbing, a significant minority preferred a military regime, despite the extensive human rights violations associated with that regime. Only about one third of respondents clearly preferred a fully liberal democratic regime, a description which most closely fits with the Radical governments which prioritized democratic procedures and processes.

The widespread preference for Peronism under Menem is interesting. Menem's government did not subjugate the Congress as fully as did Perón in the 1940s. No mobs attacked opposition party headquarters and the leader of the Radical party was not jailed. Thus Peronism under Menem was less authoritarian than it had been in the 1940s and 1950s. Yet under Menem, as under Perón himself, clientelism, vertical control, and a hierarchical leadership style predominated. Peronism's fundamental value structure was recognizably similar, and its lack of respect for democratic norms and procedures, both inside the party and within the polity, was evident in the behavior of President Menem and the party. During his presidency, Peronism's leaders relied on clientelism, secrecy, and the ability to maneuver internally bypassing democratic norms and procedures, and avoiding the transparency and institutionalized rule of law that are fundamental to democracy.[12] Despite these non-democratic practices, nearly 50% of these respondents preferred a Peronist government. We investigate the reasons for that popular preference below.

[12] Levitsky (2003).

Democracy and Its Competitors

I have argued that the geographical isolation of Argentina as a nation constituted one factor contributing to the country's ability to develop a movement with some fascist characteristics at a time when fascism was on the decline globally. Isolation from the main currents of political ideas also allowed Argentina to develop a poor people's movement only incompletely influenced by leftist ideas at a time when leftist movements were gaining strength in Europe and Latin America. National isolation thus contributed to the rise of Peronism in the first place. The data set at hand allows us to investigate individual isolation. In the public opinion data analyzed here, we will see that individual isolation contributes to a personal preference for Peronism in the contemporary period and is also associated with non-democratic values more generally. Just as horizontal ties build positive social capital and contribute to democracy, isolation that is either national or personal undermines horizontal ties and makes it much harder for democracy to work.

There are many ways in which individuals can be isolated from others in their everyday lives or from sources of new ideas or new ways of thinking. This section explores three types of isolation: social isolation in one's place of work, intellectual isolation in terms of limited exposure to education, and regional isolation. Individuals who work outside the home have less workplace isolation than those who work at home. Higher levels of education tend to open people's minds to new ideas and decrease intellectual isolation. And finally, some regions of any country are more geographically isolated than others. In the next few pages, we will investigate how different kinds of isolation have affected individual political values in the form of preferences for an authoritarian, a clientelistic, or a liberal democratic regime.

Workplace Isolation

We begin by examining the extent to which individuals work and interact on a daily basis with a large number of other people versus the extent to which social interactions are limited by their occupation. This type of isolation is partially a reflection of the physical workplace in which one spends one's time. This survey asked respondents for their occupation and reflects self-classifications. Analysis revealed a difference between the category of respondents who defined themselves as housewives and those of both genders who worked full time outside the home. I call this "workplace isolation." This is, though, an imperfect reflection of isolation since some professionals (writers, artists) may work at home, or alone, or both, and thus experience relatively little social interaction through their work while some housewives may interact socially quite often. But the distinction reflects differences in the level of daily or weekly interactions individuals have. For the purposes of this analysis, all respondents who said they were full-time or part-time students, or retired/unemployed, are excluded since they do not fit neatly into either category scrutinized here.

Figure 5.4 shows that housewives preferred a military regime or a clientelist regime in higher proportions than workers. The numbers to the right of

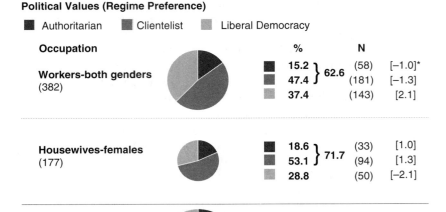

FIGURE 5.4. Regime preference by workplace isolation in Argentina.

the brackets show that 62.6% of workers but 71.7% of housewives preferred authoritarianism or clientelism. Moreover, the residuals are ≥ 2 with respect to the preference for democracy.[13] This finding is even more interesting, given that Peronism was supposed to have been a movement of the working class. This bivariate relationship is significant above the .1% confidence level in this sample.

It is important to remember that respondents who preferred a clientelist regime (any Peronist government) were selecting a regime whose president had been democratically elected and who allowed the existence of a Congress. Peronist governments in Argentina have not resorted to the level of human rights violations associated with military regimes. Thus, the preference for a clientelist regime is not the same as a preference for authoritarianism, but it is not a statement of support for a fully democratic government either. A preference for a Peronist government displays a popular willingness to accept or tolerate the multiple violations of democratic processes in which Peronism has historically engaged and in which Menem's government itself engaged in the years immediately prior to this survey.

[13] One way of seeing whether there is a statistically significant difference between cells inside a table is to examine the residuals. Residuals are given in brackets [] in Figure 5.4. Residuals that reach the level of 2.0 or higher indicate the presence of a statistically significant difference between that cell and others.

These results show the complexities of political values among Argentine citizens and underscore the weakness of liberal democratic political values. Most respondents in this analysis prefer a government that is either openly anti-democratic and authoritarian, or one that shows a willingness to disregard many aspects of democratic processes. The implications of such a finding for democratic loyalty and values in Argentina are disturbing. Finally, while the majority of respondents in this analysis show this non-democratic or partially democratic preference, those who pass their days in more isolated circumstances demonstrate this preference in higher percentages.

Education

A previous analysis in this book found a relationship between education and organizational memberships. Here we explore the relationship between educational level and preference for an authoritarian, clientelistic, or liberal democratic regime. Low levels of education, of course, are a kind of isolation, detaching the individual from new ideas and influences. Thus the examination of education is a scrutiny of intellectual or educational isolation.

There was a strong bivariate relationship between educational level and democratic values. Higher levels of education were significantly related to a declining preference for an authoritarian or a clientelistic regime. Increased levels of education were related to an increased likelihood of preferring a liberal democratic regime. The numbers to the right of the brackets in Figure 5.7 combine the percentages of those preferring an authoritarian regime with those preferring a clientelistic regime, giving a total percentage for those who preferred something other than liberal democracy for each educational group. The reader will remember from Chapter 3 the conflictual relationship Peronism has historically had both with the universities themselves and with the more educated members of Argentine society. Here we see that same historical tension reflected in public opinion. Moreover, the residuals in Figure 5.5 are strong, indicating that there are statistically significant differences between the cells as well as for the bivariate relationship overall (p = 0.000).

In considering the previous two figures (5.6 and 5.7) and the preferences of the working class and the less educated for clientelism or authoritarianism, one is reminded of Seymour Martin Lipset's argument that the lower classes are more authoritarian in their political values.[14] Here we see support for that argument in statistically significant differences. Whether class status is reflected in working class occupation or in lower educational levels, or, as is probably the case, in both, the affinity for some form of non-democratic or less democratic regime is present, at least in this national sample. We know from the Nicaraguan case that low-income citizens are not necessarily authoritarian in their belief systems and may even be among the most progressive members of society. In situations where the rhetoric of horizontal ties and bridging social capital have defined a poor people's movement, then authoritarianism is

---

[14] Lipset (1960); Lewis (1961); Adorno et al. (1969).

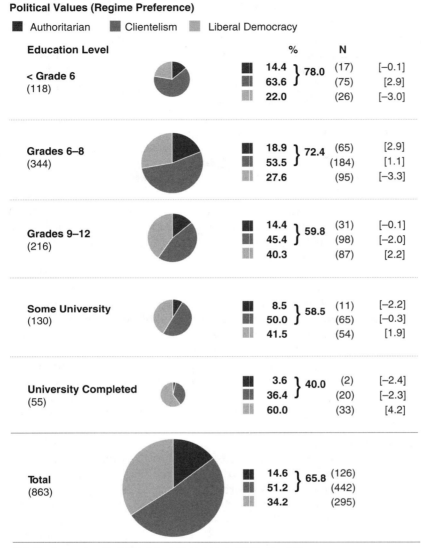

FIGURE 5.5. Political values in regime choice in Argentina by education.

more likely to be associated with the upper classes, as it occurs in Nicaragua. But where a movement favoring the poor, at least ostensibly or initially, has historically used a rhetoric of blame, victimization, and conspiracy, there can be an association between authoritarianism and the lower class. Argentina exemplifies this connection. A critical question for democratic development in

Argentina will be whether democratic values can spread themselves more fully among those who prefer and lead the Peronist party.

It is interesting to note that a bivariate relationship between income and democratic values was not significant, nor was there a direct relationship between rising income and decreasing preference for clientelism. (This relationship is not shown here.) This can be explained by the fact that Peronism has always had a dual appeal to the wealthy as well as to the poor, a by-product of its lack of consistent, defining ideology. Once Perón's charismatic ability to hold together two groups whose interests are diametrically opposed was gone, and once Menemism came to dominate Peronism (the time when these surveys were carried out), the party's support for the wealthy emerged more clearly. Menem's government pursued policies favoring big business and the upper class; it weakened the power of the unions; and, at the same time, it still relied on the emotional bond of the working class with Peronism.[15] In the Menem years, those who had more money to start with made a great deal of money, and as a consequence the gap between the rich and the poor widened. Therefore, when respondents were asked whether they preferred a Peronist government, large percentages of wealthy respondents showed as much Peronist loyalty as the working class, which made the relationship between income and Peronist preference statistically in significant. In the case of the Menem government, wealthy respondents who preferred it were reflecting a logical and self-interested preference, while low-income respondents who gave the same response were answering out of emotional loyalty and tradition.

The educational levels examined here reflect intellectual isolation just as the working class categories reveal workplace isolation. We find that intellectual isolation is related to higher authoritarian values and lower democratic values. Putnam has argued that the social capital built by bridging ties among individuals facilitates democracy. Here we find independent empirical evidence for that argument. Argentine citizens who are isolated from others – either by virtue of a socially isolated job as a housewife, or by the intellectual isolation of never having received much education – are significantly more inclined toward non-democratic or less democratic political values, and have a preference for clientelism or authoritarianism. Personal experiences that facilitate social interaction, by contrast – either higher educational levels or a job that allows the individual to interact with others – are related to higher democratic values.

Regional Isolation

Many historical considerations of Argentina's political and social development emphasize the division between the capital city of Buenos Aires and the

---

[15] The reader will remember that a key component in the popular appeal of many populist movements, including the fascist populisms, is a reliance on emotional appeal. Such emotional attachment and loyalty comes to dominate reason and rational motives for supporting a movement. Hermet (2001, p. 16).

rest of the country.[16] Observers have argued that Buenos Aires is a cosmopolitan, developed center exposed to advanced ideas and sometimes connected to the political and social thought of Europe, while the interior of the country has always been more isolated, backward, and cut off from modern ideas.[17] The data set at hand scrutinizes the cities of Cordoba, Rosario, Mendoza, and Santa Fe, as well as the city of Buenos Aires and its surrounding province. If it is true that isolation is associated with lower democratic values, we should find evidence for that argument in regional differences as well. We would expect to find higher non-democratic political values – expressed in preferences for non-democratic or less democratic regimes – and a lower preference for a Radical government outside of the capital city. The opposite would be true in Buenos Aires proper.

One question of relevance for a regional analysis is whether respondents from the province of Buenos Aires but outside of the city of Buenos Aires have opinions more closely related to those from the capital city or that more closely resemble the opinions found among respondents in the provincial cities. Statistical analysis answered this question definitively. A bivariate equation subdividing public opinion into three regional categories – Buenos Aires city, Buenos Aires province, and the provincial cities – revealed almost no differences whatsoever between the political values of respondents living in Buenos Aires province and those living in the provincial cities.[18] Because the political values of Buenos Aires province residents and provincial city residents are so similar, the more interesting subdivision of the sample is into two groups: residents of Buenos Aires city itself and residents of either Buenos Aires province or the provincial cities.

Figure 5.6 shows that there is a strong relationship between political values and place of residence. Respondents who lived outside the capital city showed a higher preference for a clientelistic regime and an almost 200% higher

---

[16] On the topic, see Crassweller (1987); Halperin et al. (1994); and especially Katra (1994).
[17] Part of the reason for the isolation of Argentina's interior provinces is geographical. Solberg (1987) has argued that, unlike the United States, Argentina's interior was not made easily accessible by a network of rivers that reached far into the interior of the heartland. Likewise, Crassweller (1987) maintains that this divide between urban Buenos Aires and the rural rest of Argentina constitutes one of the most fundamental and influential divisions in the nation's history and one that plays itself out politically, socially, and economically.
[18] Among Buenos Aires province residents, those who preferred a military regime were 17.0% while those from the provincial cities were 17.3%; residents of Buenos Aires city who preferred a military government were only 8.7%. Similarly, among Buenos Aires province residents, those who preferred a Peronist government were 54.7% and those from the provincial cities preferring a Peronist government were 54.2%. Those from Buenos Aires city who preferred a Peronist government were 44.1%. And those from Buenos Aires province who preferred a Radical government were 28.3% while the comparable percentage for the provincial cities was 28.5%. Among Buenos Aires city residents, 47.2% preferred a Radical government. The Chi Square statistic for the 3x3 bivariate equation was .000 but, for reasons of space, I do not show the equation here. Since the percentage point differences of opinion between Buenos Aires province residents and provincial city residents were minute, in Figure 5.8 I collapsed these two groups into one category, "Provinces," and I show that equation instead.

Democracy and Its Competitors

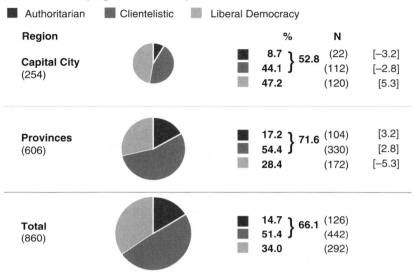

Note: ( ) = Raw numbers [ ] = Adjusted standardized residuals Chi Square = .000.
Totals may not equal 100% because of rounding.
Source: Nationwide survey across 5 cities and Buenos Aires province, October, 1997, taken by Mori Argentina.

FIGURE 5.6. Political values in regime choice in Argentina by region.

preference for an authoritarian regime, while more residents of the capital city preferred a liberal democratic regime. This bivariate relationship between democratic values and region is statistically significant, but the residuals in this figure are also quite strong, indicating that there is a significant difference between cells within the figure. The evidence is that regional isolation, like workplace or intellectual isolation, is also associated with non-democratic or less democratic values.

These results reflect Argentine history as well. Lower preferences for an authoritarian regime inside of Buenos Aires city are partially a reflection of the fact that military repression, particularly during the recent Proceso government (1976–1983), fell more heavily on the population of Buenos Aires city than it did on the populations of the interior.[19] Likewise, the results show that provincial residents would be less likely to reject an authoritarian regime. This is consistent with the fact that, while the repressive aspects of Peronism were more evident in Buenos Aires than they were in the more far-flung provinces, Perón, himself, deliberately courted provincial residents, visiting the provinces, throwing candy and toys, granting voting rights, and making former territories into national provinces with electoral access.

[19] The exception to this is the secondary city of La Plata, the location of an important university. Military repression in La Plata was severe.

Since history has contributed to the presence of higher democratic values in Buenos Aires city, the capital city may well provide the nation's impetus toward democracy, with the interior provinces and cities following the lead of the nation's capital. This is also the same path followed by other progressive ideas in the history of Argentina.[20] The regional analysis also provides guidance for policy experts who wish to increase democratic political values in Argentina. Such policy would need to focus on the provinces, including both the region around the capital and the interior cities, and could, for example, provide greater educational access – because higher educational levels are associated with an increased preference for a liberal democratic regime.

Beyond the occupational, educational, and regional differences found here, this examination of political values in Argentina reveals a moderate to high preference for authoritarianism and clientelism. It shows, as well, a high tolerance for governments that bypassed democratic processes wherever possible, particularly when those same governments delivered economic goods and appealing social policies. And it shows only a limited support for liberal democracy and, consequently, for democratic institutions and processes. The smaller group that preferred a government committed to democratic rules and procedures included the more educated and the residents of Buenos Aires city.

My findings coincide with those of another political analyst. In an earlier study drawing upon public opinion from the years immediately prior to and just after the end of the military regime in 1983, Edgardo Catterberg found deep authoritarian values among Argentine citizens, including a propensity to dismiss opinions different from ones own, and a tendency to think that those who disagreed (with oneself) should not be allowed to voice their opinions. Collected during a time strongly influenced by a severely authoritarian government, Catterberg's data might have reflected the time period rather than true political values among Argentines.[21] The data analyzed here come from a much later period and one that follows upon fourteen years of democracy. Nevertheless, this study also uncovers a deep reservoir of support for non-democratic politics among Argentine respondents. These findings illustrate the obstacles that democracy faces in Argentina. Not only does it struggle to take root in a nation that has frequently engaged in non-democratic politics at the state level; it also seeks to survive in a country where many citizens displayed either authoritarian political values or a preference for clientelism, even after fourteen years of democratically elected governments. These findings reveal the extent to which Peronism in 1997 still held a firm grip on popular political loyalties, despite its clientelistic and vertical mechanisms of operation and its very limited commitment to democratic rules, procedures, and institutions.

Nevertheless, the values uncovered by these data and the difficulties they portend for the establishment of democracy should not be considered fixed

---

[20] For example, Buenos Aires city was the first to embrace the Radical Party and its demands for universal male suffrage and rotation in power in accordance with the male vote.
[21] Catterberg, (1991).

or permanent. Collected in 1997 during a Peronist government, but at a time when public opinion had begun to turn against Menem, the data are a snapshot of public opinion at one particular moment in Argentine history. Despite the preferences for non-democratic regimes that habitually ignored democratic rules and institutions, the nation had, at that point, abided by an electoral calendar for fourteen years. Moreover, after 1997 and moving into the 21st century, Argentina was soon to enter a period of profound economic crisis and yet retain its electoral schedule. These are significant accomplishments for any new democracy. They are even more significant where democratic values are still so limited and preferences for other types of regimes so widespread.

Now we will consider a multivariate model examining workplace isolation, regional isolation, and education in relationship to political values. While each has a significant bivariate relationship to democratic values, we cannot know which among them is strongest unless we include all of them simultaneously in a regression equation (Table 5.3).

The reader will remember from the discussion above that multinomial regression analysis operates on the basis of probabilities, using the last category of each variable (dependent and independent alike) as a baseline against which to compare the probabilities of all the other relationships. It then individually compares the probability of the relationship between each subcategory of each independent variable with each subcategory of the dependent variable, and thus obtains a coefficient of probability of that relationship, as opposed to the baseline relationship.

In this equation, the first independent variable, workplace isolation, is not significant, either with respect to preferring a military government or with respect to preferring a clientelist regime over a liberal democratic regime. Occupational circumstance becomes less important in determining political values when included in an equation with both education and region. Region was always significant in this equation. Capital city residents were less likely to prefer authoritarianism by a coefficient of -1.015 (p=.004) and were less likely to prefer a clientelistic regime by coefficient of $-.512$ (p=.02). Education was always significant with respect to preference for a military government, (authoritarianism), or a Peronist government (clientelism) and respondents who had lower levels of education (grades 8 and below) were significantly more likely to prefer either an authoritarian or a clientelistic regime with respect to preferring a clientelist regime.

With respect to region, the baseline comparison is "the provinces," and the analysis grouped into this category residents of all the cities other than Buenos Aires and the province surrounding Buenos Aires. We see that residents of Buenos Aires are less likely than provincial residents to prefer authoritarianism, as opposed to liberal democracy, by a coefficient of -1.015 (p = .004) and less likely than provincial residents to support a Peronist government, as opposed to a Radical government by a coefficient of $-.512$ (p = .02). Region is a powerful determinant of non-democratic political values or of tolerance for a clientelistic government.

TABLE 5.3. *Argentina: Multinomial Regression Analysis: Dependent Variable = Political Values*

Dependent Variable	Independent Variables	Beta coef	Sig Level	Exp(B)
Authoritarian Regime	Intercept	−19.894	.000	
	Workplace Isolation			
	Worker	1.270E-02	.965	1.013
	Housewife	0		
	Education			
	< Grade 6	20.016	.000	4.9E+08
	Grades 6–8	19.822	.000	4.1E+08
	Grades 9–12	19.563	.000	3.1E+08
	Some Univ	18.346	.000	9.3E+07
	Univ Complete	0		
	Region			
	Capital City	−1.015	.004	.362
	Provinces	0		
Clientelist Regime	Intercept	1.044E-02	.978	
	Workplace Isolation			
	Worker	−.104	.640	.901
	Housewife	0		
	Education			
	< Grade 6	1.278	.007	3.591
	Grades 6–8	.818	.022	2.266
	Grades 9–12	.529	.138	1.697
	Some Univ	.242	.525	1.274
	Univ Complete			
	Region			
	Capital City	−.512	.020	.600
	Provinces			

Note: −2 log likelihood = 188.891; Sig level = .000.
Nagelkerke Pseudo R squared = .116.
Source: Nationwide survey across 5 cities and Buenos Aires province, October, 1997, taken by MoriArgentina.

This model illustrates that the strongest independent variable in the top part of the table is education, where it has both the strongest levels of significance and the largest coefficients. Low educational levels are an even stronger predictor of authoritarian political values than of clientelistic political values. The table shows that each educational category is more likely to support authoritarianism than is the educational category just above it so that every category increase in educational level decreases the propensity toward authoritarianism and increases democratic values.

The same direction of relationship appears with respect to clientelism, although the difference between university attenders and grade levels of 9 and

Democracy and Its Competitors

above were not statistically significant. Less educated respondents are more likely to prefer clientelism and more educated respondents are more likely to prefer liberal democracy. Each category increase in education was associated with a decreasing likelihood of supporting clientelism, as opposed to liberal democracy, and by a smaller and smaller coefficient. This indicates that the difference between the probability preference of university graduates for liberal democracy and that of other educational categories declines with rising educational levels. Each educational category is slightly less likely to support clientelism and slightly more likely to support a government that espouses democratic values than the educational category just below it. The lowest educational category (incomplete grade school) has a positive coefficient of 1.278 (p = .007), indicating that this least educated group is by far the group most likely to support clientelism.

One conclusion emerges from the multinomial regression analysis that is similar to conclusions from the bivariate analysis: at the time of this survey, democratic values were limited in Argentina. Multinomial regression analysis does not produce an R2 or predicted level so we do not know the predictive power of the model. We can say, however, that both residence outside of the capital city and low educational levels are associated with lower democratic values. We can say as well that the value of education and region is greater with respect to predicting authoritarianism than it is in predicting a preference for clientelism. The differences in probability preference between a clientelistic and a liberal democratic regime are small, but significant.

Although these findings reveal uncomfortably high levels of preference for an authoritarian regime and high tolerance for clientelism in Argentina, they also uncover several avenues for public policy intervention to increase democratic values. Education levels and provincial isolation can be directly and intentionally addressed through public policy. Bringing education, particularly beyond grade school level, to all Argentines, as well as developing the interior of the nation, would both increase democratic values and could be done in a relatively short period of time.

The image given here of limited support for democracy found among Argentines is disturbing. Yet were Argentines really as unconcerned about democracy as these results appear to indicate? What political values were Argentines expressing when they said they preferred a specific kind of regime? The question is particularly relevant for respondents who said they preferred a Peronist government. Fortunately, the Argentine survey allows us to answer that question. Respondents who said they preferred a specific regime were also given a closed-ended question asking about their first and second choice reasons for that preference. Their choices were: (1) because it respected human rights and democratic procedures; (2) because of its ethics or lack of corruption; (3) because of its social policies; (4) because of its economic policies; or (5) because it maintained order. Figure 5.7 shows the results for this question across all respondents.

The data in Figure 5.7 are contradictory, as is Argentine public opinion itself. On the one hand, in 1997 Argentines displayed modest support for an

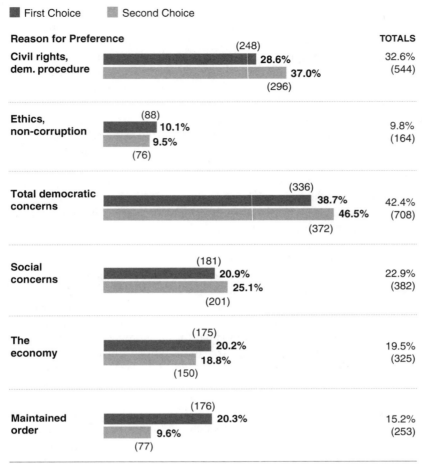

FIGURE 5.7. Argentina: reasons for preferring a government – first and second choice reasons, by percentage.

authoritarian regime and high support for clientelism. On the other hand, human rights and democratic procedure were the top reasons they gave for their government preference. The regime preferences and the priorities are in contradiction to each other. The contradiction reflects both the ambivalent nature of Peronism itself and the unconsolidated nature of Argentine democracy at that time.

Peronism in its original formulation was not committed to democratic rules and institutions. Menem's more recent Peronist government, and the government in power at the time of this survey, also circumvented many democratic rules and subverted democratic institutions. Yet, as discussed in Chapter 3,

Democracy and Its Competitors

Peronism's relationship to democracy is complex and not only hostile. Even in its original decade, Peronism held two national elections, included the Congress in those elections, and kept the Congress open. Today, as in the 1940s, Peronism follows a contradictory mixture of clientelistic practices and verticalism combined in an uneasy coexistence with electoral practices. There is a battle currently raging within Peronism over whether or not the party will continue to be clientelistic and verticalist or whether it will modernize, open itself to the light of day, and behave as an electoral party, responsive to its base both internally and within the population at large. Some Peronists would like to see the party democratize, while Menem and others, who are comfortable with vertical control over secondary leaders and followers, prefer the traditional ways. The struggle within Peronism was exemplified in the 2003 election where two Peronist candidates opposed each other and Menem spent more energy opposing reformist Peronist Nestor Kirchner than he did the opposition party candidate. With the recent victory of Kirchner's wife, Cristina, a more reformist brand of Peronism may be gaining the upper hand, but at the expense of party rotation in office and with an undercurrent of nepotism. Additionally, with the passage of time, the Kirchners have become more verticalist and authoritarian in their own control of the party.

What political values were respondents expressing when they said they preferred a Peronist government? Were they ignoring the party's anti-democratic patterns and accepting hierarchical control and clientelism because, through those channels, the Peronist party delivered economic goods to followers? Or were they concentrating on the strong role Peronism played in curbing the military after the return to democracy and upon Menem's willingness to jail officers who attempted to overthrow his government? Why did respondents prefer a Peronist or any other government?

Figure 5.8 helps answer these questions and is very useful for our understanding of political values in Argentina. It shows the correlation between preferring any given type of regime and prioritizing democratic concerns versus other types of concerns. The figure shows both the strength of democratic values among these respondents and the limits to concerns about democratic procedure, civil rights, and ethics in Argentina. It shows which types of regimes are preferred by those who prioritize democracy and democratic concerns. It also reveals the complex relationship between Peronism and democracy, and shows what level of priority Peronists place on civil rights and democratic procedure.

In the darkest bars of the graph in Figure 5.8 we see the political values of respondents who preferred a military regime. While this group is the smallest subset of the respondent pool, their reasons for preferring authoritarianism have little to do with democracy. Nearly half of this group preferred an authoritarian government because it maintained order and only 23.6% combined gave reasons of civil rights, democratic procedure, or ethics as either their first or second choice reason for preferring a military regime. These figures show that most of these citizens know very well what they are getting

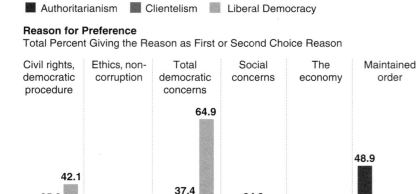

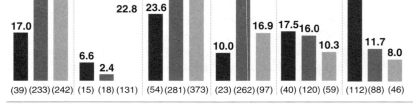

FIGURE 5.8. Argentina: reasons for preferring a government among respondents who preferred....

when they say they prefer a military regime: they are getting a government that will impose order but that has no regard for democratic process, and little concern for the state of the economy or for social concerns like poverty. In Argentine history, these priorities are precisely what military regimes have delivered and, at least at the time of this survey, they still had their strong minority of followers among the Argentine population.

The other group that showed the clearest and least confusing political values was the group that preferred a liberal democratic government, shown in the third column of Figure 5.8. Citizens who said they preferred a Radical regime (the lightest bar in Figure 5.8) clearly prioritized democratic concerns, with more than two thirds of them (64.9%) giving this preference because of the attention this type of regime shows to democratic procedure, civil rights, or ethics. Across all three columns, this group is the one that shows the highest level of democratic values, a finding in keeping with the history of Radicalism in power. We can conclude from looking at the darkest and lightest bars in the graph of Figure 5.8 that democratic values are highest among respondents who prefer liberal democracy and lowest among respondents who prefer an authoritarian regime.

The most complex set of empirical results is found in the third bars of the various categories in Figure 5.8. Among respondents who preferred a clientelistic regime, slightly more than one third (37.4%) said they did so for reasons of democratic procedure, civil rights and ethics! This type of answer is partially contradictory, given Peronism's inconsistent support for democratic procedure. But Peronism did actually respect some aspects of democratic procedure, so the answer is not completely contradictory. More easily understood and in closer correspondence with Peronism's history is the large percentage of respondents who said they preferred a Peronist government because of its social or economic policies. A total of 50.9% of respondents (34.6 + 16.0) gave these two responses as their first or second choice reasons for preferring a clientelist regime.

Respondents who preferred a clientelist regime are clearly not unconcerned about democracy. Yet the percentage of them who prioritize democratic concerns is much lower than that same percentage among respondents preferring a liberal democratic government. In comparison with the other two groups, the democratic values of Peronist supporters lie somewhere in between those of authoritarians and Radicals. Peronist supporters are much less concerned about democracy than are Radicals, but they are considerably more concerned about it than are authoritarians. We explore this preference for clientelism in greater detail in the next chapter.

We are correct to be concerned about the low level of democratic values among Argentine citizens. And we are also correct to correlate that low level of democratic values with support for Peronism. Figure 5.8 provides empirical evidence of a connection between support for a clientelistic Peronist regime and a lower level of concern about democratic process. For most of these respondents, the preference for Peronism was a clear-eyed and consistent preference for what it is that the party offers: an expressed concern for the poor, a strong economy, and an orderly society but not necessarily a government that adheres to democratic norms, procedures and institutions. But the correlation is not perfect and there is, among Peronists, a significant minority of citizens who prefer a Peronist regime and who *are also concerned* about democratic procedures, civil rights, and ethics. These individuals are caught within the inner contradictions of Peronism itself. They may well be more focused on social concerns and economic policy than are the other two groups in our sample, and the empirical evidence shows that they are. Yet they are unwilling to prioritize economic and social concerns at the expense of democratic procedure.

This personal conflict is also the conflict that is currently emerging within the Peronist party itself. At the time of this survey in 1997, Peronism had delivered a sound economy and an orderly civil society, while following some democratic procedures and circumventing many others. Within a few short years of this survey, all of that would change. Argentina's economy crashed and the Peronist role in that crash was clear to many Argentines, if not to all. Citizens responded in 2002 and 2003 by rejecting Menem, even if they did not reject the Peronist party itself.

Subsequently, citizens turned toward what they hoped would be a different version of Peronism, the leftist and reformist side of the party. Elected president in 2003, Nestor Kirchner is a Peronist. But he defined his career in opposition to former President Carlos Menem, who represents the traditional, charismatic, clientelistic, corporatist Peronism of Perón himself. The 2007 election of Cristina Kirchner, Nestor's wife, *may* mark a continuation of a more reformist brand of Peronism with respect to economic policy and overt attention to human rights. However, the Kirchners appear to be at least as autocratic as was Menem – and this is even more true of Cristina than it was of Nestor. The election of the Kirchners brought hopes that there would be a gradual process of democratization inside Peronism, moving government by the party beyond the pronounced clientelism and lawlessness of the Menem years. But greater attention to democratic procedure does not appear to be the style of the Kirchner presidencies any more than it was Menem's style. That reality leaves the empirical evidence from Figure 5.8 as internally contradictory now as it was in 1997.

It is also the case that citizens learn what their values and priorities are by living through different regimes. Argentine citizens may be learning what they value and this survey may be only a snapshot of the past, a point from which Argentines have learned in the years and crises since. Today citizens may expect Peronism to deliver social goods and a sound economy *while also* respecting democratic institutions and procedures. Peronism may now be trying to respond to such popular demands.

CONTEMPORARY ASSESSMENTS OF POLITICAL VALUES

Let us step back from the individual country data and reexamine political values in both Nicaragua and Argentina. We have seen that there were significant differences in political values between these countries in the late 1990s when memories of authoritarianism were vivid. What differences still exist today? Recent Latinobarometro data provide some answers. In this section we examine four questions asked in 2007, which reflect the value that citizens place on democracy.

1. Is democracy preferable to any other kind of government?
2. Does the government seek the welfare (bienestar) of the people?
3. How much confidence do you have in the government?
4. How satisfied are you with democracy?

These questions offer a broad comparison of the value placed by citizens on democratic governance and in the democratic government more generally. For the purposes of this study, we are fortunate that Sandinismo and Peronism were the political parties in power in 2007. In Nicaragua, Daniel Ortega had won the presidency in 2006 and had been president for about one year when these data were collected. In Argentina, Nestor Kirchner was president. The data below reflect public opinion in these two countries while the popular parties of historical importance were in power (Figure 5.9).

The differences between these two countries were not as pronounced in 2007 as they were in the late 1990s. In both countries the vast majority of

Democracy and Its Competitors

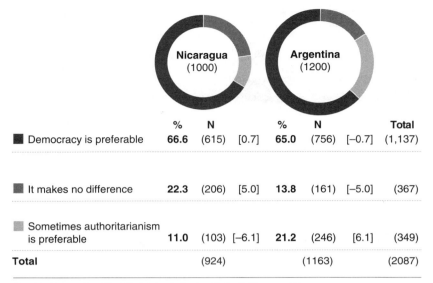

FIGURE 5.9. Is democracy preferable to any other kind of government?

respondents preferred democracy – in the first row the percentages who gave that answer in both nations are roughly similar. The bottom row tells a different story and fits with the 1996/1997 data. In 2007 more than 20% of Argentine respondents said that authoritarianism was sometimes preferable, while only 11% of Nicaraguans gave that answer. The figure reflects both progress toward democratic values in Argentina and a lingering authoritarianism there.

The second and third questions examined here address citizen confidence in the government that was in power at the time of the survey – a Sandinista government in Nicaragua and a Peronist government in Argentina. Respondents were offered four alternative responses: Do you fully agree? Agree somewhat? Disagree somewhat? Or totally disagree? The answers indicate that Nicaraguan respondents had more confidence in their government than did Argentines.

Figure 5.10 shows that Nicaraguans had more confidence in the Sandinista government of Ortega while Argentines had less confidence in the Peronist government of Cristina Kirchner. The combined positive responses indicate that 64.4% of Nicaraguans responded positively to this question while only 43.8% of Argentines did the same. By contrast, 56.2% of Argentines did not think the government sought the overall well-being of the people, while only 35.6% of Nicaraguan respondents gave a negative response. In a different question about overall satisfaction with democracy (not graphed here), 44.7% of Nicaraguan respondents said they were either very satisfied or somewhat

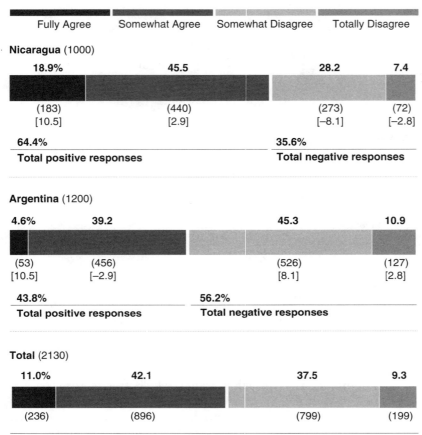

FIGURE 5.10. Does the government seek the welfare (bienestar) of the people?*

satisfied with democracy, while only 33.7% of Argentine respondents gave the same response (p = .000). Insofar as this question is a reflection of democratic values, such values were still higher in Nicaragua in 2007 than they were in Argentina.

CONCLUSION

This chapter has taken the first step toward tracing an empirical connection between social capital and democracy. The differences in social capital that we found in Chapter 4 are clearly reflected in differences in support for democracy and democratic values in the two nations. We can conclude, therefore, that social capital is indeed related to political values and that different kinds of social capital within a nation are associated with different political values, including differences in support for alternative versions of democracy and support for different kinds of non-democratic or partially democratic regimes.

Let us summarize the findings thus far. Both nations show an important reservoir of support for a non-democratic or less democratic regime. In Nicaragua, support for a non-democratic or less democratic regime is associated with being a Liberal, while Sandinistas are more likely to support a liberal or a radical democratic regime. In Argentina, higher levels of support for a liberal democratic regime were correlated with working outside the home, having a higher level of education, and living in the city of Buenos Aires. Peronists were in the middle, less concerned about issues of democratic process than those who preferred a liberal democratic regime, but more concerned about such issues than authoritarians. In the late 1990s when non-democratic and socialist regime alternatives were part of the recent past, democratic values were stronger in Nicaragua. When we review democratic values in each nation in contemporary times, again we find democratic values to be stronger in Nicaragua. Nicaraguans are somewhat more satisfied with democracy as a form of government and they have more confidence in the government in power. The next chapter will review how these differences in political values are reflected in political participation and in citizen support for democratic institutions and procedures.

6

Participation, Democratic Institutions, and Procedures

> ...we do not say that a man who takes no interest in politics is a man who minds his own business; we say that he has no business here at all.
> *Pericles' Funeral Oration, on Athenian Democracy*

> Political institutions have moral as well as structural dimensions. A society with weak political institutions lacks the ability to curb the excesses of personal and parochial desires.
> *Samuel Huntington*[1]

We move now to take a second step in tracing the empirical connection between social capital and democracy. Since, as we saw in Chapter 5, different kinds of social capital are associated with different democratic values, what difference does that make with respect to political action and attitudes about democracy's institutions and procedures? This chapter answers those questions. It is divided into three sections: political participation, support for democratic institutions, and support for democratic procedures.

The empirical bases for this chapter are several. We begin by returning to our two neighborhood data bases: Bello Horizonte in Nicaragua and La Matanza in Argentina. Those data scrutinize the specifics of political participation and do so across party lines, as well as allowing a contrast across the two nations studied here. We then continue the analysis with national data bases drawn from the Latinobarometer study. That contrast reproduces the historical perspective used in Chapter 5. The national samples begin with the late 1990s and draw upon the Latinobarometer study for 1997. We then contrast the 1997 findings with Latinobarometer data for 2007.

POLITICAL PARTICIPATION

Democrats want citizens to participate in politics. It is the essence of democracy and the linguistic foundation of the word. This desire for citizen participation goes back to the first democracy of ancient Greece. But the nature of citizen participation is as important as the fact of it. Democracy demands

---

[1] Huntington (1968, p. 24)

Participation, Democratic Institutions, and Procedures

citizen involvement and participation but it also needs citizen trust, both in the polity, in its institutions and processes, and in each other. Participation must be based in trust. For if citizens do not trust each other, they will not willingly follow democratic rules because they will not believe that they can survive to participate another day after losing on the first day or in the first round. The nature of citizen participation will depend both on social trust and on political values within society. This section explores the presence or absence of political participation, itself a reflection of political trust and democratic values in Nicaragua and Argentina. We begin the task of connecting the findings about social capital in Chapter 4 with data on political action and values. We ask what additional differences there are within and across these two societies with respect to political activism and values.[2]

We know from the previous chapter that, within our neighborhood samples, Nicaraguans are more inclined than Argentines to build horizontal ties among each other and join organizations. Social capital theory tells us that these horizontal ties themselves contribute directly to democracy. Yet such an argument *assumes* that those more inclined to associate with each other formally and informally are also more likely to engage in political action. It does not test that connection empirically. We now take our first step toward investigating whether those who are more likely to associate with each other are also more likely to engage in political action. We begin with the Nicaraguan neighborhood of Bello Horizonte. We know that Sandinistas are more likely to belong to formal organizations of various kinds. In addition to asking respondents about organizational involvement, these two neighborhood surveys also asked respondents about different kinds of political activism. The questions asked were as follows: In the last year have you

1. worked for a political party?
2. worked for any other kind of organization?[3]
3. attended a political meeting?
4. attended a political rally or demonstration?
5. written or visited a legislator?
6. written or visited any other politician?
7. signed a petition?
8. written or called the newspaper or any other news media?[4]

---

[2] The argument that activist citizen participation can facilitate democratic development builds on the work of Robert A. Dahl (1971; 1998).
[3] Pilot studies in both nations revealed that citizens did not always know that their activities had or could have political effect. For example, they might have worked for a neighborhood project on services for the neighborhood but not consider the act to have been a political one. "We were just trying to get the water pump fixed." However, as political scientists, we know that all such meetings and organizations have or may have political impact and they are the very stuff of social and political capital. Accordingly, I added this second question as a probe in order to uncover any kind of organizational or cooperative work that respondents had done, regardless of whether they thought the work was political or whether it was intended as a political act.
[4] In Nicaragua many radio stations run a daily program during which time citizens call in to make complaints about common problems, talk about bread and butter issues, and discuss

We begin by exploring the bivariate relationships between these specific actions and partisan identification in our two samples. All of the questions above ask about a kind of activism that is normal within a political democracy. Yet there are also differences in the style of activism and in the directly political nature of the actions. Questions 1–4 and 7 represent a kind of mobilized activism in which participants have engaged in a politics of numbers. Such activism depends on mobilizing a group of people – sometimes a large group of people – in order to have an effect. By contrast, questions 5, 6, and 8 are forms of political activism that rely on a specific channel into power rather than on numbers to have an effect. These actions trust that a single, common citizen can speak to a person in a place of political power or visibility and have a problem addressed in that manner rather than through group action. These are representational political activities. From these eight questions we can create a total of three indices of political activism, two of which are indices of mobilized political activism and one of which is an index of representational political activism.

There are two ways to create an index of mobilized political action. One way relies on all five questions about mobilized political action; the other relies on only the four strongest indicators of mobilized activism. If we refer again to the list of eight questions above, the reader will see that, of the 5 questions about mobilized political action, four are directly political questions that ask about actions that are or would clearly be political. These four are: (In the last year) Have you worked for a political party? Attended a political meeting? Attended a political rally or demonstration? Signed a petition? Using these four questions to create a four-level index of mobilized political activism produces an index of political activism that captures the most direct and obvious kinds of political activism.

We can also create an index of mobilized political activism that also includes the question (In the last year) have you worked for any other organization? This fifth question goes to a more diverse kind of activism and tests how broadly diffuse is the influence of partisanship upon horizontal ties. So, for example, one might spend the afternoon working for a conservation organization (stuffing envelopes, making phone calls, putting up posters for an exhibit). Such a group is not a directly political group and respondents might not include it in the first four answers about directly political activities. But a respondent would probably include it in the fifth question: Did you work for any other organization? And a conservation group clearly has a political

---

local concerns. This is a tradition that began during the Sandinista years of 1979–1990 and continues today. These complaints may involve neighborhood problems that have not been addressed, repairs that are needed to the local highway, situations in which citizens think the police were abusive or impolite, instances where the municipal authorities have been unresponsive, and a variety of similar local concerns. Citizens come on the air briefly, state their complaint, and the radio programmer repeats their concern just to make certain that he/she has understood the facts correctly. These programs are designed to publicize problems citizens are having with local government and to place pressure on government to respond.

agenda so that its activities may well have a political impact. Thus, including it in an index of mobilized activism makes that index more broadly inclusive but less directly and powerfully political.

In the analysis that follows and for both neighborhood samples, I test the relationship between partisanship and both indices of mobilized political activism. The four-level index tests the relationship between partisanship and the most directly and obvious political activities; the five-level index tests the relationship between partisanship and all mobilized activities of either a directly or indirectly political sort. I also created an index of representational political activities based on questions 5, 6, and 8. The analysis that follows also tests the relationship between partisanship in each neighborhood and representational political activities.

We will start with the Nicaraguan neighborhood. In bivariate examinations of the relationship between partisanship and activism, on all but one of the activities listed above, Sandinistas were more likely to have engaged in that type of political activism than were non-Sandinistas. But let us examine activism more closely to scrutinize the more broadly or less broadly constructed indices of mobilized political activism and to scrutinize representational activism. Figure 6.1 below compares the relationship between partisanship in the Nicaraguan neighborhood and both indices of mobilized political activism.

Figure 6.1 provides several kinds of information. First, we see that citizens who have engaged in political activism in the last year constitute less than 50% of this sample with respect to both kinds of mobilized activism and representational activism (the far right column of parts A, B, and C of Figure 6.1). Modest levels of political involvement are common in any democracy where most citizens do not necessarily have time for politics. We might expect this to be even more true among low income respondents in a developing country, since they may be working long hours with little household help or conveniences in order to make ends meet. Therefore, here, as in any democracy, we are studying a minority. The questions at hand are how large that minority is across our two samples, what kinds of activism that minority undertakes, and what partisanship that minority declares. In the Nicaraguan sample that minority is sizable, and considerably higher than what we would find in established democracies. For example, as seen in part A, more than 40% (26.3 + 16.6 = 42.9%) of respondents engaged in some form of mobilized political action over the last year. This percentage reflects Nicaragua's history of mobilized citizen action. If 40% of the U.S. population engaged in mobilized political activism in a given year, we would certainly experience a dramatic change in the character of our democracy!

We see, second, that there was a statistically significant relationship between partisanship and mobilized political activism, with Sandinistas much more likely to have undertaken mobilized action in the last year. This relationship is true with respect to both the more directly political index (indicated in part B of Figure 6.1) and the index that measures political activism in a more

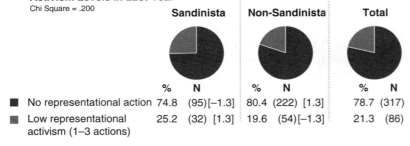

A. Index of Broadly Diffuse Mobilized Political Activism Levels in Last Year (5 level index)
Chi Square = .007

	Sandinista % N	Non-Sandinista % N	Total % N
■ No mobilized action	46.5 (59)[−2.9]	62.0 (171) [2.9]	57.1 (230)
■ Low mobilized activism (1–2 actions)	29.9 (38) [1.1]	24.6 (68)[−1.1]	26.3 (106)
▫ High mobilized activism (3–5 actions)	23.6 (30) [2.6]	13.4 (37)[−2.6]	16.6 (67)

B. Index of Directly Political Mobilized Activism Levels in Last Year (4 level index)
Chi Square = .016

	Sandinista % N	Non-Sandinista % N	Total % N
■ No mobilized action	52.8 (67)[−2.5]	65.6 (181) [2.5]	61.5 (248)
■ Low mobilized activism (1–2 actions)	24.4 (31) [0.6]	21.7 (60) [0.6]	22.6 (91)
▫ High mobilized activism (3–4 actions)	22.8 (29) [2.6]	12.7 (35)[−2.6]	15.9 (64)

C. Index of Representational Political Activism: Representational Activism Levels in Last Year
Chi Square = .200

	Sandinista % N	Non-Sandinista % N	Total % N
■ No representational action	74.8 (95)[−1.3]	80.4 (222) [1.3]	78.7 (317)
■ Low representational activism (1–3 actions)	25.2 (32) [1.3]	19.6 (54)[−1.3]	21.3 (86)

Note: ( ) = Raw numbers [ ] = Adjusted standardized residuals.
Totals may not equal 100% because of rounding.
Source: Urban Sample: Bello Horizonte, Nicaragua, 2002 (*N*=403).

FIGURE 6.1. Comparison of indices of political activism by partisanship in Nicaragua.

broad and diffuse manner (indicated in part A of Figure 6.1). The Chi Square statistics in both part A and in part B of Figure 6.1 are significant (.007 for the five-level index and .016 for the four-level index). Moreover, in both part A and part B of Figure 6.1 there are important differences between some of the cells, with adjusted standardized residuals over 2.0. At the highest and lowest levels of mobilized activism, Sandinistas look significantly different from non-Sandinistas.

This tells us that there is a relationship between partisanship and mobilized political activism, both when it is measured to capture direct political actions and when it is measured to include more broadly diffuse kinds of activism. In both instances, Sandinistas are more likely to engage in mobilized action. But the influence of Sandinismo is sufficiently strong that it can also be seen in horizontal ties and citizen activities of a less directly political nature. The influence of Sandinismo toward creating and encouraging horizontal ties is so strong that we can even see that influence when we measure political activism broadly and include kinds of activism that are only indirectly political.

Given the small size of the Nicaraguan data set, combined with the small number of individuals who engaged in representational political activism – only 21.3% of the sample –, it was difficult to discern the relationship between partisan identification and propensity toward representational political activism. However, if one compares only two levels of representational activism – no representational activism versus any level of such activism – then the relationship is visible at the .2 level. Part C of Figure 6.1 shows this relationship. This third bivariate relationship is indicative but does not reach a statistically significant level. For the most part, these Nicaraguans were uninclined to undertake representational political action, and only 21.3% of them had done so in the last year. But self-identifying Sandinistas were more likely to have engaged in representational political activism (25.2% vs. only 19.6% of non-Sandinistas). In a larger data set this difference would be statistically significant. This finding bodes well for the development of democracy in Nicaragua. Citizens who are more likely to take to the streets or to engage otherwise in mobilized forms of politics are also more likely to utilize the institutional channels of democratic process: writing to a legislator, contacting another kind of politician, or contacting the media. If mobilized politics in Nicaragua can gradually contribute to citizen participation through institutional political channels as well, then the tradition of mobilization that Nicaragua enjoys will have developed into a more stable and enduring form of institutional politics as well.

If we think back to the history of politics in Nicaragua, these empirical findings make considerable sense. Sandinismo was a highly mobilized form of political action, a social revolution that came to a society which already enjoyed some tradition of grassroots activism. The revolution then mobilized much of the population over most of the nation's geography and for a considerable length of time before taking power. After assuming state power, the revolution continued to mobilize people and relied on mobilized groups within the population as a key part of national politics during the Sandinista years. From these empirical findings it would appear that mobilization brought important lessons of empowerment to Nicaraguan citizens and became a form of politics with which they feel comfortable.

With time, the Sandinista regime also incorporated representative political bodies, particularly a legislature, that play a role in Nicaragua's democracy today.[5] Chapter 7 addresses the role of Nicaragua's legislature in detail. But representational institutions came later and more slowly, whereas mobilization was central to the revolution. Citizen political activism today reflects these patterns of political development. As the data show, even the activist Sandinistas were cautious about formal channels into power and a larger percentage of them used mobilized politics.

These findings make sense from another perspective as well. They may represent the state of Nicaraguan democracy and its level of consolidation today. In particular, these findings speak to the level of institutional consolidation, an issue we consider at greater length in Chapter 7. In new democracies, popular participation moves into political institutions only gradually and as those institutions develop. Mobilized activism, by contrast – politics in the streets, so to speak – may be easier and more natural in democracy's early years, particularly in a post-revolutionary democracy. This could be an additional explanation for the low levels of institutionalized political activism. After all, citizens *see* the results of their activism when it is mobilized. At the very least, they can see a crowd and hear a great noise, block traffic, and break rules. Representational activism carries with it no such sense of togetherness and no such heady rush. These findings about Nicaragua, a nation whose democracy cut its teeth on mobilization, tell us a great deal about the nature – and the limits – of democracy today in Nicaragua.

Let us look, now, at the same political activities within the Argentine sample. The Argentine study addressed the same eight questions about mobilized and representational activism, and I have created and tested the same three indices. Before looking at those indices, however, let us consider political activism of all kinds. If we compare the percentage from the Nicaraguan sample that engaged in any level of mobilized activism in the last year (42.9%) with the comparable percentage from the Argentine sample we find that only 20.8% of the Argentines sampled engaged in any type or level of mobilized political activism in the last year. Even before measuring the different styles of activism, this finding is important in and of itself. Just as the Nicaraguans were more likely to join organizations and to socialize informally, so they were more likely to engage in mobilized political action. This comparison provides initial support for the argument of social capital theory that those who associate with each other socially are also more likely to engage in politics.

The contrast is less marked when considering representational political activism. In these two samples, 21.3% of the Nicaraguans and 16.4% of the Argentines sampled said they had engaged in some level and some kind of representational political activism in the last year. While the Nicaraguans sampled were also more likely to use representational and institutional

---

[5] Anderson and Dodd (2002b); Anderson (2006b).

channels of political access than the Argentines, the percentage difference is less marked than it was with respect to mobilized activism.

The three indices of political activism in Argentina are shown in parts A, B, and C of Figure 6.2. Figure 6.2 provides interesting results in comparison with Figure 6.1. First, in the Argentine sample, Peronists were more likely to have engaged in mobilized political action. This relationship holds true in parts A and B of Figure 6.2. This is a fascinating finding and is living testimony to the continuing power of Peronism to mobilize followers. Yet the kinds of acts for which Peronists can be mobilized differs from the grassroots, self-directed mobilization we associate with Sandinismo. If we contrast the Chi Square statistic for part A of Figure 6.2 (.552) with the Chi Square statistic for part B of Figure 6.2 (.030) we find that only the bivariate relationship examined in part B (Directly Political Mobilized Activism) is significant. This second index includes only actions that are directly political, those more likely to result from the directives of Peronist leaders.

But when we consider a more broadly diffuse measure of political activism and an index that includes citizen actions not directly elicited by political leaders (and therefore not directly led by political leadership), then the superior capacity for mobilization among Peronists fades and the statistically significant advantage to them washes away. With respect to mobilized activism that might only have an indirect political effect, such as working for a conservation league, the need for citizens to assume the initiative and make their own decisions is more necessary. And here Peronists fall short and are lacking in such initiative. This finding corresponds to my argument that Peronism created mobilization in response to vertical leadership, but disempowered followers with respect to any capacity to initiate their own political actions or to foster horizontal ties independently of leadership.

The third interesting point in Figure 6.2 is found in part C, the bottom section of the figure. While Peronists were more likely to have engaged in mobilized activism in the last year, non-Peronists were more likely to have engaged in at least a low level of representational activism.[6] Non-Peronists are not inclined toward mobilized political activism, as measured by either index, but they are significantly more inclined to use representational political channels such as contacting a legislator, contacting another politician, or contacting the newspaper. We explore the propensity of Argentines to use institutionalized political channels in greater detail in Chapter 7. For now, however, the results of Figure 6.2 can be summarized as follows: Peronists are more likely to engage in mobilized political action *but only when such action directly*

---

[6] The third row in part C of Figure 6:2 shows Peronists more likely to have engaged in a high level of representational activity. But this difference is minute (1.9% versus 2.4%) and corresponds to a very small group of people (N = 25 out of a sample of 1200). This difference is not great enough to override the overall higher propensity of non-Peronists toward at least some level of representational action. The residuals in the final row of part C, Table 6.2 show that the difference between 1.9% and 2.4% is statistically insignificant.

180   *Social Capital in Developing Democracies*

A. Index of Broadly Diffuse Mobilized Political Activism Levels in the Last Year (5 level index)
Chi Square = .552

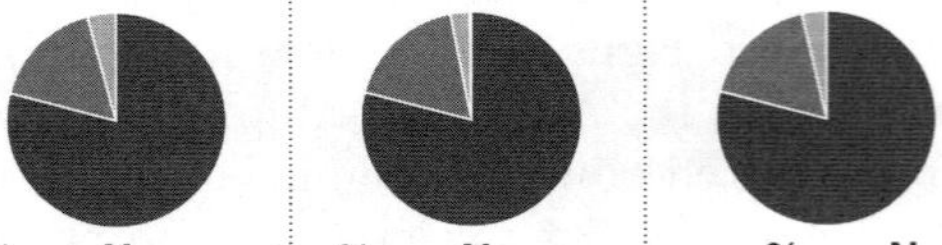

	Peronists % N	Non-Peronists % N	Total % N
■ No mobilized action	79.1 (587)[−0.1]	79.5 (360) [0.1]	79.2 (947)
▨ Low mobilized activism (1–2 actions)	16.8 (125)[−0.4]	17.7 (80) [0.4]	17.2 (205)
▤ High mobilized activism (3–5 actions)	4.0 (30) [1.1]	2.9 (13)[−1.1]	3.6 (43)

B. Index of Directly Political Mobilized Activism Levels in Last Year (4 level index)
Chi Square = .030

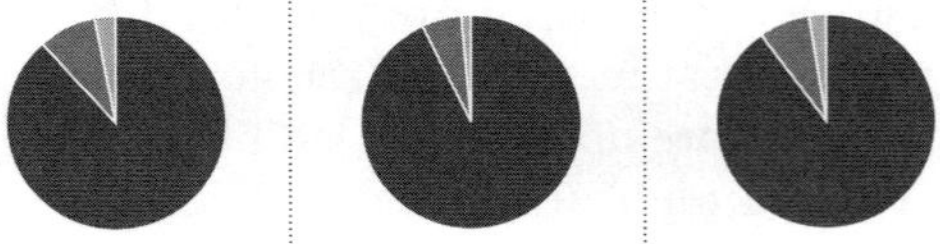

	Peronists % N	Non-Peronists % N	Total % N
■ No mobilized action	88.4 (656)[−2.5]	92.9 (421) [2.5]	90.1 (1077)
▨ Low mobilized activism (1–2 actions)	8.6 (64) [1.8]	5.7 (26)[−1.8]	7.5 (90)
▤ High mobilized activism (3–4 actions)	3.0 (22) [1.8]	1.3 (6)[−1.8]	2.3 (28)

C. Index of Representational Political Activism Levels in the Last Year
Chi Square = .001

	Peronists % N	Non-Peronists % N	Total % N
■ No representational action	86.8 (644) [3.8]	78.4 (355)[−3.8]	83.6 (999)
▨ Low representational action	11.3 (84)[−3.8]	19.2 (87) [3.8]	14.3 (171)
▤ High representational action	1.9 (14)[−0.6]	2.4 (11) [0.6]	2.1 (25)

Note: ( ) = Raw numbers [ ] = Adjusted standardized residuals.
Totals may not equal 100% because of rounding.
Source: Urban Sample: La Matanza, Argentina, 2002 (*N*=1200).

FIGURE 6.2. Indices of styles of political activism by partisanship in Argentina.

corresponds to leadership directives. Non-Peronists, when they act politically in any way at all, are more likely to use the legalized and formalized channels offered by institutional mechanisms.

If we consider popular history in these two nations, these empirical findings make sense. Like Sandinismo, Peronism was a social movement that became powerful by means of mobilizing citizens in support of the movement. While Peronism was hierarchical and accomplished mobilization through top-down directives rather than through independent, grassroots initiative, that difference does not alter the fact that it had considerable capacity to mobilize citizens in mass displays of political support. Peronist partisans now have that history as part of their political learning experience, and it is something that they can draw upon as political actors today. In fact, given the anti-institutional posture of Peronism, mobilization may be the only or the primary political experience that Peronists have or at least the one with which they feel most comfortable. And in the index of directly political mobilized activities, Peronists are superior.

Yet, unlike Sandinismo, Peronism did not encourage its supporters to think for themselves in political ways that would have a more broadly diffuse political impact in society. The broader political impact is captured by the five-level index of mobilized political activism in both Figures 6.1 and 6.2. But only among Sandinistas, trained in a movement that enhanced horizontal ties and grassroots initiative, does the effect of partisanship spread outward to more indirectly political mobilized actions. Only in Figure 6.1 does the five-level index have a statistically significant relationship to partisanship.

That broadly diffuse political effect in Nicaragua then also yields results with respect to representational political activism. There again the Sandinistas are more likely to assume the initiative and engage in politics through institutionalized channels. Non-Sandinistas are less activist in representative politics as well as in mobilized politics. By contrast, the constraining and disempowering influence of Peronism is seen both with the diffuse index of political mobilization and in the index of representational activism. In these two indices, both reflective of political actions that would emerge primarily as a result of citizen initiative, Peronists are either not highly superior or, with respect to representational activism, they clearly fall short.

Radicalism and the non-Peronist opposition in Argentina were always more oriented toward democratic institutions than was Peronism. Early Radicalism made political reality out of institutions and procedures that had previously existed in form only. Radicalism attracted its mass following by demanding real elections and an elected president. It institutionalized the first mass political party in Argentina and initiated the nation's first period of democracy. Subsequently the struggle between Radicalism and its adversaries took place inside Argentina's institutions of state. If Radicalism's power deteriorated into Yrigoyen's personalism, that did not change the fact that the original struggle had been for democracy's procedures (free elections, universal male suffrage) and institutions (a mass political party, the presidency). We see in the Argentine data that history has produced a learned political style among non-Peronists, just as Peronism has left a legacy of patterns among Peronists. Non-Peronists are more likely to take representational political actions. By contrast, Peronism had an adversarial relationship with democratic institutions and procedures. Today Peronists are less likely to contact the news media or an official political representative than are non-Peronists.

The reader will remember that the representational index includes a question asking respondents if they have contacted the newspaper in the last year. Contacting the printed media explains part of the difference in representational activism between Peronists and non-Peronists. Again, this makes sense in light of history. Peronism traditionally rejected the free press and its presentation of alternative viewpoints just as it battered the nations' institutions of higher education for the same reasons.[7] Non-Peronists and Radicals have tended to see both the written media and the universities as allies.[8] It is not surprising to find, therefore, that Peronists are less likely to contact the media than non-Peronists.

Finally, the results of these two surveys may also reflect the somewhat higher state of institutional consolidation in Argentina's democracy. While both Argentina and Nicaragua initiated their current democracies with a first election in the early 1980s, Argentina enjoyed an earlier period of democracy under Radicalism in the early part of the twentieth century while Nicaragua did not. That early period was characterized by an emphasis upon democracy's institutions and procedures. Argentina's democratic institutions have a head start over Nicaragua's, even if its current electoral calendar does not. This difference finds empirical reflection in a greater tendency toward representational and institutional activism among Argentine respondents generally, and particularly among non-Peronists. We explore this issue with respect to the legislature in Chapter 7.

These initial findings are important for our understanding of the relationship between partisanship and political activism but they are complicated with respect to the health and development of democracy in these two nations. They show that a propensity toward mobilized political activism may appear in any context where popular politics has assumed a mobilized style. It can come where there is extensive social trust, as in Nicaragua, or in a context characterized by suspicion, a lack of social trust, and weak or absent horizontal ties, as in Argentina. Mobilized politics *may* be associated with strong horizontal ties and with democratic social and political capital. But it may also simply reflect the continuing strength of vertical ties and of leaders' abilities

---

[7] Peronist President Menem allowed teachers' and professors' salaries to fall to extremely low levels and labelled striking teachers "subversives."

[8] One of the most powerful and coherent student organizations in Argentina is the Franja Morada, the student branch of the Radical Party. The Franja Morada has branches on most university campuses, an organizational capacity nearly everywhere, and participates actively in political campaigns. Polak and Gorbier (1994).

to get their followers out. If mobilized activism takes place in a context of few social and horizontal ties, then it may exist despite anti-democratic social and political capital.

The cases of Nicaragua and Argentina fit with contrasts between democratic and non-democratic popular mobilization in other nations. In France and the United States, the people have mobilized to protest authoritarian politics, international imperialism, or violations of civil rights. Similarly, in Nicaragua, the people mobilized before democracy in defiance of tyranny, and they mobilized under democracy to protest corruption, restrain power, or to demand social justice.[9] In other nations, however, mobilized citizens have had a destructive purpose driven by anger at and blame of one specific group or target. In the infamous Crystal Night of November, 1933, German citizens, many of whom supported Nazism, took to the streets to wreck and burn. They targeted Jewish businesses and smashed their windows or burned them to the ground. In 1952, whipped to anger by Perón's speech, Peronists rampaged through downtown Buenos Aires, attacking and burning the headquarters of all the other political parties. As recently as 2001, angry Argentines mobilized in the streets, attacking shops and small businesses, breaking windows and looting. These latter examples were instances of mobilized activism, but a destructive style of activism driven by blame and directed toward specific targets of "them."

At issue here is not the value of mobilized politics in and of itself, because mobilized politics can be democratic or destructive. The real question is the level of mutual faith behind mobilized politics and the extent to which citizens have learned to trust others and cooperate, as opposed to viewing others in society with suspicion and blame. We began the effort to view the strength of horizontal ties in Chapter 4. This section has now traced the connection between horizontal ties and political activism. Now we will analyze attitudes about democratic institutions.

TRUST IN DEMOCRATIC INSTITUTIONS

We turn now to an assessment of popular trust in democratic institutions in Nicaragua and Argentina. Here we examine the faith citizens have in the formal institutions of the state and in political parties. This exploration is

---

[9] In her important cross-national study of citizen responses to democratic breakdown, Nancy Bermeo, (2003) considers citizen activism across a large number of cases in Europe and Latin America in the twentieth century. Within this time frame, she does not study the French and American revolutions. In the twentieth century, she finds that, while citizens were not usually the cause or source of democratic breakdown, they also did not normally mobilize in support of democracy either. She finds one important exception to this rule: in Spain, when confronted by fascism, many Spaniards went to war in defense of democracy. The popular mobilization found in Nicaragua fits most closely with the French and American revolutions or with the Spanish case: Nicaraguans have mobilized and gone to war against tyranny and in favor of popular democracy.

important because institutions may represent an alternative resource for democratization in the absence of social capital. We explore that possibility in the next chapter. Given the potential of institutions as a resource for democratization, citizen faith in institutions would seem to be an important element in the role institutions can play. Citizens can participate in democratic politics more effectively if they understand and believe in the rules of the democratic game. Such knowledge enhances the incentive to participate because citizens know what to expect from different actions, institutions, and players. If democratic values constitute a desirable characteristic of citizen participation, broad popular comprehension of the institutions of democratic politics allows citizens to gauge political action by what they know about institutions and make realistic assessments of progress. While citizens can and will learn how democratic institutions work through the act of participation itself, an important early indicator of the strength of a new democracy is popular understanding of institutions and procedures.

We have seen in the previous two chapters that differences in political loyalties associated with being either a Sandinista or a Peronist are indeed related to different levels of organizational membership. We have also seen that different national histories, which created different kinds of social capital, are related to different democratic values. Scrutiny of democratic values moves our study of social capital considerably beyond the arguments of Tocqueville and Putnam. This section continues the examination of an empirical connection between social capital and democracy by examining citizen confidence in democratic institutions. It looks at trust in the national legislature and in political parties. It also examines trust in formal institutions of the democratic state. Finally, it scrutinizes the role of political parties in democracy.

The surveys asked two key questions that address citizen confidence in democratic institutions such as the national legislature and in the political parties. The questions asked: How much trust do you have in the work of the national legislature? How much trust do you have in the work of the political parties? Citizens could respond "a lot," "some," "very little," or "none." Figure 6.3 below gives the results across Nicaragua and Argentina.

The reader will note that trust in these democratic institutions is relatively low in both of these two societies. Trust in democratic institutions is low even in established democracies.[10] It is not surprising to find, therefore, that, in 1997, more than two thirds of Argentines (65.4%) and 60% of Nicaraguans said they had low or no trust in their national legislatures. Citizen confidence in the national legislature had dropped even further by 2007, with 65.8%

---

[10] Cooper (1999). See in particular Table A.2, on p. 190, where public trust in Congress and the Presidency is shown to have dropped steadily in the United States from 1973 to 1997. Notably, 22% of U.S. citizens said they had "a great deal" or "quite a lot" of confidence in the Congress. In comparison with U.S. citizens in the same year, Nicaraguans and Argentines appear to have a fair amount of faith in their legislature.

Participation, Democratic Institutions, and Procedures

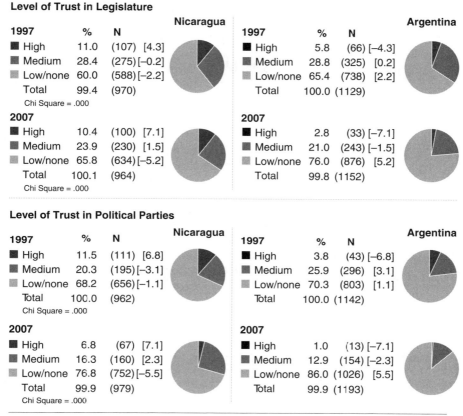

FIGURE 6.3. Nicaragua and Argentina: trust in democratic institutions – national legislature and political parties.

of Nicaraguans and 76% of Argentines (65.4%) saying they had little or no confidence in their national legislature. Similarly, evaluations of the work of the political parties was low in both countries and dropped over the decade between 1997 and 2007.

Yet despite the overall caution toward parties and the legislature in both nations that emerges from data collected first in the late 1990s and then in the late 2000s, there are statistically significant differences between these two nations. Institutional confidence is higher among Nicaraguans than among Argentines and this is true both with respect to the legislature and with respect to the work of the political parties. In 1997, nearly 40% (39.4) of Nicaraguans said they had high or medium trust in their national legislature. For Argentines, the comparable percentage was 34.6%. By 2007, 34.3%

of Nicaraguans and 23.8% of Argentines had high or medium trust in their legislature. Moreover, the residuals in the first and last row of the top half of Figure 6.3 are significant (above 2.0), indicating a statistically significant difference between the cells.

The results in the bottom half of Figure 6.3 are similar but more pessimistic. Respondents in both countries have limited faith in their political parties, a phenomenon that is evident in other new Latin American democracies as well. Yet confidence in parties is even lower in Argentina than it is in Nicaragua. In 1997 only 31.8% of Nicaraguans and 29.7% of Argentines had high or medium trust in their nation's political parties. By 2007 those percentages had dropped to 23.1% in Nicaragua and 13.9% in Argentina. Again, the residuals are strong in the bottom half of the figure, indicating that the differences in levels of confidence are statistically significant in most of the cells. Both of these bivariate relationships are significant, indicating that there is a significant overall difference between these two countries in levels of trust in the democratic institutions of the national legislature and the political parties. The higher level of social capital found in Nicaragua has caused a greater overall confidence in these national democratic institutions and that difference has continued as democracy has aged. These findings are visually evident in all four quadrants of Figure 6.3, where the darkest wedge (high trust) is always bigger in Nicaragua than in Argentina.

Note: ( ) = Raw numbers [ ] = Adjusted standardized residuals Chi square = .000.
Totals may not equal 100% because of rounding.
Source: Latinobarometer Data, 1997, 2007. The Latinobarometro sample for each year is 1000 for Nicaragua, 1200 for Argentina.
The analysis excludes interviewees who did not have an opinion or who did not respond.

FIGURE 6.4. Nicaragua and Argentina: confidence in other formal democratic institutions – the judiciary and the electoral authorities.

Questions about other democratic institutions revealed similar results in 2007. Nicaraguan respondents to the Latinobarometer survey that year had more confidence in the judiciary and in the electoral authorities. This latter is the Electoral Tribunal in Argentina and the Supreme Electoral Council in Nicaragua.

Participation, Democratic Institutions, and Procedures

Figure 6.4 shows that democracy's institutions still have a considerable distance to go in gaining public confidence in both of these nations. In the last column of Figure 6.4 we see that only 28.2% of respondents across both countries had a lot or some confidence in the judiciary and only 33.5% of both respondent pools had confidence in the electoral authorities. Yet among Argentines, confidence in these other democratic institutions was even lower than it was among Nicaraguans. Only 23.4% of Argentines gave a positive response about the judiciary while 34% of Nicaraguans gave the same. Similarly, 29.5% of Argentines had confidence in the electoral authorities, while 38.4% of Nicaraguans likewise had confidence in their electoral authorities.

The function of established democracies shows us that political parties provide a better representation of citizen interests than do temporary, factional political divisions. Parties solve problems of collective action by providing a

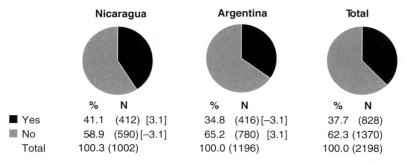

Question: Are Political Parties Indispensable for the Function of Democracy? (1997)
Chi Square = .002

	Nicaragua % N	Argentina % N	Total % N
Yes	41.1 (412) [3.1]	34.8 (416) [–3.1]	37.7 (828)
No	58.9 (590) [–3.1]	65.2 (780) [3.1]	62.3 (1370)
Total	100.3 (1002)	100.0 (1196)	100.0 (2198)

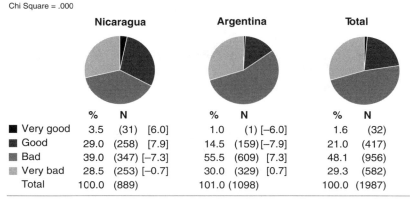

Question: How do you Evaluate the Work of the Political Parties? (2007)
Chi Square = .000

	Nicaragua % N	Argentina % N	Total % N
Very good	3.5 (31) [6.0]	1.0 (1) [–6.0]	1.6 (32)
Good	29.0 (258) [7.9]	14.5 (159) [–7.9]	21.0 (417)
Bad	39.0 (347) [–7.3]	55.5 (609) [7.3]	48.1 (956)
Very bad	28.5 (253) [–0.7]	30.0 (329) [0.7]	29.3 (582)
Total	100.0 (889)	101.0 (1098)	100.0 (1987)

Note: ( ) = Raw numbers [ ] = Adjusted standardized residuals.
Totals may not equal 100% because of rounding.
Source: Latinobarometer survey 1997, 2007.

FIGURE 6.5. Nicaragua and Argentina: Understanding of the role of political parties.

permanent institution of collective interests.[11] They allow collective interests to be articulated publicly or in the legislature in a manner that affects policy.[12] In 1997, a second question in the Latinobarometer study addressed citizen understanding of the essential role that political parties play in a democracy. That question was replaced by a similar question in 2007: How do you evaluate the work of the political parties? Figure 6.5 presents the analysis of these two questions for both countries and both years.

In 1997 (top half of Figure 6.5) the majority of respondents in both countries did not yet understand that parties are essential to democracy. This is not surprising, given citizen inexperience in both developing democracies. More importantly, however, is the percentage of respondents who identified parties as indispensable to democracy in 1997. This percentage was larger in Nicaragua, and the relationship is significant, both in the overall bivariate relationship and within the cells. By 2007 most citizens in both countries evaluated the work of political parties as "bad" or "very bad," but Argentines were more negative about their parties than were Nicaraguans. The differences between the cells are statistically significant in the top three rows of the second half of Figure 6.5. If citizens in 2007 were evaluating parties across four levels of performance, it may be that they had gained by that year a fuller comprehension of party function than they had in 1997. Unfortunately we cannot know this for certain because the Latinobarometer study in 2007 did not repeat that year the question from the top half of Figure 6.5. However, we can say that Nicaraguans are more positive about the role of parties than are Argentines, and that such relationship is statistically significant within most of these cells as well as across the bivariate relationship itself.

TRUST IN DEMOCRATIC PROCEDURES

A third aspect of the assessment of social capital and democracy is an empirical examination of citizen support for democratic procedures. As with institutions, citizens are more able to use democratic procedures if they understand them and assess them positively. We turn now to discover whether there are differences across these countries with regard to assessments of democratic procedures. In particular we seek to learn how citizens evaluate elections themselves. We also examine how citizens assess the function of their judicial system and their political parties. There were no statistical differences between the two countries in terms of citizen confidence in voting and elections. In both countries more than three fourths of the sample believed that voting mattered and that it could change the future (p = .164; N for Nicaragua = 985; N for Argentina = 1168; Total N = 2153). This is a positive finding and one that emerges despite the differences in social capital and democratic values that we have discovered across these two nations. On the other hand, there were statistically significant differences across these two countries in evaluations of

---

[11] Schwartz (1977); Aldrich (1995).
[12] Cox and McCubbins (1993).

the judiciary. In a series of three questions regarding the independent function of the judiciary and the question of its ability to deliver equality before the law, these citizens differed.[13] Table 6.1 presents these results.

We turn now to consideration from several angles of the judiciary and legal system in each of these two democracies. Let us examine Table 6.1 closely. Insights into attitudes toward the legal system and toward citizen views of how laws are upheld can also help us gain a handle on citizen faith in democratic institutions.[14] We look here at citizen confidence in the judiciary system and the fairness achieved under the system of laws. We contrast public opinion in 1997 with public opinion in 2007. These measures derive from three questions about trust in the judiciary system, opinions of how fully the laws are applied in each nation, and the extent to which citizens think that there is equality before the law. Table 6.1 provides the results of three bivariate equations testing the relationship between answers to these three questions and nationality (Nicaraguan vs. Argentine). For each section of the figure, the specific question and possible answers are provided.

Table 6.1 presents a great deal of information about citizen views of the judiciary in their country and about the equal application of the laws or equal access to justice. The questions also address citizen views about equality before the law and about the predominance of powerful groups in government. The top half of the figure considers citizen views of the judiciary and the rule of law in 1997 when memories of authoritarianism were relatively recent in each nation. The bottom half of the figure revisits views of the judicial system, the role of powerful groups, and equal access to justice in 2007, when democracy has aged in each nation.

Each of these six relationships is statistically significant and Nicaraguans always had more confidence in their judicial system and in the laws of their country than did Argentines. This is somewhat surprising since the Argentine courts played a crucial role in the return to democracy, and are the only courts in the continent to have tried military officers for human rights violations.[15] In contrast, Nicaragua's legal system has not played a visible role in the establishment of democracy. Nicaraguans, however, appear to have greater faith in their judicial system than Argentines do. In 2007 Argentines were more likely than Nicaraguans to think that the country was ruled by powerful groups and less likely than Nicaraguans to say that all citizens have equal access to justice. The residuals are very strong in each of the cells in Table 6.1, indicating that there is statistical significance in the difference between the cells.

These responses illustrate that trust in the judiciary is higher in Nicaragua than in Argentina, and confidence in the even-handed rule of law is also higher in Nicaragua than in Argentina. The responses in part C of the top half of Table 6.1 are notable. In Nicaragua, in 1997, only slightly more than half the sample, 56.5%, said there was no equality before the law while

---

[13] For other works on the independence of the judiciary and citizen views of individual equality before the law see Chavez (2004b) and Walker (2003).
[14] Walker (2003).
[15] Nino (1996).

TABLE 6.1.

SECTION I. *Nicaragua and Argentina: Trust in the judicial system as measured by three separate questions in the 1997 Latinobarometer study*

A. *Question: How Much Do You Trust the Judicial System in Your Country? Percentages (Raw Numbers) [Adjusted Standardized Residuals]*

Level of Trust	Nicaragua	Argentina	Total
High	12.2(119)[6.4]	4.5(52)[−6.4]	8.1(171)
Medium	28.0(274)[6.1]	16.9(194)[−6.1]	22.1(468)
Low or Not at All	59.8(584)[−9.4]	78.5(899)[9.4]	69.9(1483)
Total	100(977)	99.9(1145)	100.1(2122)
Chi Square = .000			

B. *Question: To What Extent Are the Laws in Your Country Followed? Percentages (Raw Numbers) [Adjusted Standardized Residuals]*

Level of Trust	Nicaragua	Argentina	Total
High	12.2(122)[9.3]	2.2(26)[−9.3]	6.8(148)
Medium	26.6(265)[4.9]	17.8(211)[−4.9]	21.8(476)
Low or Not at All	61.1(609)[−9.7]	80.0(947)[9.7]	71.4(1556)
Total	99.9(998)	100(1184)	100(2180)
Chi Square = .000			

C. *Question: Is There Equality before the Law in Your Country? Percentages (Raw Numbers) [Adjusted Standardized Residuals]*

	Nicaragua	Argentina	Total
Yes, Everyone is Equal Before the Law	43.5(435)[18.9]	8.6(102)[−18.9]	24.6(537)
There is No Equality Before the Law	56.5(564)[18.9]	91.4(1082)[18.9]	75.4(1646)
Total	100(999)	100(1184)	100(2183)
Chi Square = .000			

SECTION II. *Nicaragua and Argentina: Citizen Evaluations of the Judicial System, Predominance of Powerful Groups, and Equal Access to Justice in the 2007 Latinobarometer Study*

A. *Question: How Do You Evaluate the Work of the Judicial System?*

	Nicaragua	Argentina	Total
Very Good	5.8(50)[7.4]	0.3(3)[−7.4]	2.8(53)
Good	39.4(339)[10.0]	18.7(199)[−10.0]	27.9(538)
Bad	33.3(287)[−9.2]	54.2(577)[9.2[	44.9(864)
Very Bad	21.5(185)[−2.7]	26.8(285)[2.7]	24.4(470)
Total	100(861)	99.0(1064)	100(1925)
Chi Square = .000			

TABLE 6.1. (continued)

B. *Question: Some People Say the Country is Governed for the Benefit of Powerful Groups While Others Say the Country is Governed for the Benefit of All the People. What Do You Think?*

	Nicaragua	Argentina	Total
Governed for Powerful Groups	66.3(650)[−8.3]	81.9(935)[8.3]	74.7(1585)
Governed for the People	33.7(331)[8.3]	18.1(206)[−8.3]	25.3(537)
Total	100(981)	100(1141)	100(2122)

C. *Question: Do You Think That People in Your Country Have an Equal Opportunity to Obtain Access to Justice? Answer: Everyone...*

	Nicaragua	Argentina	Total
Has Equal Access to Justice	33.0(321)[13.3]	9.8(116)[−13.3]	20.2(437)
Does Not Have Equal Access to Justice	67.0(653)[−13.3]	90.2(1070)[13.3]	79.8(1723)
Total	100(974)	100(1186)	100(2160)

43.5% of Nicaraguans said that there was equality before the law in their country. By contrast, in 1997 Argentines were much more cynical, with 91.4% saying there was no equality before the law in their country. Only 8.6% of Argentines had faith in their country's legal system, as measured by this question. Both populations display cynicism about the judiciary, but Argentines are much more cynical and distrustful than are Nicaraguans. In 2007, Section II of Table 6.1 Argentines evaluated their judicial system more negatively than did Nicaraguans, were more likely to say that the nation was governed by powerful groups, and were less likely to say that everyone does not have equal access to justice.

The empirical findings thus far show that Nicaraguans have a higher level of engagement with political participation and a higher level of support for regimes that are liberal democratic than do Argentines. Nicaraguans are also more favorable about the legal system. But both countries are highly positive about elections.

We conclude this section by looking at recent data on democratic procedures, turning again to the Latinobarometer data of 2007. That year, the survey asked respondents a series of questions evaluating the procedures of democracy, such as the work of the legislature, the work of the political parties, and the work of the judiciary. These questions contrast with the ones above in that citizens were asked to focus their attention upon the *tasks* of democracy performed by various institutions rather than evaluating the institutions themselves. The distinction made here is small and subtle but it does

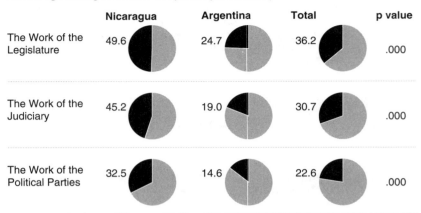

FIGURE 6.6. Nicaragua and Argentina: positive evaluations of democratic processes – the work of the legislature, the judiciary and the political parties.

give us a unique opportunity to view citizen opinions about democracy's procedures. In 2007, respondents were asked to evaluate the work of the legislature, that of the political parties, and that of the judiciary. The question was asked as follows: How do you evaluate the work of ___? They were given four alternative answers: "very good," "good," "bad," and "very bad." In each case, Nicaraguans evaluated the various democratic processes more positively (Figure 6.6).

In 2007 citizens of both nations had somewhat more confidence in the processes of the democratic institutions than they had in the institutions themselves. However, the consistent pattern is that Nicaraguans always had more confidence in these various democratic procedures than did Argentines, and the differences were always statistically significant.

CONCLUSION

The empirical findings of this chapter show that differences in social capital matter in regard to political participation and in assessments of democracy's institutions and procedures. Citizens from both countries are favorable towards elections, but apart from that similarity these two national groups are different. Nicaraguans are more likely to participate politically and to do so in an autonomous and independent manner. Nicaraguans are also more positive about democracy's institutions and more favorable in their evaluations of the work of those institutions.

Participation, Democratic Institutions, and Procedures

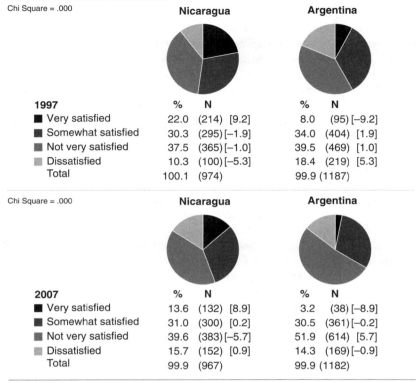

FIGURE 6.7. Nicaragua and Argentina: satisfaction with democracy 1997, 2007.

It seems appropriate, therefore, to look now at overall satisfaction with democracy. The results from Figure 6.7 correspond with what we would have expected from the findings of the chapter with respect to political participation and with regard to the confidence citizens have in the democratic institutions and procedures in their own nation. Nicaraguans have demonstrated higher levels of such confidence and here they show a higher overall level of satisfaction with democracy itself. This was true in 1997, when memories of authoritarianism were recent, and it is true one decade later. The differences in democratic satisfaction between Nicaragua and Argentina are most pronounced at the two ends of the scale: the responses "very satisfied" and "dissatisfied." On the first and last rows of Figure 6.7 the residuals are very strong. This is true with respect to both the first and the second half of the figure.

AN ASSESSMENT OF THE ARGUMENT

We now conclude Part II of this book. Chapters 4, 5, and 6 have provided an empirical exploration of social capital in Nicaragua and Argentina. They have also assessed various aspects of political attitudes and behavior, all of which are elements of political capital. As reflected in democratic values and in evaluations of democratic institutions and procedures, political capital is clearly related to social capital. In the first part of this book I suggested that social capital would contribute to political capital and that the relationship could be empirically demonstrated. These high levels of associational interaction among citizens would be found among groups who also show a higher level of appreciation for, understanding of, and participation in democracy. These are indicators of political capital, a more directly political investment upon which democracies can draw as they struggle to develop. Thus societies with higher levels of social capital would also have higher levels of political capital. Chapters 5 and 6 show that, indeed, Nicaraguans generally score higher on various indicators of democratic satisfaction, understanding, and participation. Part I gave a theoretical argument for why there is a connection between higher social capital and higher political capital. The analysis of Part II provides empirical support for that theoretical argument: Nicaragua has both higher levels of social capital and higher levels of political capital. Argentina has lower levels of both.

The historical chapters on Sandinismo and Peronism suggested reasons why social capital would be higher among Sandinistas and lower among Peronists. The empirical analysis within each nation supports the theoretical argument I have made based on the histories of these mass movements. Social and political capital are higher among Sandinistas than among non-Sandinistas, and lower among Peronists than among non-Peronists. The importance of partisan loyalties for either Sandinismo or Peronism is particularly evident in the study of a Sandinista and a Peronist neighborhood in Chapter 4. But partisan differences explored in Chapter 5 also show that Sandinistas are more likely to prefer either a liberal or a radical democratic government, whereas Peronists are more likely to prefer a clientelistic regime or authoritarianism. Partisanship is not the only factor determining political values, however. In keeping with the social capital argument, isolation and lower levels of social or educational contact are also associated with lower democratic values, lower support for democracy or a democratic regime, and a more limited understanding of democracy's procedures and institutions.

Popular political values in both nations, as measured by empirical indicators of social and political capital, advantage Nicaragua throughout this study up to this point. The data also show that the popular mobilizational experience acquired through the Sandinista revolution or the Peronist mass movement are a key part of that difference. Citizens influenced by Sandinismo show higher levels of social and political capital, while citizens influenced by Peronism show lower levels of both. Yet the experience of mass mobilization does not confine itself to citizens who are partial to the mass movements themselves. Just as Peronism and Sandinismo were themselves products of social and political trends in their respective nations, so they have also left social and political influences that extend beyond their own partisan supporters. While other influences are undoubtedly also at play, the influences of these two mass movements on their wider societies is found in higher social and political capital in Nicaragua and lower levels of both in Argentina.

Social capital theory tells us that democracy works where citizens have learned to associate with each other socially. I have expanded that argument to say that something much more directly political – political capital – will also influence democracy's successful function. I suggest that where social capital is high, political capital will also be high, and both will help democracy work more smoothly.

Recent events in Nicaragua and Argentina fit my argument about the importance of both social and political capital. In the late 1990s and early twenty-first century, Argentina's democracy has gone through an extraordinary period of political turmoil. As the nation approached and then passed twenty years of an unbroken electoral calendar in the late 1990s and early 2000s, Argentina's democracy became more troubled rather than less so. Politics over the past two years causes us to reassess democracy in these two nations anew. Argentina appears to be entering yet another period of personalistic power. The presidency has moved from one spouse to the other in consecutive terms while party competition itself is on the decline.[16] In Nicaragua, on the other hand, party competition is thriving and deepening. The left has regained the presidency after sixteen years out of power and party competition is also spreading to local elections.[17] While the personalistic leadership of the Kirchners was initially greeted positively in Argentina and is still tolerated now, Ortega's efforts at caudillista control confronted extensive opposition even before he won his narrow 2006 victory and are still criticized today.[18] If alternation in power, two or more strong parties capable of winning the presidency and amassing substantial legislative influence, party competition and citizen involvement at the local level, and opposition to personalistic and caudillista power are indicators of democratic health, then Argentina again appears to be making slower progress than one would expect given its wealthy, cosmopolitan, industrialized status. Nicaragua, by contrast, is still unfolding its democracy in a steady, if tumultuous fashion, despite being one of the poorest agrarian nations in Latin America.

If this were a book on social capital and only on social capital, we could end this study here. We could shake our heads and throw up our hands and conclude that social capital is low in Argentina. Too bad. But this is not just a book about social capital. As political scientists, we are not only interested

---

[16] Anderson (2009).
[17] Anderson and Dodd (2007; 2008; 2009).
[18] Anderson and Dodd (2009).

in organizational memberships and social capital for their own sake. We are interested in social capital as part of a broad and much more far-reaching set of questions. We are concerned about social capital because we are interested in democracy and democratization. We are interested in what makes democracy work and in how it can be made to work. We are interested in alternative working mechanisms that democracy can rest upon, including social capital, but also apart from and beyond social capital.

As students of democracy we need to look again at Argentina. Argentine democratization, while confirming arguments about social and political capital, simultaneously raises questions about such arguments. After all, despite its problems and despite its low level of social capital, Argentina is democratizing anyway. It has followed an electoral calendar since December 1983. Two different parties have won the presidency and held plurality legislative power in that time. With periodic backsliding, Argentina has honored freedom of the press throughout most of that time. It has respected human rights and begun to take its place among a community of civilized nations. This is no small achievement for a country with demonstrably low levels of social capital, troublingly high levels of social distrust, and a population with low levels of cooperative capacity and a disinclination to be involved with each other at all.

Yet these various accomplishments in the mechanics of democratic procedure are the first and not the last of Argentina's democratic achievements. Beyond such mechanics, we have also seen a measure of democratic progress within the Peronist party itself. This is an extremely important development given Peronism's semi-fascist past and the central role it is playing in Argentina's democracy today. Peronism has held national power during most of the years since Argentina's return to democracy. While Peronism in power has been autocratic and somewhat lawless, as we would expect it to be, there are also many authoritarian methods that Peronism has left behind since 1983. In power, Peronism did not attack the press or jail the Radical Party leader. It did not sack and burn opposition party headquarters. Instead, Peronism, under the leadership of Carlos Menem, carried out one of the most successful economic reforms in Latin America and it did so largely through the use of the democratic institutions of state and through democratic procedure. Peronism did all of this during the 1990s, while, as the data in this book reveal, social capital was low on every indicator in Argentina.

Moreover, Argentina's accomplishments still do not end here. More than any other nation in Latin America and more than most nations of Eastern Europe and Africa, Argentina has confronted its recent authoritarian past with a measure of retroactive justice.[19] Let us not forget that it was Argentina that put the military on trial and sent the former dictators to jail. It was able to do this despite low social capital and through the use of democratic institutions

[19] Nino (1996).

Participation, Democratic Institutions, and Procedures

and procedures, making use, in particular, of the judiciary and the legislature. Moreover, many members of the Peronist party played a central role in supporting the human rights trials. It was Peronist President Carlos Menem and not Radical President Raul Alfonsín who put a stop to the repeated attempted coups. While both presidents suffered attempted coups, it was Menem who asked the main body of the military to follow civilian orders and to fire on the soldiers seeking to overthrow the democratic state. To date and after that event, Argentina has not again seen an attempted coup. The credit for (hopefully) final subjugation of the military belongs to Menem. These are steps toward democratization, including civilian control of the military, and they were all done while social capital was low.

Therefore, for us to conclude this book by surmising that social capital is low in Argentina and walk away from the study now, would be for us to turn our backs on the truth about Argentina's democracy. Argentina is democratizing and it is doing so despite low levels of social capital. If we want to understand democratic development, it is incumbent upon us to look again at what is happening in Argentina, and to ask ourselves how a nation can take steps toward democracy while social capital is so low. Argentina raises questions about social capital arguments because such arguments say that democracy will not work where social capital is low, but it clearly demonstrates that such arguments are not true. Perhaps a more measured statement of the social capital argument would be to say that democracy will work better where social capital is high. A more cautious or restrained statement of the social capital argument is in order with respect to Argentina; democracy there is struggling forward despite the low levels of social and political capital that this book's analysis has found.

I suggest, based upon the Argentine example, that nations can democratize despite low social capital. Nations can find alternative bases upon which to build the democratic effort. In Argentina's democratic success story, that alternative basis is the nation's institutions of state. As a democratically elected president working with the legislature and an autonomous judiciary, Alfonsín put in place and then carried out one of the most impressive programs of retroactive justice in the world. As the details of that policy were hammered out, Congress played a central role in leading the policy closer to public opinion and in constructing and revising the policy details as the needs of the developing democracy emerged. Responding to the president's policy and the Congressional demands, Argentina's court system systematically worked its way through hundreds of cases of human rights violations, applying the law in an impartial manner that left it clear that human rights violations will not be tolerated in Argentina. As Argentina moved beyond the trials and toward economic reform, again, the democratically elected president, Carlos Menem, envisioned and carried out one of the most impressive and far-reaching economic reforms in any developing nation today. Like the human rights trials, the economic reform process was undertaken through the use of democratic institutions and procedures, including the involvement of many members of the cabinet and both chambers of Congress.[20] Policy vision and leadership were driven from above, through the foresight and courage of national leaders and institutions, while social capital was, is, and remains low in Argentina.

Therefore, any true picture of democracy in Argentina cannot end now with the empirical evidence on social capital alone. Something important is happening in Argentina and, as students of democracy, it is our duty to understand what that something is. It is not possible to measure all aspects of a nation's institutions. If I am correct that the democratic institutions of state are the resource upon which Argentina is building its democracy, then it would be a complicated task to construct a complete data base with which to investigate the argument. We cannot measure all aspects of every institution in a country. But we can start somewhere and we can do something. Moreover, we can do something that has been done many times before. We can study and measure the legislature. As an incomplete but initial first indicator of the power of a nation's institutions, we can scrutinize legislative function. We can draw on previously-proven measures to examine the function of Argentina's Congress, using Nicaragua's legislature as a point of comparison. A detailed study of these two legislatures constitutes an initial step toward investigating the relative power of institutions in Argentina and Nicaragua.

Other students of political development have emphasized the role of institutions in stabilizing politics and making societies able to resolve their differences peaceably when they would not otherwise be able to do so. In scrutinizing the function of the legislature and measuring its strength, we are simultaneously examining one of the state institutions most central in resolving differences peaceably, and we are avoiding the misleading conclusion that social capital is the entire picture of what matters in a developing democracy. I suggest that Argentina is able to use its institutions to democratize because they are stronger than the nation's basis in social capital. We will find empirical support for that argument in the next chapter.

[20] Llanos (2001, 2002); Diez (2002).

PART III

MAKING DEMOCRACY WORK WITHOUT SOCIAL CAPITAL: INSTITUTIONAL CAPITAL

7

If You Build It They Will Come
Institutional Capital in Democratic Development

Le Congrés ne marche pas; il danse.

La Garde-Chambonas[1]

When, in *The Social Contract*, Rousseau confronted the possibility that the people, while willing the good, might not always be able to see the good, he reached back to ancient Greek and Roman traditions and suggested the Legislator, the extraordinary individual with sufficient wisdom to establish a system of laws and institutions that would enable a society to manage its affairs in peace and justice.

Thornton H. Anderson[2]

It was a balmy South American spring night in early November. The clock read 1 a.m. in Buenos Aires, a city that never sleeps. I had been observing the debate on the floor of the Senate since 5 p.m. the previous evening, and I could not keep my eyes open any longer. As I left the National Congress, I paused for a moment on the sidewalk and looked back. On both sides of the four-story Congress, lights blazed in every window, visual testimony to the vitality, energy, and power of Argentina's contemporary Congress. On the right side of the imposing, Baroque-style building beneath its bronze dome, just outside the House of Deputies, dozens of advisors, staff people, and secretaries scurried back and forth across the now-empty street between the Congress and the House Office Building. An important vote was coming down in the lower chamber, and Deputies were demanding information from their exhausted staff as debate swelled on the floor. But that vote would not come for another several hours and I, for one, had had it. Clearly, the Congress had energy to burn, more energy than a weary observer headed home to sleep. This dramatic picture reveals energy, enthusiasm, hope, and dedication to the work of democratic procedure. At 1 a.m. I was leaving behind an institution alive with vigor and dynamism.

---

[1] La Garde-Chambonas (1843)
[2] Anderson (1993, p. xiii)

In point of fact, Argentina's legislature assumed a central role in the nation's democratic development beginning with the nation's return to democracy in late 1983. The same has also been true of the judicial system and the courts. The vibrancy of the Congress is mirrored in the role played by the Argentine judiciary in the early years of democracy. In fact, it was the courts more than any other institution that carried forward the struggle to contain authoritarianism, seek retroactive justice and build protected legal space that would guarantee human rights. After President Alfonsín proposed a human rights policy and the Congress revised and passed the policy into law, it was the court system that dealt with the legal process of trials in the many months and years after a retroactive justice system was established.

In the 1980s the activity of the judiciary proceeded on two fronts. First, Alfonsín established a special commission – CONADEP – to investigate the fate of the thousands of people who had disappeared during the dictatorship of 1976–1983. Second, the president's human rights policy, and the Congressional bills that made the policy law, set up legal proceedings and goals that have helped shape human rights trials ever since. The CONADEP investigations uncovered the shocking truth that most disappeared people had, in fact, been murdered and had not simply disappeared. They were dead.[3] The human rights trials then worked their way slowly through the many cases of disappearances in an effort to learn who had been responsible for the violations and what could be done to punish the offenders.

The extent to which the people and leaders of Argentina turned to the judicial system to redress these horrific acts, and the seriousness with which the judiciary responded, are both evidence of the strength of this particular institution and the willingness of the people within it to play a central role in moving the nation toward democracy. I have suggested that democracy can develop upon the basis of different foundations. In the absence of strong social capital, Argentines turned to the strength of their institutions because they needed to find resources that would enhance democracy and constrain authoritarianism.

In the early years after the return to democracy, Argentine democrats found strength in Congress. Although the idea of a policy of retroactive justice that would try the military commanders began with Alfonsín, the policy could not properly become law unless it was passed through Congress. That institutional requirement thereby offered Senators and Deputies a chance to influence the details of the law. They did so with such energy and enthusiasm that the policy soon departed from the path Alfonsín had originally envisioned. It was the Congress, and not the president, who decided that the human rights trials would extend far beyond the top military commanders. When the president's bill was presented to Congress and had already passed the lower chamber, a single amendment offered in the Senate fundamentally changed both the nature of the policy and the scope of its reach. In

[3] Argentine National Commission on Disappeared (1986).

If You Build It They Will Come

a final moment before the bill was to pass the Senate, Senator Elías Sapaq of Neuquen offered an amendment to require that trials of individuals could also extend to anyone who had been involved with "abhorrent or atrocious acts." Of course, since everything that happened in the clandestine detention centers and torture chambers was abhorrent and atrocious, this amendment opened the trials potentially to include every member of the military down to the lowest-ranked private. In the end the trials never extended as far as the Sapaq amendment asked, but they extended much further than Alfonsín had ever intended. Argentina's institutions had stepped forward to lead the nation's movement away from authoritarianism and toward democracy. The impetus for that democratic progress came from inside the institutions of state – in this case the Congress –, and not from citizen initiative or strong social capital.

In contrast to this exciting and encouraging picture in Argentina, the role that institutions have played in Nicaragua's developing democracy is much more limited. Neither the National Assembly nor the court system has ever to date played a major, visible, national role in constraining authoritarianism or in moving the nation forward toward democracy in a significant, far-reaching and momentous manner. When Nicaragua began its movement toward popular government with the 1979 revolution, no meaningful legislature had ever existed in Nicaragua as a place for dialogue, debate, and policy construction. The nation's judiciary was similarly weak and had played almost no role in the political development and leadership of the nation. In fact, as this chapter will show, it was the revolution itself that took the first steps toward creating a representative legislature. Likewise, the revolutionary government fortified the court system and created the Supreme Electoral Council as a fourth branch of state.

Between these two nations, it was Argentina more than Nicaragua that built its institutions of state early in the twentieth century. Therefore, when democracy arrived and the current electoral calendar began, the procedures and processes of democracy immediately had a place to go, a set of previously existing institutions which, while they had stood dormant for years, nevertheless stood ready and waiting as a possible resource for building democracy. Nicaragua's democratic procedures, by contrast, had nowhere to go, and the primary resource for democratization and for combating authoritarianism was citizen protest – the proverbial politics of the streets.

A full comparison of the institutions of state in Argentina and Nicaragua is beyond the scope of this chapter. Instead, we will take a more limited approach. As an example of institutional strength, in the remainder of this chapter we will explore the history, contemporary standing, and institutional strength of the legislature in Argentina and Nicaragua. That effort will begin with a brief history of each legislature, followed by a summary of the role of each legislature in today's democracy. The chapter concludes with an empirical investigation of institutional strength across both legislatures. We will learn that Argentina's legislature is fundamentally stronger than Nicaragua's.

That superior strength is grounded in a longer and more central historical role and is evident in recent data on both legislatures. This comparison will show a stronger institutional presence in Argentina's democracy than in Nicaragua's.

In the sections that follow, we begin with an exploration of legislative history in Argentina and Nicaragua in the early twentieth century before the advent of the two mass movements studied here. That contrast is stark because Argentina's Congress has a rich history while Nicaragua's legislature has almost no history at all. Legislative history advantages Argentina. We continue with a brief examination of the relationship between the popular movement in each nation and its respective legislature. That more recent historical overview illustrates that Sandinismo played a positive and constructive role vis-a-vis the legislature, while Peronism used the legislature to abuse power, violate many rules of debate and procedure, and generally weaken democracy. The relationship between the popular movement and the legislature advantages Nicaragua.

The chapter then summarizes the role of the two legislatures since 1990 and draws upon data from the 2000s to compare institutional strength. Since 1990 both legislatures have had moments of severe weakness as well as moments of institutional strength. As this book closes the Nicaraguan legislature is doing better than the Argentine legislature in holding the president accountable, but recent data on institutional strength still give the advantage to Argentina. The wisdom of having created a legislature over one hundred years ago places Argentina ahead of Nicaragua when we compare their institutional capacity. The contrast shows that Argentina does have resources to use in building democracy despite its lack of social capital. In the absence of citizen initiative and horizontal ties, Argentina's institutions of state can assume and have already assumed a leadership role in moving democracy forward.

EARLY LEGISLATIVE HISTORY

Studies on the subject suggest that institutions begin a process of learning and strengthening from the moment they are founded. This process begins and advances even while institutional function itself is quite imperfect. I call this accumulation of experience and enhanced function "institutional capital." In the case of a legislature, the early establishment of a legislative chamber allows institutional capacity and the development of institutional capital to begin. If a legislature exists, then representatives can look backward to previous periods of democratic function and find examples of legislative activity, the presentation and debate of bills, patterns of relationships with the executive and other state institutions, and prior experience in interaction with the public. All of these patterns of behavior then become accumulated wisdom to which legislators can refer when deciding how to act in the current democratic period. When placed in a new democratic context, prior experience, even if part of it was accumulated outside of democracy, allows a legislature and its members to become stronger and more professional at a faster pace than

If You Build It They Will Come

they would have been able to do without the accumulation of past experience. An institution that has accumulated institutional capital can constitute itself earlier, more rapidly, and in a more competent fashion than it would do if it started without any accumulated institutional capital in the form of past experience. In the case of a legislature, that mission is essential to democracy.

This section will demonstrate that Argentina's early effort to establish a legislature allowed the nation to accumulate institutional capital in a way that was not possible in Nicaragua. Argentina's first coherent national government was the ruthless dictatorship of Juan Manual de Rosas, who unified the nation under one government and reined from 1829 to 1852. After Rosas' ouster, a set of political leaders comparable to the framers of the United States Constitution tried to formalize and institutionalize the Argentine government by writing a Constitution in 1853. They hoped to avoid in the future the style of lawless, personalistic rule that Rosas exhibited. Like the U.S. Constitution, the Argentine document established a presidential democracy with a bicameral Congress.[4] Members of the lower chamber, the House of Deputies, were directly elected from legislative districts on a proportional basis, and thus responded to the need to represent the people numerically. Deputies were elected for six years, and one third were up for election every two years. Also following the U.S. example, the Senate was not directly elected.[5] Instead, Senators were chosen in pairs by the legislatures of each province, thus responding to the need for geographical representation in Argentina's federal system. Senators served for nine years and one third could be replaced every three years.

The 1853 Constitution reflected a desire to protect the young nation from the various threats it confronted, of which a Rosas-style dictatorship was one. Those writing the new constitution sought to minimize both the danger of tyranny and the centrifugal chaos of excessive provincial autonomy. It was an effort at balance, not unlike the U.S. effort to balance the strength of the national government against the retained powers of the States. Seeking to construct an institutionalized democracy with a key role for the legislature, Argentina's framers were simultaneously fearful of democracy and of the rash decisions and popular influence it could bring.[6] They produced a Congress that was functional but sluggish.

Despite these promising beginnings, Argentina's subsequent governments did not follow the 1853 Constitution and made no effort to use the cumbersome legislative institution. Instead, for the next forty years Argentina functioned as an exclusive society of elites, rather than as a democracy. Politics was the province of the wealthy, particularly cattle ranchers. Parties were

---

[4] For a general perspective on the development and current configuration of Argentina's Congress see Molinelli (1991; 1996).
[5] For a study of the change from indirect to direct election in the U.S. Senate see King and Ellis (1996).
[6] Such dilemmas, tradeoffs, and compromises also confronted constitution-makers in the United States. Anderson (1993); Dahl (2002, esp. chaps 1 and 2); Wirls and Wirls (2004).

organizations of notables rather than mass electoral parties. Presidents were selected behind closed doors without popular input. Legislators were selected through fraudulent votes, and they accomplished little real legislation while in office. The Senate, in particular, became a club of cronies of the provincial governors, selected on the basis of personal friendships. It was a disappointing outcome to a promising beginning.

Even so, the formal establishment of a Congress provided a considerable advantage for Argentine democratic development, positioning Argentina ahead of other Latin American nations that had no legislature, much less a written law establishing one. The existence of a legislature provided Argentine democrats with a forum for debate and a popular mandate separate from the executive. As Argentine democracy developed in fitful and sporadic periods of forward movement, the legislature gave political leaders an institution from which to challenge the president and present alternative perspectives and within which to engage in debate over policy.

Scholars of democratic transition have suggested that the establishment of democracy's institutions represents an important first step, even if those institutions are not immediately put to use.[7] The fact that they exist provides a crack in the armor of dictatorship, and it is through that crack that democracy itself can eventually enter.[8] As we will see in the next section, having a Congress and not using it for its intended purpose became a weapon that advocates of democracy could use against the polity of notables that characterized Argentine governance in the late eighteenth century. The importance of Argentina's early Congress will also become evident when we consider Argentine democratization in contrast with that of Nicaragua, where no such Constitution or legislature were created in the nineteenth century.

Argentina's Congress in the Radical Years: 1916–1930

The Radical Party, established in 1890, demanded that the mechanisms of democracy written in the Constitution be made reality. They organized protests in support of national elections for both the presidency and the Congress. Although such an agenda may seem natural today, in the late nineteenth century and in the face of a closed, elitist political system, the request for democracy met with considerable resistance. The Radical Party would agitate for elections for nearly fifteen years before Argentina had its first democratically elected president in 1916. That year also brought the Congress more fully into national government. Argentina's first experience with a popularly elected executive (1916–1930) would offer an opportunity for critical institutional learning inside Congress. These were the first years that Congress actually functioned as a forum for debate and a source of an independent

---

[7] Linz and Stepan (1978).
[8] For a study of the extent to which the existence of a Congress in Peru represented a crack in the armor of authoritarianism in that country see Aguayo, (2004).

legislative agenda. The Radical Party leader, Hipolito Yrigoyen, easily won the presidency in 1916. That same year saw elections to the lower chamber, while the Senate continued to be filled by indirectly elected representatives of the provinces.

While the Radical Party had sufficient electoral reach to win the presidency, it had not yet penetrated all the districts to win a majority of seats in the lower chamber as well. As a result, the Congress that was elected with Yrigoyen was an opposition Congress, controlled by the conservative parties that opposed the Radicals as well as by representatives of wealthy ranching and mining interests. The year 1916 thus ushered in a divided government, making democratic governance an even more difficult task.[9] However, in the struggle between President and Congress, we see the democratic learning process moving forward in Argentina generations before it would be possible in any nation that lacked a Congress.

President Yrigoyen was legally elected and would leave the presidency in 1922 on schedule with the electoral calendar. He stood back while Marcelo T. de Alvear, his hand-picked successor, won the next presidential election and governed for six further years of democracy. Yrigoyen then ran for the presidency a second time and won in 1928. In all of these ways, his behavior was democratic and that of a duly elected popular leader. Nevertheless, Yrigoyen behaved in an imperious fashion toward the Congress and the provinces, exercising powers far beyond those intended for the presidency. His attitudes toward federalism and the legislature were closely connected. He

---

[9] On divided government see Mayhew (1991). On divided government in new democracies see Linz (1994). Although he does not include the Yrigoyen government in the cases he studies, Linz argues that divided government causes democratic breakdown. Examining cases of the late twentieth century, he suggests that presidential democracy, requiring as it does a separate mandate for the executive and legislative branches, has the potential of delivering a divided government in a manner impossible in a parliamentary system. Divided government then makes the implementation of presidential policy initiatives more difficult or impossible.

The story of Yrigoyen's relationship with the Congress and of the subsequent democratic breakdown in 1932 fit Linz's argument. However, as will become clear, democratic breakdown in 1930 was more directly due to the high-handed intransigence of the president and to the willingness of Argentina's military to end democracy than to the institutional configuration of the new democracy. The same can be said of other more recent instances of democratic breakdown where a president more willing to compromise and more committed to democracy could have avoided breakdown.

The theory holds true in Peru, where an imperious, anti-democratic president, faced with divided government, responded by closing the Congress and thus initiating democratic breakdown. The theory is contradicted by the Nicaraguan case during the late Chamorro years, when a president unwilling to end democracy tolerated an opposition Congress that deliberately moved to curtail her power. The argument does not explain instances where divided government did not end in democratic breakdown, such as Vicente Fox's presidency in Mexico in the early twenty-first century or Alfonsín's administration (1983–1989), both of which faced opposition Congresses without overseeing democratic breakdown. It also ignores multiple instances of successful divided government in older democracies. On the Peruvian case see Kenney (2004). On the Nicaraguan case see Anderson and Dodd (2005); Anderson (2006b).

maintained that the legislators held no electoral mandate because in their provinces they had been elected via corrupt elections. The lack of a popular mandate particularly hurt the Senators' legitimacy, since they were only appointed because of their close association with the provincial governors. In view of these practices, Yrigoyen maintained that he was the only official of the democracy who had any electoral mandate, and therefore the only leader entitled to make decisions or rule the country. In addition, Yrigoyen used electoral corruption in the provinces as an excuse to intervene militarily, particularly in those provinces where opposition parties had won. When the Radicals themselves also used questionable electoral practices in some provinces, Yrigoyen did not object. His double standard showed that his opposition to electoral fraud was only meant to serve his drive for power and was not a position in support of democracy itself.

Legislators in both chambers objected to Yrigoyen's treatment of the provinces. They challenged the legal and constitutional grounds for military intervention, asked the president to explain his behavior, suggested that he withdraw military intervention, and demanded to be included in intervention oversight. In all of these positions, the Congress stood on strong legal ground. The legislators were correct that the interventions fell under constitutional rules and, accordingly, should include the Congress in any decision making. They were also correct that interventions, in general, were intended to involve Congressional oversight and not to be a unilateral move by the executive. Most importantly, in calling Yrigoyen to account, they were exercising their constitutional duties of checking and balancing the president. In addition, the constitution specifically gives the Congress the right of interpellation, somewhat like the Question and Answer sessions in which the British parliament questions the Prime Minister. In the Congressional response to provincial interventions, we see the Argentine Congress resist the executive for the first time. The challenge was not well-received by Yrigoyen, but it was nonetheless the Congress' first step toward fulfilling its constitutional mandate of checking the power of the presidency.

Yrigoyen's response to Congressional challenge was confrontational. He sent written messages to the legislature informing legislators that they had no business overseeing his provincial policies. He told them that they lacked an electoral mandate and therefore had no standing from which to challenge him. He prohibited his ministers from responding to Congressional interpellation calls and himself refused to appear before the Congress. Yrigoyen wrote to the Congress that if they wished to approach him by asking for instructions, he would be happy to oblige by telling them what functions they could undertake, but he explicitly rejected any equal executive/legislative relationship and denied any Congressional right to supervise the executive.[10] Hostility between the president and Congress continued throughout Yrigoyen's six years in office. By the end of his term, even members of his own party came to think

---

[10] Mustapic (1984); Mustapic and Goretti (1992); Mustapic and Ferretti (unpublished manuscript).

that a president with a more amicable approach to the legislature would be desirable.

Despite Yrigoyen's attitude, the early Argentine Congress sometimes won its contest. Yrigoyen was entirely defeated by Congressional vote in his effort to nationalize the mines. By the early twentieth century, Argentina, like many wealthy nations, had begun to focus on the wealth contained in minerals, particularly oil, iron, and coal. Argentine mines, like those elsewhere, were privately owned. In keeping with his radical democratic agenda, Yrigoyen sought to nationalize the mines in the name of the people. Private individuals, he said, should not hold such vast economic power over the nation. In an uncharacteristic effort to work with Congress, Yrigoyen used sympathetic legislators in the lower chamber to introduce a bill nationalizing the mines. Like his interventions in the provinces, Yrigoyen's nationalization bill encountered extensive opposition, particularly from wealthy conservative interests closely aligned with the traditional parties of notables and mine owners. Unlike the opposition to intervention in the provinces, opposition to nationalization was based upon economic interest.

Now the Congress proved capable of checking the executive. In systematic fashion, conservative legislators challenged the bill, raising one legal question after another. They also skillfully used parliamentary obstructionist tactics to draw out the debate interminably, accomplishing a kind of filibuster. Yrigoyen's supportive legislators, Deputies Carlos Melo and Rudolfo Moreno, were not up to the task. They took the opposition at its legalistic face value and failed to recognize the conservative economic interests behind the opposition position. They continually answered legal challenges with legal responses without calling public attention to the conservative self-interest behind the legal front. When Melo and Moreno appeared to have won the day temporarily with legal arguments, conservative legislators would wander out of the chamber, one by one, until the chamber lacked the required quorum and debate had to be suspended.

In seeking to nationalize the mines, Yrigoyen needed the Congress. Despite his belief that he was the only fairly elected official, even he could not conduct such a massive economic reform using executive powers alone. But since his party did not control the legislature and he had made many enemies in the chambers, Yrigoyen did not have the votes he needed to push through a truly radical economic reform. In addition, he and his supporters did not adequately use even the forces they could muster. They could have publicly exposed conservative Congressional opposition for the self-serving wealthy agenda that it was. In the prevailing populist atmosphere, such an exposé might have built popular pressure against the conservative legislators and for the bill. But Yrigoyen and his supporters, inexperienced in legislative politics, failed to use the supportive public atmosphere to their own advantage. In his dismissive attitude toward the Congress, Yrigoyen had also failed to learn how to influence Congressional debate to further his own agenda. After being stalled for more than two years, the bill was finally defeated. The sad irony of this story is that where Yrigoyen's measures were legally questionable, the

Congress did not succeed in stopping him, but where his policies followed the law and would have furthered a progressive agenda, there the Congress successfully used its checking powers.

With the 1922 election of Marcelo T. de Alvear, Argentina's next president, the executive-legislative relations improved, though at the cost of Radicalism's reformist agenda. Alvear was also a Radical but was less driven toward rapid, extensive reforms. Yrigoyen became disgusted with the slow pace of progressivism during Alvear's administration and ran again in the next election. He returned to the presidency in 1928. By that time, however, conservative interests had regained the upper hand and were unprepared to tolerate another radical, confrontational Yrigoyen administration. The economy foundered with the 1929 Depression, and in 1930, Yrigoyen was overthrown by a military coup. Argentina returned to non-democratic governance.[11]

The Yrigoyen years left a complex legacy for Argentine democratic development. First, it provided the first step toward the creation of legislative institutional capital. To future executives and elected presidents, Yrigoyen left an example of an elected president who behaved in an authoritarian manner. This example undermined the movement toward democracy that Radicalism had accomplished by bringing about Argentina's first free elections. But the Yrigoyen years also left a model for future legislatures, despite his leadership style. The Congress of 1916 to 1930 and particularly that of 1916 to 1922 exemplified a legislature checking executive excess. Legislators in that period made it clear that they had a legal role to play in national governance, and they expected to be allowed to play it. They scrutinized executive policies, challenged them on the floor of Congress, and placed written records of their objections into the historical archives. Where they did not prevail, the fact of their protest and the legal grounds for it remained. And, in one key policy that would have altered the nation's economic landscape, the Congress stopped the executive agenda. The fact that this victory went to conservative forces that opposed the democratic and popular agenda does not diminish the fact that conservatives used legislative means to achieve their goals and gained democratic experience from the exercise. In the face of a hostile executive, the Congress kept open a forum for dissent and disagreement throughout this first period of democracy. Despite Yrigoyen's own agenda and policies, Argentina terminated its first democratic experiment having learned that an attentive national Congress – one capable of checking and balancing the executive – was a part of democratic governance. It was an important example for democracy that went beyond the advent of elections themselves.

Nowhere to Go, Nothing to Build On: Nicaragua's National Assembly

In contrast to congressional history in Argentina, Nicaragua's legislative history is minimal. While legislative experience and historical learning are

[11] Luna (1958).

If You Build It They Will Come

not entirely absent in the Nicaraguan case, the nation saw no written constitution and no popularly selected legislature until after the downfall of the Somoza dictatorship in 1979. In the nineteenth and early twentieth centuries, Nicaragua's government alternated between parties of notables who took power militarily. The Somoza dictatorship took control in the 1930s, but no people's party like the Radicals appeared. Somoza created a rubber-stamp legislature made up of his friends and economic allies, but it was not a forum for debate. It lacked any coherent group of opposition legislators who offered an alternative agenda. It did not debate policy or consider laws. It was simply a figurehead of appearances designed, like the Somoza regime itself, to deceive the United States (which did not look closely) into thinking that Somoza's dictatorship was a presidential democracy. The early twentieth century history of Nicaragua's legislature left the nation without the early steps toward institutional development and learning that Argentina had taken. These constituted important steps for democratization and for the institutional development and professionalization in a nation. Where Argentina's legislature lurched forward problematically, in Nicaragua no learning process began at all.

LEGISLATIVE DEVELOPMENT IN THE SHADOW OF MASS MOVEMENTS: PERONISM AND SANDINISMO IN INTERACTION WITH THE LEGISLATURE

If early twentieth century history favored the development of institutional capital in Argentina more than in Nicaragua, the mid-to-late twentieth century history of the two popular mass movements of Sandinismo and Peronism did exactly the opposite. Peronism undermined the strengths of Argentina's Congress while Sandinismo itself became the force that established a meaningful legislature in Nicaragua when no previous government had been willing to do so.

As we saw in Chapter 3, Peronism was a contradictory movement that followed the outward appearance of democratic procedure while simultaneously undermining democratic functions with its everyday actions. As president, Perón expanded the electorate to include social groups (women) and far-flung territories that had previously been disenfranchised. Yet from 1946 to 1955, Perón undermined and punished dissent, attacked opposition parties, jailed the Radical Party leader and the leaders of non-Peronist unions, and restricted freedom of the press.

Perón's relationship with Congress was likewise contradictory. On the one hand, he held legislative elections as mandated by the Constitution and, through those, achieved a majority in both chambers. The Congress then engaged in energetic policy making following the President's agenda of labor reform, social rights, and an improved living standard for the poor. The activist legislators gave Peronism a democratic appearance and involved the Congress in policy. On the other hand, the Congress was deeply subservient to Perón, acted as a rubber stamp for him, and paid official homage to him regularly. Moreover, the Peronist Congress used its majority status to enact highly undemocratic policies and to treat the opposition with contempt when they objected to the new laws. In this way, Peronism only appeared to be democratic in its use of the Congress. In the hands of the Peronists, the Congress became another weapon in the abuse of power.

Two key Peronist policies serve as examples of the movement's undemocratic agenda and its willingness to use the Congress to impose authoritarian policies. These were the imposition of religious education in the primary schools and Perón's intervention into the universities, which have already been discussed in Chapter 3 when reviewing the history of Peronism. Here we revisit these policies and consider how they exemplified Peronism's authoritarianism, but also inadvertently allowed the development of institutional capital in the legislature.

Modeling upon the United States constitution, Argentina's 1853 Constitution separated church and state, making primary education a public affair and protecting it from church influence. This law was one of Argentina's attractions for the waves of immigrants from Germany and Eastern Europe, many of whom were Protestant or Jewish. All subsequent governments had followed this law. Perón, however, violated it by mandating Catholic education in primary schools. He did this by presidential decree, and then sent the law to Congress for its rubber stamp of approval. That step gave the opposition an opportunity for symbolic resistance. Radicals and Socialists mustered extensive legal, scholarly, and philosophical arguments against the law, urging the Congress to overturn the decree. They said the law violated the Constitution. They argued for freedom of conscience, saying that schools were for teaching students to think, not for indoctrination. The Radical deputies predicted that the public opposed the measure and would protest its continuation. The debate lasted for more than a week, ran late into the night every day, and filled over 150 pages of congressional records.[12] As the Radicals foresaw, the measure attracted public opposition, which swelled even under Peronist oppression. Eventually, public opposition became so pronounced that, at Perón's request, the Congressional majority repealed the measure in the second Peronist presidency, using many of the original Radical arguments as reasons for the repeal.[13] When challenged about Peronism's policy reversals, Peronist deputies retorted that the new law was Perón's personal wish and that was all the reason they needed for its passage.

---

[12] Vol IV (September 5–19, 1946, p. 390); Vol X (January 30–March 20, 1947, pp. 538–539) (sending the bill to committee), 568–621, 684–738, 757–768, 770–879. The bill that was the cause of so much debate was actually nothing more than a ratification of a law made by decree and signed by Juan Perón. The presidential decree imposing religious education in primary schools was first signed into law on June 4, 1943 while Perón was still Minister of Labor. It was later modified on June 3, 1946.

[13] Perón (1955, Vol. 1, p. 187), overturning of law 12.978 which had imposed religious education in public schools.

If You Build It They Will Come 213

The other Peronist policy that generated extensive Congressional opposition was the executive intervention into the nation's universities. Perón intervened into all six of the nation's universities because he said they were bastions of opposition, as, indeed, they were.[14] His personally appointed interveners fired faculty, expelled students, decimated entire departments and programs, and imposed mandatory retirement at age 55 because the "older faculty" were "outdated" in their thinking. The interveners particularly targeted the social sciences and humanities. The interventions became witch hunts in which critical thinkers and non-Peronist faculty and students were persecuted, ostracized, fired, or expelled. Many faculty left Argentina rather than have their work subjected to the ongoing censorship around them. Under the Peronist intervention, Argentina's universities began the long decline from which they have never recovered.

As with the debate on religious education, the Radicals brought their considerable oratorical and legal skill to bear in their speeches. They argued for academic freedom and freedom of conscience. They trumpeted the universities as among the greatest in Latin America and cited statistics on the number of foreign students who came to study in Argentina. They tried to appeal to national pride, human empathy, and the sense of fair play. They noted that the expelled students and fired professors had not been breaking any law. They argued that the universities were being destroyed and would lose their international reputation. They were correct in all of this. The Peronist bench, whose responses, interruptions, and expressions of open contempt are recorded in Congressional transcripts, gave no indication that they even understood what academic freedom or critical discourse were, much less why they were valuable. When the opposition spoke, the majority bench hissed and jeered. When the Peronists got tired of making disrespectful comments or felt that the Radicals were winning the debate, they resorted to parliamentary maneuvers to avoid a vote on the proposed Radical resolutions. They tabled resolutions. They voted to move on to issues of "greater importance." They left the chamber, enabling the Peronist Speaker of the House to declare no quorum and suspend debate. They sent the motions to a committee where they were buried and never considered again. The Radicals raised their objections about the destruction of the universities in May, July, September, October, November, and December 1946, and again in February 1947. At times when the debate in the chamber became particularly heated or hostile, the Radicals withdrew the resolution only to present it again a month later. Their persistence was never rewarded. The Congress never declared a resolution in support of the universities or in

---

[14] Universities are always bastions of opposition, precisely because they are and should be bastions of critical thinking. The more monolithic policy is, the more critical the university community will become. According to Gutmann, this is the job of the university and is a task essential to both democratic and university survival. See Gutmann (1987, chaps 6 and 7, esp. pp. 181, 184, 192, 229, 230). Nowhere was the anti-democratic nature of Peronism revealed more starkly than in its relations with the universities.

opposition to Perón's intervention into them. The interventions continued until all university opposition had been ousted or had left of their own accord.

For those who believe in the inseparability of democracy and free thought, these are demoralizing stories.[15] The imposition of religious education and the destructive, partisan micro-management of the universities are examples where the democrats were defeated, despite valiant efforts to keep public education free of religious influence and to protect higher education. But if we step back from these losses to consider the larger picture, we can see that institutional learning progressed in these years, and the battle the Radicals waged still created democratic institutional capital, despite the immediate loss of political and academic freedom. In the first Peronist Congress, Argentina learned how Congress could be a forum for debate and the presentation of alternative political views. The transcripts preserved the record of a united opposition bench working efficiently to present an argument. In addition, a large number of impressive speeches and arguments in favor of educational freedom were recorded on transcripts, and they stand as testimony to the power of rhetoric and informed argument in the debate that is so essential to democracy.

The story of the legislature during Perón's first nine years is a story of much loss and some gain. On the positive side, Argentina's Congress remained open throughout those years and was only closed by the military at Perón's ouster in 1955. When Perón won a second six-year term in 1952, his party again won majority support in both chambers while a few seats went to the opposition. The Radical bench of the mid-1950s was less intellectual and less oratorically gifted than the bench of the mid 1940s, but they used their seats to press for changes in the repressive Peronist laws and for repeal of the most damaging reforms. Thus, even to the very end of Perón's first administrations (1946–1955) Congress held some voices of opposition.

On the negative side, however, while Congress remained open, much of its purpose had been defeated, with a resulting decline in its power, importance, and efficacy. Peronism undermined Congress' independent, democratic function so severely that the institution ceased to move forward toward greater professionalization and stood instead as a reminder of the freedom lost. Congress was less impressive in the 1950s than it had been between 1946 and 1948. The days of eloquent opposition were over. Many Radicals who had opposed early Peronism left the Congress, exhausted by the futile effort to stop Peronism and beaten down by persecution and contempt. The head of the Radical bench, Ricardo Balbín, was jailed for over a year for his Congressional dissent. As a result of Congressional decline, debate was shorter and less impassioned; many policy issues never reached the legislature at all. The Congress met fewer hours and fewer days. By defeating and humiliating the opposition so thoroughly and by *never* allowing them to pass a single law or win a single resolution, by

---

[15] Gutmann argues that, in fact, democracy and higher education cannot exist without each other and that each provides indispensable support for the other (1987).

If You Build It They Will Come

demonstrating that different opinions, no matter how eloquently presented, nor how firmly grounded in law, would never win, the Peronist majority also defeated itself. In following Perón so closely, the Congress had gone a considerable distance toward eliminating its own job, leaving more and more of the legislative task in the hands of the executive.

We see the decline of Congress in the Congressional transcripts, which by the mid-1950s are slim volumes, a shadow of what they had been between 1946 and 1948.[16] Moreover, in the 1954 and 1955 transcripts, Peronism was itself beginning to backpedal in response to critics, undoing its most odious laws, including the 1948 law imposing Catholic education in primary schools. By leaving the legislature open, despite its debilitated state, Peronism had a venue where policy could be gradually reformed. Historical descriptions of Perón's final two years portray him as uncompromising as ever. But on the floor of Congress, a different image emerged. Peronist deputies sensed a decline in Perón's popularity. Many of his early allies, including the Church, had turned against him, and growing sectors of the population were disillusioned with his heavy-handed government. Peronist deputies took conciliatory steps toward the opposition, and these efforts were evident in Congress, even if they did not become public knowledge. In the Congressional transcript one can see Peronism trying to undo some of the damage it had done, realizing that it needed to compromise if it wanted to retain at least its following, let alone national power. The late Peronist Congress provides evidence of both a continued opposition to Peronism and of a growing flexibility and responsiveness within Peronism. The presence of dissent and the Peronist responsiveness to the opposition set apart late Peronism from the European fascisms which had never permitted a Congress, had never been forced to recognize opposition, and had never considered it necessary to respond to the opposition. It was in Congress where one could see that the small space that remained for dissent began to widen, even under Perón. Inside Congress in those final years, one could also see Peronism attempting to change in ways that were not immediately evident to society at large, and that were more in keeping with the proper function of a Congress.

From the 1954–1955 Congressional debate, particularly in the lower chamber, it appears that the worst of Peronism has already come and gone, and Peronist legislators were increasingly willing to negotiate. If Peronism was becoming more flexible, then the 1955 coup came when the movement was ready to compromise. Judging from the Congressional debate, it seems as if the voices of opposition might have been ready to reform Peronism sufficiently to allow democracy to reappear gradually, if only Congress had been left open. Instead, by closing the Congress in 1955, the military precluded any

---

[16] The decline of Congress is visibly evident in the number of volumes recording Congressional debate during Perón's first two presidencies. For 1946 eleven such volumes exist. The numbers for the subsequent years are as follows: 1947: 7; 1948: 6; 1949: 7; 1950: 4; 1951: 4; 1952: 3; 1953: 3; 1954: 4; 1955: 2.

chance for democracy to work itself out by making Peronism a more democratic populist movement and making opposition voices more respected and influential. Instead of allowing repeated Congressional elections gradually to change the character of Congress and of the laws it passed, the military took matters into their own hands and outlawed democracy altogether. Although Peronism had deprived Congress of most aspects of democratic function, it was the 1955 coup that denied it the opportunity for self-correction. Of course, one can never know what the course of events would have been. But the Congressional transcripts make evident that, even in the face of an authoritarian populism, some semblance of democracy remained alive in one corner of Peronist Argentina while the Congress remained open.

Whatever its limitations, the institutional capital that developed in the Argentine Congress periodically in the twentieth century had no counterpart in Nicaragua until after 1979. After the revolutionary victory, a legislature emerged in Nicaragua, and the nation began the process of creating legislative memory and institutional capital. Because the learning period is much shorter in Nicaragua, the level of institutional development and professionalization is much lower there. Yet, because the learning process has not been interrupted by a coup, institutional learning has proceeded more quickly in Nicaragua than it did in Argentina. This section of the chapter considers recent legislative history in Nicaragua and the more limited legislative development there. That story shows that Nicaragua's legislature is beginning to institutionalize but that it lags far behind Argentina's. This section, like the section above, also scrutinizes the relationship between legislative development and the nation's powerful mass movement, in this case Sandinismo.

As we have seen, Peronism left open the legislature partly as a result of its democratic facade and partly because Congressional control increased and broadened Perón's power. Insofar as democratic practices existed inside Congress during the first nine Peronist years, they did so *despite* Peronism and in the face of active Peronist efforts to suppress the opposition. The relationship between Sandinismo and the legislature was precisely the opposite. Sandinista leaders took the initiative in founding and encouraging a legislature when no meaningful chamber had existed previously. Sandinismo did much to encourage debate and differences of opinion within the legislature. That support left the democratic aspects of Nicaragua's legislature developing in harmony with the popular mass movement, rather than in opposition to it.[17]

After the Sandinista victory in 1979, Nicaragua's new national leadership replaced Somoza's legislature of cronies with a representative unicameral sectoral legislature: the Council of State.[18] The Council included representatives of the mobilized groups (trade unions, peasant organizations, women's and

---

[17] Anderson (2006).
[18] In their study of the United States Senate, Lee and Oppenheimer write that bicameral legislatures were an "eighteenth century norm." By contrast, unicameral legislatures have become more common in the twentieth century (1999, pp. 26–29). The Argentine and Nicaraguan cases fit this pattern.

student groups, and associations of public employees, each elected by their organization[19]), but it was not a traditional representative legislature.[20] Instead of representing districts or provinces, the sectoral legislature allocated seats in conjunction with the size of the mobilized sector in question. Nicaragua's low-income groups were the majority, but the Council also included a limited number of representatives of the upper classes: industrialists, coffee growers, ranchers, and business owners. In this way, Nicaragua's new National Assembly followed its Constitutional mandate more closely than Argentina's Congress in its early years. Yet the mandate for the National Assembly was further from the role of a traditional legislature in a presidential system than was the official role of Argentina's Congress.

While the new Council of State was Nicaragua's first representative legislative body, it began its existence deeply subordinate to the president. Its institutional configuration was close to what Yrigoyen would have preferred for Argentina's first Congress. It provided a forum for debate but did not initiate legislation in disagreement with the executive. Since most legislators were Sandinistas,[21] the Council did not question presidential policy or offer an alternative agenda. The sectoral and revolutionary legislature allowed Nicaragua's president Daniel Ortega to avoid divided government. Its members were not geographical representatives. It reflected the mass mobilized nature of Nicaraguan society and was a first step toward institutionalizing popular voices.

Gradually, in response to domestic demands and pressure from abroad for elections, Sandinismo decreased the Council's electoral and procedural limits by holding an election in 1984 and by expanding the legislature's powers. With the 1984 election, which was legislative as well as presidential, the Council of State was replaced by a National Assembly, whose members represented the national popular vote rather than the sectoral interests of an occupational or demographic constituency. In 1984, former sectoral representatives could run for the National Assembly, and many from both low income and wealthy backgrounds did. The new legislature included representatives of different classes just as the Council had.[22]

The 1984 reforms were another step in institutionalizing popular representation in national government, yet the new National Assembly also had limits.[23] Despite proportional representation and the presence of opposition

---

[19] For an enumeration of these sectors see Vilas (1985, esp. pp. 122–123, 126–130).
[20] The early U.S. Congress reflected agrarian, regional, and parochial perspectives, was suspicious of national government in general, and, as a branch of state power, was passive and factionalized. Young (1966).
[21] Interview with Edmundo Castillo, sectoral legislator, 1979–1984 and deputy to the National Assembly for the Conservative Party, 1990–1996, Managua, March, 1995.
[22] Thomas Walker calls the post-1984 years "the constitutional period. He contrasts it with the first five transitional years of Sandinismo, which he calls "the Government of National Reconstruction." (1997, pp. 1–20).
[23] Reding (1991). For Nicaragua as a representative democracy see Serra (1991, esp. p. 74).

parties, the 1984 Sandinista electoral victory was so sweeping that Sandinismo again controlled the legislature after 1984 as it had before. Like Argentina's Peronist-controlled Congress, Nicaragua's post-1984 Assembly was politically disinclined to disagree with executive policy. It offered no alternative political agenda and did not attempt to check or question the executive in any way. Nevertheless, the Assembly undertook some legislative functions, the most important of which was a 1987 constitutional reform. The reform established an electoral calendar, confirming the scheduling of another national election for 1990, and it also institutionalized a Supreme Electoral Council to oversee that and subsequent elections. While the Sandinista years had initiated steps toward a legislature, Nicaragua's legislature in the early years of democracy was still more subservient to the executive than Argentina's Congress was by 1983.

INSTITUTIONAL CAPITAL IN TODAY'S DEMOCRACIES

Argentina's institutions of state played a central role in establishing today's democracy and creating a context of respect for human rights. After the Alfonsín presidency, the strength of both the legislature and the judiciary declined, largely owing to the deliberate efforts of the next president, Carlos Menem, to undermine the autonomy of both. Yet Menem was never entirely successful in marginalizing these two institutions and by the end of his term both had begun to reassert their own power. Moreover, Menem was also forced to work with the Congress because many of his sweeping economic reforms could not be put into place without Congressional involvement and consent. Thus Congress granted Menem special extraordinary powers to act on the economic emergency engulfing the nation in 1989. Congress scrutinized every major privatization bill that Menem proposed and approved them all. As the economic emergency abated, Congress increased its scrutiny of Menem's bills and took time to amend them. While Congressional involvement in Menem's extensive economic reforms of the 1990s was not as high as some might have preferred, it was never entirely absent.

As Menem's power and influence declined and his autocratic style became increasingly unacceptable, it was the Congress that gave early warning signs that his popularity would end. In the 1997 mid-term elections the Peronist Party lost the lower chamber, and from that point onward Menem faced divided government. Congress, working with the judiciary, subsequently ended Menem's quest for permanent power by signaling that it would not support the ten-year, two-term president's effort to hold office yet a third term. Thus it was the nation's institutions that offered the first and the most effective opposition to Menem's effort to remain in power.

After Menem finally left the presidency, Argentina suffered a period of weak executive authority when the elected Radical president, Fernando de la Rua, resigned. During these months, Congress assumed the leadership of the nation, appointing new presidents and organizing new elections to

If You Build It They Will Come

allow the population to choose a new president. The new elected president was Nestor Kirchner, who served a full term and then succeeded in having his wife, Cristina, elected as his successor. Both Kirchners have tried to subordinate Congress at least as much as did Menem but, like him, they have not been entirely successful. When Cristina encountered a paralyzing agricultural strike in 2008, it was Congress that stepped forward to resolve that crisis.

While this chapter focuses primarily upon the legislature in each nation as an example of institutional strength, the story of the legislature is also paralleled by a similar story in the judiciary. Throughout both the Menem and Kirchner years, Argentina's judiciary has continued to function with some degree of autonomy. While it has not been as autonomous as we might ideally like, it never ceased to function. In fact, the Kirchners' return to an emphasis upon human rights policy and retroactive justice has revitalized the judiciary in recent years.

In contrast with the Argentine Congress, Nicaragua's National Assembly has played a lesser leadership role in democratization and has never engaged in extensive policy formulation or crisis resolution. Yet even Nicaragua's National Assembly has sometimes made an important contribution to the development of democracy. From 1990 to 1996, Nicaragua's legislature enjoyed one of its most impressive periods. During those years, a coalition of rightist parties, the Liberals and Conservatives, held the presidency under Violeta Chamorro, while the Sandinistas stood in the opposition. Given the positive historical relationship between Sandinismo and the legislature, this particular power configuration produced a period of autonomous legislative action. In those six years, Nicaragua's legislature stood up against autocratic executive behavior across two issues. One involved nepotism and the other constitutional reform.

As Chamorro's presidency evolved, it became increasingly clear that she was a disinterested president who lacked the drive toward policy initiatives after her initial success in ending the war and the command economy and in reopening diplomatic relations with the United States. Her disinterest created a power vacuum which her son-in-law, Antonio Lacayo, stepped into. Chamorro was happy to have him take the leadership role and she gave him a cabinet position, which he used to assume more and more presidential powers. He even reached a point where he conducted presidential press conferences while Chamorro sat silently on the sidelines. Lacayo looked increasingly like an unelected, de facto president.

The National Assembly responded negatively. Taking up the cause of a Constitutional reform, which Chamorro had promised and then forgotten, the legislature wrote constitutional amendments denying Lacayo or any contemporary office holder the right to run for office while holding office. This was an effort to prevent office holders from using their power to keep themselves in office. Instead candidates would be required to resign one year prior to the next election or to stay out of power for one term. The new constitution also explicitly forbade family members of the current president from running for office immediately. The 1995 Constitutional reform exemplified legislative authority constraining executive power. Predictably, the executive resisted and the Constitution's legality went to the courts. However, Nicaragua's other institutions of state upheld the validity of the Constitutional reform and the new Constitution became law.

Partly as a result of the unexpected showing of legislative independence, Nicaragua's next president, Arnoldo Alemán, was determined to constrain legislative autonomy and prevent any such challenge to himself. He did this through a combination of bribery and majority seats. He guaranteed to himself the loyalty of his own party members by purchasing their support through substantial economic favors. From 1996 to 2001 this bought him an obedient, subservient legislature, which gave him a self-amnesty or immunity law by which he sought to avoid corruption charges after he left office.

But like Menem in Argentina, Alemán was never able to guarantee himself complete legislative subservience. As soon as he left office, the National Assembly came under pressure from incoming president, Enrique Bolaños, to repeal Alemán's legal immunity and try him for corruption. This the legislature did only reluctantly and under severe mobilized popular pressure in the form of mass demonstrations against legislative inaction. The legislature finally repealed Alemán's immunity and the former president was found guilty of corruption. At this point, the judiciary stepped forward to play an impressive autonomous role in curtailing presidential excess. Over the next ten years the multiple counts of corruption brought against Alemán were systematically investigated and redressed where possible. For example, a helicopter purchased with state funds for Alemán's personal use was sold and the funds returned to state coffers. Warrants were issued for the arrest of Alemán's adult children, each of whom owned hefty bank accounts of stolen state funds. To date those adult children remain in exile in Miami, unable to return to Nicaragua for fear of arrest. Thus both the legislature and the judiciary assumed a central role in curtailing executive corruption and authoritarianism. While the trial of Alemán was an important moment for Nicaragua's legislature, it was short-lived. For the rest of the Bolaños presidency the National Assembly did not again assume a central role in democratizing the nation. After the legal victory against Alemán, Bolaños did not again come forward with an important leadership role for the legislature and, left to its own devices, the legislature proved incapable of offering a strong, independent policy agenda of its own.

With the 2006 re-election of Ortega, Nicaragua's legislature is again entering a period of some autonomy. Ortega has tried to govern in an autocratic manner and has sought to bypass the legislature in the process. But he has encountered significant resistance, in large part because the National Assembly is dominated by the right. In every instance where he has needed legislative aquiescence to enhance his own power, the National Assembly has resisted. For example, where he tried to establish citizen councils in the nation's municipalities which would have allowed him to control local government, the legislature has tried to stop him from doing so and refused to pass laws which would make such councils mandatory.

In summary, Nicaragua's legislature has reached its most impressive and autonomous moments during periods of time when it has resisted executive excess and constrained executive authority. This is an important contribution and should not be dismissed. Nevertheless, the Nicaraguan legislature has not to date witnessed a sustained period of independent policy vision during which it pursued its own agenda apart from executive initiative. By contrast, Argentina's Congress has done both. It has stepped forward to constrain executive excess and curb executive authoritarianism. It has even assumed the executive leadership role momentarily. But Argentina's Congress has also had sustained periods of offering an independent policy agenda of its own. This is the dramatic difference in institutional power and capacity that exists between these two legislatures and the explanation lies in the greater institutional experience – institutional capital – that the Argentine Congress has accumulated throughout its longer history. Figure 7.1 illustrates that Argentina's Congress began its current democratic involvement earlier and at a higher level than did Nicaragua's legislature. Both institutions have then had downward and upward swings in autonomy and power. The trend for both is upward toward more independence and autonomy, but the Argentine Congress continues to function at a higher level than does the Nicaraguan National Assembly.

CONTEMPORARY CONTEXT AND EMPIRICAL EVIDENCE

If Argentina's legislature is stronger and more professional, we should find evidence of that in the contemporary function of the two legislatures. A higher level of institutional capital in Argentina should be evident in greater professionalism in that nation's Congress than in Nicaragua's National Assembly. Nicaragua's National Assembly should appear to be a more amateur legislature at an earlier stage of development.[24] Comparison with the U.S. Congress is useful and places the developing nature of these two legislatures in a broader comparative context.

---

[24] The term "amateur legislature" is associated with the field of American politics and with the study of Congress there. See, for instance, Polsby (1968) and Weisberg et al. (1999). By contrast, the field of comparative politics uses the term "marginal legislature" to describe a legislature early in its development process. See, for example, Mezey (1979) and Taylor-Robinson and Diaz, (1999). The term "amateur legislature" underscores the inexperience and sometimes unprofessional behavior of individual legislators themselves while the term "marginal legislature" refers to the extent to which the legislature fails to check executive power in the manner appropriate to a presidential system. Both of these terms are useful for understanding these two legislatures and particularly the Nicaraguan legislature. Both legislatures have sometimes been "marginal"; the Nicaraguan legislature shows many more attributes than does the Argentine Congress of also being an "amateur legislature."

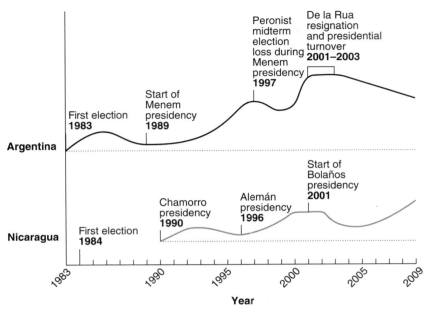

FIGURE 7.1. Level of Legislative Function since the First Election of the Contemporary Electoral Calendar: Argentina and Nicaragua.

Physical Plant and Staff Resources[25]

Studies of the United States Congress in its developing stages have found that legislators initially had few constituent demands upon their time and meager staff and resources to help them. As the legislature professionalized, constituent demands expanded, support staff and resources increased, and legislators moved from being part-time unpaid officials to being full-time representatives.[26] A review of the physical plant and staff resources available to legislators in Argentina and Nicaragua illustrates the difference in professionalism between the two assemblies.

The Argentine Congress is an imposing Baroque structure that occupies an entire city block in downtown Buenos Aires; the office buildings around it fill several more. Legislators circle the block and enter the Congress through the back entrance, which is barricaded and secluded so that they can arrive quietly. One rarely sees the legislators on the street or in the halls of Congress and the office buildings. By contrast, the National Assembly that Somoza built stands abandoned in what was once Managua's center. That center was destroyed by the 1972 earthquake and is seismically unsafe for reconstruction. Instead, Nicaragua's legislature is a single building in a state of disrepair,

---

[25] The data for this section draw upon two surveys of legislators, one each in Nicaragua and Argentina. For details on these two data bases see the Appendix.

[26] Price (1971, pp. 18–19); Weisberg et al. (1999, pp. 22, 27).

uphill from Lake Managua and away from the former center of town. It is neither beautiful nor remarkable, and one would not even know that it was a legislature except for the protective fencing around it, the presence of guards at the entrance, and the high level of daytime activity. In Nicaragua, both legislators and the public use the front entrance, and it is easy to see deputies coming and going in their daily activities at the front of the building.

Argentine legislators have offices in their respective office buildings, as well as advisors, secretaries, and receptionists to help them with their duties. Each legislator has a telephone line directly into the office and a receptionist to answer the phone. Argentina's legislature has an entirely separate mail department for each chamber and mail is delivered directly to their offices by postal clerks who work for the Congress. Until very recently, Nicaraguan Deputies did not have offices at all, and instead worked out of their own professional offices or their homes. In the last few years, Nicaragua's national deputies (20 of the 92) have received offices while departmental deputies (nearly all the others) have only cubicles. Nicaraguan legislators have very low salaries and during most of the years of democracy have not earned enough to live on. They have stayed in office only while they could live on personal savings, and have returned to paid work once they could no longer meet their own expenses. They have very little staff, and land lines are so poor that most legislators communicate using personal cell phones. Nicaraguan Deputies have a mail room and separate mail boxes, but mail delivery is unreliable.

In Argentina, a member of the public or a scholar doing research must make an appointment to visit a legislator in his or her office. After the appointment has been made over the phone, meeting that appointment requires the visitor to enter the first floor lobby of the office building, either the lower chamber office building or one of the buildings that house Senate offices. The visitor must present identification and other credentials to a staff of employees at the security check. In the lower chamber office building public lines sometimes extend out the door just to get to the counter and present credentials. Once a visitor has presented her credentials, the lobby staff telephone the office of the legislator in question to double check that an appointment really exists. If that office agrees that an appointment has been made and the legislator is able to keep the appointment, the visitor is then given a pass and told to go to a specific floor and a specific office number. Any visitor found away from the floor to which she has been given access can be escorted out of the building by guards.

Nicaragua's legislature is more open and chaotic, less cloistered and officious, and its legislators are much less protected. There is a guard at the fence outside the legislature and one internal security check. In the years since 1990 when I first began studying the Nicaraguan legislature, the chamber has moved from being quite open to being somewhat more protected. In the 1990s the chamber was as open as is the mail room in an academic department, and one could make an appointment with a legislator simply by wandering among them in the thirty minutes before a legislative session began. Now, to make an appointment, one calls the main switchboard and gets either a secretary or the personal cell phone number of the legislator. Many Nicaraguan legislators still schedule their own appointments.

The Nicaraguan style is partly a result of legislative size. Nicaragua's single chamber has ninety-two Deputies. If you wander among them, you can usually find the one you are looking for. If you can't find the legislator you are looking for, ask another Nicaraguan legislator. They usually know each other's schedules. Argentina's legislature, in contrast, has more than 240 Deputies in the lower chamber alone, and more than seventy Senators in the upper chamber. Since they meet in separate chambers, Deputies and Senators do not enter together and there is no central lobby where all legislators can be found together. Although Senators usually know each other, Deputies often do not. Deputies are even less likely to know the Senators. The formality of having office staff is much more essential in such a huge legislature.

The Nicaraguan legislature is still what legislative scholars have termed an "amateur legislature," with limited staff and resources and minimal salaries for legislators. The fact that ninety-two individuals are willing to serve as legislators at all under such circumstances is a testament to the commitment to democracy in Nicaragua. The Argentine legislature has many more of the characteristics of a professional legislature: staff, offices, telephone lines, and salaries. Although it falls far short of the level of professionalism found in legislatures in older democracies, it is considerably ahead of Nicaragua's National Assembly. This difference in staff and resources helps understand why the Argentine Congress has been more central in democratic governance.

Length of Time in Session

Both of these legislatures have gradually increased the amount of time that they are in session, moving from being more amateur to becoming more professional. The increase of time in session has expanded the numbers of weeks that they are in session as well as the number of hours per day that they are meeting. However, the expansion that each nation has experienced advantages Argentina: its legislature is in session more weeks per year and more hours per day. Because of the rapid expansion of duties, there is no regular schedule of sessions for either of these two legislatures, although the Argentine legislature is more predictable because it is in session nearly all the time. The Argentine Congress was originally supposed to meet for only four to five months during the south American winter, but now is in session about eleven months of the year. Nicaragua's legislature meets only periodically, with two weeks of sessions followed by two weeks or more when the legislature is not in session. This schedule is irregular and difficult to predict. The only way to know when the National Assembly is meeting is to be in touch with the Deputies directly. Nicaraguan sessions often start around 11 am or noon, and run until three or four in the afternoon – about three- to five-hour sessions. Argentine sessions begin at 3 pm and run all night long, or at least until 3 or 4 am, resulting in sessions that are about twelve hours long.

Experience in Government

Empirical indicators of governing experience and service provide another perspective on legislative professionalization. John Hibbing studied legislator career lengths. His studies suggest that House careers in the United States were not really an attractive option until after 1890. Other literature on established legislatures in older democracies provides a series of empirical indicators of professionalization and institutionalization. These include length of legislative careers and levels of constituency service. In the United States, longer careers and higher levels of constituency contact were associated with the growing professionalism of the United States Congress.[27] Longer careers are generally considered a sign of increased institutional professionalization because the power that accompanies office makes remaining in Congress desirable.[28] A contrast of career lengths and constituency service in the Argentine and Nicaraguan legislatures reveals different levels of professionalism there. The analysis here compares these indicators across the two legislatures, but also draws upon legislators' recent memories to consider changes in these indicators over recent years. The data sets analyzed here consist of eighty-three Argentine legislators from both chambers of Congress and fifty-three Deputies from the Nicaraguan National Assembly.

Empirical evidence on career length draws on two separate indicators, one about general experience in government of the legislator's family and one about the length of time in office of the individual legislator himself or herself. Not surprisingly, 17% of Nicaraguans but 77.1% of Argentines had family members elsewhere in local or national government. Argentines had a mean number of months in office of 51.86 (a little over four years) while the mean number of months for the Nicaraguan legislators was 40.49 (a little over three years). A simple frequency on both legislatures revealed that 64% of the Nicaraguans had been in office eighteen months or less while that same percentage of the Argentines had been in office fifty-six months or more, which amounts to about four years and eight months. Taken overall, most Argentine legislators had considerably more experience than most Nicaraguan legislators and, in fact, had been in office three times as long or more.

Breadth of Campaign Activities

A second indicator of experience is the breadth of campaign activities. Legislators in both nations were asked whether they had engaged in five different types of campaign activities during their last campaign for office:

[27] Hibbing (1991, p. 3); Price (1971, pp. 16–19).
[28] Abramson et al. (1987, pp. 3–35).

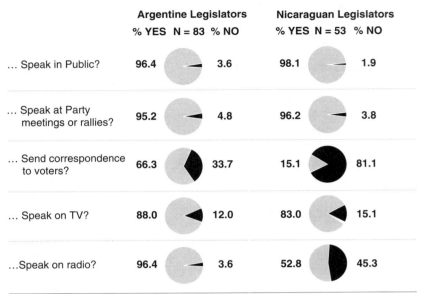

FIGURE 7.2. Breadth of campaign activities in last campaign: Argentine and Nicaraguan legislators (percentages).

(1) speak in public, (2) speak at party meetings or rallies, (3) send correspondence to voters (did not include email), (4) speak on TV, and (5) speak on the radio. The comparison showed that where both groups of legislators engaged in a particular campaign activity, the Nicaraguans were every bit as active as were the Argentines. However, the Argentine legislators had a broader range of campaign activities and most had engaged in all five of the activities listed above, whereas the Nicaraguans had mostly engaged in only three or four of the five activities. The data suggest that Argentine legislators are somewhat more professional, both in the experience they bring to office and in the breadth of their campaign activities (Figure 7.1).[29]

Availability to Constituents

Studies of legislators in the United States find that professionalism increases as the level of resources to support the legislator increases. Professionalism is

---

[29] Unlike the U.S. system from which these types of measures have been taken, both Nicaragua and Argentina are proportional representation systems. This means that candidates for office are or may be advertising their party as much or more than they are campaigning for

If You Build It They Will Come

often measured in terms of the legislator's availability to his or her constituents. The next two indicators scrutinize the legislators' availability to their constituents by asking how much time they spend in the capital city versus in their province or district, and how many voters they see in a given week. This last question referred to personal visits to the legislator's office.

These data show a higher level of professionalism among Argentine legislators but also reveal that the Nicaraguan legislators are taking their jobs very seriously, despite their more limited experience and resources. Legislators in both nations are making a serious effort to be at their elected posts in the capital city and also to meet with their constituents.[30] In the top half of Figure 7.2, both groups of legislators spent more than half of each week in the capital city, with means in each group above 5.0 (or five days per week). The literature on older legislatures argues that time spent in the capital city is an indicator of higher levels of professionalism. On this particular measure, the Nicaraguan legislators appear to spend even more time in the capital city than the Argentine legislators, although that is easier in a small nation.

The literature on more established legislatures also takes the number of voters seen on a regular basis as another indicator of professionalism. This indicator is applied to these two legislatures in the bottom half of Figure 7.2. We see that the Argentine legislators have a higher mean level with respect to the number of citizens they see in a given week, an indicator of higher availability and greater professionalism in that legislature. Yet the mean for the two groups in the second half of the figure shows that the differences between them are not as great as we might expect, given the longer history enjoyed by Argentina's Congress.

The reader will remember that the Argentine legislators have a greater level of resources and office staff at their service to assist them in making appointments with and seeing constituents. This higher level of resources may well help them achieve higher levels of contact with constituents, despite the fact that their districts are much bigger in population size than are the Nicaraguan districts. The interplay between higher staff resources and higher consitutency service shows how greater legislative professionalism encourages more of the same: once legislatures have at their disposal enough resources to allow them to do their jobs more thoroughly, they can use those resources to attend to the public more fully.

---

themselves individually. By contrast, the single-chamber district, first past the post system used in the United States means that candidates primarily campaign for themselves, with their party only part of the background context within which they present themselves to voters.

[30] The reader will remember that these are self-selected samples in which respondents were asked to take the survey but were free to decline. This probably means that the more conscientious, serious, and attentive legislators in both nations were the ones who chose to answer the survey. The bias in each sample gives a somewhat higher measure of professionalism to each sample since it probably includes the more professional legislators.

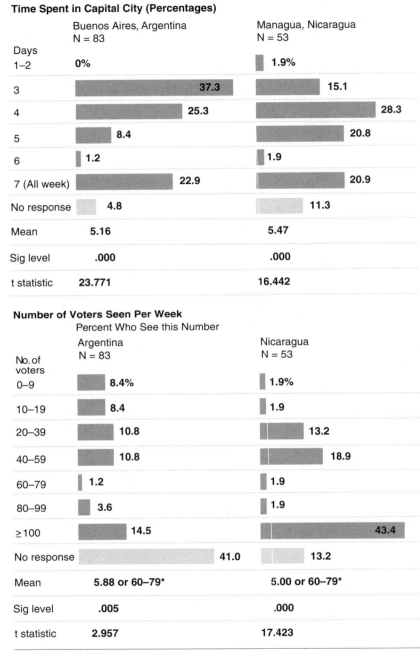

FIGURE 7.3. Availability to constituents: Argentine and Nicaraguan legislators.

Increase in Constituency Service

In order to compare the level of availability that legislators have toward the public with recent changes in that availability, I collected data on several aspects of constituency service and public contact. Respondents in both legislatures were asked to estimate the level of constituency service that they had provided in the last two years. The historic overview showed that the Argentine legislature has been functioning at a high level of national leadership for much of the last two decades, whereas the Nicaraguan legislature has vacillated in its level of professionalism. These differences are reflected in the estimates legislators gave. The Nicaraguans have experienced a recent jump in constituency service, but the Argentines, whose constituency service developed sooner in the current democracy, have not. Among the Argentine legislators, 73.4% said they had experienced an increase in the number of voters they saw in the last two years; all of the Nicaraguan legislators were seeing more voters today than they had two years previously.[31]

According to their own estimates, the Nicaraguan legislators had experienced a greater increase in demands on their time over the last two years than the Argentine legislators. No Nicaraguan legislators had experienced a zero increase in numbers of voters seen or in time spent with voters over the last two years. By contrast, a little under a third of Argentine legislators had seen no increase on these two measures in the last two years. This difference is due to the fact that Argentina's Congress has been functioning at a higher level of professionalism, including constituency service, for a longer period of time than Nicaragua's National Assembly. More importantly, however, the data in Figure 7.3 show that attention to voters has increased in both legislatures. Since time spent with voters is often considered another indicator of professionalism in the more established democracies, these estimates show that serious attention to voter concerns is increasingly part of the job that these legislators perform.

The questionnaire for this study included two additional questions about the amount of public contact between legislators and the public. Respondents estimated how many letters and phone calls they received per week and how much that number had increased in the last two years. These two questions provide information that contrasts nicely with the information given previously in Figure 7.3. That figure provided two estimates of the amount of service or attention legislators are devoting to their constituents and how much that has increased over the last two years. By contrast, Figure 7.4 below estimates the amount of attention the public is devoting to their representatives, either by sending letters or by making phone calls. Here, we see much higher levels

---

[31] Many legislators found it difficult to make these estimates and many respondents in each sample said they could not answer these questions. The data in Figure 7.3 are based upon the estimates of legislators who were willing to answer the questions.

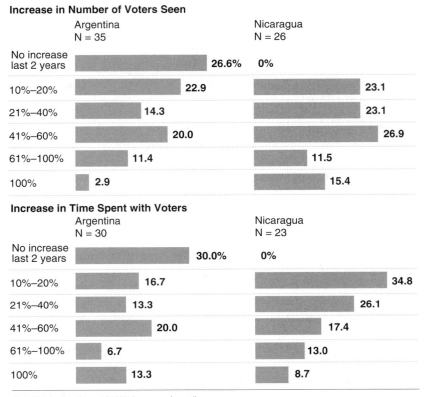

FIGURE 7.4. Argentina and Nicaragua: increases in number of voters seen and time spent with voters, last two years.

of public contact in the Nicaraguan case and also higher levels of increase in the amount of contact.

The data in Figure 7.4 show the extent to which the public in Argentina and Nicaragua are increasingly turning toward their legislators as a resource. Legislators in both samples said they were receiving a large number of letters and phone calls per week. Among the Argentine legislators, 57.7% said they were receiving between 10 and 39 letters per week (combining the third and fourth categories in the top half, left column of Figure 7.4) while the comparable percentage among the Nicaraguan legislators was 55.1%. More than 15% of the Argentine legislators and more than 20% of the Nicaraguan legislators received one hundred or more letters from voters per week.

The numbers of phone calls received also shows a considerable level of citizen attention to their legislators. Looking again at the two categories with the largest numbers of responses in the Argentine sample, 45.5% of

If You Build It They Will Come

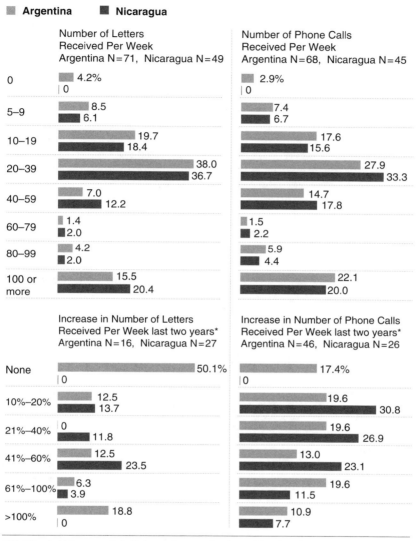

FIGURE 7.5. Argentine and Nicaraguan legislators: letters and phone calls received per week.

Argentine legislators estimated receiving between 10 and 39 phone calls per week from voters, while 22.1% receive one hundred or more phone calls per week. Among the Nicaraguan legislators, estimates of phone calls received were even higher, and the largest middle categories were 20–39 phone calls per week and 40–59 phone calls per week. Combining these two categories for the Nicaraguan sample shows that 51.1% of Nicaraguan legislators were receiving between twenty and fifty-nine phone calls per week from voters and 20% were receiving one hundred phone calls per week or more. The bottom half of Figure 7.5 shows the legislators' estimates of increases in the numbers of letters and phone calls received over the last year. Most members of both groups of legislators estimated that they had received a considerable increase in the number of letters and phone calls received per week over the last two years.

The data in Figure 7.5 provide an additional contrast as well. With respect to the number of letters received, both groups of legislators made similar estimates, despite the fact that the numerical population size of the Argentine constituencies is much larger. Nonetheless, Nicaraguan legislators estimated that they were receiving about the same number of letters per week. However, Nicaraguan legislators estimated a much larger level of increase in the number of letters received per week. Again, this difference reflects the greater amount of change that has occurred and the more rapid professionalization that has happened recently in the Nicaraguan legislature. In contrast, the Argentine legislature appears to have a more stable relationship with the public, less subject to rapid change over the past two years. Its period of rapid professionalization took place in the 1980s. By the early 2000s its rate of institutionalization and professionalization had slowed down.

Legislative/Executive Relations

A key part of legislative strength and professionalism in a presidential democracy is the capacity of the assembly to check and balance the executive. Executive authoritarianism is one of the most dangerous problems for new Latin American democracies. Both of these countries have had problems with presidents who have assumed more power than the constitution granted them. In the history of these two assemblies, the Argentine legislature has done much better than the Nicaraguan legislature in restraining executive power. With this essential balancing role in mind, legislators in both countries were asked to consider the relationship between the legislature and the executive and to comment on the relative power of the legislature vis-a-vis the executive (Figure 7.6).

The Nicaraguan legislators were fairly evenly divided on both of these questions. By contrast, the Argentine legislators were more likely to feel that Congress did not have enough power vis-à-vis the president and that Congressional power had not increased in the last two years. In addition, the more professional legislature is also the one where respondents wanted more power vis-à-vis the executive. This difference in perceptions about power is, itself, a reflection of the level of professionalism in each legislature. Two responsibilities of an assembly in a presidential democracy are to provide an agenda separate from the president and to balance the president's power. The Argentine legislature is performing those tasks at a superior level, but Argentine legislators are also more aware of the limits of the power they hold

If You Build It They Will Come

Source: Surveys of legislators in Argentina's Congress (2002) and Nicaragua's National Assembly (2003).

FIGURE 7.6. Argentina and Nicaragua: legislative power vis-à-vis the executive.

to perform those responsibilities. Nicaraguan legislators have a lower level of understanding of their responsibilities in this regard and, since they use their checking power much less, they find fewer problems with the level of power they have.[32]

Legislative Duties

A final question for each group of representatives asked them to rank the importance of five separate duties that legislators must normally fulfill: (1) check the president, (2) represent the people, (3) represent the district or province, (4) make laws, and (5) protect their own self-interest (Tables 7.1 and 7.2).

These two tables, together and separately, present a very different profile of duties as the two sets of legislators define them for themselves. Among the

---

[32] Even in the United States, the Congress does not always fulfill its responsibility of checking the power of the executive, including in instances where the president has reached beyond the appropriate limits of his power. Recently in the United States George W. Bush "moved to claim extraordinary executive powers" in his war on terrorism. In response, the U.S. Congress did virtually nothing to check or even question such sweeping powers. Fortunately for U.S. democracy, the powers of the executive were checked by a Supreme Court decision where even a conservative Court concluded that Bush had gone too far. *The Economist* (July 3–9, 2004, pp. 23–24).

TABLE 7.1. *Argentina and Nicaragua: Ranking of Legislative Duties*

Duty	Argentina: % of Respondents Ranking This Duty					
	1st	2nd	3rd	4th	5th	N
Check President	2.5	42.5	37.5	13.8	3.8	80
Represent People	10.1	7.6	5.1	17.7	59.5	79
Represent dist/prov	3.8	26.3	18.8	33.8	17.5	80
Make Laws	2.5	13.8	35.0	31.3	17.5	80
Protect Self interest	85.5	0	0	0	14.5	62

Duty	Nicaragua: % of Respondents Ranking This Duty					
	1st	2nd	3rd	4th	5th	N
Check President	2.2	4.4	17.8	71.1	4.4	45
Represent People	63.5	23.1	9.6	3.8	0	52
Represent dist/prov	21.6	47.1	21.6	9.8	0	51
Make Laws	39.6	15.1	41.5	3.8	0	53
Protect Self interest	0	0	0	2.9	97.1	35

Source: Surveys of legislators in Argentina's Congress (2002) and Nicaragua's National Assembly (2003).

TABLE 7.2. *Argentina and Nicaragua: % of legislators ranking this duty first or second*

	Argentina	Nicaragua
Check President	45%	6.6%
Represent People	17.7%	86.6%
Represent District or Province	30.1%	68.7%
Make Laws	16.3%	54.7%
Protect Self-interest	85.5%	0%

Source: Surveys of legislators in Argentina's Congress (2002) and Nicaragua's National Assembly (2003).

Nicaraguan legislators, representing the people constitutes a very high priority, followed closely by the duty to represent one's district. Among the Argentine legislators, by contrast, these two duties ranked somewhat lower. Nearly half of Argentines said that one of their primary duties was to check the president, a finding closely in keeping with the data saying that they feel the Congress lacks sufficient power vis-à-vis the presidency. Among the Nicaraguan legislators, only 6.6% of respondents said that checking the president was one of their top two duties. A second interesting contrast comes with respect to the final category, protecting self-interest. There, most Argentines ranked this duty very high, and 85.5% said it was one of their top two priorities; Nicaraguans, by contrast, ranked this duty very low and none of them said it was one of their top two duties.[33] The data on the way legislators prioritize their duties corresponds closely with the responses legislators gave in Figure 7.5 earlier. There Argentine legislators seem to be much more focused on the need for the Congress to balance the president's power while the Nicaraguan legislators are surprisingly inattentive to that responsibility, despite the clear need for it in the contemporary politics of Nicaragua.

These empirical differences reflect the fact that Argentina started early in its effort to incorporate a legislature into its government while Nicaragua started late. That simple variation in timing has made an enormous difference, because, as Weaver and Rockman have illustrated, institutions represent an opportunity. Legislative institutions in particular represent an opportunity for problem solving, a forum for dialogue and compromise, and an alternative source of power in a democratic system.[34] The more experienced legislators become across generations of learning, the more skilled they will be in using that opportunity to its full advantage.

CONCLUSION

This contrast of state institutional strength shows that Argentina has stronger institutions and, in particular, a stronger legislature. Argentine institutions have played a leadership role in democratizing the nation, despite low social capital. When the Argentine people could not or would not rely on each other, they have relied on their institutions and those institutions have allowed them to democratize. Nicaragua's institutions of state have less history and less institutional capital, and have played a more minor role in democratization. In times of crisis in Nicaragua, it is still citizen initiative that has provided the most important bulwark against authoritarianism.

If you build it they will come. If you build democratic institutions of state, democracy and its advocates will come to those institutions and use them to combat authoritarianism, constrain tyranny, and bring about a more just and humane society. Part II of this book illustrated that social capital constitutes a resource for democratization and a strong foundation upon which to build a more inclusive and just society. The findings demonstrate that Nicaragua has strong social capital while Argentina does not. But the question of how Argentina can be democratizing anyway forces us to look for alternative resources upon which Argentines can be drawing, in the absence of social capital, in order to democratize their country. This chapter has illustrated that Argentina has a rich source of democratic resources in its institutions. The strength of those institutions lies partly in the fact that they have survived

---

[33] It is also notable that non-response on this final question was the highest of all the duties and this was true across both groups of legislators. This may be due to the fact that some legislators felt uncomfortable with this question or felt uncomfortable saying (admitting) that self-interest was a high priority.

[34] Weaver and Rockman (1993).

both authoritarianism and Peronism. In contrast, Nicaragua's democratic institutions of state are newer, less experienced and resilient, and less effective. Both the history and the empirical comparison of legislative function has shown this to be true.

Nelson Polsby argues that legislatures must be institutionalized and professionalized in order to make a positive contribution to democratic governance. He uses the three criteria for institutionalization: autonomy, complexity, and universalism. Autonomy means that the legislature can function without inappropriate interference into its task from its immediate environment. Complexity means that the legislature has multiple levels of staff and professionals, including committees, that allow it to handle and complete a high work load swiftly. Universalism means that standards and expectations about performance and rewards are applied similarly to all members and particularistic rules of favoritism are absent or mostly absent.[35]

His standard of institutionalization, with its three subcomponents, is still in the distance ahead of these two assemblies. These legislatures are not fully autonomous, much less as complex or universalized as they would need to be to accomplish their full-intended purposes. Therein lies one of the key reasons for the weakness of these new democracies and for viewing them as consolidating democracies, with a level of institutional function that lags behind that of the established democracy Polsby studied (the United States). And yet, these legislatures are not impossibly amateur and both have contributed to democracy.

Public opinion evaluating the function of these two legislatures reveals an intuitive citizen understanding of their strengths and limits. In answer to a question about the specific importance of legislatures in democracy, both populations were skeptical. But Argentines gave more importance to their legislature than Nicaraguans. Thirty-seven percent of Argentines and 20% of Nicaraguans said legislators were "indispensable" for their country (p=.000; N for Nicaragua = 1002; N for Argentina = 1196).[36] In addition, Argentines were significantly more likely than Nicaraguans to say that democracy cannot function without the National Congress (p = .05) Whatever skepticism Argentines harbor about their institutions, they would rather have them than not. Nicaraguans, in contrast, seem to think that their institutions are well and good, but if they fail, the population will simply take to the streets and solve their problems through mobilization. Indeed, the history of democracy in Nicaragua bears out this assumption and illustrates that mobilized politics is usually effective and democratic in that country. One quality that is remarkable about these answers is the extent to which the people know (sense, feel, intuit) their democracy, and how they understand both its strengths and weaknesses. Respondents in each nation are correct. Institutions *are* the best bet Argentina has for continued democratization, and institutions *are* less

[35] Polsby (1999).
[36] Latinobarometer (1997).

essential in a highly mobilized and participatory democracy like Nicaragua's. In both nations, the people are right, at least in the immediate sense.[37]

But the people are also wrong. A strong democracy needs both social and political capital in the form of a mobilized society that has the capacity to act together *and* a strong institutionalized legislature that protects democratic process should popular mobilization weaken or take a non-democratic turn. Institutionalization and the formalization of rules and procedures under the rule of law can serve as a safety belt for mobilized politics when the people become destructive and attack the democratic state or break democratic laws. Argentine popular history, both recent and less recent, has shown that the potential for destructive populism certainly exists there. Yet under different circumstances and in the wake of a different popular history, popular mobilizational capacity can instead be a safeguard when it is the institutions that fail, as they have on several occasions in Nicaragua. When institutions show themselves to be so fully corrupted that they cannot or will not enforce the law, or fulfill their own mandate even *after* an authoritarian president has stepped down, then institutions cannot be trusted to uphold democracy. The events of the early 2000s showed that this was a distinct possibility in Nicaragua and, in that event, democracy there must still rely upon mobilized politics for self-correction and continued democratization.

In advocating a legislature, Rousseau thought that legislators would be wise. This chapter shows how that can sometimes be true and that, when true, it can be the salvation of a threatened new democracy, making the legislature a bulwark against an authoritarian president. But this book is also about the potential wisdom of the people themselves, and about how that wisdom can make democracy work when institutional wisdom, including wisdom among the legislators, is lacking. In the end, democracy needs both – social and political capital on the one hand and institutional capital on the other hand. There are times when the legislator will be wiser, but there are times when the legislature and legislators may be distinctly less wise than the people, especially when the legislature is functioning in an amateur mode. Democracy needs access to both kinds of wisdom so that if one fails, hopefully the other will not. Each nation considered here has one of the two ingredients that democracy needs in order to work – either social and political capital, or institutional capital – but neither has high levels of both. This leaves each nation vulnerable to anti-democratic elements in the state, in the population at large, or both. When each of these two countries has developed the capacity that the other one already has, then democracy will be safer in each nation.

[37] One exceptional example of pro-democratic grassroots organization in Argentina is the well-known story of the Mothers of the Plaza de Mayo. Without receiving directives from any party, mothers of young people kidnapped by the dictatorship marched weekly in downtown Buenos Aires, demanding the return of their loved ones and a return to democracy. Madres de Plaza de Mayo (1995).

8

Conclusion

> Too many people expect wonders from democracy, when the most wonderful thing of all is just having it.
>
> *Walter Winchell*
>
> You may be deceived if you trust too much, but you will live in torment if you don't trust enough.
>
> *Frank Crane*

This book offers many lessons about the relationship between "the people" and democracy. The book grew out of a theory, dating back to Tocqueville that posits a positive relationship between the people and democracy: democracy will be better, grow stronger, be healthier, if the people participate in their polity to a fuller rather than to a lesser extent. Contemporary perspectives on social capital pick up this positive view of popular involvement, suggesting that "the people," vis-à-vis their organizations, can make democracy work and keep it alive. Without them, democracy is in trouble.

Considering the origins of the word "democracy," this is hardly a surprising conclusion. Indeed, we would be alarmed if conclusions ran otherwise. And yet, the comparison of Nicaragua and Argentina shows that popular involvement in politics is very complex, and that it cannot be qualified with a simple term, such as "positive." The relationship between citizen politics, mass movements, social movements, and democracy may very well be positive, but, then again, it may not. Scrutiny of the nature of different popular movements and the values they inspire leaves us knowing more about the relationship between citizen politics and democracy, and this same scrutiny has led us to reflect more deeply upon the relationship between social trust and democratic politics. That reflection includes thinking about political participation; attitudes and beliefs about democracy's rules, institutions, and procedures; and, perhaps most fundamentally of all, democratic values. We now understand that certain kinds of popular movements and involvement bear a direct and positive relationship to democracy and democratic development, but such a conclusion is not universally true of all popular politics and all popular organizations. Attention to the nature of popular organizations and the belief systems behind those associations is essential if we are to know whether there is a supportive relationship between those associations and democracy.

SOCIAL CAPITAL, POLITICAL CAPITAL, AND DEMOCRACY

Scrutiny of the relationship between social trust and democracy also leads us to extend our analysis to incorporate a dimension not previously included in studies of social capital: political capital, which, we now know, is influenced and enhanced by the existence of social capital. The empirical analysis of this book shows that citizen values influence social capital, as previous theories led us to expect. But citizen values are also reflected in political capital, defined as specifically political organizations, acts, and activities. Hence we have now moved considerably beyond previous theories about social capital. We have found that political capital relates directly to political activities and is connected to attitudes about political processes and institutions. Political capital is more directly connected with democratic development than social capital is because it has a more direct empirical relationship to specifically political values and behavior. Moreover, we also find that political capital is closely related to and determined by the nature of citizen politics and by the belief systems within citizen associations. Chapters 5 and 6 show that the citizens who are more likely to belong to organizations and to socialize with others are also more likely to engage in positive, democratic citizen participation, more likely to trust democracy's institutions and procedures, and more likely to value democracy in its own right, including when recent memory offers alternative regime configurations.

Chapter 1 suggested that equality among citizens was a crucial ingredient in developing democracy. Tocqueville stressed this in his explanation for democratic development in the United States, although studies of social capital have often forgotten that aspect of Tocqueville's argument. The study of social and political capital presented here suggests that equality is also part of the difference in the development of these assets in Nicaragua and Argentina. A nation like Nicaragua, whose mass popular movement depended on cooperation, enhanced equality among citizens by encouraging them to see each other as partners in the struggle. The kind of social and political capital that emerged in Nicaragua encouraged equality among citizens by enhancing horizontal ties and by asking them to depend upon each other.[1] In contrast, a nation like Argentina, whose mass popular movement encouraged vertical dependency, did not facilitate horizontal ties. Peronism encouraged citizens to focus upon inequality – their own subordination relative to Perón – and

---

[1] Socialism has elsewhere been associated with a legacy of relative egalitarian social relations. Bunce (1999) makes this argument with respect to the formerly socialist nations of Russia and Eastern Europe.

ignored or undermined any capacity for mutuality or horizontal cooperation that might have emerged.

But even considering social and political capital together does not provide the full picture for a study about democracy, unless we factor in the role of institutions. Considering the role of institutions within the development of democracy moves this study to an entirely different dimension. Parts I and II of this book are about citizen politics, a kind of politics of the streets. Those parts help magnify and refine our understanding of the implications of street politics, but they also illustrate that citizen politics of the street has its limits, even with respect to their contribution to democracy. When those limits are reached, institutional capital demands our attention.

CITIZEN VALUES AND THE PRE-DEMOCRATIC STATE

The theoretical argument of this book emerges gradually through the historical narrative of Chapters 2 and 3, and is then examined empirically in Part II. The historical narrative makes clear that a book scrutinizing both Sandinismo and Peronism offers a unique opportunity to study the role of social capital in helping a new democracy develop or inhibiting it from doing so. These two popular movements offer examples of very different kinds of social capital; between them we have a kind of social laboratory that allows us to consider the role of social capital in democratization in two very different situations.

I focus on Sandinismo and Peronism for two important reasons. First, they each marked a coherent and defined moment in time when specific political goals and styles became highly pronounced. As such they allow us to scrutinize those moments in order to discern what those political goals and styles were. As emphatic moments in national popular history, they etched in bold specific characteristics with which the developing democracies must now reckon. But second, as key moments in popular history, their advent also caused each movement to become a part of popular identity, a subject of popular loyalty, and a source of popular values. Today, in Nicaragua and Argentina, Sandinismo and Peronism are political parties central to the developing democratic process. Each has a core of supporters who mobilize, vote, think and respond to others in ways that reflect their fundamental political identity and the core values of their originating movements. As individuals who identify with Sandinismo or Peronism, they provide us with an opportunity to study political loyalties and values in relation to social and political behavior and public opinion. They divide their respective societies into obvious and meaningful subgroups whose opinions and behaviors can be compared with those outside the subgroup.

Yet the value of a contrast between Nicaragua and Argentina goes beyond the study of these two popular movements. Studies of social capital in Italy and the United States illustrate that the nature of social relations in any given society is a product of many decades, even generations of social patterns.

Conclusion

Although Sandinismo and Peronism each accented a particular type of social pattern, they were themselves also a product of social patterns already at play in their own societies. In each case, those broader patterns were strongly influenced by the state long before the state became democratic.

A brief focus on the nature of the state in each of these two cases reveals a deep irony: less may be more when constructing the pre-democratic state. This is an irony that studies of democracy have often missed. The strength of the pre-democratic state matters long before elections and even before the arrival of popular movements. In political science, much attention has been directed to the strength of the modern state. But scant attention has gone toward the strength of the state in the early years of state building. In both the cases at hand, those years took place in the early nineteenth century; shortly after, each received independence from Spain.

In the Argentine case, nineteenth-century founders tried to construct a strong, formal national state, especially after the downfall of Rosas in 1852. They wrote a constitution, established a Congress, set up a three-branch presidential system, created formal electoral laws, forging the structure for a powerful central government. As we saw in Chapter 3, the Argentine government subsequently ignored many of its own rules and laws. But one element of the nineteenth century goals remained: the desire for a powerful state. Whether or not the Argentine national government followed its own rules, it certainly tried to make certain that the population followed rules and was well under the control of the state.

With the early strong state in Argentina came considerable control over the population, as well as an emphasis on exclusion.[2] These tendencies kept citizen initiative weak and subject to state control. The strong state entered into people's lives, controlling their immigration status, their right to work, their access to land, and their ability to become citizens. Argentines had less room to maneuver, organize themselves, solve their own problems, and take responsibility for their own condition than they would have had under a weak state. A strong state that was simultaneously a non-democratic state greatly undermined citizen capacity for independent initiative and citizen opportunities for social organization. This would have long-term consequences for Argentine social capital, particularly for the kind of popular movement that would emerge and receive a loyal following.

The Nicaraguan case provides the opposite scenario. While the nineteenth century Argentine founders sat down to write a formal constitution, Nicaraguan elites thundered around on horseback in armies, taking control of

---

[2] The tendency toward an exclusionary political culture sometimes assumed an authoritarian character and sometimes a populist character. In either guise, however, it encouraged individuals to view others negatively and lent itself to the development of authoritarianism. Argentina's exclusionary political culture contrasts with that of Uruguay, which emphasized the building and use of political parties and political governance by consensus. Spektorowski (2000, pp. 81–99).

the state in violent and chaotic fashion. No group of thoughtful and reflective state builders sat down to write a formal, elaborate, and thorough constitution along the lines of those being followed in Argentina. In contrast to the Argentine state, the nineteenth century Nicaraguan state was weak, haphazard, and fragile. Each government was subject to being abruptly overturned by the invading army of the other party. Indeed, the Liberal and Conservative parties were themselves the only indicators of any formal political organization in Nicaragua at all. And neither of them showed any inclination, either together or alone, to establish a formal set of rules and institutions for the governance of Nicaragua.

The chaos and tumult of nineteenth century Nicaraguan politics was experienced by average citizens as a weak, distant, and sometimes even absent state. Politicians and leaders themselves were inclined to use any means possible to change the government or take power. There was little following of rules among the elites. The state was certainly unable to determine citizenship status, work permits, and various other aspects of private lives. For the most part the state, was too disorganized and too weak to take over such particulars in the lives of average citizens. The weak and absent state left citizens with considerable room to maneuver and to undertake their own initiatives. If they wanted to accomplish something, it was best to do it themselves, since the state was mostly absent and political elites were otherwise preoccupied with their own power struggles. A non-democratic state that was also a weak state had a low capacity to undermine citizen initiative. Consequently, citizens were left largely to their own resources to take independent action and to organize socially as they saw fit.

The irony here is the relationship between the early state and the creation of social patterns that would later become a type of social capital. In most nations, the early state is a non-democratic state. This has been true in both Europe and Latin America. The United States is one of the few examples that began by deliberately establishing a democracy. And, even in the United States, the breadth of democratic participation was quite limited in the first century. Therefore the strength of the early state matters. Judging from these two cases we can draw some tentative conclusions: Where the early non-democratic state is weak, room for citizen initiative and independent citizen association will be greater; where the early non-democratic state is strong, citizen lives and initiatives will be much more curtailed and in a non-democratic manner. Room for citizen association will be much more limited.

One general conclusion appears. The ideal scenario is for the early state to be democratic, even if participation is limited. But if the early state is to be non-democratic – and most early states are – then it is far better that it be weak. At least it is better from the standpoint of social capital. For the weak non-democratic state will allow more room for social relations to develop independently while the strong non-democratic state will have a more forceful and debilitating non-democratic impact on popular association and initiative. This conclusion bears further investigation beyond the two cases at hand.[3] Other societies with strong or weak pre-democratic states will also reveal cultural patterns that affect the kinds of national popular movements that emerge. But one fact seems clear: a strong state is not necessarily a better state when the state is still non-democratic.

CITIZEN VALUES AND CONTEMPORARY POLITICS IN NICARAGUA AND ARGENTINA

This book is as much about history as about contemporary politics, and we have sought explanations for the contemporary political situation in a deeper understanding of the past. Yet the understanding we have gained does not provide all the answers about democratic development in Nicaragua and Argentina. We have found no crystal ball. We know that democracy is still developing in these two nations and that it is deeply imperfect, problematic, troubled, and unconsolidated. We also know that both of these democratizing societies contain within them the seeds of their own destruction, domestic elements that would certainly destroy democracy if they could. The process of democratization, by its very nature, implies a long-term struggle between those who cherish democracy and those who reject it, those who hold democratic values and those who do not. The democratization struggle is successful only if the former win and the latter learn to tolerate that victory, even if they do not accept it.

Each of the nations studied here has non-democratic actors (both citizens and leaders) within society and even within the polity. These actors have struggled against the democratization of their nations and have done so throughout the twenty-odd years of the unbroken electoral calendar that these nations currently boast. We can only expect that these anti-democratic actors will continue their struggle into the foreseeable future, as long as they believe they may eventually prevail. Therefore, the uncertainties that these democracies face and the threats to democratic consolidation will remain for some time into the future.

As we have demonstrated, Nicaragua has significant advantages favoring its democratization. These advantages help explain why the nation has moved toward democracy with as much success as it has – even in the face of other disadvantages such as poverty, a limited industrial base, low educational levels, long years of dictatorship and anti-democratic foreign intervention, and extremely weak institutionalization.[4] Nicaragua's democratic advantages

---

[3] An important new study of Mexico and Peru in the nineteenth century pursues the question of the development of social capital in the pre-democratic era in both nations. Forment (2004) finds that there were distinct differences in the level of associational life in different Latin American nations.
[4] Although this book has not been about local level politics, new scholarship on local politics in Nicaragua and Argentina again advantages Nicaragua, indicating that Nicaraguans are already able to understand and use local politics to help meet their own daily needs, a capacity that is related to their ability to work together and cooperate to accomplish development tasks.

lie primarily in the nature of popular values and the way that popular associations have encouraged horizontal ties, citizen cooperation, and social trust.[5]

But citizen politics are not always democracy's ally and are not democracy's only ally. Even in Nicaragua, popular politics and citizen opinion pose some threats to continued democratization. The repeated presidential victories accruing to the right in 1990, 1996, and 2001 were disturbing. While a rightist coalition of center-right and far-right leadership won in 1990 by backing moderate rightist Violeta Chamorro, who appeared genuinely to believe in democracy, the far-right Liberals won by themselves in national elections in 1996 and 2001. During those years, Liberal Party leadership was strongly influenced by Arnoldo Alemán, who did much as president to undermine Nicaraguan democracy from 1996 to 2001.[6] He also sought to undermine democracy after leaving the presidency, acting like a caudillo in his control over the Liberal Party and its members. Despite his corrupt and authoritarian style, his party won again in 2001 anyway. The data in this book show that Liberals have lower social capital and lower democratic values than Sandinistas. Liberal elite leadership and Liberal citizen values do not necessarily support democracy in Nicaragua. A vote for the right, then, brings into power a party whose supporters have only limited commitment to democracy.

Immediately prior to the 2006 election and after its loss in that election, the right has experienced an ongoing struggle over democratization within the Liberal Party itself. Its strong loyalty to Alemán certainly contributed to the electoral loss by Jose Rizo, who was widely seen as closely connected with Alemán. Yet, rather than jettison Alemán entirely, the right has divided, with only part of the Liberal Party, led by Eduardo Montealegre, rejecting Alemán, while the other part still continues to embrace and follow him. This struggle within the right is a struggle over the democratization of the right and of the

---

Argentines, by contrast, appear not to understand how local politics works. They continue to judge local political performance by focusing on national policy decisions, faulting national politicians for local problems and expecting national politics to resolve local issues. On this issue in Nicaragua see Anderson and Dodd (2008; 2009). On Argentina see Gelineau and Remmer (2006). The pattern found in Nicaragua is similar to that found in El Salvador where local politics and holding local politicians accountable to public opinion has enhanced democratic development. On El Salvador see Manning (2008).

[5] A related but different argument appears in the work of Elisabeth Jean Wood (2000; 2001). She maintains that popular mobilization can be a pathway toward democratization when it becomes so disruptive that it inhibits elite investment and capital development. Even in oligarchic and anti-democratic governments, elites will move toward democratization when they find that they can no longer do business because popular disruption has prevented the stability that a lucrative business environment needs. Wood's argument centralizes the impact popular mobilization has on elite behavior; my argument stresses the influence popular mobilization has on citizen values and on ordinary people themselves. Yet in both arguments the outcome of popular mobilization is democratization.

[6] Part of Alemán's agenda was to target NGO's that were working on social programs and to make their continued operation difficult or impossible. His antagonism toward NGOs particularly targeted women directors of these organizations, many of whom were forced to leave Nicaragua. Kampwirth (2003).

Liberal Party itself, and the winners in that struggle remain unknown as this book goes to press.

A similar struggle is also occurring on the left, inside the Sandinista Party. As this book goes to press, the Sandinista party is electorally in the minority at the national level, but holds the most local government seats nationwide. At the national level, Sandinismo lost three consecutive elections to a united right. The 2006 Sandinista presidential win was owing largely to division on the right over the continuing predominance of Alemán. It is disturbing that the 2006 popular choice, Daniel Ortega, has shown scant regard for the law since being elected. This behavior has not undermined popular support for his party in most local elections, where Sandinista mayors continue to be more faithful to the original development and democratic ideals of the party than Ortega is himself. What we see here is a struggle inside the Sandinista party for the heart and soul of Sandinismo. Will it remain the democratic and participatory instrument it was intended to be? Or will it become a corrupted party of a new caudillo named Daniel Ortega? That struggle also reaches into the future, goes beyond this book and is part of the ongoing democratization of Nicaragua.

For these reasons, a vote for either left or right in Nicaragua is more complicated now than it was earlier in its electoral era. On both left and right, democrats and non-democrats face each other. Within each party some leaders are a better bet for democratic development, while others actively seek to undermine democracy. But reaching below the level of party leadership, the empirical findings of this book remain predominant. The values of Sandinismo itself support democracy more thoroughly than do the values of non-Sandinistas. That reality serves as a source of encouragement since the current Sandinista leader can no longer be counted among the nation's democrats.

Is the positive bridging social capital derived from the Sandinista revolution fading ever further into the past with each passing year? Will Ortega's corrupt and authoritarian behavior undermine the values of the very party that supports him? Is it possible that political values even among Nicaraguans are gradually becoming less democratic? Or will the predominant values of social capital and democratic support within Sandinismo undermine Ortega, re-democratizing the party from below and removing Ortega in the process? And will the right gradually adopt the democratic values of Sandinismo as the right itself moves away from caudillismo and toward more transparent democratic politics? Only time will fully answer these questions, but informed consideration can help place such questions in perspective. Liberal electoral victories and citizen self-identification with Liberalism do not necessarily mean a decline in democratic values in Nicaragua, although these developments warrant close attention. Likewise, leftist electoral victories that come from voters with high social capital do not necessarily usher in a democratic president, at least as long as Ortega dominates the party. The analysis of social capital in this book and the comparison of Nicaragua with Argentina indicate that Nicaraguans are highly sociable and exhibit high levels of social capital.

While Sandinistas are more trusting and sociable than non-Sandinistas, Nicaraguan *society* has relatively high social capital, even among Liberals. Additionally, the data on social capital analyzed in this book were collected after Bolaños' election in 2001, indicating that a second Liberal victory did not immediately undermine social capital in Nicaragua, although the long-term effects of such a victory are unknown.[7]

Third, even during the Alemán term of 1996–2001, the authoritarian values of the party in power did not keep the population as a whole from reacting against the president once he had left office. The population mobilized against Alemán in 2001, insisting that his self-declared immunity be removed and that laws against corruption be applied to him. Mobilization against Alemán indicates that the contentious citizen "politics of the streets," that distinguish Nicaraguans from other populations were still alive and well, despite two Liberal victories, the extended rightist hold on presidential power, and the long period of Sandinista exclusion from presidential power.[8] This citizen politics of the streets still represents Nicaragua's best bet for continued democratization. Liberal victories did not undermine Nicaragua's capacity for mobilized politics. In fact, the 2006 electoral outcome indicates that citizens eventually tired of flagrant Liberal violations of democratic law and corruption.[9] If people have no need to march, they will not march because marching takes time and energy from a low-income population that needs both just to survive. But if government insists on breaking the law and institutions do nothing to stop that, then the people will march – or at least the Nicaraguan people will march. It is their revolutionary heritage and their social capital. On them still rests their democracy.

Fourth, some leaders on the right do respect democratic law and procedures. The last Liberal president, Enrique Bolaños, reacted against Alemán's authoritarianism. His first efforts were to separate both himself and his administration from Alemán. Moreover, he encouraged mobilized politics and helped organize the streets in the effort to remove Alemán's immunity and bring him to trial. Another potential leader is Eduardo Montealegre of the center-right Liberal Alliance. He appears less personalistic than Alemán and, in the 2006 election, appeared willing to abide by democratic law. He continues to challenge Alemán for leadership of a reunified rightist coalition. Bolaños and Montealegre are rightist leaders who are or may be more prepared to accept the rule of law than Alemán was. Bolaños, in particular, was willing to utilize mobilized citizen politics in order to continue the democratization process. If the entire political spectrum is willing to resort to a politics of the streets,

---

[7] At a more general level, Weyland (2004) has argued that neo-liberal reforms throughout Latin America have weakened democracy in the continent because they have weakened leftist parties generally. This pattern is clearly visible in the Nicaraguan case and extends across both the Alemán and Bolaños presidencies.
[8] Luciak (1990; 1995); Isbester (2001).
[9] Anderson and Dodd (2007).

Nicaraguan politics may continue to be extremely tumultuous, but at least the capacity for mobilization will not atrophy.

Finally, since ending his term, Alemán has been punished for his corruption and lawlessness, even if that punishment falls short of what it should have been. He was arrested, tried for corruption, and found guilty despite all his extraordinary efforts to legalize his own immunity, buy a legislative bloc, and otherwise live quite comfortably above the law. These developments indicate that while some Nicaraguans may support Liberalism as a party, they reject those aspects or the individuals within it who are least democratic. Montealegre and his Liberal Alliance did better than the Liberal Party in 2006, both with respect to presidential votes polled and with respect to seats in the legislature.[10]

The long-term outcome of the ongoing battle for democratization in Nicaragua is unknown as this book goes to press. Charles Tilly has suggested that democratic nations engage in "de-democratization" as well as in democratization.[11] Other scholars have seen "de-democratization" as only a temporary period of backsliding on the democratization scale, two steps forward and one step backward. Another way to look at democratic development in Nicaragua is to say that democratization is occurring at the local level and at the level of the nation's legislature, but de-democratization is temporarily underway in the presidency.[12] The outcome of that contest will be only partly determined by citizens' mobilizational capacity. It also depends on the strength of Nicaragua's democratic institutions, particularly the legislature. If Nicaragua were to develop stronger democratic institutions, then it would matter considerably less if the presidency were held by a party or an individual of low democratic values. The institutions of state would themselves constitute a safeguard for democracy, quite apart from the state of public opinion or the behavior of a leader at one moment in time.[13] But as long as Nicaragua's institutions remain as weak as they were by the time this book was written, then the strength of social and political capital among the public remains crucial, since they determine the nature of mobilized politics in Nicaragua. Precisely because Nicaragua's institutions are so weak, the state of social capital among the public and what leaders do while in power have a hefty importance.[14]

---

[10] Anderson and Dodd (2007).
[11] Tilly (2007).
[12] Anderson and Dodd (2009).
[13] For a discussion of changes in the strength of Nicaragua's legislature in particular and of the waxing and waning of its power see Anderson (2006b). For a study of horizontal accountability in the judiciary institution see Dodson and Jackson (2004). For a study of horizontal accountability in Argentina see Chavez (2004).
[14] Nicaragua's social capital also matters because its leaders have often been reluctant to compromise among themselves and reach agreement upon matters that instead become the subject of considerable controversy. Anderson and Dodd (2005) argue that elite reluctance to reach agreement or to pact among themselves has characterized Nicaragua both historically and contemporarily. O'Shaughnessy and Dodson (1999) illustrate that, in similar social context, elites in El Salvador were much more willing to reach agreement among themselves.

In his argument for social capital as a conductor for democracy, both in *Making Democracy Work* and in *Bowling Alone*, Putnam never describes or explains the exact connection between social capital and democratic institutions.[15] He assumes that where the one is strong the other will also be strong. In the case of Nicaragua, however, twenty-five years after the onset of elections, social and political capital are quite strong but institutions are still weak. Will political and social capital eventually strengthen Nicaraguan's institutions of state? One would hope so, and there are certainly indications of political development in this general direction. Yet as of this study, Nicaragua is still a democracy that demonstrates strong political and social capital, but relatively weak democratic institutions. Those weak institutions constitute a danger for Nicaragua's democracy, particularly in view of the fact that the current president governs in a lawless and personalistic style.

Argentina's problems of democratization are quite different. This book shows that Argentina has much lower social and political capital than Nicaragua. Within Argentina, the strongest and largest political party is associated both with lower social capital among its followers and with less democratic behavior, both historically and recently.[16] The data analyzed here show that Peronism is in fact one of the key causes of Argentina's low levels of social and political capital.[17]

Argentine democracy must develop despite Peronism and not because of it. Since Peronism is the strongest electoral party, the weakness of political parties with higher democratic values leaves the nation facing a significant obstacle to democratization: its strongest party has only tepid democratic loyalty.[18] Argentina is unique in undertaking such a task. No other democracy has ever tried to develop while also retaining a political party with fascist historical traits at the heart of its electoral system.[19] Every other nation that

---

[15] Putnam (1993; 2000).
[16] In an important new study, Matthew Cleary and Susan Stokes (2006) likewise find that social capital is low in Argentina, as well as in Mexico.
[17] When the new democratic government in Germany began its effort to reestablish democracy immediately after World War II, it recognized that trust was weak everywhere in society after Nazi rule. The government consciously sought to establish trust within society by following norms of humaneness and even-handed application of the rule of law. Frei (2002).
[18] In contrast to Peronism, some scholars note that democratic values are higher within the Radical Party which has deliberately undertaken policy to further democratic values. See, for example, Fournier (1999). Peronist president, Néstor Kirchner, showed more willingness to abide by democratic rules and work with democratic institutions than Menem ever did or, for that matter, than do many other Peronist leaders. *The Economist*, May 17–23, 2003, p. 33. But his recent successful effort to install his wife in the presidency raises anew questions about personalistic politics within Peronism and many observers think that her autocratic treatment of the Congress is even worse than was Menem's. On the limits of Argentina's democracy in the face of lack of party competition see Anderson (2009).
[19] Burgess and Levitsky (2003) argue that populism is adaptable and that, among populisms, Peronism is one of the more adaptable kinds. The question at hand is whether Peronism can adapt to democracy, demonstrating itself willing to abide by democratic rules internally and externally and absorb democratic norms. Peronism's adaptability at that level remains to be seen, although there are some positive indicators in that general direction.

ever developed an authoritarian populist party in its midst (all of them in Western Europe) found that it needed to eliminate that party before it could democratize. No nation has ever tried to tame a party with fascist traits, or tried to convince its leaders and followers to play by democratic rules and respect the human and civil rights of their opponents. In Italy, the citizens moved against Mussolini and ousted him before beginning their return to democracy. In Germany, foreign military intervention was necessary before the Nazi party could be destroyed, and while the foreign powers intervening in Germany came with a democratic agenda, they were under no illusion that democracy could be instituted by including the Nazis as one of the possible electoral contenders. In Spain, the nation waited until the fascist leader died before even beginning the democratization process. Argentina is the only known case attempting to democratize while including an authoritarian mass party within its new electoral system. Little wonder, then, that they are having such difficulties.

The problems Peronism presents for democracy run deep. This book has demonstrated the devastating effect Peronism has had on social capital and on citizen abilities to create horizontal ties upon which to build cooperation. Peronism has gotten inside the heads of its followers and supporters. As the data show, these people fundamentally do not trust others. They do not join organizations; they do not want to. They do not want to associate or cooperate. They have a dark view of others and rate low on trust questions. And how could they be otherwise when their basic political socialization experience was shaped by a party and a leader with a conspiracy-theory view of the world? Peronists lack the most basic tools for human cooperation that Tocqueville discovered in America, those that Putnam has called for in every democracy, and those that Nicaraguans have found so helpful in developing their own democracy.

The problem of distrust and lack of cooperation also exists at the level of Peronist party leadership and in the Peronist party machine that is so electorally effective.[20] This means that even when the party conducts much-needed economic reforms, as under Menem, it does so in a clientelistic manner, thus undermining public trust both in the reforms and in the state itself.[21] As a party, either in power or in electoral competition, Peronism has no rules and no reliable inner procedures that are respected by party members and leaders. The party has no inner institutionalization and no accepted career paths upward. Instead, inside the party and in interactions with each other, Peronists constantly break rules and try to leap-frog over one another in the

---

[20] McGuire (1995); Jones (1997). For an overall perspective on parties in Latin America see Mainwaring (1991).
[21] Teichman (2004). Similarly, Leaman (1999) argues that Menem's style of leadership reduced the democratic discourse that had begun to develop in Argentina under Alfonsín's presidency. Thus Menem's liberal economic reforms, conducted under an ostensibly democratic government, had a conservative class content and democratic shortcoming that made them similar to comparable reforms done under an authoritarian regime.

advancement of individual careers. Person X, whose career is newer and who is younger than person Y, can be counted on *not* to respect Y's experience and seniority but rather to try to best Y in any way possible, including by breaking the rules. This is standard practice within the Peronist party; Peronist leaders expect such behavior of one another and engage in it themselves. Thus Peronists must constantly monitor each other and each leader must play the watchdog for his/her own interests against the lawlessness of all the other leaders. Each leader must watch his own back to be certain that all the other leaders do not betray him. Peronism's non-institutionalization has two paradoxical results: its flexible and pragmatic capacity allows it to change always to meet a new situation and a new electoral contest, but, on the other hand, it suffers centrifugal disintegration when out of power because it has no institutions or procedures and no one respects or obeys any rules or procedures.[22] This lack of party institutionalization is a weakness, not a strength, because in a democracy any viable political party must be able to survive defeat and to remain coherent, cooperative, and internally united in order to present a better campaign at the next election.[23]

A party whose members are utterly devoid of trust, mutual respect, internal rules, or cooperation is a party with little capacity to survive over the long term in a truly competitive environment. The members of such a party are rational actors who, as Mancur Olson predicted, have no incentive to cooperate. But parties, like democracies, must cooperate to survive. A party with no internal capacity for cooperation must depend entirely upon market mechanisms to compete and win votes. This is what Peronism does. As a highly clientelistic party, it has considerable access to pork, which it uses to buy votes.[24] So far this has been a widely successful electoral strategy. But it depends on economic good times, times which may now be ending, on a global scale, as this book goes to press. A party that has no capacity for inner cooperation and mutual trust is not a strong party, no matter how much pork it can deliver nor how many elections it can win in the early decades of democracy. It is a weak party based on individual self-interest and greed. But democracy, as we have seen, is based on cooperation.[25]

---

[22] Levitsky (2003b; 2003a; 2000); Murrillo (2001).

[23] A similar case is that of the Congress Party in India which, despite a strong early beginning, has, in recent decades, deteriorated into being a highly personalistic, corrupt party given to thugery in some regions of India. Like the Peronist party, as the result of such internal conflict, India's Congress Party appears "... to lose all sense of purpose and political initiative" when out of power. Kohli (1990) raises questions about whether India's Congress Party can survive over the long term, given its deteriorated state. The party's repeated failure to build institutional roots has undermined both its future and the possibility of good government in India.

[24] Levitsky (2003).

[25] A similar story describes the demise of the highly corrupt and clientelistic Mexican PRI in the final years before its electoral defeat. In economic good times it was able to remain in power by buying votes. But as elections became more competitive, beginning in 1988, its effort to purchase votes eventually became so costly that the PRI bankrupted the Mexican economy

The deep internal democratic weakness of Peronism, combined with its integral involvement in Argentine democracy, leaves the democracy itself weak in fundamental ways. For democracy must also have norms, ideas, vision, and dreams.[26] It cannot rely entirely on self-interest and pork. The greed, habitual corruption, and self-centered behavior within the Peronist party, the willingness of leaders to compromise with whatever interests bid the highest price at the moment – these habits –, leave Argentine democracy fragile at its inner core. The willingness to ally with the highest bidder of the moment, the utter lack of norms, ideas, vision and dreams are all part of the price Argentina and Peronism have paid for the lack of bridging social capital that Peronism engendered. If hierarchy, charisma, personalism, and exclusion all existed before Perón, his movement solidified and exacerbated all of these traits to the point that social and political capital, human trust, and the basic faith people must have for democracy to work are all in woefully short supply in Argentina. As a result, a wealthy, educated, industrialized, and highly cosmopolitan society struggles desperately to improve its democracy. Whether it can do so remains to be seen. If trust and cooperation are lacking in Argentine society as a whole, where they are most conspicuously absent is within Peronism and among Peronists.

The capacity for grassroots initiative and horizontal ties is still lacking in Argentina due to Peronism. Even many of the disruptive events that brought down the De la Rua government were organized or at least partially organized by the Peronist Party. Recent work by Javier Auyero reveals that low-level Peronist organizers openly admit the role of the party in organizing food looting and the massive destruction of small stores while higher level Peronist Party officials (predictably) deny any such involvement. This proves that these riots were not necessarily spontaneous. In fact, they show more affinity with Crystal Night in Germany than they do with the famous bread riots studied by E.P. Thompson. Moreover, these actions rejected democracy's institutions and the legitimacy of electoral procedures and their outcome. Thus mass citizen action in crisis and post-crisis Argentina still may be no more democratic than Nazi violence was in Germany.[27]

---

and then was defeated in open elections anyway. Magaloni (2006, esp. chap. 4). The Peruvian state under Fujimori likewise attempted the purchase of votes but with considerably less success. Stokes (2001). And investment into provincial economies in Argentina is directly related to the electoral cycle and follows partisan lines. Remmer (2007).

[26] One Peronist leader who did have long-term vision was Juan Bramuglia who envisioned Peronism as a democratic political party competing for power under an electoral system but without the personalism and coercion that characterized the behavior or Peron himself. Peron destroyed Bramuglia's chances of becoming an electoral candidate for the party. Rein (2008).

[27] On Peronist organization of the recent lootings see Auyero (2007, esp. pp. 110–118). For an alternative view of recent citizen activism as representing a potentially democratic citizen politics see Merklen (2002). Seeing these events as democratic, Merklen argues that Argentina's poor have two obstacles to overcome rather than one: (1) their own poverty and marginalization (an obstacle which confronts all poor people) and (2) the heritage of their Peronist past

Argentine democracy thus faces formidable odds. As we have seen, one of its greatest difficulties is the historical character of Peronism itself. Populisms, including authoritarian populisms, tend to be quite flexible, able to change their outward appearance to respond to political demands or trends of the moment.[28] But the chameleon-like quality of such movements means that changes toward democratic appearances do not necessarily reflect greater commitment to democracy within the populist movement. Peronism in the 1990s under Carlos Menem shared with Peronism of the 1940s the use of personalism to gain electoral support, a willingness to bend or break democratic rules, and the vertical control over its followers.[29] Peronism in the 2000s again reflects personalism, this time going so far as to keep the presidency between spouses. Additionally, the Kirchners are making full use of the undemocratic Peronist party machine. Hence Peronism's limited loyalty to democracy remains at the center of Argentina's democratization process and continues to cause difficulties. Its anti-democratic character is found in the severe clientelist control it holds over its followers through its extensive clientelistic network. Clientelism limits poor peoples' ability to move their loyalties away from Peronism. The severe and widespread poverty that characterizes Argentina in the early twenty-first century forces poor people to participate, for short-term survival, in the same vertical mechanisms that disempower them over the long run.[30]

(which confronts only Argentina's poor). Merklen asks whether a true politics of the left – and of the poor – can develop in Argentina and suggests that these recent spontaneous events indicate that it can.

For a more cautious view of these same events see Iñigo and Cotarelo (2003). Iñigo Carreras and Cotarelo say that these disruptive initiatives came from citizens rather than from Peronist party directors but the potential of such actions to have a constructive political or social impact still remains to be seen. Dinerstein (2003) argues that the popular riots which ousted President de la Rua were a "popular insurrection" and a "negative politics" which rejected everything about the state, including both its liberal economic policy and its liberal democratic institutions. Edgardo Manero (2002) argues that crime in the post-2001 period has become another form of social protest and a very *negative* form of social action. One suspects that crime, in fact, only serves to undermine social trust further.

[28] On the flexibility of Latin American populisms see Ellner (2003). On the flexibility of Peronist populism see Levitsky (2001).

[29] With respect to breaking democratic rules, Menem was notorious for his illegal subordination of the judiciary Chavez (2004). Menem subordinated the judiciary to his control at the national level while other Peronist leaders at the provincial level did so with respect to local-level judiciary institutions. On the use of personalism, Teichman argues, in comparing market reforms in Argentina and Chile, that while similar types of reforms were undertaken in each of these two nations, they went forward in a more personalistic and caudillistic manner under the elected government of Menem than under the dictatorship of Pinochet! Conducting such reforms in a manner that placed Menem at the center of caudillismo has accented the non-democratic nature of such reforms in Argentina. Consequently, the popular reaction against these reforms has been stronger and more angry. The Argentine economic crisis "is characterized by deep public disillusionment and anger with both the political leadership and the manner in which policy reforms have been carried out." Teichman (2004, p. 37).

[30] Auyero (2001). In contrast with Auyero, Sidicaro (2003) argues that Menemism destroyed the populist character of Peronism and that Peronism's capacity for mobilization is today greatly

Conclusion 253

That participation then limits their capacity to create more independent, long-term solutions to their own poverty and marginalization. Peronist clientelism delivers much-needed goods, allowing survival in situations of personal poverty and desperation. Yet such goods are only obtained through individualistic self-help mechanisms that rely on vertical ties. The use of such mechanisms simultaneously undermines cooperative mechanisms of group help which themselves generate bridging social capital.[31]

Yet, like some elements within the Liberal Party in Nicaragua, some elements within the Peronist party and some portions of the Argentine electorate reacted against the craven character, corruption, and authoritarian tendencies of former president Menem. After his presidency, popular opinion turned against him over the growing evidence of his corruption and over his disregard for the law. Ultimately, legal steps taken against him forced Menem to leave Argentina and take up residence in Chile for a temporary period. As of 2009 he resides in Argentina, and efforts to bring him to justice on corruption counts continue.

Elsewhere I have argued, and other observers have agreed, that Argentine culture is also changing in a more democratic direction, albeit not through the efforts of the Peronist party.[32] Like Liberalism, Peronism has become less undemocratic and progress in that direction may continue. Even under Menem, progress toward democracy unfolded. Like Alemán, there were limits to which Menem would not go while in power. He did not seize power extra-legally but was elected twice in fair elections. He changed the constitution to allow his reelection rather than staging a military coupe. He left office on schedule.[33] He did not bribe legislators on the scale that Fujimori did in Peru and he did not close the Congress.[34] In fact, Menem tolerated an increasingly quarrelsome Congress toward the end of his decade in power.[35] And, when popular opinion in yet a third election appeared to go against him, he withdrew from the contest. While Argentina might have hoped for more democratic behavior from Menem, it could have received even less. In the aftermath of the Menem decade, the majority of voters in Argentina have remained loyal to the Peronist party while rejecting Menem.[36] Their behavior is not unlike Nicaraguans'

reduced. Although they see modern Peronism differently, both of these authors nonetheless conclude that poor people who follow Peronism today have little or no capacity for self-mobilization.

[31] For a similar discussion with respect to Peruvian clientelism see Schonwalder (2002).
[32] Anderson (2002); Peruzzotti (2001). Popular willingness to protest against authoritarianism and repression that have taken place under the democratic government continues to reappear in minor but nonetheless hopeful and promising instances. See, for example, Denisson et al. (2004).
[33] Setting aside Menem's non-democratic behavior and concentrating only on this list of legal actions, Szusterman (2000) argues that Menem moved Argentine democracy forward during his decade in power.
[34] On executive-legislative relations in Peru see Kenney (2004) and Aguayo (2004).
[35] Llanos (2002).
[36] Unlike what occurs in Nicaragua, continued popular loyalty to Peronism in Argentina is due to a lack of strong electoral competition from any other party. Anderson (2009).

loyalty to Liberalism in the 2001 election and rejection of Alemán at the same time. Since Menem's departure from office in 1999, the Argentine electorate has chosen two new Peronist presidents who reject and are rejected by Menem. In Nicaragua, the popular choice of Bolaños and the growing popular support for Montealegre reveal a possibility that Liberalism could reform itself from within.[37] It is much less clear, however, that the Kirchner presidencies represent a similar force for reform coming from within Peronism itself. Although the Kirchners are more progressive than Menem, they are at least as autocratic. But even if the Kirchners were more law abiding than Menem, the Peronist party cannot reform itself by simply relying on personalities, since these, as Huntington tells us, can be unpredictable and variable.[38]

As we illustrated in Chapter 7, there are some reasons for guarded optimism in Argentina. That optimism relates to the nation's apparent capacity and willingness to institutionalize, a legacy of its formality.[39] First, it has institutionalized an electoral calendar and followed it with almost no efforts to subvert the electoral process with fraud. Moreover, Argentina has practiced clean elections without the need to have electoral observation teams, such as those that have regularly been necessary in Nicaragua.[40] In its ability to conduct and honor elections, another example of institutionalization, Argentina is far ahead of Nicaragua. With respect to elections, even the Peronist party and its leaders have abided by the rules. Their tendency to subvert rules and ignore procedures that guarantee fair play is a tendency that they prefer to keep behind closed doors in the internal operations of the party.[41] In the open arena of national elections, where the spotlight of national and international attention is more likely to uncover lawless behavior, Peronists are more inclined to submit to democratic rules and procedures.

Elections are of crucial importance for Argentine democracy because they allow the people to enter into the political process in a manner that is regulated by formal rules and procedures.[42] Regulated in such a manner, citizen

[37] The German case immediately after World War II likewise demonstrates that the state can act deliberately, particularly under enlightened leadership, in a manner that facilitates democratization by following the rule of law, acting with magnanimity and forgiveness, and by insisting that democratic process and procedures be followed. Frei (2002).
[38] (1968).
[39] For a study of the relationship between Argentine democracy and its formal electoral laws, see Jones (1995).
[40] Nicaraguan elections in 1984, 1990, 1996, and 2001 were all closely watched by foreign observers. For reports on two of those elections by the scholarly team of observers see Latin American Studies Association (1984; 1990).
[41] Similarly, Laura Tedesco (2004) argues that corruption and the failure to apply or follow the rule of law equally across all members of society constitutes the most important reason for the difficulty of governance in new Latin American democracies such as Argentina.
[42] My optimism about the role of elections in Latin American democracy is not shared by Manuel Antonio Garreton (2003) who evaluates more negatively the possibilities of democratic development in Chile and throughout Latin America. Garreton's pessimism in shared by José Antonio Rivas Leone (2003) and George Philip (2003). These three authors underrate the gradual progress toward democracy that elections and other democratic procedures

participation does not have a chance to lash out in the angry, destructive way we saw with the urban riots in 2001. Because of their distrust of each other and of others, the Argentine people, unfortunately, do not appear to have the extensive capacity for positive and democratic mobilization that the Nicaraguans have learned how to use so effectively. The politics of the streets in Nicaragua are democratic; at least at the present time, they tend to be blaming and destructive in Argentina. As long as social capital remains as low as it is, the politics of the street are dangerous and potentially anti-democratic in Argentina.

Instead, it is mostly through the formal, regulated institution of elections that Argentine citizens have had a very positive democratic influence, including against the non-democratic behavior of Peronism. In 1997, in the face of increasing authoritarian behavior from President Menem, Argentine citizens delivered a crushing midterm defeat to the Peronist party. That defeat changed the balance of power in the Congress for the remainder of Menem's presidency and foretold the Peronist electoral defeat in the presidential elections of 1999. A president who defies rules of democratic procedure, is perceived as corrupt, and shows limited concern for civil rights may go a long way inside a political party that values those behaviors, but may have a foreshortened future in the electoral arena of Argentine democracy. Such has been Menem's experience.[43]

Elections hold out hope for Argentine democracy because Argentine voters have shown moments of real wisdom and a true capacity to participate in a democratically constructive fashion.[44] Examples of this are the 1997 midterm election whose outcome was against Menem and the 1999 popular rejection of him as a candidate. Such electoral wisdom is not surprising. On all public opinion indicators, Argentine citizens show that they support democracy. Their confidence in democracy is considerably higher than similar indicators for democracy in other large Latin American nations, such as Peru, and Argentine confidence compares favorably with all other Latin American nations.[45] Argentines *believe* in democracy. They just don't believe in each other.

have brought. Instead, they share an expectation that democracy should unfold rapidly in Latin America and should deliver a minimum of economic support to the population, as well as political rights. This broad array of political and economic accomplishments has never been seen in early democracies anywhere in the world, nor been expected of them. Anderson (2005b).

[43] *The Economist*, May 17–23, 2003, p. 33
[44] The extent to which elections are fair and honest versus subject to clientelistic manipulation is a subject of disagreement. On the one hand, Auyero argues that Peronism uses material goods to purchase political support. On the other hand, Brusco, Nazareno and Stokes suggest that vote-buying is less prevalent than imagined and that Argentina is generally less clientelistic than is widely perceived. On the two sides of this argument see Auyero (2000; 2001) and Brusco et al. (2004).
[45] These data are available in the Latinobarometer study for 1997. See also Anderson and Aragon (2003) and McClintock (1978; 1981).

A second reason for guarded optimism about Argentine democracy beyond the electoral calendar is the positive contribution of the institutions of state and particularly the legislature. Again, this is an institutional reason for optimism. Whatever rule-breaking behavior Peronists may display in the internal operations of their party, when their behavior is more subject to public scrutiny – on the floor of the legislature, or during elections – Peronists are more willing to abide by democratic rules. Congress represents one of the greatest hopes for Argentine democracy. If the legislature can continue to institutionalize and professionalize, it will become an even stronger national force favoring democracy.[46]

Institutionalization, then, the *institutionalization of democracy*, constitutes the best hope for continued democratization in Argentina and the nation's best bet for the future. Most obviously in need of institutionalization is the Peronist party itself. As a non-institutionalized organization lacking either informal norms of fair play or formal mechanisms of rules and procedures, Peronism will remain weakened by its inability to cooperate and by leaders' inability to trust one another. This book has shown that citizens' faith in each other is fundamental to democracy. That finding holds true as well for citizens who are political leaders and party militants, especially if they are members of a party with a long history of non-democratic patterns.

Argentina is democratizing, just as is Nicaragua, but on the basis of strong institutions and despite weak social and political capital. While social capital certainly constitutes a critical base upon which democracy can develop, its absence clearly does not mean that democracy cannot take hold. Its absence causes severe problems for democratization and renders it extraordinarily difficult for democracy to develop, but it can still do so on an alternative basis: in this case, institutions. Democracy can develop on the basis of institutions even in the face of negative and non-democratic social capital drawn from a popular experience that engendered non-democratic political values, clientelism, and vertical ties. In fact, it may be Argentina's very history of top-down control that has facilitated an institutionally-based process of democratization. While Nicaragua is democratizing from the bottom up and on the basis of social capital, Argentina is democratizing from the top down and on the basis of institutions.

---

[46] In both Argentina and Nicaragua the legislature has passed through moments of weakness and failure when the executive has moved toward authoritarian and extra-legal dominance. While this has been more true in Nicaragua than in Argentina, the pattern has been present in both nations. It is not surprising that executive aggression should have this effect on the legislature when even power aggrandizement *within* the legislature can have a negative impact on legislative function in an established legislature. Lawrence C. Dodd argues that the quest for power by individuals *within the U.S. Congress* perpetually generates pressure toward organizational fragmentation of that legislature and its immobilization. Reform then becomes necessary to address such fragmentation and immobilization, just as has been the case with the Nicaraguan legislature during the new Bolaños administration. On this dynamic in the U.S. Congress see Dodd (1977).

Public opinion in Argentina also shows reason for guarded optimism. For nearly every indicator, social and political capital increased in Argentina with levels of education. In particular, citizens' trust in and willingness to engage with others, socially and politically, came with high school levels of education. Here is another place where Argentina can facilitate its own democratization. By investing in education, particularly education beyond middle school, Argentina can increase social capital among its citizens. And it can do this despite the legacy of Peronism.

Nicaragua can democratize by institutionalizing the mobilized strength of citizen participation. Argentina can democratize by continuing to institutionalize its polity, educating its citizens, erecting procedures and rules, establishing mechanisms for fair play, and exposing to public scrutiny the behavior of all those who do not follow the rules. Each nation has choices and can implement policies that can encourage democratization by enhancing social and political capital, or by supporting institutions, or both. Human agency is available in both cases and neither needs to remain captured by events up to the current moment.

OTHER RELEVANT THEORIES: MODERNIZATION, TRADITIONALISM, AND MORALISM

This overview of contemporary events and ongoing democratization processes in Nicaragua and Argentina brings to mind the applicability and limitations of other theories about democratization, development, and cooperation. One school of thought about democratization that predates social capital theory and moulds expectations about democratization is modernization theory. Modernization theory and development strategies built upon it focus upon the availability of economic resources at the individual or national level. A focus upon wealth cannot explain the findings of this study. In fact, modernization theory would have incorrectly predicted a clear advantage to Argentine democracy when compared to Nicaragua.

Similarly, World-Values data, which do not include Nicaragua but do subdivide societies into "traditional" and "less traditional" categories, also predict that post-modern values will be lower in traditional societies. Traditional societies are defined as those displaying higher levels of religiosity or religious action, lower socioeconomic levels, and an economy based more on agriculture and less on industry. These characteristics all apply to Nicaragua. Insofar as Nicaragua fits the description of a more traditional society, then world-values theory would also predict less modern values in Nicaragua and more post-modern values in Argentina.[47]

Social capital theory and the findings of this study have a response to these assumptions about modernization and traditionalism. From this study it

---

[47] For a new study of religion and values based on world-values data see Inglehart and Norris (2008).

appears that social capital itself represents a kind of resource, although it cannot be measured in monetary terms. Where societies, for historical reasons, have developed higher social capital they have a head start on democratization even if they lack the monetary resources that modernization theory finds so important. Democracy can then build itself upon the basis of an alternative resource, namely social capital, even if it lacks extensive financial resources. Social capital may then modernize what would otherwise be a traditional society far more thoroughly and more rapidly than world values conclusions would lead us to believe.

Two recent works that focus specifically on Nicaragua and Argentina yield findings that are in keeping with what we have found in this study. In an earlier work co-authored with Lawrence Dodd[48], we conclude that the Nicaraguan revolution gave Nicaraguans a kind of resource that is not strictly measurable in monetary terms. Instead, the capacity to cooperate and support each other toward a common political goal is a resource that Nicaraguans now have as a result of the revolution, even though they remain financially poor, both as individuals and as a nation. Following this argument, Nicaraguans do have a level of resources superior to the level of resources available to citizens in a nation that never experienced a popular revolution. It is therefore not surprising to find that Nicaraguans have higher social capital than Argentines. Similarly, in their recent study of Mexico and Argentina, Matthew Cleary and Susan Stokes find that social trust is lower in Argentine regions where Peronism is more influential.[49] Their findings with respect to Argentina are similar to the findings of this study. Since their data are drawn from cities outside Buenos Aires, the similarity of patterns across their study and mine indicates that Peronism is associated with lower trust and lower social capital, both within the capital city and in the provinces of Argentina.

As with the argument of modernization theory, the findings of this book are compatible with World-Values conclusions if we redefine our terms. Just as social capital can constitute a kind of resource, so the revolutionary experience may force citizens of a nation to break with traditional ways of thinking – even if they remain religious in their behavior and if their nation remains poor and agricultural. If this argument is true then Nicaragua may not fit the traditional society profile after all. Including Nicaragua in the World-Values study would allow more detailed exploration of the extent to which Nicaragua fits or fails to fit the description of a traditional society.

A third relevant theory that focuses upon cooperation rather than directly upon democratization is Daniel Elazar's classic work *Cities of the Prairie*.[50] Elazar looks closely at the urban and metropolitan development of the United

---

[48] Anderson and Dodd (2005).
[49] Stokes (2006).
[50] Elazar (1970). Other scholars have also found a connection between a higher sense of "we" or of common community on the one hand and lower corruption on the other hand. Amanda Maxwell and Richard F. Winters find that corruption is lower where leaders perceive homogeneity in the society around them and higher where the surrounding society is more

States, particularly in the areas of the mid-west and west. He argues that the rural and agrarian foundation of American society is a source of "moralism" or positive and cooperative values that allow individuals and communities to identify and work toward the common good. Elazar's argument is similar to one I made about peasant communities in which village life allows citizens to see beyond individual self-interest to a more inclusive and longer-term self-interest that includes the good of the community.[51]

In the study at hand, a citizen capacity to cooperate is the essence of bridging social capital and, according to Putnam, a foundation for democracy. By contrast, its absence forces democracy to search for other foundational resources and assets because cooperative social capital is absent. We have seen that both social capital and cooperation are higher in Nicaragua, owing in part to the revolutionary experience, which forced citizens to cooperate with each other. Argentines, contrarily, went through a heirarchial social movement that undermined horizontal cooperation and they lack that asset as a foundation for democracy. The conclusions of this study fit with Elazar's findings about cooperation or moralism in the United States. It is interesting that Elazar does *not* see the American Revolution as a foundational source of the capacity for citizen cooperation, although, of course, the United States, like contemporary Nicaragua, is founded upon a citizen revolution.

Elazar's work also has relevance because of the existence of corruption in the two societies under study here. He suggests that corruption is higher where the sense of common interest or moralism is lower or absent while corruption will be lower where citizens identify with a cooperative sense of community. While corruption is present in both Argentina and Nicaragua, it is worse in Argentina, just as Elazar's conclusions would suggest. Menem's presidency was internationally notorious for its corruption. In general, Peronism is associated with high levels of corruption – in fact, through the use of corruption, the party succeeds in binding its leaders to the party and in holding popular support and loyalty. In Argentina, high levels of corruption are associated with Peronist political leaders, with the Peronist trade unions, and with Peronist party control in many different provinces. If corruption is present and objectionable in Nicaragua, it is a way of life for Peronism.[52]

---

heterogeneous. Eric M. Uslaner found that lower social trust predicted higher corruption levels. More recent studies of Elazar's moralism, operationalizing it in various ways, find moralism to be one of the strongest predictors of corruption in equations including several variables: high moralism (politics as being about community) is associated with lower corruption levels. See Maxwell and Winters (2004) and Uslaner (2006). On recent operationalizations of Elazar see Nice (1983); Hill (2003); and Rosenson (2009).

[51] Anderson (1994).

[52] Probably the most notorious example of corruption in Nicaragua came with the 1996–2001 presidency of Liberal Arnoldo Alemán who stole hundreds of thousands of dollars out of the treasury and purchased a personal helicopter for $750,000,000. Unlike in Argentina, Arnoldo was tried and jailed for his corruption, although Daniel Ortega has significantly lightened the enforcement of his sentence. Although the Sandinistas, including Ortega, have engaged in corrupt acts, in general, the right in Nicaragua has been associated with higher

THE INTERPLAY OF SOCIAL CAPITAL AND INSTITUTIONAL CAPITAL

Robert Putnam tells us that social trust, manifested in the form of social capital, is essential for making democracy work. He also argues that trust breeds trust: once a society has begun to establish trust among members, it is easier for more trust to grow. Where citizens have learned to work together in civic associations, they will also work together more easily in politics. They will be more able to cooperate and compromise. Samuel Huntington, on the other hand, tells us that a society must institutionalize in order for it to become viable and stable. Democratic polities that have not institutionalized remain vulnerable to disorder and breakdown.[53] In an institutionalized political system, it is easier to know where the pressure points are and any changes to the rules can be enforced more easily. In the absence of institutionalization, politics are more likely to succumb to the dominance of elites, patrimonialism, and clientelism, patterns of relationships that favor a few select individuals at the expense of improving the position of an entire class or social sector.[54]

Both of these positions are correct, but only partially. An emphasis on social trust and the creation of a citizen capacity to cooperate is essential. But looking only at that capacity misses the contribution and the consequence of institutions, and the protection that they can provide in moments when the people become imprudent in their electoral choice or in their use of mobilization. At the same time, focusing only or exclusively upon the contribution of institutions misses the positive contribution that comes from mobilized politics and the capacity for social trust that some kinds of social movements generate. Putnam and Huntington each provide an important part of the picture but only a part. The separate stories of Nicaragua and Argentina show that democratization can move forward on the basis of either social and political capital, or institutional capital alone. But the limitations of democracy in each case also show that a new democracy requires *both* a capacity for citizen mobilization and cooperation *and* a minimum level of institutionalization. Each of these two capacities provides a kind of safety belt against the deficiencies of the other. Where the people mobilize against democracy, institutions hold democracy in place anyway. When institutions petrify, stagnate, or become corrupted, mass mobilization can break them out of its fossilized state and force them back toward democratic function. A democratic society needs both a capacity for mobilized politics and an institutionalized polity.

This study also underscores the need to scrutinize the internal operation of both mobilized and institutionalized politics. To suggest that mobilized citizen

---

levels of corruption. That fact is keeping with Elazar's argument that those who see less affinity with others around them will find it easier to use political office to engage in theft.
[53] Huntington (1968; 1965a; 1965b).
[54] Waylen (2000). Even where institutionalization is moving forward, its progress can be uneven and some aspects of institutionalization may be incompatibility with other aspects of institutionalization. Foweraker and Krznaric (2002).

Conclusion

politics, a politics of the streets, is always a positive contribution to democracy is to romanticize mobilized politics and, quite often, the politics of the poor. Such romanticization does not help our understanding of how citizen politics can help make democracy work because sometimes citizen politics can also make democracy fail. Poor peoples' movements *may* be romantic, heroic and inspiring. They have produced moments in human history when the poor have reached upward out of their disadvantaged condition to point toward a more just future and a better world. But the politics of the poor and the movements they create also have some possibility of being politics of hate and movements of anger. When they foment conspiracy theories and blame-based understandings of the world, they are neither visionary nor heartening nor inspirational nor heroic, although at times it may be difficult to tell the difference.[55] The politics of anger do not point toward a better world or empower their participants. Rather, anger becomes an anti-democratic and even dangerous political force that must then be overcome or at least tamed if democracy is to develop.

Likewise, to idealize the role of institutions at the expense of mobilized citizen politics is also an error that dims rather than illuminates our understanding of how democracy develops.[56] First, institutions for their own sake are not necessarily a positive good for democracy. To insist that institutions develop first, before citizen participation is permissible or before mobilized citizens are allowed to march, is only a recipe for oppression.[57] Institutional development and citizen mobilization are best developed simultaneously, although at some moments, a society's capacity for one will outstrip its capacity for the other. Democracy and its development cannot be controlled. Second, even where institutions exist, they may have periods where they do not contribute to democracy or even when they become a hindrance to democratization. The Argentine Congress under most of Perón's first two presidencies and the Nicaraguan legislature under Alemán both are good examples of institutions that became part of the problem and not part of the solution. Third, such institutional failures are not reasons to close the institutions themselves or to resort back entirely to a mobilized citizen politics of the streets. Institutions have a capacity to self-correct, and they may have a greater such capacity than citizen politics precisely because they are formalized and bound by a set of rules. Despite periods of failed and non-democratic function, both the legislatures studied here show that they have a capacity for self-correction and they have used that capacity after periods of institutional failure. It is important to remember, though, that the self-corrective capacity of institutions is only available if the institutions are allowed to remain open so that institutional learning can continue forward and institutional capital can continue to develop.

---

[55] Anderson (2006a).
[56] Cavarozzi (1997) argues that the state-centered model so prevalent in Latin America and that emphasizes institutions is in decline in Latin America more generally. Revesz (1997).
[57] Tilly (1973).

Mine is essentially an argument for a hands-off approach to democratization and for allowing the process to muddle through. The hands that need to remain off of the process include not only the hands of foreign meddling and bullying, but also the hands of internal military coupes. When democratization is allowed to move forward with less rather than more interference, the process itself often has a capacity for self-correction. Winston Churchill said that democracy was the worst kind of government in the world...except for all others. He was referring to the messiness and uncertainty of democracy. As observers, we find it stressful to watch democracy unfold, wondering all the while if it will survive its own muddling, especially in its very early stages. Observers of these two societies have, at times, given in to the urge to intervene. The Argentine military intervened against Peronism. The United States government intervened against Sandinismo. And yet, as we can now see in historical perspective, such interventions did more harm than good to the process of democratic development. In both cases, leaving the society alone to mobilize, institutionalize, and democratize was more likely than not to facilitate the development of democratic learning and a democratic polity. For all of the tumult that it caused, making the United States so nervous, Sandinismo did more than anything else in Nicaraguan history to create the bridging social capital so essential to democracy. And Peronism, for all of its perversion of the nation's institutions and its creation of social distrust, nonetheless left open essential democratic institutions and, with them, the possibility for the creation of institutional capital that is also vital to democracy.[58]

TUMULTUOUS VERSUS REGULARIZED DEMOCRACY

This book has also implicitly raised the following question: What difference does a revolution make for democratic development? The question goes to the heart of the utility of social capital for democracy. Theories of social capital as they are currently in vogue in political science stress the importance of slow and gradual development of citizen capacities for cooperation. Additionally, such slow development is necessarily peaceful. Students of slow-developing social capital have made their case convincingly. This book leaves us with no reason to doubt such assertions. But it also shows that the rapid development of social capital is another distinct possibility, and, when it comes quickly, social capital is no less able to contribute to democracy than it is when it comes gradually.

Revolution, therefore, makes a great difference.[59] Under certain circumstances, it can contribute to the rapid development of citizen cooperation

---

[58] In suggesting that democratization must move forward drawing upon both institutionalization and upon popular mobilizational capacity, I recognize that these two aspects are ultimately inseparable and, in fact, democratization is best that way. For an argument on the related nature of multiple aspects of democratization see O'Donnell (2001).

[59] Whereas I see a connection between social revolution and democratic development, Alan Knight (2001) sees them as alternatives. He explains the recent rise of democracy in Latin

skills and, with them, social capital. The scholars who traced a connection between revolution and democracy – in France, the United States, and now in Nicaragua – were and are correct.[60] But their argument fits within theories of social capital rather than opposing them. An argument that grants that citizens can learn cooperation rapidly as well as gradually only broadens the relevance of social capital theory to make it applicable in places that have developed democracy quickly and after a revolution. In fact, revolution may jump start the development of social capital, making it possible to develop citizen cooperation sooner than would have otherwise been possible without a revolution. Revolution, as well as the danger and need for mutual reliance that revolution and tumultuous politics bring, may force citizens to learn cooperation skills in order to survive. This book and the connection it illustrates between revolution and democracy shows that there is a place for tumultuous politics in the development of democracy. In certain conditions, tumultuous politics may be the best option.

But tumultuous politics are also unpredictable and can inflict considerable harm.[61] They are not automatically a democratic form of politics and they do not always enhance citizen cooperation skills. One path toward democratic development is not always appropriate to all situations. The appropriate path toward democracy depends in part on the values and culture within a given society.[62] In places where tumultuous politics are anti-democratic politics, regularized participation, as through elections, may contribute more constructively toward the development of democracy. Argentina shows us what the role is for regularized politics: elections, rules and procedures, a legislature. Where citizen participation skills are underdeveloped and where the politics of the streets are often anti-democratic, regularized citizen participation, channeled through routines, procedures, and institutions, may make a more positive democratic contribution than the tumultuous politics of the streets. Even in Nicaragua, regularized, institutionalized elections greatly contributed to extracting the positive advantages of revolution (citizen empowerment) without the disadvantages that inevitably spring from continuation in power (unaccountable leadership). When leaders who came to power supported by mobilized politics were then also forced to respond to repeated, democratic elections, democracy has been enhanced. In other nations where revolutionary leaders have not been forced into elections, revolutions have resulted in totalitarian regimes.

America as a *failure* of revolution as a viable alternative. I do not see the contrast as being so stark and suggest that, in Nicaragua, the development of democracy is due to revolutionary *success*. For an earlier version of my argument see Anderson and Dodd (2005).

[60] For a general consideration of the connection between revolution and democracy see Munck (1997). For a specific consideration of the Nicaraguan case see Vanden and Prevost, (1993) and Brown (1990). Other scholars have found that, due to its revolutionary history, Nicaragua today has higher levels of popular participation than are found in older and more established democracies. Davis et al. (1999).

[61] Anderson (2001).

[62] Fukuyama (1995).

Thus the interplay of tumultuous and regularized politics is constant and everywhere. One single form of politics does not answer every purpose. And a form of politics that worked well at one point in time may need to be tempered with another variety of politics later on. While we should not be blind to the positive democratic possibilities than can emerge from social revolution, we also should not expect tumultuous politics to be the only path toward democratic development. While revolution makes a difference, it does not make the only difference. The goal is that human agency be facilitated. Democratization proceeds best and is most likely where the process allows entry points for individuals and civil society to become involved. Whether such involvement is facilitated through institutions, or through a tradition of mobilized politics, or both is less important than that the process allows individual and social involvement in the politics of the nation.[63]

PARTICIPATORY AND REPRESENTATIVE DEMOCRACY

This book has also raised another question: What difference do institutions make for democratic development? The question is directed at the tradeoffs in time, energy, and scope that can be achieved through grassroots and participatory democracy versus representative, institutionalized democracy. The tradeoff is also between politics conducted by citizens versus politics conducted by experts and professionals. Each has its advantages and drawbacks. The question speaks directly to the role of institutions in political development and the extent to which those institutions are influential in defining how politics unfold. In the face of low levels of social capital, institutions can make a great difference.

One school of political thought sees participatory democracy as clearly superior to representative democracy. In fact, from this perspective, the only "true" democracy is participatory, bypassing legislatures and representation as temporary crutches on the pathway toward complete democracy.[64] A related argument is that direct participation or deliberation enhances the quality of democracy because direct involvement in democracy's functions is a superior form of democracy. It is better to work with one's neighbors in the task of governing oneself rather than turning the matter over to professional representatives. Drawing on Jurgen Habermas, Simone Chambers makes this argument with respect to the growth of democratic values. By going through the process of democratic deliberation, she argues, we incorporate a deeper belief in democracy and come to be better democratic citizens than we were before we began the dialogue.[65] "Face-to-face participation will make us better

---

[63] For an argument on the importance of agency see O'Donnell (2001).
[64] Within this tradition see the work of Mary Wollstonecraft (1995) and her advocacy of the French Revolution, and Pateman (1970). Wollstonecraft's support for the tumultuous politics of the French revolution is expertly presented in O'Neill (2007). I am indebted to Dan for helping me articulate this position. Doubtlessly he will disagree with some of what I have written but he cannot deny that I have listened.
[65] Chambers (1996; 1998); Habermas (1996).

Conclusion

citizens by educating us about our communities and teaching us to be tolerant and cooperative."[66] Thus, participatory democracy breeds social capital, even while it depends on the preexistence of social capital in order to get started in the first place. Putnam makes this argument: social capital breeds social capital. Places rich in it tend to get richer[67].

In fact, the assumption that participatory democracy is superior lies behind current concerns about the decline of social capital in established democracies, particularly in the United States.[68] Social scientists who believe that American democracy is in decline take this position because they see a decline in citizen participation. Skocpol argues that democracy in the twentieth century relies more on representative interest groups and less on voluntary organizations than it did fifty or one hundred years ago.[69] Berry and Crawford and Levitt suggest that direct citizen participation at the local level has dropped.[70] If all of this is true, and if participatory democracy is in fact superior, then democracy has indeed diminished in the United States.

Also, if this is true, then Nicaraguan democracy is superior to Argentine democracy. Nicaraguan citizens are more able to mobilize in a democratic manner, so they must be ahead of Argentines. With their superior capacity to cooperate and mobilize, Nicaraguans have more ready access to their political system and appear more comfortable in addressing their political leaders. By participating directly, Nicaraguans learn more about their government and learn to become more tolerant of each other. Those who already have high social capital work use that social capital regularly, thereby increasing it, simply by engaging in participatory governance. By contrast, Argentines, who participate primarily through elections and otherwise rely on representational democracy through their legislature, have an inferior form of democracy. Their system works for Argentina better than mobilized participation would, but it is a lesser form of democracy. Even more sadly, those who have low social capital do not increase their national stock of social capital by exercising their form of democracy.

But is participatory democracy indeed superior? In an in-depth study of participatory democracy within social movements across much of the twentieth century, Polletta finds strengths but also serious limits to participatory democracy[71]. Among its strengths, participatory democracy is a form of democracy that is more likely to lead to the discovery of new leadership talent and is simultaneously more likely to bring that talent forward to a leadership level. Additionally, participatory democracy contributes to a

---

[66] Berry (1999). For general arguments in favor of participatory democracy see Barber (1984); Pateman (1970); Berry et al. (1993); and Mansbridge (1980).
[67] Putnam (2000).
[68] For an important challenge to the position that American democracy is in decline see Wolfe (1998; 2006).
[69] Skocpol (2003).
[70] Berry (1999); Crawford and Levitt (1999).
[71] Polletta (2002).

feeling of empowerment, enhanced self-worth, and self-esteem among participants. This is particularly important for the low-income and marginalized citizens whose movements Polletta studies, and it is particularly important for Nicaraguans. Polletta finds that participatory democracy maximizes solidarity among participants and that leaders are more accountable under participatory democracy.

Each of these assets of participatory democracy is relevant to the democracies studied here. A more participatory form of democracy could help Argentina where solidarity is certainly in short supply. The advantage of calling leaders to account has helped Nicaragua where citizens have used participatory mobilization to call leaders to account.[72] In the nation where participatory democracy prevails (Nicaragua), its advantages have been those Polletta anticipated; in the nation where participatory democracy is mostly absent (Argentina), some of its advantages could be put to good use.

But there are also problems with participatory democracy. It is cumbersome, time consuming, and exhausting. People get tired of participating. George Bernard Shaw said that socialism would take up too many evenings. Much the same can be said of participatory democracy, particularly one that has its foundation in socialism. As the exhausted participants withdraw, if they have not left in place representatives ready to take up the task on a full-time basis, then democracy itself will disappear. In addition, participatory democracy may do wonders for the participants but accomplish less real political change in policy. Many of Polletta's participatory organizations found their policy impact limited unless and until they found ways to work through democracy's institutions. Often this meant institutionalizing aspects of their own movements.

There are also ways that participatory democracy is less than fully democratic. These liabilities are related to participatory democracy's non-institutionalized status. First, the participatory context always includes some groups and individuals more fully and fairly than it does others. The informal mechanisms that characterize participatory democracy allow no way of addressing these inequalities. There are no formulae for ensuring equal participation, so some participants are always marginalized or excluded altogether. Second, and related to the first, in the absence of formal mechanisms, participants try to use friendship to ensure equality and inclusion. Friendship entails long-term relationships whose longevity facilitates the trust and mutual respect upon which democracy relies. At first glance, therefore, friendship appears to be an ideal basis for democracy and one that enhances participatory mechanisms. But upon closer scrutiny friendship turns out to be no asset for democracy. In fact, the first democracy, in Athens, was eventually destroyed by friendship. Groups of friends voted in blocs, bribed and intimidated officials to exclude other groups, and attempted to control and manipulate group assemblies

---

[72] For considerations of recent elections in Nicaragua see Oquist (1992); Barnes (1990; 1992); Booth and Richard (1997); Anderson and Dodd (2002a; 2002b; 2007; 2008; 2009).

Conclusion

where the one-person-one-vote rule should have prevailed. "In practice," writes Polletta, "*friendship was quite at odds with democracy.*"[73] Organizations that rely on friendship actually weave into their operations deliberate mechanisms of exclusion because friendship is as much a mode of exclusion as it is a mode of inclusion. Having "friends" by definition means that certain others are *not* friends. In the participatory democratic environment, those "others" end up being excluded or treated unfairly precisely because they are not "friends." Third, the participatory democratic movement was always vulnerable to the rise of personalized leadership, which, lacking formal rotational mechanisms, eventually became unaccountable. Even the best-intentioned leaders, including Martin Luther King, eventually succumbed to relying too much on personalized power. Thus non-institutionalized participatory democracy has some of the very dangers that Peronism presented: favoring some groups over others; the creation of a world view of "us" and "them" in which "they" are excluded from participation, political equality, representation, and even respect; and vulnerability to a charismatic leader.

Institutions can make a considerable difference. For each of these dangers inherent to participatory democracy, some form of institutionalization could lessen or even eliminate these problems. Formal representational mechanisms would go further to ensure the representation of marginalized groups. This is particularly true for proportional representation, the method of representation used in Argentina's Congress. Formal mechanisms of participation, like elections, institutionalize the one-person-one vote rule so that bloc voting and intimidation become more difficult and less effective. Formal mechanisms for rotating leadership reduce the power of personalism and charisma. It is perhaps no accident that the nation that has been so badly damaged by personalized leadership, Argentina, is the nation that has more fully developed its representational democratic mechanisms. On the other hand, Nicaraguan democracy is vulnerable to some of the drawbacks of participation that Peronism exemplified.

There are elements of the Nicaraguan democracy that make participation more appropriate. These characteristics are not as strong or are not present in Argentina, and thus participatory democracy yields its benefits less fully there. "Participatory democracy's solidary benefits are most evident where the costs of participation are high and the incentives for it weak," writes Polletta.[74] This description characterizes Nicaragua during the revolutionary insurrection when the foundation of Nicaragua's participatory democracy was laid. Participatory democracy works best for groups that are small, homogeneous, and unhurried, a description more relevant for Nicaragua than for Argentina.[75] Argentine society is large, heterogeneous, and always in a rush. For groups that are more oriented toward personal enhancement

---

[73] Polletta (2002, p. 212); Hutter (1978).
[74] Polletta (2002, p. 212).
[75] Polletta (2002, p. 219).
[76] Polletta (2002, p. 219).

than toward institutional change, participatory democracy works better.[76] Nicaraguans may have been more oriented toward personal enhancement in the early revolutionary years when political participation was also personal liberation. They may still see that as a key part of their political experience. Liberation is less central to Argentine political development. Argentines are trying to run a huge, complex nation and resurrect one of the continent's largest economies. Personal enhancement may have to wait in Argentina, or be achieved by means outside political participation. So far, at least, Nicaraguan democracy has managed to access the positive aspects of participatory democracy while avoiding the drawbacks that participatory democracy entails. But Nicaragua's democracy needs to institutionalize soon, before the drawbacks catch up to the democratization process and undermine the assets of participation. Installation of a regular electoral calendar has been an important step in that direction; increased professionalization of the legislature will also contribute in this regard.

The comparison of democratization in Nicaragua and Argentina takes us directly into the debate over the relative advantages of participatory versus representational democracy. It is a debate that political theorists have not resolved among themselves, and we are not likely to resolve it here. But contrasting the experiences of these two nations does underscore the extent to which that discussion is relevant to the study of democratization. Scrutiny of different pathways to democracy in today's world speaks to dialogues within political theory. The experiences of Argentina and Nicaragua illuminate the two theoretical positions with recent information from contemporary democratic examples. The contrast of these two democratizing contexts shows us that there are, in fact, advantages to each kind of democracy such that one may be better in one context and the other better in another context. Moreover, developing one first may be more appropriate in a given context, even if the eventual goal is to develop both. It is true that participatory democracy enhances social capital. Yet, as Argentina shows, social capital is not the only pathway to democracy. The institutionalists have their argument. On the other hand, Nicaraguan democracy would be safer if its institutions were stronger. Some theorists argue that it is difficult for any political system to survive for a long time without institutionalizing itself. If this is correct, Nicaraguan democracy has a fatal flaw until it institutionalizes.

As with the contrast between Putnam's argument for social capital as essential to democracy and Huntington's argument for institutionalization, both positions have value. In this section we conclude that there are places, times, and ways in which participatory democracy is better. There are also places, times, and ways in which it is not optimal – in a complex nation, for instance, it may be highly impractical. Those instances, those democratizing nations, may be better served by representative, institutionalized democracy. One approach to democracy does not suffice for all democratizing contexts everywhere. That conclusion returns us to a consideration of the contemporary concern about the decline of social capital in the United States. Is it the problem that scholars say it is? Are there representative mechanisms that replace social capital adequately? Has representation gotten better? Is representative democracy more appropriate for the large, complex, heterogeneous, hurried society the United States has become? Is the decline of social capital a crisis after all? These are questions for another study and another book. But the study at hand raises these questions before us and leaves us wondering if the answers are quite as simple as we thought they were.

IMPLICATIONS FOR OTHER DEMOCRACIES: LATIN AMERICA AND BEYOND

As has become apparent in the preceding discussion, the questions raised by this book reach far beyond the cases of Nicaragua and Argentina. These selected examples of the relationship between popular values and democracy are especially useful because of their ability to enlighten the study of social capital. As nations which experienced powerful mass movements that won deep emotional loyalty among supporters and followers, Nicaragua and Argentina allow us to scrutinize the values that these social movements established and encouraged. From these experiences, we can draw conclusions about the values of social and political capital in these societies more broadly. We can see from the empirical analysis that these values play an important role in shaping popular participation in a new democracy and, with that, the nature and ease of democratization. The history of a mass movement and the loyalty it inspired make Nicaragua and Argentina easy and obvious places to begin the study of the role and limits of social capital in the development of democracy.

Beyond this book, there is much more that can be done with this approach to understanding democratization. One question left open is the deeper exploration of the role of mass movements and the popular values they engender within the process of democratization. Within Latin America, other nations that have also experienced a powerful mass movement have unexplored popular cultures and popular values that contribute to or detract from the development of social capital. Other nations that experienced powerful mass movements include Mexico, El Salvador, and Bolivia, among others. Some mass movements in Latin America, such as the Mexican Revolution, occurred much longer ago than both Sandinismo or Peronism. Others were less successful than Sandinismo and Peronism in seizing the state and remolding politics in their own image. These movements may nonetheless have left behind a reservoir of popular values that enhance or undermine social capital and citizen abilities to cooperate and build horizontal ties. These histories bear exploration as we seek to understand democratic development in settings where mass movements have come and gone.[77] Such exploration will broaden our

---

[77] A recent book that shows how mass insurrection contributed to democratization in El Salvador and South Africa is Wood, (2000).

understanding of the role of mass mobilization and participatory democracy in the process of democratization more generally.

Nations in the Western hemisphere that have not experienced mass movements or revolutions include, among others, Venezuela, Peru, and Chile. Some of these nations, particularly Chile, have stressed the development of their institutions, even when their histories have lacked strong mass movements. Nations like these also have popular political values that interact today with their developing and troubled democracies. We would understand that interaction better and how it supports or opposes democratization if we had more knowledge about the nature of social capital in these new democracies and about the popular ability to cooperate and draw upon horizontal ties. A comparison of the popular values in nations that have not experienced a mass movement with those in nations that have would help us understand how mass movements or their absence affect democratic development. Moreover, studying the role of institutions within nations that have not had mass movements will enhance our understanding of the role of representative democracy in the process of democratization.

Another unexplored question is about the relationship between institutions and electoral democracy and the development of democratic values. We have seen in Argentina and Nicaragua a capacity to resist authoritarianism, and this capacity has saved the democracy in each case. In Nicaragua, that capacity for resistance to authoritarianism came from the citizen's capacity to mobilize. In the Argentine case, it came from the strength of democratic institutions. What does the capacity for resistance to authoritarianism look like in a nation that has had neither the mass mobilized experience nor the institutional strength presented by the Nicaraguan and Argentine cases? If a nation has developed the institutional and electoral mechanisms of democracy but has not developed these on the basis of a mass social movement and also lacks Argentina's long history of institutional development, what capacity exists to resist an authoritarian executive? What do popular values look like in such an instance, and how stable and robust are they in the face of incipient authoritarianism? Only in-depth studies of social capital in other contexts will answer such questions.

The story told here has relevance in understanding democracy as it has developed elsewhere. For example, students of Britain and France have often noted the formal, institutionalized nature of democratic development in Britain and contrasted it with tumultuous French politics. Contrasting Britain and France with Argentina and Nicaragua leads to further insights about the democratic trajectories of new democracies that have either strongly participatory or highly formal and institutional traditions.[78] Argentina's story of democratization in a hierarchical way also replicates many aspects of democratization

---

[78] On England see Howell (1977). On France see Tilly (1986). On Germany see Frei (2002). On Spain see Pérez-Díaz (1993).

Conclusion

in Germany, Italy, and Spain. Today, democracy is developing in many places that have histories of mass movements, or institutional development, or both, or neither. The findings of this study have relevance there as well. The new democracies of Eastern Europe are examples where institutional democratic development has received particular attention, but mass social movements have a more erratic profile. What does social capital look like in these new European democracies? Social capital may be less developed in contexts where institutional development has received more support, but mass movements are more rare. Studies of popular values in these new European democracies will answer such questions.

A question that lies beyond the scope of this study but that piques the curiosity now is the question of whether social and political capital can create institutional capital and vise versa. Although each of these nations is strong in one of these two and is working to develop the other, exactly *how* the presence of strong social and political capital can help institutions to develop and vise versa remains an unanswered question as this study ends.[79] Putnam implies that strong social capital will develop strong institutions by virtue of the fact that individuals have already learned to cooperate. Perhaps he is correct, although the precise connection remains unexplored. If he is correct, then institutionalization in Nicaragua will proceed more easily than does the advancement of social and political capital in Argentina. On the other hand, in settings that are more authoritarian than Argentina, the creation of institutional cooperation at the grassroots level has been shown to help create political trust and therefore social capital.[80] This remains a fascinating area for further study.

Finally, this study has relevance for the United States and speaks to the contemporary concern about the decline of social capital here.[81] Participatory democracy undoubtedly has its advantages and the findings of this book underscore those. But other democratic assets such as institutions and procedures also contribute to making democracy work and have advantages that participatory democracy lacks. As this book goes to press and the national and global disaster of the George W. Bush years confronts us all, many democrats

---

[79] I am grateful to Anne Pitcher for raising the question of how social and political capital relate to institutional capital. I have not answered the question, but the query certainly points toward the need for further research.

[80] Fox (1996). My sense of the Mexican situation Fox describes is that it is very different from the one studied in this book. The institutions he scrutinizes in Mexico are international institutions such as NGOs, not the formal institutions of state studied here. Thus his findings that institutions can enhance social capital may or may not apply to the Argentine case. Fukuyama also considers institution-building essential to democratic development and suggests that social capital can aid in democratic development, but likewise does not address the question of how social capital can help build strong institutions. Fukuyama (2004; 2002).

[81] The concern over the decline of social capital in the United States has also extended to include the other advanced industrial democracies in North America, Western Europe, and Japan. See the collection of essays on this subject in Pharr and Putnam (2000).

in the United States are feeling grateful for the power of Congress in constraining arbitrary, warlike, and incompetent power in the hands of the executive.[82] That constraint was institutional more than popular, since the majority of voters not only elected George Bush but then re-elected him as well. In the United States perhaps we should look more carefully both at the advantages of representational democracy and at its contribution to making a complex, established democracy continue to work. If citizens of the United States have turned more toward representational organizations, it may be because those institutions have something to offer to a modern large-scale democracy that participatory democracy does not provide. It may also be that representational organizations and institutions limit the anti-democratic elements of participatory democracy or constrain poor choices that have been made by the electorate until it has a chance to vote again. Democratic and bridging social and political capital are clearly positive assets for democracy and resources for moving forward with the task of democratic governance. But they are not democracy's only allies. Institutions likewise constitute assets and resources. As such, they may not be getting the attention and credit they deserve in the contemporary debate about the quality of democracy in the United States and elsewhere.

[82] On the constraint placed by the Congress upon George W. Bush's war policy see Howell and Kriner (2009, esp. pp. 323–330). On the problems of Bush's economic policies see Jones and Williams (2008). On the continuation of Congressional constraint upon the executive, including incoming president Barak Obama see Dodd and Oppenheimer (2009).

Appendix

The analysis of this book relies on seven separate data bases collected by different pollsters in Nicaragua and Argentina between 1996 and 2003. Of those seven data bases, five were public opinion polls and two were elite opinion polls. This appendix describes these data sources. Of the five public opinion polls described here, one was a Latinobarometer survey that included both Nicaragua and Argentina. The other four public opinion surveys were national or neighborhood samples of public opinion, two each in Nicaragua and Argentina. The two elite opinion surveys were directed at current legislators who held seats in the national legislatures of these two countries at the time that our study took place.

I. THE 1997 AND 2007 LATINOBAROMETER SURVEYS

Sections of Chapters 4, 5, and 6, as well as the final paragraphs of Chapter 7, draw on data collected by the continent-wide survey known as the Latinobarometer. These data are publically available. As it is explained in the text, the late 1990s was a period of regime change in both Nicaragua and Argentina. Public opinion surveys collected then were most appropriate to uncover public attitudes toward different types of governmental regimes. Because it matched in terms of timing with the two national surveys (discussed below), the year 1997 represented an ideal year for using the Latinobarometer data. The 1997 Latinobarometer data were collected by local pollsters and supervised by FLACSO, Chile. In 1997 the Latinobarometer data collected surveyed 1000 respondents from a national sample in Nicaragua and 1200 respondents from a multisite sample in Argentina. At the time this book went to press, the 2007 Latinobarometro data were the most recent data available, allowing us to make contemporary comparisons with the 1997 data.

II. THE NEIGHBORHOOD SURVEYS

Chapter 4 relies on empirical analysis of public opinion from two working class neighborhoods, one in Managua, Nicaragua, and one in Buenos

Aires, Argentina. The data base drawn from Bello Horizonte has an N of 403 and comprises .04% of Managua's population; the data base drawn from La Matanza has an N of 1200 and comprises .012% of the Buenos Aires population.[1] In both neighborhoods I was closely involved with constructing the surveys. I wrote the survey instrument, worked with the pollsters to fund and conduct a pilot study in each neighborhood, and remained in close contact with the pollsters while the data were being collected.

The data from Bello Horizonte were collected by the Nicaraguan polling firm, CINASE, and funded by a grant from the Department of Political Science at the University of Florida. CINASE stands for Centro de Investigacion Social y Economica (Center for Social and Economic Investigation). CINASE is directed by Sergio Alberto Santamaria, an experienced Nicaraguan pollster who also collects data for various development projects funded by NGOs, including the United Nations and the Nicaraguan NGO INPROHU (Instituto Para la Promoción Humana). These data are then used to make policy and investment decisions about development projects throughout Nicaragua. CINASE also regularly conducts preelectoral polls for political parties and the media in Nicaragua.

The data from La Matanza were collected by the Argentine polling firm, KNACK, funded by a Humanities Award from the College of Liberal Arts and Sciences at the University of Florida. KNACK is directed by Gerardo Androgue, who was himself trained by working with MoriArgentina (see

---

[1] Unlike public opinion surveys that are voting studies, public opinion surveys designed to uncover levels of social capital in society are still quite new in Latin American societies. Accordingly, while citizens might readily respond to questions about vote choice, candidate preference, and various kinds of evaluations of candidates, we are breaking new research ground when we ask about membership organizations. With respect to the collection of data, this discovery meant that respondents often did not understand, at first, what was being asked of them. When asked if they belonged to organizations, they often did not bring to mind which organizations they did engage with. This discovery was made in both Nicaragua and Argentina when the pilot studies in each nation were launched.

In response to this discovery, I worked closely with the respective pollsters in each nation to develop survey instruments with probes that would uncover associational memberships in each nation. In each country this meant, in essence, using multiple probes after the first question was posed in order to uncover the full extent of organizational memberships. The survey instruments also gave examples, along with the questions, so as to make it clear to respondents what kinds of answers we were soliciting. Thus a question went as follows: Do you belong to any neighborhood organizations? For example, do you belong to an organization such as an organization concerned with the local schools, the local water supply, the condition of the neighborhood streets, or the public transport availability? Following a question like this, respondents were asked another similar question? What about an organization that concerns itself with neighborhood crime? In both countries, the pollsters learned that a series of probes like these would eventually uncover the full extent of organizational memberships. In addition, in each case the pollsters asked final probes: Are there any other organizations you belong to? And any others? In Nicaragua we used a total of eight probes to uncover the full extent of organizational memberships; in Argentine we used five.

Appendix

below). KNACK conducts a large number of public opinion polls, both for scholars and for scholarly institutions and for various marketing firms collecting market data in Argentina.

III. THE NATIONAL SURVEYS IN NICARAGUA AND ARGENTINA

The empirical analysis for Chapters 5 and 6 rely in large part on national surveys in Nicaragua and Argentina. As discussed in the text, the year 1996 in Nicaragua and the year 1997 in Argentina represented opportunities to ask participants about their preference for different types of governing regimes. These two years represented midpoints in each nation when regimes of distinctly different character had been part of the recent past.

The Nicaraguan national sample drew data from every department (province) in Nicaragua except for Rio San Juan in the far south, along the Costa Rican border. The number of individuals surveyed (N) for the Nicaraguan study was 2700. The Nicaraguan national data were collected by the Venezuelan polling firm, DOXA, and funded by a grant from the National Science Foundation. Located in Caracas, Venezuela, DOXA takes its name from the Greek word that means "to know." DOXA is the firm involved in conducting the ongoing Latinobarometer study and also was selected by the Venezuelan government to conduct its national census.[2] It also had repeatedly conducted polls in other Central American countries such as El Salvador and Panama at times when elections were tense and the population inexperienced, timid, and reticent. DOXA's director, Gustavo Mendez, was trained in survey research at the University of Michigan and thus had a professional and systematic approach to survey research. He has spent his career immersed in survey analysis of Latin America, particularly in the Caribbean basin, including Central America.

The Argentine multi-site sample took place in five major cities and the province of Buenos Aires, and the survey was taken in 1997. The N for the Argentine study was 1000. The data were collected by MoriArgentina and funded by a grant from the Institutions Program, Department of Political Science, of the University of Florida. MoriArgentina is directed by Maria Braun. Braun was originally trained by the British polling firm, Mori. MoriArgentina is highly respected within Argentina and is the firm that collected the Latinobarometer data on Argentina. MoriArgentina also collects data for numerous scholarly enterprises in Argentina, for several marketing research firms, and for some of the political parties.

---

[2] The Latinobarometer models the Eurobarometer, spearheaded by the work of Ronald Inglehart and designed to probe for values and changing values within the European community. The Latinobarometer does the same for Latin America, testing, in particular, for the rise and health of democratic values and other attitudes supportive of political pluralism.

IV. THE ELITE SURVEYS

Between 2002 and 2003 I conducted a survey of opinion among legislators in the Argentine Congress and the Nicaraguan National Assembly. In Nicaragua the surveys included 53 Nicaraguan deputies who were legislators at the time of the survey. At that time, the Nicaraguan legislature included a total of 92 deputies. The deputies surveyed came from all three major political parties – the Sandinistas, the Conservatives, and the Liberals, and also included several members of minor parties in Nicaragua. In Argentina the legislative survey included responses from 83 members of Congress across both chambers and all political parties. At the time of the survey, the Argentine Congress held 240 deputies in the lower chamber and 73 Senators. The legislative surveys in both Argentina and Nicaragua were funded by research awards from the Department of Political Science at the University of Florida. In collecting the legislative data I received expert assistance from two doctoral students in the Department of Political Science: Guillermina Seri helped with the data collection from the Argentine legislators; Maria Mora assisted in the collection of data from the Nicaraguan legislators. I am very appreciative of these two students as the collection of elite opinion would have been far more difficult without their assistance.

Works Cited

Abramowitz, Alan I., and Jeffrey Sepal. 1992. *Senate Elections.* Ann Arbor, MI: University of Michigan Press.
Abramson, Paul, John Aldrich, and David Rohde. 1987. "Progressive Ambition Among U.S. Senators, 1972–1988," *Journal of Politics,* 49: 3–35.
Adorno, Theodor W., Else Frenkel-Brunswick, Daniel L. Levinson, and R. Nevitt Sanford. 1969. *The Authoritarian Personality.* New York: W. W. Norton.
Agresti, Alan. 1996. *Introduction to Categorical Data Analysis.* New York: John Wiley and Sons.
　2002. *Categorical Data Analysis.* 2nd ed. New York: Wiley-Interscience.
Agüero, Felipe. 1995. *Soldiers, Civilians and Democracy: Post-Franco Spain in Comparative Perspective.* Baltimore, MD: Johns Hopkins University Press.
Aguayo, Javier. 2004. "The Legislature Strikes Back: The Role of Congress in the Demise of Fujimori in 2000," PhD dissertation, University of Florida.
Aldrich, John H. 1993. *Why Parties? The Origin and Transformation of Political Parties in America.* Chicago, IL: University of Chicago Press.
Anderson, Leslie E. 1991. "Mixed Blessings: Disruption and Organization Among Costa Rican Peasant Unions," *Latin American Research Review,* 26: 111–143.
　1993. "Agrarian Politics and Revolution: Micro and State Perspectives on Structural Determinism," *Journal of Theoretical Politics,* 5(4): 495–522.
　1994. *The Political Ecology of the Modern Peasant: Calculation and Community.* Baltimore, MD: Johns Hopkins University Press.
　1995. "The Nicaraguan Legislature as a Reflection of Democracy," *Legislative Studies Section Newsletter,* Extension of Remarks, American Political Science Association, July.
　2001. "Fascists o Revolutionaries? Politica Izquierdista y Derechista de la Poblacion Pobre Rural," *Politica y Sociedad* (Madrid), 38: 129–151.
　2002. "Of Wild and Cultivated Politics: Conflict and Democracy in Argentina," *International Journal of Politics, Culture, and Society,* 16: 99–132.
　2004. "La Contribucion de partidos pre-democraticos a una democracia en transicion: el caso de Nicaragua," in *Selected Proceedings of the First Central American Congress of Political Science,* San Jose, Costa Rica: EDUCA.
　2005. "Idealism, Impatience and Pessimism: Recent Studies of Democratization in Latin America," *Latin American Research Review,* 40(3): 390–402.

2006a. "Fascists or Revolutionaries? Left and Right Politics of the Rural Poor," *International Political Science Review*, 27(2): 191–214.
2006b. "The Authoritarian Executive? Horizontal and Vertical Accountability in Nicaragua," *Latin American Politics and Society*, 48(2): 141–169.
2009. "The Problem of Single-Party Predominance in an Unconsolidated Democracy: The Case of Argentina," *Perspectives on Politics*, 7(4): 767–784.

Anderson, Leslie E., and Lawrence C. Dodd. 2002a. "Comportamiento Electoral y Democracia en Nicaragua: 1990–2001," *America Latina Hoy* (Salamanca), 30: 205–230.
2002b. "Nicaragua Votes: The Elections of 2001," *Journal of Democracy*, 13: 80–94.
2004. "Démocratie Envers et Contre Tout; Comportement Électoral et Démocratic au Nicaragua, 1990–2001," *Le Banquet* (Paris), 21(October): 293–323.
2005. *Learning Democracy: Citizen Engagement and Electoral Choice in Nicaragua, 1990–2001*. Chicago, IL: University of Chicago Press.
2007. "A Nip and Tuck Victory: The 2006 Election and Ortega's Return to the Presidency in Nicaragua," paper prepared for presentation at the Annual Meeting of the American Political Science Association, Chicago, IL, August 30–September 2.
2008. "Electoral Democracy in Nicaragua: From Ideology to Pragmatism. The Value of Local Politics in Fostering Democratic Stability," paper prepared for presentation at the Annual Meeting of the Southern Political Science Association, New Orleans, LA, January 10–12.
2009. "Nicaragua: Progress Amid Regress?" *Journal of Democracy*, 20(3): 154–167.

Anderson, Leslie E., and Jorge Aragon. 2003. "What Difference Could a Revolution Make? Political Values in Nicaragua and Peru," paper presented at the XXIV International Congress of the Latin American Studies Association, Dallas, TX, March 27–29.

Anderson, Thornton H. 1993. *Creating the Constitution: The Convention of 1787 and the First Congress*. University Park, PA: The Pennsylvania State University Press.

Anonymous. 1971. "La Organización A Traves del Pensamiento de Perón," Buenos Aires: Editorial Freeland.

Arditi, Benjamin. 2004. "Populism as a Spectre of Democracy: A Response to Canovan," *Political Studies*, 52(1): 135–143.

Argentine National Commission on Disappeared. 1986. *Nunca Mas: A Report by Argentina's National Commission on Disappeared People*. London: Faber and Faber. First published in Spanish (Buenos Aires: Editorial Universitaria de Buenos Aires, 1984).

Associazione Nazionale Sandro Pertini. 2003. *Biography of Sandro Pertini*. Rome: Associazione Nazionale Sandro Pertini.

Auyero, Javier. 2000. "The Logic of Clientelism in Argentina: An Ethnographic Account," *Latin American Research Review*, 35: 55–81.
2001. *Poor People's Politics: Peronist Survival Networks and the Legacy of Evita*. Durham, NC: Duke University Press.
2007. *Routine Politics and Violence in Argentina: The Gray Zone of State Power*. New York: Cambridge University Press.

Baker, Ross K. 1989. *House and Senate*. New York: W. W. Norton.

Baracco, Luciano. 2004. "The Nicaraguan Literacy Crusade Revisited: The Teaching of Literacy as a Nation-Building Project," *Bulletin of Latin American Research*, 23(3): 339–354.
Barnes, William. 1990. "Pre-Election Polling in Nicaragua," in *Interamerican Public Opinion Report*, Washington, DC: Interamerican Foundation.
  1992. "Rereading the Nicaraguan Pre-Election Polls," in eds., Castro, Vanessa and Prevost, Gary, *The 1990 Elections in Nicaragua and Their Aftermath*. Lanham, MD: Rowman and Littlefield.
Barber, Benjamin. 1984. *Strong Democracy*. Berkeley, CA: University of California Press.
Bardina, Roberto. 1984. *Eden Pastora: Un Cero en la Historia*. Mexico City: Mex-sur Editorial SA.
Berman, Sheri. 1997. "Civil Society and the Collapse of the Weimar Republic," *World Politics*, 49(3): 401–429.
Bermeo, Nancy. 2003. *Ordinary People in Extraordinary Times: The Citizenry and the Breakdown of Democracy*. Princeton, NJ: Princeton University Press.
Berry, Jeffrey M. 1999. "The Rise of Citizen Groups," in eds., Skocpol, Theda and Fiorina, Morris P., *Civic Engagement in American Democracy*. Washington, DC: Brookings Institution Press.
Berry, Jeffrey M., Kent E. Portney, and Ken Thomson. 1993. *The Rebirth of Urban Democracy*. Washington, DC: Brookings Institution Press.
Berryman, Philip. 1989. *The Religious Roots of Rebellion: Christians in Central American Revolutions*. Maryknoll, NY: Orbis Books.
Bianchi, Susana. 2001. *Catolicismo y Peronismo: Religion y Politica en la Argentina, 1943–1955*. Buenos Aires: Instituto de Estudios Historico-Sociales.
Booth, John A. 1985. *The End and The Beginning: The Nicaraguan Revolution*. 2nd ed. Boulder, CO: Westview Press.
Booth, John A., and Patricia Bayer Richard. 1997. "The Nicaraguan Elections of October 1996," *Electoral Studies*, 16: 386–393.
Borroni, Otelo, and Roberto Vacca. 1968. *Historia del Peronismo: La Secundia Presidencia – XI*. Buenos Aires: Primera Plana. Year VI, # 290, July 16–22, pp. 51–53.
Brown, Doug. 1990. "Sandinismo and the Problem of Democratic Hegemony," *Latin American Perspectives*, 17: 39–61.
Brusco, Valeria, Marcelo Nazareno, and Susan C. Stokes. 2004. "Vote Buying in Argentina," *Latin American Research Review*, 39(2): 66–88.
Buenos Aires Herald. 1985. "Massera Reproaches Martinez de Hoz," 1.
Bullock, Alan. 1971. *Hitler: A Study in Tyranny*. Abridged version. New York: Harper and Row.
Bunce, Valerie. 1999. *Subversive Institutions: The Design and the Destruction of Socialism and the State*. New York: Cambridge University Press.
Burgess, Katrina, and Steven Levitsky. 2003. "Explaining Populist Party Adaptation in Latin America: Environmental and Organizational Determinants of Party Change in Argentina, Mexico, Peru and Venezuela," *Comparative Political Studies*, 36(8): 881–911.
Burke, Edmund. 1782. "Speech on Reform of Representation of the Commons in Parliament," in ed., Langford Paul, *The Works of Edmund Burke*, vol. 7. Oxford: Clarendon Press.
  1790. "Reflections on the Revolution in France," in ed., Pocock, J.A., *The Works of Edmund Burke*, vol. 3. Indianapolis, IN: Hackett.

Burrin, Phillippe. 1984. "La France dans le Champ Magnetique des Fascismes," *Le Debat*, 32: 52–57.
Butler, David J. 1969. "Charisma, Migration, and Elite Coalescence: An Interpretation of Peronism," *Comparative Politics*, 1: 423–439.
Calvert, Susan, and Peter Calvert. 1989. *Argentina: Political Culture and Instability*. Pittsburgh, PA: University of Pittsburgh Press.
Cammack, Paul. 2000. "The Resurgence of Populism in Latin America," *Bulletin of Latin American Research*, 19(2): 149–161.
Canovan, Margaret. 1999. "Trust the People! Populism and the Two Faces of Democracy," *Political Studies*, 47(1): 2–16.
Cardoza, Anthony L. 1982. *Agrarian Elites and Italian Fascism: The Province of Bologna, 1901–1926*. Princeton, NJ: Princeton University Press.
Carey, John M. 1997. "Strong Candidates for a Limited Office: Presidentialism and Political Parties in Costa Rica," in eds., Mainwaring, Scott and Shugart, Matthew Soberg, *Presidentialism and Democracy in Latin America*. Cambridge: Cambridge University Press.
Cavarozzi, Marcelo. 1997. "Grandeur et Decadence du Model Etat-Centrique en Amerique Latine," *Cahiers des Ameriques Latines*, 26: 173–182.
Cavarozzi, Marcelo, and Manuel Antonio Garretón, eds. 1989. *Muerte y resurrección: Los partidos políticos en el autoritarismo y las transiciones del cono sur*. Santiago: FLACSO.
Catterberg, Edgardo R. 1991. *Argentina Confronts Politics: Political Culture and Public Opinion in the Argentine Transition to Democracy*. Boulder, CO: Lynn Rienner Publishers.
Chambers, Simone. 1996. *Reasonable Democracy*. Ithaca, NY: Cornell University Press.
  1998. "Contract or Conversation? Theoretical Lessons from the Canadian Constitutional Crisis," *Politics and Society*, 26: 143–172.
Chamorro Cardenal, Pedro Joaquín. 1948. "El Derecho del Trabajo," thesis presented to the National School of Jurisprudence and Social Sciences, National Autonomous University of México, Mexico City.
  1961. "Diario De Un Préso: Testimonio de la Cárcel," *Revista Conservadora*, 2(9): 1–16.
  1970. *Los Pies Descalzos de Nicaragua: Monografia Sobre la Frontera Sur y el Eje Hidrografico Gran Lago-Rio San Juan*. Managua: Editorial Artes Gráficas.
  1980. *Estirpe Sangrienta: Los Somoza*. 2nd ed. Mexico City: Editorial Diogenes SA.
  1981. *La Patria de Pedro: El Pensamiento Nicaraguense de Pedro Joaquín Chamorro*. 2nd ed. Managua: La Prensa.
Chavarria, Ricardo E. 1982. "The Nicaraguan Insurrection," in ed., Walker, Thomas W., *Nicaragua in Revolution*. New York: Praeger.
Chavez, Rebecca Bill. 2004a. "The Evolution of Judicial Autonomy in Argentina," *Journal of Latin American Studies*, 36(3): 451–478.
  2004b. *The Rule of Law in Nascent Democracies: Judicial Politics in Argentina*. Stanford, CA: Stanford University Press.
Cleary, Matthew R., and Susan C. Stokes. 2006. *Democracy and the Culture of Skepticism: Political Trust in Argentina and Mexico*. New York: Russell Sage.
Congreso de la Nación. 1946–1955. Camara de Diputados. *Diario de Sesiones*. All volumes.
Congreso de la Nación. 1946–1955. Camara de Senadores. *Diario de Sesiones*. All volumes.

Conway, Margaret M. 2000. *Political Participation in the United States*. Washington, DC: Congressional Quarterly Press.
Conway, M. Margaret, Gertrude A. Steuernagel, and David W. Ahern. 1997. *Women and Political Participation: Cultural Change in the Political Arena*. Washington, DC: Congressional Quarterly Press.
Cooper, Joseph, ed. 1999. *Congress and the Decline of Public Trust*. Boulder, CO: Westview Press.
Corner, Paul. 1975. *Fascism in Ferrara, 1915–1925*. London: Oxford University Press.
Cox, Gary W. and McCubbins, Matthew D. 1993. *Legislative Leviathan: Party Government in the House*. Berkeley, CA: University of California Press.
Crassweller, Robert D. 1987. *Peron and the Enigmas of Argentina*. New York: W.W. Norton.
Crawford, Susan, and Peggy Levitt. 1999. "Social Change and Civic Engagement: The Case of the PTA," in eds., Skocpol, Theda and Fiorina, Morris P., *Civic Engagement in American Democracy*. Washington, DC: Brookings Institution Press.
Dahl, Robert A. 1958. *A Preface to Democratic Theory*. Chicago, IL: University of Chicago Press.
   1971. *Polyarchy: Participation and Opposition*. New Haven, CT: Yale University Press.
   1998. *On Democracy*. New Haven, CT: Yale University Press.
   2002. *How Democratic Is the American Constitution?* New Haven, CT: Yale University Press.
Davis, Charles L., Edwin E. Aguilar, and John G. Speer. 1999. "Associations and Activism: Mobilization of Urban Informal Workers in Costa Rica and Nicaragua," *Journal of Interamerican Studies and World Affairs*, 41(3): 35–66.
Denisson, Marieke, Mirella Van Dun, and Kees Koonings. 2004. "Social Protest against Repression and Violence in Present Day Argentina and Peru," *European Review of Latin American and Caribbean Studies*, 77: 91–99.
Dewey, John. 1993. "Democratic Ends Need Democratic Methods for their Realizatiton," *New Leader*, 22 (October 21, 1938). Reprinted in John Dewey, *The Political Writings*, Morris, Debra and Shapiro Ian, eds. Indianapolis: Hackett, 1993.
Diaz, Rodolfo. 2002. *Prosperidad o Ilusion? Las reformas de los 90 en la. Argentina*, Buenos Aires, Editorial Abaco de Rodolfo Depalma.
Dietlind, Stolle. 1998. "Bowling Together, Bowling Alone: The Development of Generalized Trust in Voluntary Associations," *Political Psychology*, 19(3): 497–525.
Dinerstein, Ana C. 2003. "¡Que Se Vayan Todos! Popular Insurrection and Asambleas Barriales in Argentina," *Bulletin of Latin American Research*, 22(2): 187–200.
Dodd, Lawrence C. 1977. "Congress and the Quest for Power," in eds., Dodd, Lawrence C. and Oppenheimer, Bruce I., *Congress Reconsidered*. 1st ed. New York: Praeger.
   1981. "Congress, the Constitution, and the Crisis of Legitimation," in eds., Dodd, Lawrence C. and Oppenheimer, Bruce I., *Congress Reconsidered*. 2nd ed. Washington, DC: Congressional Quarterly Press.
   1986. "The Cycles of Legislative Change," in ed., Weisberg, Herbert, *Political Science: The Science of Politics*. New York: Agathaon.
   2001. "Re-Envisioning Congress," in eds., Dodd, Lawrence C. and Oppenheimer, Bruce I., *Congress Reconsidered*. 7th ed. Washington, DC: Congressional Quarterly Press.

Dodd, Lawrence C., and Bruce I. Oppenheimer, 2009. "Congressional Politics in a Time of Crisis: The 2008 Elections and Their Implications," in eds., Dodd, Lawrence C. and Oppenheimer, Bruce I., *Congress Reconsidered*. 9th ed. Washington, DC: Congressional Quarterly Press.

Dodd, Lawrence C., and Scot Schraufnagel. 2007. "Legislative Conflict and Policy Productivity: The Role of Member Incivility and Party Polarization in the Enactment of Landmark Legislation, 1873–2004 – Based on Evidence from the *New York Times* and *Washington Post*," paper prepared for presentation at the annual meeting of the American Political Science Association, Chicago, IL, August 30–September 2.

Dodson, Michael, and Donald Jackson. 2004. "Horizontal Acountability in Transitional Democracies: The Human Rights Ombudsman in El Salvador and Guatemala," *Latin American Politics and Society*, 46(4): 1–27.

Dodson, Michael, and T.E. Montgomery. 1982. "The Churches in the Nicaraguan Revolution," in ed., Walker, Thomas W., *Nicaragua in Revolution*. New York: Praeger.

Downs, Anthony. 1957. *An Economic Theory of Democracy*. New York: Harper.

Duverger, Maurice. 1954. *Political Parties: Their Organization and Activity in the Modern State*. London: Metheun.

Eaton, Kent. 2001. "Decentralisation, Democratisation and Liberalisation: The History of Revenue Sharing in Argentina, 1934–1999," *Journal of Latin American Studies*, 33(1): 1–28.

Eckstein, Harry. 1992. *Regarding Politics: Essays on Political Theory, Stability, and Change*. Berkeley, CA: University of California Press.

Eckstein, Susan. 1989. *The Poverty of Revolution*. Princeton, NJ: Princeton University Press.

The Economist, "Business Notes: Dollars for Argentina, May 27, 1950, p. 1182; "Don't Cry for Menem," May 17–23, p. 33; "It Takes Two to Tango," June 5–11, 2004, p. 10; "Pickets and Police," July 3–9, 2004, p. 30.

Edmisten, Patricia Taylor. 1990. *Nicaragua Divided: La Prensa and the Chamorro Legacy*. Pensacola, FL: University of West Florida Press.

Elazar, Daniel J. 1970. *Cities of the Prairie: The Metropolitan Frontier and American Politics*. New York: Basic Books.

Elkins, Stanley, and Eric McKitrick. 1993. *The Age of Federalism*. New York: Oxford University Press.

Ellner, Steve. 2003. "The Contrasting Variants of the Populism of Hugo Chávez and Alberto Fujimori," *Journal of Latin American Studies*, 35(1): 139–162

Enriquez, Laura J. 1991. *Harvesting Change: Labor and Agrarian Reform in Nicaragua, 1979–1990*. Chapel Hill: University of North Carolina Press.

Fagen, Richard R. 1969. *The Transformation of Political Culture in Cuba*. Stanford, CA: Stanford University Press.

Fajardo, Jose. 1978. "Porque no ha caido Tachito?" *El Tiempo*, Bogota, Colombia, October 9.

Fallada, Hans. 2002. *Seul Dans Berlin* Paris: Denoel and D'ailleurs; originally published as Jeder Stirbt Fur Sich Allein, (Berlin: Aufbau-Verlag, 1965).

Farquharson, J.E. 1976. *The Plough and the Swastika: The NSDAP and Agriculture in Germany, 1928–45*. London: Sage Publications.

1986. "The Agrarian Policy of National Socialist Germany," in ed., Moeller, Robert G., *Peasants and Lords in Modern Germany*. Boston, MA: Allen Unwin.

Ferla, Salvador. 1974. *La Tercera Posicion Ideologica y Apreciaciones Sobre el Retorno de Perón*. Buenos Aires: Ediciones Meridiano.
Fernandez, Roberto M., and Emilio J. Castilla. 2001. "How Much Is That Network Worth? Social Capital in Employee Referral Networks," in eds., Lin Nan, Cook Karen, and Burt, Ronald S., *Social Capital: Theory and Research*. New York: Aldine de Gruyter.
Fiorina, Morris P. 1996. *Divided Government*. 2nd ed. Boston, MA: Allyn & Bacon.
  1999. "Extreme Voices: A Dark Side of Civic Engagement," in eds., Skocpol, Theda and Fiorina, Morris P., *Civic Engagement in American Democracy*. Washington, DC: Brookings Institution Press.
Fitch, J. Samuel. 1998. *The Armed Forces and Democracy in Latin America*. Baltimore, MD: Johns Hopkins University Press.
Fonseca, Carlos. 1984. *Vive Sandino*. Managua: Department of Propaganda and Education.
Forment, Carlos. 2004. *Democracy in Latin America*. Chicago, IL: University of Chicago Press.
Fournier, Dominque. 1999. "The Alfonsín Administration and the Promotion of Democratic Values in the Southern Cone and the Andes," *Journal of Latin American Studies*, 31(1): 39–74.
Foweraker, Joe, and Roman Krznaric. 2002. "The Uneven Performance of Third Wave Democracies: Electoral Politics and the Imperfect Rule of Law in Latin America," *Latin American Politics and Society*, 44(3): 29–60.
Fox, Jonathan. 1994. "The Difficult Transition from Clientelism to Citizenship," *World Politics*, 46(2): 151–184.
  1996. "How Does Civil Society Thicken? The Political Construction of Social Capital in Rural Mexico," *World Development*, 24(6): 1089–1103.
  2008. *Accountability Politics*. Oxford: Oxford University Press.
Frei, Norbert. 2002. *Adenauer's Germany and the Nazi Past: The Politics of Amnesty and Integration*. Translated by Joel Golb. New York: Columbia University Press. Originally published in German (Munich: Verlag C.H. Beck., 1997).
Fukuyama, Francis. 1995. "Confucianism and Democracy," *Journal of Democracy*, 6: 20–33.
  2002. "Social Capital and Development: The Coming Agenda," *SAIS Review*, 22(1): 23–37.
  2004. "The Imperative of State-Building," *Journal of Democracy*, 15(2): 17–31.
Galitelli, Bernardo. 1987. *Argentina From Anarchism to Peronism: Workers, Unions, and Politics, 1855–1985*. London: Zed Books.
García Sebastiani, Marcela. 2003. "The Other Side of Peronist Argentina: Radicals and Socialists in the Political Opposition to Perón, 1946–1955," *Journal of Latin American Studies*, 35(2): 311–339.
Garreton, Manuel Antonio. 2003. *Incomplete Democracy: Political Democratization in Chile and Latin America*. Chapel Hill, NC: University of North Carolina Press.
Garrioch, David. 2002. *The Making of Revolutionary Paris*. Berkeley, CA: University of California Press.
Gelineau, Francois, and Karen Remmer. 2006. "Political Decentralization and Electoral Accountability: The Argentine Experience 1983–2001," *British Journal of Political Science*, 36(1): 133–157
Germani, Gino. 1978. *Authoritarianism, Fascism, and National Populism*. New Brunswick, NJ: Transaction Books.

1980. "Categoría de ocupación y voto político en el Capital Federal," in eds., Manuel Mora y Araujo e Ignacio Llorente, *El Voto Peronista: Ensayos de Sociologia Electoral Argentina*. Buenos Aires: Editorial Sudamericana. Originally published in *Estructura Social de la Argentina*, Chapter XVI, 251–263 (Buenos Aires: Raigal, 1955).

Giliomee, Hermann. 2003. *The Afrikaners: A Biography of a People*. Charlottesville: University of Virginia Press.

Goodin, Robert E. 1996. "Institutions and Their Design," in ed., Goodin, Robert E., *The Theory of Institutional Design*. New York: Cambridge University Press.

Gould, Jeffrey L. 1990. *To Lead As Equals: Rural Protest and Political Consciousness in Chinandega, Nicaragua, 1912–1979*. Chapel Hill, NC: University of North Carolina Press.

Green, James R. 1978. *Grass-Roots Socialism: Radical Movements in the Southwest 1895–1943*. Baton Rouge: Lousiana State University Press.

Green, Melanie C., and Timothy C. Brock. 1998. "Trust, Mood and Outcomes of Friendship Determine Preferences for Real Versus Ersatz Social Capital," *Political Psychology*, 19: 527–544.

Griffin, Roger. 1995. *Fascism*. Oxford: Oxford University Press.

Guilhot, Nicolas, and Philippe C. Schmitter. 2000. "De la Transition a la Consolidation: Une Lecture Retrospective des 'Democratization Studies,'" *Revue Francaise de Science Politique*, 50: 615–631.

Gutmann, Amy. 1987. *Democratic Education*. Princeton, NJ: Princeton University Press.

Gutmann, Amy, and Dennis Thompson. 1996. *Democracy and Disagreement*. Cambridge, MA: Belknap Press of Harvard University Press.

Haberman, S. J. 1978. *Analysis of Qualitative Data, Vol 1: Introductory Topics*. New York: Academic Press.

Habermas, Jürgen. 1979. *Communication and the Evolution of Society*. Translated by Thomas McCarthy. Boston, MA: Beacon Press.

1996. *Between Facts and Norms: Contributions to a Discourse Theory of Law and Democracy*. Translated by William Rehg. Cambridge, MA: The MIT Press.

Halperin Donghi, Tulio, Ivan Jaksic, Gwen Kirkpatrick, and Francine Masiello, eds. 1994. *Sarmiento: Author of a Nation*. Berkeley, CA: University of California Press.

Hamann, Brigitte. 1999. *Hitler's Vienna: A Dictator's Apprenticeship*. Translated by Thomas Thornton. Oxford: Oxford University Press.

Harris, Leslie M. 2003. *In the Shadow of Slavery: African Americans in New York City, 1626–1863*. Chicago, IL: University of Chicago Press.

Harris, Richard L. 2000. *Death Of A Revolutionary: Che Guevara's Last Mission*. Revised Edition. New York: W. W. Norton.

Harris, Rosemary. 1972. *Prejudice and Tolerance in Ulster: A Study of Neighbors and Strangers in a Border Community*. Manchester: Manchester Press.

Hartlyn, Jonathan. 1998. *The Struggle For Democratic Politics in the Dominican Republic*. Chapel Hill, NC: University of North Carolina Press.

Held, David, and Christopher Pollitt, eds. 1986. *New Forms of Democracy*. London: Sage Publications.

Held, David. 1987. *Models of Democracy*. Stanford, CA: Stanford University Press.

Hermet, Guy. 2001. *Les Populismes dans le Monde: Une Histoire Sociologique XIXe-XX siècle*. Paris: Fayard.

Hero, Rodney E. 2003. "Social Capital and Racial Inequality in America," *Perspectives on Politics*, 1(1): 113–122.

Herzog, Don. 1998. *Poisoning the Minds of the Lower Orders*. Princeton, NJ: Princeton University Press.

Hibbing, John R. 1991. *Congressional Careers: Contours of Life in the U.S. House of Representatives*. Chapel Hill, NC: University of North Carolina Press.

Hill, Kim Q. 2003. "Democratization and Corruption: Systematic Evidence from the American States," *American Politics Research*, 31: 613–631.

Howell, Jr. Roger. 1977. *Cromwell*. Boston, MA: Little Brown.

Howell, William G., and Douglas L. Kriner. 2009. "Congress, the President, and the Iraq War's Domestic Front," in eds., Dodd, Lawrence C. and Oppenheimer, Bruce I., *Congress Reconsidered*. 9th ed. Washington, DC: Congressional Quarterly Press.

Hulliung, Mark. 2002. *Citizens and Citoyens: Republicans and Liberals in America and France*. Cambridge, MA: Harvard University Press.

Hunt, Lynn. 1984. *Politics, Culture, and Class in the French Revolution*. Berkeley, CA: University of California Press.

Huntington, Samuel P. 1965a. "Political Development and Political Decay," *World Politics*, 17: 386–430.

1965b. "*Congressional Response to the Twentieth Century*," in ed., Truman, David, *The Congress and America's Future*. 2nd ed. Englewood Cliffs, NJ: Prentice Hall.

1968. *Political Order in Changing Societies*. New Haven, CT: Yale University Press.

Hutter, Horst. 1978. *Politics as Friendship*. Waterloo, ON: Wilfred Laurier University Press.

Inglehart, Ronald, and Pippa Norris. 2008. *Sacred and Secular: Religion and Politics Worldwide*. Cambridge: Cambridge University Press.

International Center for Journalists. 2003. *Medios y Libertad de Expressión en las Americas*. Washington, D.C: International Center for Journalists. Reprinted in *Actualidad* (Buenos Aires), November 14.

Iñigo Carreras, Nicolás, and María Celia Cotarelo. 2003. "Social Struggles in Present Day Argentina," *Bulletin of Latin American Research*, 22(2): 201–213.

Isbester, Katherine. 2001. *Still Fighting: The Nicaraguan Women's Movement, 1977–2000*. Pittsburgh: University of Pittsburgh Press.

James, Daniel. 1978. "Power and Politics in Peronist Trade Unions," *Journal of Interamerican Studies and World Affairs*, 20(1): 3–36.

1979. "The Development of Peronist Trade Unionism, 1955–1966," PhD dissertation, University of London.

1988. *Resistance and Integration: Peronism and the Argentine Working Class, 1946–1976*. New York: Cambridge University Press.

Janos, Andrew C. 1992."Political Dynamics of the Post-Communist Transition: A Comparative Perspective," in ed., Bermeo, Nancy, *Liberalization and Democratizatoin: Change in the Soviet Union and Eastern Europe*. Baltimore, MD: Johns Hopkins University Press.

Jones, Bryan D., and Walter Williams. 2008. *The Politics of Bad Ideas: The Great Tax Cut Delusion and the Decline of Good Government in America*. New York: Pearson Longman.

Jones, Mark. 1995. *Electoral Laws and the Survival of Presidential Democracies*. Notre Dame, IN: Notre Dame University Press.

1997. "Evaluating Argentina's Presidential Democracy: 1983–1995, " in Scott Mainwaring and Matthew Soberg Shugart, *Presidentialism and Democracy in Latin America*. New York: Cambridge University Press.

Kaimowitz, David, and Joseph R. Thome. 1982. "Nicaragua's Agrarian Reform: The First Year (1979–1980)," in ed., Walker, Thomas W., *Nicaragua in Revolution*. New York: Praeger.

Kampwirth, Karen. 2003. "Arnoldo Alemán Takes on the NGOs: Antifeminism and the New Populism in Nicaragua," *Latin American Politics and Society*, 45(2): 133–158.

Karush, Matthew B. 1999. "Workers, Citizens and the Argentine Nation: Party Politics and the Working Class in Rosario, 1912–3," *Journal of Latin American Studies*, 31(3): 589–616.

Katra, William. 1994. "Rereading Viajes: Race, Identity and National Destiny," in eds., Donghi, Tulio Halperin , Jaksic, Ivan , Kirkpatrick, Gwen, and Masiello, Francine, *Sarmiento: Author of a Nation*. Berkeley, CA: University of California Press.

Kenney, Charles D. 2004. *Fujimori's Coup and the Breakdown of Democracy in Latin America*. Notre Dame, IN: University of Notre Dame Press.

King, Ronald, and Susan Ellis. 1996. "Partisan Advantage and Constitutional Change: The Case of the Seventeenth Amendment," *Studies in American Political Development*, 10: 69–102.

Klein, Marcus. 2001. "Argentine Nacionalismo Before Peron: The Case of the Alianza de la Juventude Nacionalista, 1937–1943," *Bulletin of Latin American Research*, 20(1): 102–121.

Klesner, Joseph L. 2007. "Social Capital and Political Participation in Latin America: Evidence from Argentina, Chile, Mexico and Peru," *Latin American Research Review*, 42(2): 1–32.

Kohli, Atul. 1990. *Democracy and Discontent: India's Growing Crisis of Governability*. Cambridge: Cambridge University Press.

Kohn, Margaret. 1999. "Civic Republicanism Versus Social Struggle: A Gramscian Approach to Associationalism in Italy," *Political Power and Social Theory*, 13: 201–235.

Kornblith, Miriam. 1991. "Constitutions and Democracy in Venezuela," *Journal of Latin American Studies*, 23: 61–90.

Knight, Alan. 2001. "Democratic and Revolutionary Traditions in Latin America," *Bulletin of Latin American Research*, 20(2): 147–186.

La Garde-Chambonas, Auguste, comte de. 1843. *Souvenirs de Congrés de Vienne, 1814–5*. Paris.

La Duke Lake, Ronald, and Robert Huckfeldt. 1998. "Social Capital, Social Networks, and Political Participation," *Political Psychology*, 19: 567–584.

Laclau, Ernesto. 1979. *Politics and Ideology in Marxist Theory: Capitalism, Fascism, Populism*. London: Verso Editions.

Lamont, Michèle. 1991. *Money, Morals, and Manners: The Culture of the French and American Upper Middle Class*. Chicago, IL: University of Chicago Press.

Latin American Studies Association. 1984. *Electoral Process in Nicaragua: Domestic and International Influences: Report of the LASA Delegation to Observe the Nicaraguan General Election of November 4, 1984*. Austin, TX: Latin American Studies Assocation.

1990. *Electoral Democracy Under International Pressure: The Report of the Latin American Studies Association Commission to Observe the 1990 Nicaraguan Election*. Pittsburgh, PA: Latin American Studies Assocation.

Lazar, Sian. 2004. "Personalist Politics, Clientelism and Citizenship: Local Elections in El Alto, Bolivia," *Bulletin of Latin American Research*, 23(2): 228–243.

Leaman, David E. 1999. "Populist Liberalism as Dominant Ideology: Competing Ideas and Democracy in Post-Authoritarian Argentina, 1989–1995," *Studies in Comparative International Development*, 34(3): 98–118.

Lee, Frances E., and Bruce I. Oppenheimer. 1999. *Sizing Up the Senate*. Chicago, IL: University of Chicago Press.

Lernoux, Penny. 1982. *Cry of the People: The Struggle for Human Rights in Latin America – The Catholic Church in Conflict with U.S. Policy*. New York: Penguin Books. First published as *United States Involvement in the Rise of Fascism, Torture and Murder and the Persecution of the Catholic Church in Latin America*, New York: Doubleday, 1980.

Levine, Daniel H. 1992. *Popular Voices in Latin American Catholicism*. Princeton, NJ: Princeton University Press.

Levine, Robert A., and Donald T. Campbell. 1972. *Ethnocentrism: Theories of Conflict, Ethnic Attitudes, and Group Behavior*. New York: John Wiley and Sons.

Levitsky, Steven. 2000. "The 'Normalization' of Argentine Politics," *Journal of Democracy*, 11: 56–70.

2001. "An Organised Disorganisation: Informal Organisation and the Persistence of Local Party Structures in Argentine Peronism," *Journal of Latin American Studies*, 33(1): 29–65.

2003a. "Chaos and Renovation: Institutional Weakness and the Transformation of Argentine Peronism, 1983–2002," paper presented at the XXIV International Congress of the Latin American Studies Association, Dallas, TX.

2003b. *Transforming Labor-Based Parties in Latin America: Argentine Peronism in Comparative Perspective*. New York: Cambridge University Press.

Lewis, Oscar. 1961. *The Children Of Sánchez: Autobiography of a Mexican Family*. New York: Vintage Books.

Lin, Nan. 2001. *Social Capital: A Theory of Social Structure and Action*. New York: Cambridge University Press.

Lin, Nan, Karen Cook, and Ronald S. Burt. 2001. *Social Capital: Theory and Research*. New York: Aldine de Gruyter.

Linz, Juan J. 1994. "Presidential or Parliamentary Democracy: Does It Make A Difference?" in eds., Linz, Juan J., and Valenzuela, Arturo, *The Failure of Presidential Democracy*. Baltimore, MD: Johns Hopkins University Press.

Linz, Juan J., and Alfred Stepan, eds. 1978. *The Breakdown of Democratic Regimes*. Baltimore, MD: Johns Hopkins University Press.

1996. *Problems of Democratic Transition and Consolidation: Southern Europe, South America, and Post-Communist Europe*. Baltimore, MD: Johns Hopkins University Press.

Lipset, Seymour Martin. 1959. "Some Social Requisites of Democracy: Economic Development and Political Legitimacy," *American Political Science Review*, 53: 69–105.

1960. *Political Man: The Social Bases of Politics*. Garden City, NY: Doubleday.

1963. *The First New Nation: The United States in Historical and Comparative Perspective.* New York: Basic Books.

Lipset, Seymour Martin, and Stein Rokkan, eds. 1967. *Party Systems and Voter Alignments: Cross-National Perspectives.* New York: Free Press.

1967. "Cleavage Structures, Party Systems, and Voter Alignments: An Introduction," in eds., Lipset, Seymour Martin, and Rokkan, Stein, *Party Systems and Voter Alignments: Cross National Perspectives.* New York: Free Press.

Llanos, Mariana. 2001. "Understanding Presidential Power in Argentina: A Study of the Policy of Privatisation in the 1990s," *Journal of Latin American Studies,* 33(1): 67–99.

2002. *Privatization and Democracy in Argentina: An Analysis of President-Congress Relations.* New York: Palgrave Macmillan.

Llorente, Ignacio. 1980. "La Composicion Social del Movimiento Peronista," in eds., Manuel Mora y Araujo e Ignacio Llorente, *El Voto Peronista: Ensayos de Sociologia Electoral Argentina.* Buenos Aires: Editorial Sudamericana.

Luca de Tema, Torcuato, Luis Calvo, and Esteban Peicovich, eds. 1976. *Yo, Juan Domingo Peron: Relato Biografico.* Barcelona: Editorial Planeta.

Luciak, Ilja A. 1990. "Democracy in the Nicaraguan Countryside: A Comparative Analysis of Sandinista Grassroots Movements," *Latin American Perspectives,* 17: 55–75.

1995. *The Sandinista Legacy: Lessons from a Political Economy in Transition.* Gainesville, FL: University of Florida Press.

Luna, Felix. 1958. *Alvear.* Buenos Aires: Libros Argentinos.

Madres de Plaza de Mayo. 1995. *Historia de las Madres de Plaza de Mayo.* Buenos Aires: Asociación Madres de Plaza de Mayo.

Madsen, Douglas, and Peter G. Snow. 1991. *The Charismatic Bond: Political Behavior in Time of Crisis.* Cambridge, MA: Harvard University Press.

Magaloni, Beatriz. 2006. *Voting for Autocracy: Hegemonic Party Survival and its Demise in Mexico.* New York: Cambridge University Press.

Manero, Edgardo. 2002. "Pratiques et Discours de l'Alterité Négative Dans le Cadre de la Crise Argentine: Une Approche des Violences," *Cahiers des Ameriques Latines,* 41: 55–76.

Mainwaring, Scott. 1991. "Politicians, Parties and Electoral Systems: Brazil in Comparative Perspective," *Comparative Politics,* 24(1): 21–44.

1993. "Presidentialism, Multipartism, and Democracy: The Difficult Combination," *Comparative Political Studies,* 26(2): 198–228.

Mainwaring, Scott, and Timothy R. Scully, 1995. "Introduction: Party Systems in Latin America," in eds., Mainwaring, Scott, and Scully, Timothy R., *Building Democratic Institutions: Party Systems in Latin America.* Stanford, CA: Stanford University Press.

Mann, Michael. 2004. *Fascists.* New York: Cambridge University Press.

Manning, Carrie. 2008. *The Making of Democrats: Elections and Party Development in Post-War Bosnia, El Salvador, and Mozambique.* New York: Palgrave Macmillan.

Mansbridge, Jane J. 1980. *Beyond Adversary Democracy.* New York: Basic Books.

Mao Tse Tung. 1927. "Report on an Investigation of the Peasant Movement in Hunan. March 1927," in *Selected Works of Mao Tse-Tung,* Vol 1. Peking: Foreign Languages Press.

March, James G., and Johan Olsen. 1989. *Rediscovering Institutions: The Organizational Basis of Politics.* New York: Free Press.

Maxwell, Amanda, and Richard F. Winters. 2004. "A Quarter-Century of (data) on Political Corruption," paper presented at the Midwest Political Science Association.
Mayhew, David R. 1991. *Divided We Govern: Party Control, Lawmaking, and Investigations, 1946–1990*. New Haven, CT: Yale University Press.
Mazo, Eduardo. 1984. Autorizado a Vivir, 24, 4th ed. Barcelona, no publisher given.
McLean, Scott, David Schultz, and Manfred Steger, eds. 2002. *Social Capital: Critical Perspectives on Community and "Bowling Alone."* New York: New York University Press.
McClintock, Cynthia. 1978. "The Ambiguity of Peru's Third Way: Costs and Benefits," Working Paper no. 23. Latin American Program. Washington, DC: The Woodrow Wilson International Center for Scholars.
    1981. *Peasant Cooperatives And Political Change in Peru*. Princeton, NJ: Princeton University Press.
McGuire, James. 1995. "Political Parties and Democracy in Argentina," in eds., Mainwaring, Scott, and Scully, Timothy, *Building Democratic Institutions: Party Systems in Latin America*. Stanford, CA: Stanford University Press.
    1997. *Peronism Without Peron: Unions, Parties, and Democracy in Argentina*. Stanford, CA: Stanford University Press.
Merklen, Denis. 2002. "Entre Ciel et Terre: Les Sciences Sociales et la Mobilisation Populaire en Argentine," *Cahiers des Ameriques Latines*, 41: 33–54.
Mezey, Michael. 1979. *Comparative Legislatures*. Durham: Duke University Press.
Miguez, Daniel. 1995. "Democracy, Political Machines and Participation in the Surroundings of Buenos Aires," *European Review/Revista Europea*, 58: 91–106.
Molinelli, Guillermo. 1991. *Presidentes y Congresos en Argentina: Mitos y Realidades*. Buenos Aires: Grupo Editor Latinoamericano.
    1996. "Las relaciones Presidente-Congreso en Argentina 1983–1995," *PostData*, 2(November): 59–90.
Moore, Barrington. 1966. *Social Origins of Dictatorship and Democracy: Lord and Peasant in the Making of the Modern World*. Boston, MA: Beacon Press.
Montgomery, Tommie Sue. 1982. *Revolution in El Salvador: Origins And Evolution*. Boulder, CO: Westview Press.
Mora y Araujo, Manuel. 1980. "Las Bases Estructurales del Peronismo," in eds., Manuel Mora y Araujo e Ignacio Llorente, *El Voto Peronista: Ensayos de Sociologia Electoral Argentina*. Buenos Aires: Editorial Sudamericana.
Morone, James A. 2003. *Hellfire Nation: The Politics of Sin in American History*. New Haven, CT: Yale University Press.
Munck, Gerardo L. 1997. "Bringing Post-Communist Societies into Democratization Studies," *Slavic Review*, 56: 542–550.
Murrillo, Maria Victoria. 2001. *Labor Unions, Partisan Coalitions, and Market Reforms in Latin America*. New York: Cambridge University Press.
Mustapic, Ana Maria. 1984. "Conflictos Institucionales Durante el Primer Gobierno Radical: 1916–1922," *Desarollo Economico*, 24: 85–108.
Mustapic, Ana Maria, and Matteo Goretti. 1992. "Gobierno y Oposicion en el Congreso: La Practica de la Cohabitacion Durante La Presidencia de Alfonsin (1983–1989)," *Desarollo Economico: Revista de Ciencias Sociales*, 32(126): 251–269.
Mustapic, Ana Maria, and Natalia Ferretti. Forthcoming. El Veto Presidencial Bajo Alfonsín y Menem (1983–1995). Manuscript in process.

Negretto, Gabriel, and José Antonio Aguilar-Rivera. 2000. "Rethinking the Legacy of the Liberal State in Latin America: The Cases of Argentina (1853–1916) and Mexico (1857–1910)," *Journal of Latin American Studies*, 32(2): 361–397.
Nice, David C. 1983. "Political Corruption in the American States," *American Politics Quarterly*, 11: 507–517.
Nino, Carlos. 1996. *Radical Evil on Trial*. New Haven, CT: Yale University Press.
Norton, Mary Beth. 2002. *In the Devil's Snare: The Salem Witchcraft Crisis of 1692*. New York: Alfred Knopf.
O'Donnell, Guillermo. 1994. "Delegative Democracy," *Journal of Democracy*, 5(1): 55–69.
  1995. "Democracias y exclusion," *Agora*, 1(2): 165–172.
  1999. "Horizontal Accountability in New Democracies," in eds., Schedler, Andreas, Diamond, Larry, and Plattner, Marc F., *The Self-Restraining State: Power and Accountability in New Democracies*. Boulder, CO: Lynne Rienner.
  2001. "Democracy, Law, and Comparative Politics," *Studies in Comparative International Development*, 36(1): 7–36.
O'Donnell, Guillermo, and Philippe Schmitter. 1986. *Transitions from Authoritarian Rule: Tentative Conclusions About Uncertain Democracies*. Baltimore, MD: Johns Hopkins University Press.
O'Neill, Daniel I. 2007. *The Burke-Wollstonecraft Debate: Savagery Civilization and Democracy*. College Station, TX: Pennsylvania State Press.
Oppenheimer, Bruce. 1996. "The Representational Experience: The Effect of State Population On Senator-Constituency Linkages," *American Journal of Political Science*, 40: 1280–1290.
Oquist, Paul. 1992. "Sociopolitical Dynamics of the 1990 Nicaraguan Elections," in eds., Castro, Vanessa, and Prevost, Gary, *The 1990 Elections in Nicaragua and Their Aftermath*. Lanham, MD: Rowman and Littlefield.
O'Shaughnessy, Laura Nuzzi, and Michael Dodson. 1999. "Political Bargaining and Democratic Transitions: A Comparison of Nicaragua and El Salvador," *Journal of Latin American Studies*, 31(1): 99–127.
Oxhorn, Philip. 2001. *When Democracy Isn't All That Democratic: Social Exclusion and the Limits of the Public Sphere in Latin America*. North South Agenda Paper 44. April. Coral Gables, FL: North-South Center, University of Miami.
Page, Joseph A. 1983. *Peron: A Biography*. New York: Random House.
Pateman, Carol. 1970. *Participation and Democratic Theory*. Cambridge: Cambridge University Press.
Paxton, Robert O. 1997. *French Peasant Fascism: Henry Dorgeres's Greenshirts and the Crises of French Agriculture, 1929–1939*. Oxford: Oxford University Press.
Payne, Stanley G. 1987. *The Franco Regime, 1936–1975*. London: Phoenix Press.
  1995. *A History of Fascism, 1914–1945*. Madison, WI: University of Wisconsin Press.
  1999. *Fascism in Spain, 1923–1977*. Madison, WI: University of Wisconsin Press.
Pereyra, E. Pavon. 1973. *Peron: El Hombre del Destino*. Number 1, November (series of magazines).
Pérez-Díaz, Víctor M. 1973. "Processus de changement dans les communautes rurales de Castille," *Etudes Rurales*, 51: 7–25.
  1993. *The Return of Civil Society: The Emergence of Democratic Spain*. Cambridge, MA: Harvard University Press.
Peron, Juan. 1971. *Peron: Actualizacion Politica y Doctrinaria Para La Toma del Poder*. Interview. Buenos Aires: Movimiento Revolucionario Peronista.
  1973. *Habla Peron*. Buenos Aires: Editorial Freeland.

n.d. *La Tercera Posicion: Doctrina del General Peron.* Buenos Aires: Presidencia de la Nacion, Secretaria de Prensa y Difusion.
Peruzzotti, Enrique. 1997. "Civil Society and the Modern Constitutional Complex: The Argentine Experience," *Constellations,* 4: 94–104.
   2001. "The Nature of the New Argentine Democracy: The Delegative Democracy Argument Revisited," *Journal of Latin American Studies,* 33(1): 133–155.
Peterson, Anna, Manuel Vásquez, and Philip Williams, eds. 2001. *Christianity, Social Change, And Globalization in The Americas.* New Brunswick, NJ: Rutgers University Press.
Pharr, Susan J., and Robert D. Putnam, eds. 2000. *Disaffected Democracies: What's Troubling the Trilateral Countries?* Princeton, NJ: Princeton University Press.
Philip, George. 2003. *Democracy in Latin America.* Oxford: Polity Press.
Pitcher, M. Anne. 2002. *Transforming Mozambique: The Politics of Privatization, 1975–2000.* Cambridge: Cambridge University Press.
Piven, Frances Fox, and Richard A. Cloward. 1977. *Poor People's Movements: Why They Succeed, How They Fail.* New York: Pantheon Books.
Platt, D. C. M., and Guido di Tella, eds. 1985. *Argentina, Australia and Canada: Studies in Comparative Development, 1870–1965.* New York: St. Martin's Press.
Polak, Laura, and Juan Carlos Gorbier. 1994. *El Movimiento Estudiantil Argentino. Franja Morada, 1976–1986.* Buenos Aires: Centro Editor de América Latina.
Polletta, Francesca. 2002. *Freedom is an Endless Meeting: Democracy in American Social Movements.* Chicago, IL: University of Chicago Press.
Polsby, Nelson W. 1968. "The Institutionalization of the U.S. House of Representatives," *American Political Science Review,* 62: 144–168.
   1999. "The Institutionalization of the U.S. House of Representatives," in eds., Weisberg, Herbert F., Heberlig, Eric S., and Campoli, Lisa M., *Classics in Congressional Politics.* New York: Longman.
Price, H. Douglas. 1971. "The Congressional Career: Then and Now," in ed., Polsby, Nelson W., *Congressional Behavior.* New York: Random House.
Pruitt, Dean G., and Jeffrey Z. Rubin. 1986. *Social Conflict: Escalation, Stalemate and Settlement.* New York: Random House.
Putnam, Lara. 2002. *The Company They Kept: Migrants and the Politics of Gender in Caribbean Costa Rica, 1870–1960.* Chapel Hill, NC: University of North Carolina Press.
Putnam, Robert D. 2000. *Bowling Alone: The Collapse and Revival of American Community.* New York: Simon and Schuster.
Putnam, Robert D., Robert Leonardi, and Raffaella Y. Nanetti. 1993. *Making Democracy Work: Civic Traditions in Modern Italy.* Princeton, NJ: Princeton University Press.
Randal, Margaret. 1983. *Cristianos en la Revolucion.* Managua: Editorial Nueva Nicaragua.
Ranis, Peter. 1995. *Class, Democracy and Labor in Contemporary Argentina.* New Brunswick, NJ: Transaction Press.
Rawls, John. 1971. *A Theory of Justice.* Cambridge, MA: Belknap Press of Harvard University Press.
Reding, Andrew A. 1991. "The Evolution of Government Institutions," in ed., Walker, Thomas W., *Revolution and Counterrevolution.* Boulder, CO: Westview Press.
Rein, Raanan. 2008. *In the Shadow of Peron: Juan Atilio Bramuglia and the Second Line of Argentina's Populist Movement.* Translated by Martha Grenzeback.

Stanford, CA: Stanford University Press. Originally published as *Juan Atilio Bramuglia: Bajo la sombra del líder. La segunda linea de liderazgo peronista* (Buenos Aires: Ediciones Lumiere, 2006).

Remmer, Karen. 2007. "The Political Economy of Patronage Expenditure Patterns in the Argentine Provinces, 1983–2003," *Journal of Politics*, 69(2): 363–377.

Revesz, Bruno. 1997. "Redefinition de L'Etat et Gouvernabilite Democratique," *Cahiers des Ameriques Latines*, 26: 75–93.

Ripley, Randall B. 1969. *Power in the Senate*. New York: St. Martin's Press.

Rippy, J. Fred. 1963. "The Anguish of Bolivar," in ed., Wilgus, A. Curtis, *South American Dictators During the First Century of Independence*. New York: Russell and Russell.

Rivas Leone, José Antonio. 2003. *El Desconcierto de la Politica: Los Desafios de la Política Democrática*. Mérida, Venezuela: Ediciones del Vicerrectorado Académico.

Rokkan, Stein. 1970. *Citizens, Elections, Parties: Approaches to the Comparative Study of the Process of Development*. New York: McKay.

Rosenson, Beth A. 2009. "The Effects of Political Reform Measures on Perceptions of Corruption," *Election Law Journal: Rules, Politics, and Policy*, 8(1): 31–46.

Ross, Marc Howard. 1985. "Internal and External Conflict and Violence: Cross-Cultural Evidence and a New Analysis," *Journal of Conflict Resolution*, 29: 547–579.
  1986. "A Cross-Cultural Theory of Political Conflict and Violence," *Political Psychology*, 7: 427–469.
  1993. *The Culture of Conflict: Interpretations and Interests in Comparative Perspective*. New Haven, CT: Yale University Press.

Rubin, Jeffrey W. 2004. "Meanings and Mobilizations: A Cultural Politics Approach to Social Movements and States," *Latin American Research Review*, 39(3): 106–142.

Ruchwarger, Gary. 1987. *People in Power: Forging A Grassroots Democracy in Nicaragua*. South Hadley, MA: Bergin and Garvey.

Sabato, Hilda. 1992. "Citizenship, Political Participation and the Formation of the Public Sphere in Buenos Aires 1850s-1889s," *Past and Present*, 136: 139–193.

Sábato, Ernesto R. 1988. *The Tunnel*. Translated from the Spanish by Margaret Sayers Peden. 1st ed. New York: Ballantine Books. Originally published in Spanish as *El Tunel* (Buenos Aires: Sur, 1950).

Saldaña, Rodolfo. 2001. *Fertile Ground: Ché Guevara and Bolivia: A Firsthand Account*. Mary-Alice Waters, ed. New York: Pathfinder. Originally published as *Terreno fértil: Ché Guevara y Bolivia: relato testimonial de Rodolfo Saldaña* (La Habana: Editora Política, 2001).

Sandino, Augusto C. 1981. *Augusto C. Sandino: El Pensamiento Vivo*. Vol. 1. 2nd ed. Managua: Editorial Nueva Nicaragua. Reprinted in 1984. First published in San Jose, Costa Rica: Editorial Universitaria Centroamericana, 1974.

Sartori, Giovanni. 1976. *Parties and Party Systems: A Framework for Analysis*. New York: Cambridge University Press.

Sawers, Larry, and Raquel Massacane. 2001. "Structural Reform and Industrial Promotion in Argentina," *Journal of Latin American Studies*, 33(1): 101–132.

Schonwalder, Gerd. 2002. *Linking Civil Society and the State: Urban Popular Movements, the Left, and Local Government in Peru*. College Station, TX: Pennsylvania State Press.

Schwartz David C. 1973. *Political Alienation and Political Behavior*. Chicago, IL: Aldin Publishing Company.
Seligson, Amber L. 1999. "Civic Association and Democratic Participation in Central America: A Test of the Putnam Thesis," *Comparative Political Studies*, 32(3): 342–362.
Selser, Gregorio. 1984. *Nicaragua de Walker a Somoza*. Mexico City: Editorial Mex-sur.
Serra, Luis. 1982. "The Sandinista Mass Organizations," in ed., Walker, Thomas W., *Nicaragua in Revolution*. New York: Praeger.
    1985. "The Grassroots Organizations," in ed., Walker, Thomas W., *Nicaragua: The First Five Years*. New York: Praeger.
    1991."The Grass-Roots Organizations," in ed., Walker, Thomas W., *Revolution and Counterrevolution in Nicaragua*. Boulder, CO: Westview Press.
Shapiro, Ian. 1999. *Democratic Justice*. New Haven, CT: Yale University Press.
Shepsle, Kenneth A. 1986. "Institutional Equilibrium and Equilibrium Institutions," in ed., Weisberg, Herbert F., *Political Science: The Science of Politics*. New York: Agathon Press.
Shumway, Nicolas. 1991. *The Invention of Argentina*. Berkeley, CA: University of California Press.
Sidicaro, Ricardo. 2003–2004. "Les transformations du péronismo," *Problemes d'Amerique Latine*, 51(Hiver): 37–56.
Sinclair, Barbara. 1989. *The Transformation of the U.S. Senate*. Baltimore, MD: Johns Hopkins University Press.
Skocpol, Theda. 1992. *Protecting Soldiers and Mothers: The Political Origins of Social Policy in the United States*. Cambridge, MA: Harvard University Press.
    1995. *Social Policy in the United States: Future Possibilities in Historical Perspective*. Princeton, NJ: Princeton University Press.
    1999. "How Americans Became Civic," in eds., Skocpol, Theda, and Fiorina, Morris P., *Civic Engagement in American Democracy*. With the assistance of Marshall Ganz, Ziad Munson, Bayliss Camp, Michele Swers, and Jennifer Oser. Washington, DC: Brookings Institution Press.
    2003. *Diminished Democracy: From Membership To Management in American Civic Life*. Norman: The University of Oklahoma Press.
Skocpol, Theda, and Morris P. Fiorina. 1999. "Making Sense of the Civic Engagement Debate," in eds., Skocpol, Theda, and Fiorina, Morris P., *Civic Engagement in American Democracy*. Washington, DC: Brookings Institution Press.
Skowronek, Steven. 1982. *Building a New American State: The Expansion of National Administrative Capacities, 1877–1920*. Cambridge: Cambridge University Press.
    1993. *The Politics Presidents Make: Leadership from John Adams to George Bush*. Cambridge, MA: Belknap Press.
Smith, Elizabeth S. 1999. "The Effects of Investments in the Social Capital of Youth on Political and Civic Behavior in Young Adulthood: A Longitudinal Analysis," *Political Psychology*, 20: 553–580.
Smith, Graham, William Maloney, and Gerry Stoker. 2004. "Building Social Capital in City Politics: Scope and Limitations at the Inter-Organizational Level," *Political Studies*, 52(3): 508–530.
Smith, Peter. 1972. "The Social Basis of Peronism," *Hispanic American Historical Review*, 52: 55–73.
    1980. "Las Elecciones de 1946 y las Inferencias Ecologicas," in ed., Manuel Mora y Araujo e Ignacio Llorente, *El Voto Peronista: Ensayos de Sociologia Electoral Argentina*. Buenos Aires: Editorial Sudamericana.

Snow, Peter G. 1972. *Argentine Political Parties and the 1966 Revolution*. Buffalo, NY: Council on International Studies.
Snowden, Frank. 1989. *The Fascist Revolution in Tuscany, 1919–1922*. Cambridge: Cambridge University Press.
Solberg, Carl. 1987. *The Prairies and the Pampas: Agrarian Policy in Canada and Argentina, 1880–1930*. Stanford, CA: Stanford University Press.
Spalding, Rose J. 1994. *Capitalists and Revolution in Nicaragua: Opposition and Accommodation, 1979–1993*. Chapel Hill, NC: University of North Carolina Press.
Speer, Albert. 1970. *Inside the Third Reich: Memoirs*. New York: Collier Books.
Spektorowski, Alberto. 2000. "Nationalism and Democratic Construction: The Origins of Argentina's and Uruguay's Political Cultures in Comparative Perspective," *Bulletin of Latin American Research*, 19(1): 81–99.
Stahler-Sholk, Richard. 1995. "The Dog That Didn't Bite: Labor Autonomy and Economic Adjustment in Nicaragua under the Sandinista and UNO Governments," *Comparative Politics*, 28: 77–102.
Stokes, Susan C. 2001. "Economic Reform and Public Opinion in Fujimori's Peru," in ed., Stokes, Susan C., *Public Support for Market Reforms in New Democracies*. New York: Cambridge University Press.
Swift, Elaine K. 1996. *The Making of an American Senate: Reconstitutive Change in Congress, 1787–1841*. Ann Arbor, MI: University of Michigan Press.
Szusterman, Celia. 2000. "Carlos Saul Menem: Variations on the Theme of Populism," *Bulletin of Latin American Research*, 19(2): 193–206.
Taylor-Robinson, Michelle, and Christopher Diaz. 1999. "Who Gets Legislation Passed in a Marginal Legislature and is the Label 'Marginal Legislature' Still Appropriate?," *Comparative Political Studies*, 32(5): 589–628.
Tcach, Cesar. 1991. *Sabattinismo y Peronismo: Partidos politicos de Córdoba, 1943–1955*. Buenos Aires: Editorial Sudamericana.
Tedesco, Laura. 2004. "Democracy in Latin America: Issues of Governance in the Southern Cone," *Bulletin of Latin American Research*, 23(1): 30–42.
Téfel, Reinaldo Antonio. 1976. *El Infierno de los Pobres: Diagnostico Sociologico de los Barrios Marginales de Managua*. 3rd ed. Managua: Distribuidora Cultural.
Teichman, Judith. 2004. "Merging the Modern and the Traditional: Market Reform in Chile and Argentina," *Comparative Politics*, 37(1): 23–40.
Tella, Torcuato di. 1965. "Populism and Reform in Latin America," in ed., Veliz, C., *Obstacles to Change in Latin America*, pp. 47–74. London: Oxford: Oxford University Press.
Theen, Rolf H. W., and Frank L. Wilson. 1992. *Comparative Politics: An Introduction to Seven Countries*. 2nd ed. Englewood Cliffs, NJ: Prentice Hall.
Thelen, Kathleen. 2004. *How Institutions Evolve: The Political Economy of Skills in Germany, Britain, the United States and Japan*. New York: Cambridge University Press.
   Forthcoming. "How Institutions Evolve: Insights from Comparative-Historical Analysis," in eds., Mahoney, James, and Rueschemeyer, Dietrick, *Comparative Historical Analysis in the Social Sciences*. New York: Cambridge University Press.
Thelen, Kathleen, and Sven Steinmo. 1992. "Historical Institutionalism in Comparative Politics," in eds., Steinmo, Sven, Thelen, Kathleen, and Longstreth, Frank, *Structuring Politics: Historical Institutionalism in Comparative Analysis*. New York: Cambridge University Press.

Thompson, E. P. 1966. *The Making of the English Working Class*. New York: Vintage Books.
   1971. "The Moral Economy of the English Crowd," *Past and Present*, 50: 76–136.
   1975. *Whigs and Hunters: The Origin of the Black Act*. 1st ed. (American). New York: Pantheon Books.
   1991. *Customs in Common*. London: Merlin.
Tilly, Charles. 1973. "Does Modernization Breed Revolution? A Reply to Huntington," *Comparative Politics*, 5: 425–448.
   1986. *The Contentious French: Four Centuries of Popular Struggle*. Cambridge, MA: Harvard University Press.
   1995. *Popular Contention in Great Britain, 1758–1834*. Cambridge, MA: Harvard University Press.
   2007. *Democracy*. Cambridge: Cambridge University Press.
Tilly, Louise. 1992. *Politics and Class in Milan, 1881–1901*. New York: Oxford University Press.
Tocqueville, Alexis de. 1956. *Democracy in America*. New York: Signet.
Torre, Juan Carlos. 1990. *La Vieja Guardia Sindical y Peron: Sobre Los Origines del Peronismo*. Buenos Aires: Editorial Sudamericana.
Torres, Edelberto. 1984. *Sandino*. Mexico City: Editorial Dantun.
Tourrain, Alain. 1988. *La Parole et le Sang: Politique et Societé en Amerique Latine*. Paris: Editions Odile Jacob.
Uslaner, Eric M. 2006. "The Civil State: Trust, Polarization and the Quality of State Government," in ed., Cohen, Jeffrey E., *Public Opinion in State Politics*. Stanford, CA: Stanford University Press.
Valenzuela, Samuel. 1992. "Democratic Consolidation in Post-Transitional Settings," in eds., Mainwaring, Scott, O'Donnell, Guillermo, and Valenzuela, Samuel, *Issues in Democratic Consolidation: The New South American Democracies in Comparative Perspective*. Notre Dame, IN: University of Notre Dame Press.
Vanden, Harry E. 1982. "The Ideology of the Insurrection," in ed., Walker, Thomas W., *Nicaragua in Revolution*. New York: Praeger.
Vanden, Harry, and Gary Prevost. 1993. *Democracy and Socialism in Sandinista Nicaragua*. Boulder, CO: Lynne Rienner.
Vanhanen, Tatu, ed. 1992. *Strategies of Democratization*. Washington, DC: Crane Russak.
   1997. *Prospects for Democracy: A Study of One Hundred Seventy-two Countries*. New York: Routledge.
Vásquez, Manuel A., and Marie Friedmann Marquardt. 2003. *Globalizing The Sacred: Religion Across The Americas*. New Brunswick, NJ: Rutgers University Press.
Vilas, Carlos. 1986. *The Sandinista Revolution: National Liberation and Social Transformation in Central America*. New York: Monthly Review Press.
   1992. "Family Affairs: Class, Lineage, and Politics in Contemporary Nicaragua," *Journal of Latin American Studies*, 24: 309–342.
Walker, Lee D. 2003. "The Democratic Arbiter: The Role of the Judiciary in the Democratic Consolidation Process in Nicaragua and Costa Rica," PhD dissertation, Political Science, University of Florida.
Walker, Thomas W. 1997. *Nicaragua Without Illusions, Regime Transition and Structural Adjustment in the 1990s*. Wilmington, DE: SR Books.
Walsh, Rodolfo. 1969. *Quien Mato a Rosendo?* Buenos Aires: Ediciones de la Flor.

Waylen, Georgina. 2000. "Gender and Democratic Politics: A Comparative Analysis of Consolidation in Argentina and Chile," *Journal of Latin American Studies*, 32(3): 765–793.
Weaver, R. Kent, and Bert A. Rockman. 1993. "Institutional Reform and Constitutional Design," in eds., Kent, Weaver, R., and Rockman, Bert A., *Do Institutions Matter? Government Capabilities in the United States and Abroad*. Washington, DC: Brookings Institution Press.
Weber, Max. 1947. *The Theory of Social and Economic Organization*. Translated by H. R. Henderson and Talcott Parsons. New York.
Weisberg, Herbert F., Eric S. Heberlig, and Lisa M. Campoli. 1999. "How Do Legislatures Develop?," in eds., Weisberg, Herbert F., Heberlig, Eric S., and Campoli, Lisa M., *Classics in Congressional Politics*. New York: Longman.
Weyland, Kurt. 2001. "Clarifying a Contested Concept: Populism in the Study of Latin American Politics," *Comparative Politics*, 34(1): 1–22.
  2004. "Neoliberalism and Democracy in Latin America: A Mixed Record," *Latin American Politics and Society*, 46(1): 135–157.
Williams, Philip J. 1989. *The Catholic Church and Politics in Nicaragua and Costa Rica*, Pittsburgh, PA: University of Pittsburgh Press.
  1994. "Dual Transitions from Authoritarian Rule: Popular and Electoral Democracy in Nicaragua," *Comparative Politics*, 26(2): 169–185.
Wirls, Daniel, and Steven Wirls. 2004. *The Invention of the United States Senate*. Baltimore, MD: Johns Hopkins University Press.
Wolfe, Alan. 1998. *One Nation After All: What Middle Class Americans Really Think About God, Country, Family, Racism, Welfare, Immigration, Homosexuality, Work, The Right, The Left and Each Other*. New York: Viking Press.
  2006. *Does American Democracy Still Work?* New Haven, CT: Yale University Press.
Wollstonecraft, Mary. 1995. *A Vindication of the Rights of Men and a Vindication of the Rights of Women*, edited by Sylvana Tomaselli. Cambridge: Cambridge University Press.
Woloch, Isser. 1994. *The New Regime: Transformations of the French Civic Order, 1789–1820s*. New York: W.W. Norton.
Wood, Elisabeth Jean. 2000. *Forging Democracy From Below: Insurgent Transitions in South Africa and El Salvador*. Cambridge: Cambridge University Press.
  2001. "An Insurgent Path to Democracy: Popular Mobilization, Economic Interests and Regime Transition in South Africa and El Salvador," *Comparative Political Studies*, 34(8): 862–888.
Wood, Gordon S. 1969. *The Creation of the American Republic, 1776–1787*. Chapel Hill, NC: University of North Carolina Press.
  1974. *Revolution and the Political Integration of the Enslaved and Disenfranchised*. Washington, DC: American Enterprise Institute for Public Policy Research.
  1992. *The Radicalism of the American Revolution*. New York: A. A. Knopf.
Wood, Richard L. 2002. *Faith in Action: Religion, Race, and Democratic Organizing in America*. Chicago, IL: University of Chicago Press.
Wynia, Gary. 1978. *Argentina in the Post-War Era: Politics and Economic Policy Making in A Divided Society*. Albuquerque: University of New Mexico Press.
Young, James Sterling. 1966. *The Washington Community, 1800–1826*. New York: Columbia University Press.
Zimmermann, Matilde. 2000. *Sandinista: Carlos Fonseca and the Nicaraguan Revolution*. Durham, NC: Duke University Press.

Index

activism
  citizen, 183n9, 238, 251–2n26
  grassroots, 50–8, 50n52, 64, 91–8, 181, 271
  mobilized political, 174–7, 178, 180–1, 182, 183, 237, 261
  political, 139, 176f, 178–81, 180f, 182
  representational political, 174–5, 177–9
affluence, national, 2, 13
age
  democratic values and, 142, 142f, 145
  organizational membership and, 126, 127–8, 133–4
  political values in regime choice, in Nicaragua and, 142f
agrarian movement, 80–1n41, 80n40
agrarian reform, in Nicaragua, 52–3, 55–6
Aguado, Enoc, 52
Aguilar-Rivera, José Antonio, 33n7
Além, Leandro, 72
Alemán, Arnoldo, 14, 134n12, 244, 253
  corruption trial of, 220, 246, 247, 259–60n50
Alfonsín, Raul, 152, 197, 218
  human rights policy, 202
Alianza de la Juventude Nacionalista, 79n37
Alonso, Amado, 102
Alonso, José, 76
de Alvear, Marcelo T., 207, 210
American Revolution, 21, 51, 259, 263
anti-democratic social capital, 22
anti-imperialism, 35, 69, 85, 108
anti-Marxism, 69–70, 82
Arce, Bayardo, 59
Argentina. *See also* democratic development, of Argentina; legislature, in Argentina
  anti-imperialism in, 108

Catholic Church in, 105, 122
clientelism of, 252
Constitution of, 71, 205, 241
democracy preference of, 169f, 255
democratic institutions of, 17, 182, 198, 202–3
democratic values in, 165
democratization of, 196, 198, 248–9
dictatorship in, 53, 56, 70, 71, 91–3, 138, 140, 150, 205, 211, 241
European influence on, 69
exclusionary political culture of, 241, 241n2
government preference, 164f, 166f
horizontal ties, lack of in, 182, 239, 259
labor unions in, 30, 77–8, 94, 100, 108, 111, 135, 157
legislative developments and, 23, 205–6
middle class, 100
mine nationalism and, 209
mutual cooperation, lack of, in, 14, 16
nepotism in, 13
non-democratic history of, 150
North Atlantic distance from, 68–9
organizational membership in, 120f
personalistic leadership of, 70, 70n10, 71, 72, 91–2, 195, 205, 241, 252, 253, 253n28
political activism in, 178–81, 180f
political values in, 150–70, 159f
poor of, 69
Radicalism of, 72, 116, 152, 166, 167, 181–2, 206–10
regime preference reasons, 163, 164f, 166f
representational democracy of, 265
representational political activism in, 178–9

297

Argentina (*cont.*)
  retroactive judicial system of, 202, 219
  social capital, lack of, 136, 197, 202, 255
  social movement against injustice, 69
  standard economic indicators of, 12t
  state centered democratization of, 20
  universal male suffrage in, 70, 72, 92, 181–2
  vertical dependency in, 239
  working class in, 69n6, 73–5, 82, 84, 94, 133
  WWII and, 74
Arguello, Leonardo, 52
Association of Rural Workers (ATC), 55–6
associations
  citizen, 7, 11, 22, 51, 242
  political, 5–6, 22, 23, 134–5
  social, 4, 5, 6, 58, 123, 125
  voluntary, 7, 120–1, 124, 125
ATC. *See* Association of Rural Workers
authoritarian personalism
  of Brazil/Peru/Mexico/Dominican Republic, 16
  of Menem, 252, 252n28, 253
  in Nicaragua, 248
  de Rosas, 70, 71, 91–2, 205, 241
  of Venezuela/Germany/Italy/Spain, 16
authoritarian populism, 79–91, 252
  hierarchical, of Argentina, 13
  Peronist, 80, 216
authoritarianism, 1, 16, 18, 140–2, 141f, 154f, 167, 169
  of Alemán, 246
  of Argentina, 160, 202
  dictatorial, in Argentina, 150
  education and, 163
  lower class and, 156
  military, of Argentina, 152
  Nicaragua citizen initiative against, 235
  Peronism, 212
  political values and, 162t
  resistance to, 270
Auyero, Javier, 251

Balbín, Ricardo, 88–9, 101, 214
Balestrini, Alberto, 116
Baracco, Luciano, 57
Barahona, Humberto, 36
Barber, Benjamin, 6n19
Bello Horizonte, Nicaragua, 59, 115, 117, 123t, 172, 173
  organizational membership in, 119–34
  party organizational memberships and, 125f

Bermeo, Nancy, 15n40, 183n9
Berry, Jeffrey M., 265
Blair, Tony, 80n40
Bloch, Ernest, 44
Bloody Lineage: The Somozas (Chamorro, P.), 61
Boff, Leonard, 44
Bolaños, Enrique, 14, 220, 246, 254
bonding social capital, 9, 110
  Peronism and, 68–112
Borge, Tomas, 37–8, 40, 59
Borlenghi, Angel, 75n10
Bowling Alone (Putnam, R.), 248
Bramuglia, Juan Atilo, 75n10, 251n25
Brandt, Willy, 59
Brazil, 16, 45
bridging social capital, 8, 9, 31–67, 91, 95, 112
  cross-class ties and, 58–64
  democracy and, 81
  mutual cooperation and, 259
  in Nicaragua, 32
  non-Peronist, 98
  Sandinismo and, 262
  Sandinista revolution and, 245
Buenos Aires, 158, 158n17, 183
  Argentine Congress in, 222
Bunce, Valerie, 18n42
Burke, Edmund, 19n43
Bush, George W., 271–2, 272n78
Butler, David, 95, 110

Caliber, Victor, 96n108
Calvert, Peter, 99
Calvert, Susan, 99
capitalism, 85
  agro-export, 31
  group phenomenon of, 3
  of Nicaragua, 139
  Peronism and, 87, 107
Cardenál, Ernesto, 45, 47
Castro, Fidel, 61
Catholic Church, 10, 65, 84, 97, 123
  Argentine, 105, 122
  FSLN practical collaboration with, 49
  liberation theology of, 43, 44
  Peronism conflict with, 104–6
  poverty attention by, 44–5
  religious movement of, 48
Catholicism
  cross-class ties and, 59
  Peronism support of education of, 212, 215
  reformist, 41, 49
  revolution and, 47

Index

Catterburg, Edgardo, 160
caudillista, 13, 15, 195, 252n28
Chambers, Simone, 264
Chamorro, Pedro Joaquin, 60–4
   assassination of, 62
Chamorro, Violeta Barrios, 28, 60, 62–3, 140, 145, 219, 244
charismatic leadership, 81, 82, 83, 98, 267
Chavez, Hugo, 79n35
Chichigalpa, Nicaragua, 62
Chile, 45, 270
China, 16
   leftist revolutionary movement of, 40, 42
Chinandega, Nicaragua, 52
Churchill, Winston, 262
Cities of the Prairie (Elazar), 258
citizen activism, 183n9, 251–2n26
   democracy and, 238
citizen associations, 7, 22
   causality and, 11
   pre-democratic state and, 242
   revolution and, 51
citizen values
   contemporary politics and, 243–57
   pre-democratic state and, 240–3
   social capital influenced by, 239
civic life, 118
   religiosity v., 123
class conflict, liberation theology and, 44
Cleary, Matthew, 120n7, 258
clientelism, 16, 19, 22, 80, 91, 91n83, 154f
   of Argentina, 252
   Argentine preference for, 166–7
   democracy competition with, 150, 151n10
   education and, 162–3
   of Peronist government, 249, 253
   political values and, 162t
CONADEP investigations, of Alfonsín, 202
Congress, of Argentina, 229, 256, 261, 267
   Menem and, 253
Conservatives, of Nicaragua, 140, 141f, 219, 242
   democratic regime preference by, 141
   dictatorship opposition by, 59–60
   Moncada truce and, 51
   national elections of, 14
   Sandino and, 41
   U.S. allies and, 33
Constitution (1853), of Argentina, 71, 205, 241
corruption
   Alemán trial for, 220, 246, 247, 259–60n50

lower social trust and, 258–9n48
   of Menem, 253, 255, 259
COSEP. *See* Superior Council of Private Enterprise
Council of State, in Nicaragua, 55
   president subordination of, 216–17
Crawford, Susan, 265
"Crazy Little Army," 41, 41n28
cross-class ties, 98
   bridging social capital and, 58–64
   business community and, 63
   Catholicism and, 59
cross-cutting ties theory, 8, 8n26
Crystal Night, 183, 251
CST. *See* Sandinista Workers Central
Cuba, 16, 61
   leftist revolutionary movement of, 40, 42
   U.S. rejection by, 43
Cuban Marxism, 40

dangerous personalities, 19
Darío, Rubén, 40
de-democratization, 247
"Delegates of the Word," 47, 48, 63
democracy. *See also* liberal democracy; participatory democracy; representative democracy
   Argentina preference for, 169f, 255
   association relationship with, 4, 11
   bridging social capital and, 81
   citizen activism and, 238
   clientelism competition with, 150, 151n10
   elections for Argentine, 254–5
   faith in each other and, 1, 256
   horizontal ties contribution to, 171
   implications for, 269–72
   institutional capital for, 237, 256
   mass movements and, 23, 24, 194–5, 211–18, 238, 269, 270
   mutual cooperation and, 239
   Nicaragua preference of, 169f
   Nicaragua/Argentina satisfaction with, 193f
   Peronism relationship to, 164
   political capital for, 237
   political parties and, 187
   revolution connection to, 263
   social associations and, 5
   social capital for, 237
   social movement and, 238
   social trust and, 1, 81, 239
   tumultuous v. regularized, 262–4
Democracy and the Culture of Skepticism (Cleary/Stokes), 120n7

democracy development, 24
  Argentina through democratic institutions, 17, 182, 198, 202–3
  institutional capital in, 201–37
  political capital influence on, 239
  revolution and, 21
  without social capital, 18–19
  state/society centered, 20
democratic development, of Argentina
  hierarchical authoritarian populism and, 13
  Peronist social organization and, 12
democratic development, of Nicaragua
  egalitarian revolutionary movement and, 13
  Peronist social organization and, 12
  social relations and, 15
democratic institutions, 183–7
  Argentina democratization through, 17, 182, 198, 202–3
  electoral authorities, 186f
  judiciary, 186f
  national legislature, 185–6, 185f
  Nicaragua confidence in, 192
  Nicaragua weak, 248
  political parties, 185–6, 185f
  Radicalism, of Argentina and, 181–2
  trust in, 184, 185f, 186f
democratic procedures, 187–98
  Latinobarometer study on, 191
democratic processes, Nicaragua/Argentina evaluation of, 192f
Democratic Union for Liberation (UDEL), 61–2
democratic values, 117, 184, 270
  age and, 142, 142f, 145
  in Argentina, 165
  citizen participation and, 184, 264
  democratic/authoritarian/clientelistic, in Argentina, 138
  education and, 142, 144f, 145, 147, 155
  gender and, 142
  income and, 157
  liberal/radical/non-democratic, in Nicaragua, 138
  party identification and, 140–2, 141f, 145, 149
  political values and, 146t
  Sandinismo and, 149
  Sandinistas, of Nicaragua and, 149
democratization
  Argentina problems with, 248–9
  from institutional capital, 260
  Liberals, of Nicaragua struggle with, 244
  Nicaragua advantages for, 243–4
  Nicaragua right victories and, 244
  Peronism and, 240
  popular mobilization toward, 244n5
  resources and, 2
  from social capital, 260
  society centered, of Nicaragua, 20
  state centered, of Argentina, 20
dictatorship, 136, 150
  Conservatives, of Nicaragua opposition to, 59–60
  of de Rosas, 70, 71, 91–3, 205, 241
  of Somoza, 53, 56, 138, 140, 211
distribution, relatively equal, of resources, 2
divided government
  of Menem, 218
  in Mexico, 207n9
  Ortega, David, and, 217
  of Peru, 207n9
  of Yrigoyen, 207–10, 207n9
Dodd, Lawrence, 2, 258
Dominican Republic, 16
Dorgeres, Henrí, 83, 84, 99

Eckstein, Susan, 151n10
economic affluence, social capital v., 2–6
economic capital, Marx and, 2–3
education, 161–2
  Argentina teachers' salary and, 134
  clientelism and, 162–3
  democratic values and, 143f, 144, 145, 147, 155
  indoctrination during, 132
  isolation, 153, 155–7
  organizational membership and, 126–32, 128f
  political values, in regime choice, in Argentina and, 156f
  political values, in regime choice, in Nicaragua and, 144f
  Sandinista literacy crusade, 129
  social trust and, 130
egalitarian revolutionary movement, of Nicaragua, 13
El Salvador, 45, 269
Elazar, Daniel, 258–9
Electoral Tribunal, in Argentina, 186
electoralism, 87–9
Estrada, Francisco, 37
Europe, 69
  fascist movements in, 81, 83–4, 85, 87, 109, 110

Index

populist movements in, 79, 79n35
Eva Perón Foundation, 77
exclusionary political culture, of Argentina, 241, 241n2
executive, checking the, 209

faith
  democracy and, 1, 256
  education level and, 132, 257
  mutual, 2, 135
  in system, 1
fascism
  Europe movements of, 81, 83–4, 85, 87, 109, 110
  of France, 99
  of italy, 88, 92, 99, 249
  of Peronism, 22, 79–91, 248–9
female suffrage, 88
Ferla, Salvador, 85–7
Figueres, José, 59
Fonseca, Carlos, 37–8, 39–40, 59
Fox, Jonathan, 151n10
France, 15. *See also* French Revolution
  democratic development of, 270
  fascism, 99
  Jansenist movement in, 46
  mobilized political activism in, 183
  organizations of, 51
  revolution of, 16
Franco, Francisco, 82
French Revolution, 7n23, 19n43, 21, 51, 66, 84, 263
Frondizi government, 76, 152
FSLN. *See* Sandinista National Liberation Front

Garrioch, David, 51, 66
Gay, Luis, 94–5
gender
  democratic values and, 142
  organizational membership and, 126, 127–8, 133–4
Germani, Gino, 79–80n39
Germany, 16, 69, 82, 90, 249
Gil, Emilio Portes, 35
Gonzales, Jose Constantino, 35
Gould, Jeffrey L., 53
government. *See also* divided government
  Argentina preference for, 164f, 166f
  people welfare by, 170f
  representational, 272
grassroots activism, 91, 271
  mutual cooperation in, 57

Peronism, lack of, 91–8
  of Sandinismo, 50–8, 50n52, 64, 97, 181
group cooperation, social capital and, 5
Group of 27, 61
guerrilla movement, 37–8, 45, 53, 59, 115
  mutual support of, 54
Guevara, Ché, 53, 61

Habermas, Jurgen, 264
Hermet, Guy, 81–2
Herrera, Leticia, 39, 59
Hibbing, John, 225
Hitler, Adolf, 82, 83, 84, 87
horizontal cooperation
  in Italy, 9–10
  U.S. and, 9
horizontal ties, 9–10, 11, 64, 124, 181, 270
  Argentina lack of, 182, 239, 259
  literacy and, 129
  of mutual cooperation, 13
  of Nicaragua, 57, 173, 239, 244
  Peronism undermining of, 135, 249, 251
  Sandinismo fostering of, 135, 177
  in social capital, 117, 153
Hulliung, Mark, 118
human agency, 17
human rights
  Alfonsín policy for, 202
  in Argentina, 196–7
  Kirchner, Cristina/Nestor, policy on, 219
Hunt, Lynn, 66
Huntington, Samuel, 19, 19n43, 254, 260, 268

Illia government, 76, 152
income
  democratic values and, 157
  organizational membership and, 126, 127, 133–4
Independent Liberal Party, of Nicaragua, 62
Independents, of Nicaragua, 140, 141f
  authoritarian regime preference by, 141
  Sandinistas v., 147, 149
injustice, Argentina social movement against, 69
institutional autonomy, 236
institutional capital, 18
  Argentina's strong, 235
  in Argentine Congress, 216
  legislative development through, 218–21
  social capital and, 260–2, 271
institutional complexity, 236
institutional consolidation, 178

institutional universalism, 236
institutionalization
    Argentina willingness for, 254
    autonomy/complexity/universalism for, 236
    idealizing of, 261
    Peronism lack of, 250
    of political system, 260
institutions. *See also* democratic institutions
    electoral democracy and, 270
    isolation, workplace/education/regional, 152–4
Italy, 7, 16, 69, 82, 90
    fascism, 88, 92, 99, 249
    horizontal cooperation in, 9–10
    social capital in, 240

James, Daniel, 78, 95, 96n108
Jansenist movement, in France, 46
Jarguin, Edmundo, 15n39
John Paul II (pope), 46
judiciary
    Argentina retroactive judicial system, 202, 219
    Latinobarometer study on, 186
    Menem subordination of, 252n28
    Nicaragua confidence in, 189, 191
    Nicaragua development through revolution, 203
    role in Argentine democratization, 197
    trust in, 186f, 189, 190–1t

Kirchner, Cristina, 165, 169–70, 195, 219, 252, 254
Kirchner, Nestor, 165, 168, 195, 219, 252, 254
Kohn, Margaret, 139n2

La Matanza, Argentina, 116, 117, 119, 172
    organizational membership in, 119–34
    Peronists/non-Peronists of, 124
La Prensa, 60, 62–3, 89
de la Rua, Fernando, 218, 251
La Vanguardia, 89
"Labor Law in Nicaragua" (Chamarro, P.), 60
labor reform, in Nicaragua, 52, 53
labor unions
    in Argentina, 30, 77–8, 94, 100, 108, 111, 123, 135, 157
    organizational membership in, 121, 122f
    Peronism organization of, 100, 108, 111
    Sandinistas, of Nicaragua and, 55
Lacayo, Antonio, 219–20
Latin America
    democracy implications for, 269–72
    leftist revolution and, 40
    Pope Paul and, 44
    poverty in, 44
Latinobarometer study
    on democratic procedures, 191
    on judiciary, 186
    on organizational membership, 134–5
    on political activism/values, 139
    on political participation, 172, 187
    on political values, 168
leadership
    charismatic, 81, 82, 83, 98, 267
    dictatorial, 53, 56, 70, 91–3, 136, 140, 150, 205, 211
    mobilized political activism, in Argentina, 180–1
    personalistic, 70, 70n10, 71, 72, 91–2, 195, 205, 241, 252, 253, 253n28
    of Sandinismo, 32–40, 48, 64
learning,, social associations and, 6
leftist revolutionary movement, 81n43, 82
    of China/Cuba, 40, 42
    of Latin America, 40
    of Mexico, 40
    Peronism and, 69
    of Sandinismo, 32
legal system, trust in, 186f, 189
legislative development
    Argentina and, 205–6
    contemporary context/empirical evidence for, 221–35
    early history of, 204–11
    institutional capital in, 218–21
    mass movements and, 211–18
    Nicaragua through revolution, 23, 203
    trust and, 184
legislature, in Argentina, 256n45
    amateur, 221, 221n24
    campaign activities and, 225–6, 226f
    Congress, in Radical years, 206–10
    constituency service increase in, 229–32, 230f, 231f
    constituent availability of, 226–7, 228f
    contemporary standing of, 203
    function level in, 222f
    government experience of, 225
    history, 203
    institutional strength of, 203, 256
    legislative duties in, 233–5, 234t
    legislative/executive relations and, 232–3, 233f
    length of time in session of, 224–5
    Peronism abuse of, 204

Index

physical plant/staff resources of, 222–4
stronger institutional strength of, 235, 256
legislature, in Nicaragua, 256n45
  under Alemán, 261
  amateur, 221, 221n24, 224
  campaign activities and, 225–6, 226f
  constituency service increase in, 229–32, 230f, 231f
  constituent availability in, 226–7, 228f
  contemporary standing of, 203
  executive authority resistance by, 219–21
  function level in, 222f
  government experience of, 225
  history, 203
  institutional strength of, 203
  legislative duties in, 233–4, 233t
  legislative/executive relations in, 232–3, 233f
  length of time in session of, 224–5
  National Assembly, 210–11
  physical plant/staff resources in, 222–4
  Sandinismo role in development of, 204, 216
Leon, Nicaragua, 52
Levine, Daniel H., 47n41, 96–7
Levitt, Peggy, 265
Liberal Alliance Party, 246, 247
Liberal Constitutional Party (PLC), of Nicaragua, 15n39
liberal democracy, 154f
  in Argentina, 152, 171
  education and, 155
  in Nicaragua, 139–40, 141f, 145, 149
  Peronists/Sandinistas and, 171
  political values and, 166
  Sandinismo and, 194
Liberals, of Nicaragua, 140, 141f, 219, 253
  authoritarian regime preference by, 141, 149
  democratization struggle within, 244
  internal reform of, 254
  national elections of, 14
  political organization and, 242
  Sacasa support by, 51
  Sandino and, 36, 41
  Somoza and, 58, 60
  upperclass and, 33–4
liberation theology
  clerical practice change and, 44
  of Sandinismo, 41, 43–7
Lin, Nan, 3
Linz, Juan J., 20
Lipset, Seymour Martin, 2, 155
literacy, horizontal ties and, 129

Making Democracy Work (Putnam, R.), 248
Managua, Nicaragua, 27, 31, 48, 55, 59, 115
  National Assembly in, 222–3
Mann, Michael, 81n43
Marx, Karl, 2–3
Marxism, 40, 47, 48–9, 59, 65, 85.
  See also anti-Marxism
  orthodox, 82
  poverty and, 42
  Sandinismo and, 42
  Sandino and, 36, 41
Masaya, 115–16
mass movements, 23, 238, 269, 270
  legislative development and, 211–18
  of Peronism, 194–5
  populist, 24
  of Sandinista revolution, 17
Mayorga, Silvio, 37–8, 39–40, 59
McGuire, James, 75, 76
Medellin meeting, 44, 45, 46, 47
Melo, Carlos, 209
men
  organizational membership of, 126, 127
  universal suffrage of, 70, 72, 92, 181–2
Menem, Carlos, 79–80n39, 134, 152, 161, 164, 170, 196, 197, 252, 252n28
  Argentina rejection of, 167
  corruption of, 253, 255, 259
  democracy progress and, 253
  divided government and, 218
  economic reforms of, 249
  labor unions and, 157
  Peronist government of, 152
  vertical control by, 165
Mercante, Domingo, 75n10
Mexican Revolution, 269
  U.S. rejection by, 43
Mexico, 16, 33, 258, 269
  divided government in, 207n9
  leftist revolutionary movements of, 40
military conquest, of Nicaragua, 39
military interventions
  against Peronism, 262
  of Yirgoyen, 208
mobilized political activism, 174–5, 182
  in Argentina, 178
  early in democracy, 178
  leadership directives for, in Argentina, 180–1
  Nicaragua future reliance upon, 237
  Nicaragua history of, 175
  partisanship relationship with, 175–7
  romanticism of, 261
  in U.S., 183

Index

modernization theory, 136, 257–9
Moncada, 33–4, 37, 41, 51
Montealegre, Eduardo, 244, 246, 254
Moore, Barrington, 2
moralism theory, 257–9
Moreno, Rudolfo, 209
movement(s)
   agrarian, 80–1n41, 80n40
   Catholic Church religious, 48
   egalitarian revolutionary, of Nicaragua, 13
   European fascist, 81, 83–4, 85, 87, 109, 110
   European populist, 79, 79n35
   guerrilla, 37–8, 45, 53, 54, 59, 115
   Jansenist, in France, 46
   labor union, 77–8, 94
   leftist revolutionary, 32, 40, 42, 69, 81n43, 82
   mass, 17, 23, 24, 194–5, 211–18, 238, 269, 270
   MRS, 32n5
   peasant, 33, 40, 58
   populist mass, 24
   Quebec separatist, 80–1n42, 80n40
   social, 69, 238
MRS. *See* Sandinista Renovationist Movement
Mussolini, Benito, 82, 83, 87, 90, 92, 249
mutual cooperation, 2, 65, 258–9
   Argentina, lack of, 14, 16
   bridging social capital and, 259
   democracy and, 239
   in grassroots activism, 57
   horizontal ties of, 13
   in Nicaragua, 15, 50, 244, 249
   revolution and, 262–3
mutual faith, 2, 135

National Assembly, of Nicaragua, 210–11, 229
   Constitutional reform of, 219–20
   limits of, 217–18
   Ortega, D., resistance from, 220
National Democratic Party, 102
National Union of Farmers and Ranchers (UNAG), 55–6
nationalism, 40–1
Navarro, Wilfredo, 15n39
Nazism, 83, 183, 249
Negretto, Gabriel, 33n7
neighborhood organizations, 121, 122f, 123
nepotism, in Argentina, 13
Neruda, Pablo, 40
NGO. *See* nongovernmental organization

Nicaragua, 45, 58. *See also* Conservatives, of Nicaragua; democratic development, of Nicaragua; legislature, in Nicaragua; Liberals, of Nicaragua; Sandinistas, of Nicaragua
   anti-imperialism in, 108
   bridging social capital in, 32
   capitalism of, 139
   de-democratization of, 247
   democracy preference of, 169f
   demographic values in, 138
   education investment by, 133–4
   horizontal ties and, 57, 173, 239, 244
   judiciary confidence of, 189, 191
   judiciary development and, 203
   labor reform in, 52, 53
   legislative developments in, 23
   liberal democracy in, 139–40, 141f, 145, 149
   military conquest of, 39
   mutual cooperation, lack of and, 15, 50, 244, 249
   organizational membership in, 120f, 173
   participatory government of, 265, 267–8
   party competition in, 195
   political activism in, 176f
   political values in, 139–50, 142f, 148t
   poverty, individual/national in, 2, 14, 31, 36, 132
   radical democracy in, 139, 141f
   revolutionary history of, 16, 21
   revolutionary movement of, 17, 37
   social capital of, 136, 246, 259
   social trust, lack of and, 244, 249
   society centered democratization of, 20
   standard economic indicators of, 12t
   U.S. military domination of, 35–6
   U.S. ouster of, 33–4, 36–7
nongovernmental organization (NGO), 28, 271n76
   Alemán's target of, 244n6
non-Peronists, 98, 124, 181, 182
Novoa, Ramon, 106
Nuñez, Carlos, 38, 59

Obando y Bravo, Miguel, 47, 63
Olson, Mancur, 250
organizational membership, 117, 119n5
   activism and, 134–5
   age/gender/education/income and, 126, 127–8, 133–4
   in Argentina, 120f
   Bello Horizonte party identification and, 123t

Index

influences on, 126–34
labor unions in, 121, 122f
of men, 126, 127
national assessments of, 134–5
neighborhood organization, 121, 122f, 123
in Nicaragua, 120f, 173
across parties, 122–38
by party, 125f
of Peronist, 184, 249
political participation and, 239
religious club, 121, 122f, 123, 124
of Sandinista, 184
social club, 121, 122f
organizations, 4, 9
of France, 51
Peronism and, 94
relationships within, 11
Ortega, Camilo, 38, 59
Ortega, Daniel, 168, 195, 217, 245, 259–60n50
insurrection survival by, 38
National Assembly resistance to, 220–1
personalistic control by, 14–15
as revolutionary leader, 59
Sandinismo and, 32
Ortega, Humberto, 38, 59

Palme, Olaf, 59
participatory democracy, 24, 269
friendships and, 266–7
liabilities of, 266–7
personalized leadership and, 267
in U.S., 265
partisanship, 124, 151, 151n11
mobilized political activism relationship with, 175–7
political activism and, 182
political activism in Argentina comparison, 180f
political activism in Nicaragua comparison, 176f
Pastora, Edén, 38, 39n14
patronage, 19, 22
Paul VI (pope), 43, 46
peasant movement, 40
of Nicaragua, 33, 58
of Sandino, 33
Péna, Saenz, 72
Pérez-Diaz, Victor, 92
Perón, Eva, 71, 77
Perón, Juan, 29, 70–1, 152, 159, 251
electoralism of, 87–9
exile, to Spain of, 71, 76, 96
grassroots initiative and, 93
hostility of, 98n111, 101
labor union movement and, 77–8, 94
military ouster of, 214
working class and, 73–5
Peronism, 12, 17, 21, 22, 23, 29, 39, 116, 118, 269
anti-imperialism and, 69, 85
anti-Marxism of, 69–70, 82
anti-socialism and, 82
bonding social capital and, 68–112
capitalism and, 87, 107
Catholic Church and, 104–6
Catholic education, support by, 212, 215
class hostility and, 98–109
class in Argentine society and, 70
clientelistic, 152, 194
cooperation disinclination by, 126, 239–40, 249–50, 251
corruption of, 259
democratization and, 240
grassroots activism/initiative, lack of, 91–8, 181, 251
horizontal ties undermined by, 135, 249, 251
inconsistent ideas of, 79–91, 211–12
institutional capital and, 262
isolation in, 153
labor organization and, 100, 108, 111
leadership style of, 70
leftist revolutionary movements and, 69
legislature interaction with, 211–16
mass movements of, 194–5
military intervention against, 262
mobilized political activism of, 179
non-institutionalization of, 249–50
personalistic leadership and, 72
population preference for, 152–3, 154
Sandinismo v., 112
social capital lower among, 194, 248
social movement of, 69
socialism and, 87
third position of, 86
universities, hostility toward by, 101–4, 155, 212–13, 213n14
vertical control of, 70, 165, 179
vertical ties of, 125
violence and, 89, 99–100, 99n115
working class and, 69n6, 73
Peronist government. *See also* clientelism
clientelistic manner of, 249, 253
of Menem, 164
Peronist High School, 78, 78n13
Peronist populism, 80, 215

Peronist social organization, Argentina democratic development and, 12
Peru, 16, 270
　divided government of, 207n9
Pierri, Alberto, 116
Plaza de Mayo, 116
PLC. *See* Liberal Constitutional Party
political activism. *See also* mobilized political activism; representational political activism
　in Argentina, 178–81, 180f
　Latinobarometer study on, 139
　in Nicaragua, 176f
　partisanship and, 176f, 180f, 182
political associations, 5–6, 22, 23
　in Argentina/Nicaragua, 134–5
political attitudes, 23
political capital, 22
　institutional capital and, 271
　social capital relationship with, 194, 239
political development, institution role in, 264
political participation, 117, 172–83
　Latinobarometer study on, 172, 187
　mobilized, 174
　Nicaragua engagement in, 191, 193
　organizational membership and, 239
　representational, 174
　social trust and, 173
political parties
　collective interests and, 187
　political values in regime choice, in Nicaragua, 141f
　understanding role of, 187f
political values, 146t, 194–5
　age, Nicaragua regime choice and, 142f
　in Argentina, 151–4
　Argentina regime preference and, 159f
　authoritarianism and, 162t
　clientelism and, 162t
　contemporary assessment of, 168–70
　democratic development and, 239
　democratic values and, 146t
　education, in regime choice, in Argentina, and, 156f
　education, in regime choice, in Nicaragua, and, 144f
　educational level and, 156f
　Latinobarometer study on, 168
　liberal democracy and, 166
　in Nicaragua, 139–50, 148t
　party identification and, 149
　political party, Nicaragua regime choice and, 141f

region, regime choice, in Argentina and, 159f
　residence and, 158–9
　workplace isolation, regime choice in Argentina, and, 154f
politics, human face of, 27–30
Polletta, Francesca, 265–7
Polsby, Nelson, 236
populism, 80, 80n40. *See also* authoritarian populism
populist mass movement, 24
poverty, 12, 82, 119–20
　in Argentina, 252
　Catholic Church attention to, 44–5
　Eva Perón Foundation and, 77
　illiteracy and, 57
　individual/national, 2
　in Latin America, 44
　Marxism and, 42
　in Nicaragua, 2, 14, 31, 36, 132
　Sandinismo and, 42
pre-democratic state
　citizen values and, 240–3
　strength of early, 241
Proceso government, 151, 159
Protestant Reformation, 43
Putnam, Lara, 6–7n20
Putnam, Robert, 4, 7, 23, 24, 92, 117, 123, 127, 136–7, 157, 184, 248, 259, 260, 265, 268, 271

Quebec separatist movement, 80–1n42, 80n40

Radical Civic Union (UCR), of Argentina, 70
radical democracy, in Nicaragua, 139, 141f
Radical Party, in Argentina, 88, 92, 101, 102
　education as positive by, 134
　educational freedom support by, 213–14
　for national elections, 206–7
Radicalism, of Argentina, 152, 166, 167
　Congress during years of, 206–10
　coup and, 72
　democratic institutions and, 181–2
　la Matanza support of, 116
Ramirez, Sergio, 38
reformist Catholicism, 41, 49
regional isolation, 161
　political values, regime choice, in Argentina and, 159f
religiosity, civic life v., 123
religious club, 121, 122f, 123, 124
representational democracy, 264–9
representational government, 272

Index

representational political activism, 174–5
 in Argentina, 178–9
 of Sandinistas, of Nicaragua, 177–8
resources
 democratization and, 2
 political power and, 2
 relatively equal distribution of, 2
retroactive justice system, of Argentina, 202
 Kirchner, Cristina/Nestor, and, 219
revolution, 7, 8. *See also* Sandinista revolution
 Catholicism and, 47
 citizen associations and, 51
 of Cuba/Russia/China/France/U.S., 16
 democratic development and, 16, 21
 leftist, 40, 42, 69
 mutual cooperation and, 262–3
Reyes, Cipriano, 94–5
Rizo, Jose, 244
Roca, Julio Argentino, 104
Rockman,, Bert A., 235
de Rosas, Juan Manual, 70, 71, 91–2, 205, 241
Rubin, Jeffrey, 15n40
Ruchwarger, Gary, 58
Ruckauf, Carlos, 116
rural social reform, 40–1
Russia, 16, 42, 90
Russian Revolution, 40
 U.S. rejection by, 43

Sabato, Hilda, 70
Sacasa, Juan, 33, 36–7, 59–60
Sandinismo, 23, 27, 31–67, 48, 66, 100, 245, 269
 associational interaction by, 135
 bridging social capital and, 262
 cooperation within, 126
 democratic values and, 149
 democratization and, 240
 educational level/social trust of, 131
 grassroots activism of, 50–8, 50n52, 64, 97, 181
 horizontal ties fostered by, 135, 177
 ideology of, 41, 65
 leader educational backgrounds, 39–40
 leadership interchangeability of, 32–9, 64
 leadership of, 32–40, 48, 64
 legislature interaction with, 216–18
 liberal democracy and, 194
 liberation theology of, 41, 43–7
 Marxism and, 42
 as moderated socialism, 39–50
 mutual faith and, 135
 Nicaraguan legislature and, 204, 216
 Peronism v., 112
 poverty and, 42
 religion role of, 43–7
 resistance/nationalism/leftism of, 32
 social capital higher among, 194
 social trust and, 132
 university support by, 130
 U.S. intervention against, 262
 U.S. poverty perpetuation and, 43
Sandinista National Liberation Front (FSLN), 39n14, 51, 64
 Catholic Church practical collaboration with, 49
 guerrilla movement of, 37–8, 45, 53, 54, 115
 military ability of, 55
Sandinista Renovationist Movement (MRS), 32n5
Sandinista revolution, 12, 21, 28, 45, 122, 150, 194, 258
 bridging social capital derived from, 245
 grassroots initiative of, 91
 mass movement of, 17, 37
 national institutions, of state and, 67
 Nicaragua clergy support of, 47, 63
 peasant movement and, 33
Sandinista social organization, Nicaragua democratic development and, 12
Sandinista Workers Central (CST), 55
Sandinistas, of Nicaragua, 14, 118
 democratic regime preference by, 140–1
 democratic values and, 149
 education/literacy crusade, 129
 horizontal ties of, 124, 181
 Independents v., 147, 149
 labor unions and, 55
 leaders of, 48
 liberal democracy and, 171
 mobilized political activism of, 177
 nationalism of, 59
 organizational membership of, 184
 representational political activism of, 177–8
 resource redistribution by, 48
 trust of, 124
Sandinistas Renovating Movement, 15n39
Sandino, Augusto, 34, 51
 background of, 40–1
 Central America support of, 35
 Marxism and, 36, 41
 military struggle against U.S., 40–1
 murder of, 37
 peasant movement of, 33

Sapaq, Elías, 203
Schick, René, 52, 61
Second Ecumenical Council (Vatican II), 43, 46–7
  Latin American perspective from, 43–4
Second World Congress of Anti-imperialism, 35
self-determination, 33, 41
Seligson, Amber L., 121n8
Shaw, George Bernard, 266
Skocpol, Theda, 5, 7, 51, 66, 117, 127, 136–7, 265
social associations, 4, 123
  democracy and, 5
  diversity within, 58
  learning and, 6
  of Peronists, 125
social capital, 18–19. *See also* bonding social capital; bridging social capital
  anti-democratic, 22
  Argentina, lack of, 136, 197, 202, 255
  causality and, 11
  citizen values influenced by, 239
  creation of, 6–8
  for democracy, 237
  economic affluence v., 2–6
  empirical assessment of, 194–8
  group cooperation and, 5
  horizontal ties in, 117, 153
  institutional capital and, 260–2, 271
  in Italy, 240
  mobile, 6–7n20
  mutual faith/cooperation and, 2
  of Nicaragua, 136, 246, 259
  Peronism and, 194, 248
  personal connections and, 4
  political capital relationships with, 194, 239
  as resource, 258
  sources of positive, 126
  de Tocqueville and, 5, 6–7n20
  in U.S., 240, 271
social capital theory, 81, 93, 95, 173, 195, 257, 262
social involvement
  education level and, 131
  Peronism mitigation of, 131–2
social justice, 33, 35–6, 85
social movement
  democracy and, 238
  of Peronism, 69
social organization, nature of, 8–11
social trust, 23, 81, 120n7
  Argentina, lack of, 182

corruption and, 258–9n48
democracy and, 1, 81, 239
  in democratic institutions, 184, 185f, 186f
  education and, 130, 131, 257
  in Nicaragua, 182
  political participation and, 173
socialism, 82–3, 239n1, 266
  in Nicaragua, 139
  Sandinismo as moderated, 39–50
Socialist Party, 102
society centered democratization, of Nicaragua, 20
Solentiname experiment, 45, 46, 47
Somocismo, 54, 61
Somoza Debayle, Anastasio, 27, 42, 47, 61, 115, 122, 150, 216
  dictatorship of, 53, 56, 138, 140, 211
  Nicaraguan Liberals and, 58, 60
  overthrow of, 58
Somoza Debayle, Luis, 52, 61
Somoza Garcia, Anastasio, 37, 52, 59–60
Spain, 16, 69, 82, 90, 92, 249
  hierarchical social control in, 10
  Perón exile to, 71, 76, 96
Spanish Empire, 68
standard economic indicators, of Nicaragua/Argentina, 12t
state centered democratization, of Argentina, 20
Stepan, Alfred, 20
Stokes, Susan, 120n7, 258
Superior Council of Private Enterprise (COSEP), 63
Supreme Electoral Council, in Nicaragua, 186

Tato, Manuel, 106
Téfel, Reinaldo Antonio, 61, 64
Tellez, Dora Maria, 38
Thompson, E.P., 251
Tilly, Charles, 247
de Tocqueville, Alexis, 2, 5, 6–7n20, 66, 136, 184, 238, 249
top-down dictatorship, in Argentina, 92–3
traditionalism theory, 257–9
trust. *See* social trust

UCR. *See* Radical Civic Union, of Argentina
UDEL. *See* Democratic Union for Liberation
Umanzor, Juan Pablo, 37
UNAG. *See* National Union of Farmers and Ranchers
Unigenitus Bull, 46
Union of Nicaraguan Agricultural Producers (UPANIC), 56–7

Index

United States (U.S.), 16
  horizontal cooperation and, 9
  mobilized political activism in, 183
  moralism in, 259
  Nicaragua hostility toward, 43
  participatory government in, 265
  social capital in, 240, 271
  voluntary associations in, 7
universal male suffrage, 70, 72, 92, 181–2
university
  Peronism hostility toward, 101–4, 132
  Sandinismo support of, 130
University of Cordoba, 104
UPANIC. *See* Union of Nicaraguan Agricultural Producers
U.S. *See* United States

Vandor, Augusto, 76, 90, 96
Vanhannen, Tatu, 2
Vatican II. *See* Second Ecumenical Council
Venezuela, 16, 61, 270
vertical ties, 11, 19, 78
  Argentina dependency of, 239
  clientelist support of, 9–10
  cultural tendency toward, 16
  Menem and, 165
  Peronism and, 70, 125, 165, 179
voluntary associations, 7, 120–1, 124
  of Peronists, 125
voting, citizen confidence in, 188–9

Weaver, R. Kent, 235
Weber, Max, 82–3
Wheelock, Jaime, 38–9, 59
Woloch, Isser, 66
women
  female suffrage and, 88
  organizational membership of, 126, 127
Wood, Elisabeth Jean, 244n5
workplace isolation, 153–5, 161
  political values, regime choice in Argentina, and, 154f
World War II (WWII), 35, 86, 108
World-Values study, 257, 258
WWII. *See* World War II
Wynia, Gary, 107–8

Yrigoyen, Hipolito, 70, 72, 181, 217
  Congressional challenge to, 208–9
  divided government and, 207–10, 207n9
  military coup overthrow of, 210
  military interventions of, 208

Zapata, Emiliano, 40